THE
CHARLES STRONG LECTURES
1972-1984

THE
CHARLES STRONG LECTURES
1972-1984

EDITED BY

ROBERT B. CROTTY

LEIDEN
E. J. BRILL
1987

ISBN 90 04 07863 0

Copyright 1987 by E. J. Brill, Leiden, Netherlands

All rights reserved. No part of this book may be reproduced or translated in any form, by print, photoprint, microfilm, microfiche or any other means without written permission from the publisher

PRINTED IN THE NETHERLANDS BY E. J. BRILL

CONTENTS

Introduction. Religion, Culture and Society: the Direction of Charles Strong's Thought... VII
Robert B. Crotty

Aboriginal Religion

Some Aspects of Aboriginal Religion (1976) 3
W. E. H. Stanner

A Profile of Good and Bad in Australian Aboriginal Religion (1979) 21
Ronald M. Berndt

Aboriginal Women and the Religious Experience (1982) 37
Diane Bell

Eastern Religions

Some Reflections on the Japanese World of Meaning (1975) 55
Joseph Kitagawa

The Essence of Taoism (1981)... 70
Liu Ts'un-yan

Tibet in its Place (1983).. 86
Peter Bishop

The Body of God (1983) 103
Klaus Klostermaier

Western Religions

Moses in the Qur'an (1982).. 123
A. H. Johns

Jerusalem: Holy City of three Religions (1972) 139
Zwi Werblowsky

Methodology

Universal Religion for Universal Man (1978)........................ 157
Eric J. Sharpe

Interpreting Babel (1981) 172
Rowan Ireland

Studying Religion in Australian Schools (1984) 190
Graham Rossiter

INTRODUCTION

ROBERT B. CROTTY

Religion, Culture and Society
The Direction of Charles Strong's Thought

In April 1956 the Charles Strong (Australian Church) Memorial Trust was established to honour the memory of a remarkable person. Charles Strong (1844-1942), born in Ayrshire, Scotland, studied Arts and Divinity at the University of Glasgow. Ordained into the Presbyterian Church he was inducted as minister of Scots Church, Melbourne in 1875. Theologically liberal and politically radical (comparatively speaking for the latter part of the nineteenth century) he had been implicated in theological innovation, in upholding the rights of workers, championing the unemployed, the imprisoned, the destitute, the handicapped. Yet one of his more extraordinary facets was his interest in the study of world religions. In the 1890s he founded a Religious Science Club which was devoted to the study of religions other than Christianity.[1] There he met with others to consider empathetically the beliefs and sacred writings of these religions. He urged those for whom he accepted pastoral responsibility to search sympathetically amid religious traditions that differed, at times radically, from their own.

He was not unique in his thought. At that time Liberal Protestantism was espousing the principles of biological evolution and applying the ideas to culture. A natural progression was seen from the 'nature religions', which would today be called primal religions, to the 'ethical religions' of which Christianity was the highpoint.[2] The liberal Protestant movement of the nineteenth century tended to identify religion with practice, therefore, rather than belief, with 'doing' as against 'seeing'. In Kantian terms religion was to be situated in the domain of practical reason. Liberal Protestantism, like Roman Catholic Modernism, was confident that it could draw a demarcation line between the ethical and social reality proclaimed in the Christian gospel and the expendable elaboration of dogmatic teaching. Strong was aware of these

---

[1] Details on the life and writings of Charles Strong are taken from C. R. Badger, *The Reverend Charles Strong and the Australian Church* (Melbourne, 1971).
[2] Badger, *op cit.*, p. 232. Excellent background to the intellectual situation in the nineteenth century can be found in M. Charlesworth, 'Philosophy of Religion — Retrospect and prospect', in J. A. Henley (ed.), *Imagination and the Future* (Melbourne, 1980).

developments and felt at home with them. But his contemporaries were not aware of the philosophical substratum of his thought. They saw only the negative side of his position, the challenge to established Christian beliefs. In 1883, he was forced to sever his formal connections with the Presbyterian Church over his interpretation of Christian beliefs. A motion, passed in 1881, which censured his religious views read:

> The Presbytery having considered the paper on the Atonement, published in the *Victorian Review* for 1880 and signed Charles Strong, and having also considered the Committee's report on the same, express their sincere concern and pain at the negative character of the teaching in Mr. Strong's paper, the absence from it of all direct mention of the Divine Presence of the Lord Jesus Christ as the Mediator, and Reconciler, working out the Atonement, as well as the omission of all reference to the supernaturally given Revelation: and inasmuch as the Christian faith rests upon and the Christian consciousness takes hold of, certain objective supernatural historic facts, especially the Incarnation, the divine life and death and the Resurrection and Ascension of Our Lord, the Presbytery earnestly and in a spirit of brotherly kindness urge upon Mr. Strong that in future utterances he make these essential facts prominent.[3]

While it is most doubtful that his colleagues of the time understood the theological thought of Charles Strong, it seems equally obvious that Strong was moving away from the mainstream of even liberal Protestantism. His writings show him disdaining any form of religion that pretended to be based on logic and history. A telling description of Strong's position can be seen in lines penned by John Stanley James in 1877:

> The Holy Church Universal is to him composed of all who believe in the principles of a Christian life, no matter how they call their belief. In rites and ceremonies we see childish aids to religion to those who have not arrived at a stage in which they can do without these.[4]

It was to be expected that the Australian Church which he established in 1885[5] after his ostracism from the Presbyterian Church would not be hampered by dogmatic boundaries and would, on the contrary, be open and receptive to all forms of new thinking. A resume of the Australian Church's prospectus, intended for the general public, reads:

> The Australian Church aims at being a comprehensive Church, whose bond of union is the spiritual and the practical rather than creeds or ecclesiastical forms. It recognises the principles that where the Spirit of the Lord is, there is liberty, that 'by one Spirit are we baptised into the one Body' and that it is

---

[3] Cited in Badger, p. 47.
[4] *Vagabond Papers: Sketches of Melbourne Life in Light and Shade* (Melbourne, 1877), p. 103.
[5] Strong maintained that he was not the actual founder of the Australian Church, only its first appointed minister. However the encomium delivered at his death by the Australian Church names him as "the founder of our Church." See Badger, p. 153.

hurtful to truth, honesty and spiritual life to hamper either minister or people by imposing on them the interpretation of the Gospel or the theologies handed down from olden time. The conditions of membership in the Australian Church are sympathy with the general spirit and aims of the society, the honest effort to carry into modern life and thought the religion of Reason and Love and contribution to the funds of the society according to ability.[6]

The very establishment of the Australian Church was a statement that Strong did not believe in church institutions as such. A church, in his view, was to be an agency, a centre for the profession of the values put forward in the Christian gospel, such values as freedom, justice, peace, charity, compassion and reconciliation. For Strong, religion was a part of life, its core values should permeate all human activity.

In order to follow Strong's religious development it is necessary to lay down a framework within which it is interpretable. It would be my contention that, in fact, his religious thought is most understandable when seen against the background of everyday life, the backdrop of human culture. Culture means the total shared way of life of any given human group. It is made up substantially by that group's modes of thinking, acting, feeling, valuing. Cultural expression takes the form of artifacts, clothing, technology and such non-material output as language, law, religion, art. Clifford Geertz describes culture as

> An historically transmitted pattern of meaning embodied in symbols, a system of inherited conceptions expressed in symbolic forms by means of which men communicate, perpetuate, and develop their knowledge about and their attitudes toward life.[7]

Culture however is not something static. It is always growing and developing. In order to clarify this, it is necessary to introduce the concept of tradition.[8] Tradition can have several meanings, but its essential meaning is the attitude of any given generation to its own past, which attitude may amount to either approval of disapproval of its cultural heritage. The current generation either identifies with its predecessors, the 'ancients', from whom the heritage is deemed to have derived, or dissociates itself from them. The present generation of a given group can select a certain aspect of the cultural heritage and evaluate it, reform it or adjust it to its present needs. In the hands of each group, therefore, culture becomes malleable. A group inherits a way of life and then adapts that way of life to its present circumstances.

---

[6] Badger, p. 104.
[7] C. Geertz, *The Interpretation of Cultures*, New York, 1973, p. 89.
[8] J. Szacki, 'Three Concepts of Tradition', *The Polish Sociological Bulletin*, 2 (1969), pp. 17-31; J. J. Smolicz, 'The Concept of Tradition: A Humanistic Interpretation', *The Australian and New Zealand Journal of Sociology*, 10 (1974), pp. 75-83.

Culture is human, dependent on human consciousness and memory. It is an organic thing. Without human beings there could be no such thing as culture. Anthropologists would even claim that without culture there would be no such thing as a human being.[9] A human being is a physical entity that has been programmed by culture. While animals, to a large extent, have their behavioural patterns predetermined by genetic structure, human beings are less physically regulated. They must put a construction on events and do so by means of symbols, a system of symbols, a culture. Human thinking consists of the use of significant symbols, which are largely presumed within any given human community. Again, Geertz writes:

> Undirected by culture patterns—organized systems of significant symbols—man's behaviour would be virtually ungovernable, a mere chaos of pointless acts and exploding emotions, his experience virtually shapeless. Culture, the accumulated totality of such patterns, is not just an ornament of human existence but—the principal basis of its specificity—an essential condition for it.[10]

Humans are essentially incomplete animals. They complete themselves through culture and, indeed, through particular forms of culture.[11]

Culture consists basically of a system of symbols. A symbol can be anything—object, colour, sound, smell, style of clothing, story and so forth. The meanings of symbols are derived from and determined by those who use them, the human beings of the group. Symbols do not speak for themselves. The colour red means what the group decides the colour red to mean. After value and meaning have been bestowed on a symbol then the symbol can become a sign. A sign is deemed to be present when there is an intrinsic relationship between two things either because they are physically related (smoke is a sign of fire) or because, in *this* cultural context, they are related (a crown is a sign of kingship). Symbols can become signs and within an established culture they do, but only for the adherents. Observers have to learn symbols which, for the believers, are signs. Only human beings, it seems, can so manipulate things to become symbols and signs.

From being a vague, intangible entity, culture takes on a somewhat frightening objectivity. Anthropologists seem to be perennially divided over the degree of reality possessed by a particular culture.[12] There would be those who would see culture as a super-reality, existing over and

---

[9] Geertz, 'The Impact of the Concept of Culture on the Concept of Man' in A. Dundes, *Every Man His Way*. New Jersey, 1968, p. 108.
[10] Geertz, *ibid*.
[11] P. Berger and T. Luckmann, *The Social Construction of Reality*, ch. 1.
[12] G. F. Kellner, *Educational Anthropology*, New York, 1965, ch. 2.

beyond the human group.[13] Ways of thinking, acting and feeling are independent of and external to the human individual. They exercise a power of control over the individual. Thus Emile Durkheim defined culture as:

> a collaborative consciousness ... a psychic being that has its own particular way of thought, feeling, and action different from that peculiar to the individuals who compose it.[14]

Human behaviour, according to this view, would be culturally determined.[15] The individual's cultural imprisonment has been thus described:

> The individual does the thinking and feeling—by definition. But ... *what* he thinks and feels is determined not by himself but by the sociocultural system into which the accident of birth has placed him.[16]

Culture thereby becomes something like the script of a play and we are the actors who can do no other than perform according to the script. Such a determinist view does not ring true. It does not explain the evident influence of tradition in the sense explained above. Genuine human choice, at least within certain limits, always seems to be a possibility.

At the opposite end of the spectrum is the conceptualist view.[17] For the conceptualist, culture is simply a handy, anthropological tool. It synthesises, for the convenience of the trained observer, the many forms of learned and shared behaviour with the material output that accompanies such behaviour. In this view culture can be compared to a map. A map is not the real terrain. It is an abstract and formalized representation of the terrain. Culture is an abstract description of certain uniform trends in language, activity, artifacts of a certain group. Culture really only exists in the mind of the investigator. Accordingly, what pass for cultural ideas and practices are simply the result of a group living together and coping with each other. They can be explained sociopsychologically.

Such a theory would seem to explain away the pervasiveness of culture. A realist view of culture would maintain that while culture is an abstraction, since it can never be experienced as a totality, it is still a reality. There is a distinctive mode of actual historical living in human society which corresponds to the abstraction. Such existential culture is

---

[13] Thus, L. A. White, *The Science of Culture: A Study of Man and Civilization*, New York, 1949.
[14] E. Durkheim, *Moral Education: A Study in the Theory and Application of the Study of Education*, New York, 1961, p. 65.
[15] White, *op. cit.*, p. 167.
[16] *Ibid.*, p. 183.
[17] Thus, C. Kluckhohn, *Mirror for Man: The Relation of Anthropology to Modern Life*, New York, 1949.

the precondition for the logical construct in the mind of the observer. A cultural heritage is a reality, handed on by tradition from one generation to another. Those who receive the heritage are limited by its ordered dimensions and boundaries but they are able to evaluate. In times when there is widespread dissatisfaction with the culture then creative individuals can introduce new culture patterns that may be accepted by others. A cultural revolution can take place and be recognised as a revolution by the observer. In short, culture exists in reality and in the mind of the investigator.

A further question that needs to be asked is whether all cultures are basically similar.[18] There are some who hold that any similarity is illusory. Every culture is unique, formed by unique experience in the life of this group, shaped by non-recurrent historical events. Each element of a culture can only be judged by what it contributes to the totality of its own culture. A particular form of government therefore cannot meaningfully be compared to another form in another culture. It only has meaning within the total culture of the one group. Others hold to common universal characteristics in all cultures.[19]

A variant of relativism can be posited, important for our later consideration of Charles Strong's position. The case could be put that while the behaviour patterns of animals are genetically determined and the genetic code orders their activity within a narrow range of variation, human beings are only endowed with very general response capacities.[20] These capacities allow flexibility but they require regulation. Thus we have an innate capacity to speak but our capacity to speak English is culturally determined. The speech patterns of all languages work on a few basic principles. Beneath all languages there are deep structures, as Noam Chomsky calls them.[21] Surface grammars are simply variants of the deep structures. Perhaps this principle can be applied to the whole of culture. Capacity is determined by the biological species. How this capacity will be activated and manifest itself will depend upon the culture into which the individual is socialized. Just as an individual is free to depart from the 'rules' of language and speak nonsense so too the individual can depart from the 'rules' of culture generally and so behave, think and value is a nonsensical way. A human being, with capacities

---

[18] C. Kluckhohn, 'Universal Categories of Culture' in A. L. Kroeber (ed.), *Anthropology Today*, Chicago, 1953, pp. 507-523. Geertz argues against cultural universals which are too broad. See his 'The Impact of the Concept of Culture on the Concept of Man'.

[19] M. J. Herskovits, *Cultural Anthropology*, p. 364.

[20] Geertz, *The Interpretation of Cultures*, pp. 108-109.

[21] N. Chomsky, *Language and Mind* (New York, 1972): *Rules and Representations* (New York, 1980).

only, is an incomplete animal. It is culture that completes the human being by activating the capacities in a certain direction.

What does such a culture offer to the human being? The human individual has a need for order. To make sense of the universe, self and others the individual within the group requires a direction, a purpose, a basic meaning. Culture, every culture, offers this. In order to survive, both individuals and the group must adapt to the present environment and this demands the adaptation and evaluation of the present cultural heritage. However, the group acts to retain its cultural heritage with the same tenacity as the individual displays in maintaining personal, physical life. Hence there is always an element of continuity about culture.

In general, it is the universal need for order, accompanied by the universal capacities generated by human biology, psychology and geophysical context that give rise to so-called cultural universals. Kluckhohn writes:

> Every society's patterns for living must provide approved and sanctioned ways for dealing with such universal circumstances as the existence of two sexes; the helplessness of infants, the need for satisfaction of the elementary biological requirements such as food, warmth, and sex; the presence of individuals of different ages and of differing physical and other capacities. The basic similarities in human biology the world over are vastly more massive than the variations. Equally, there are certain necessities in social life for this kind of animal, regardless of where that life is carried on or in what culture. Cooperation to acquire subsistence and for other ends requires a certain minimum of reciprocal behavior, of a standard system of communication, and, indeed, of mutually accepted values. The facts of human biology and of human gregariousness supply, therefore, certain invariant points of reference from which cross-cultural comparisons can start without begging questions that are themselves at issue.[22]

The capacities of the human group are activated and directed by a culture and this culture itself can be affected substantially by subsequent human experience and non-recurrent historical events. Tradition will shape and reshape the cultural totality in response to ongoing human need. Diversity will remain with universalism.

Religion is a cultural pattern or, as many would see it, a cultural system. Like all culture it is, at base, a meaning-seeking activity that, from the viewpoint of the observer, is interpreted as a human construct. Like all culture it consists of a system of symbols. The symbols are principally myths and rituals but they also include objects, natural phenomena, clothing, smell, sights and so forth. For those observers who study a religion from outside, the symbols must be learned. What for ex-

---

[22] Kluckhohn, 'Universal Categories of Culture', pp. 520-521.

ample is the meaning of a serpent? For the Canaanite religion it was the symbol of fertility, for ancient Greek religion it was the symbol of healing, for Hebrew religion it was the symbol of evil, for Australian aboriginal religion it is the symbol of creativity. The symbol must be learned and, indeed, the whole gamut of symbolism must be learned. For the believer, the enculturated, the symbols have become signs. Intuitively they bespeak their meaning. Conversion indicates that the symbols of a religious culture have become signs.

But religion, seen as religious culture, must be appreciated in its vital function of attaining order. We have seen that culture, in general, bestows order and human beings depend upon their symbol systems for viability. Should there be the remotest indication that these symbols systems might not prove able to cope with human experience, for example the experience of death and dying, then anxiety is aroused. Human beings, accordingly, find themselves pitted against chaos, ultimate lack of interpretability. Culture, everyday culture, allows human beings to bestow order on human experience, to explain historical events, to solve problems of identity and destiny. However there are certain points where chaos could reassert itself. Insuperable ignorance, the experience of suffering and the problem of evil with the concomitant problem of cosmic injustice can threaten an ordered world and threaten the interpretability of human experience. At this point there is need for religious culture.[23] The religious person construes the world and self in terms of Ultimacy, of ultimate order. Ultimacy has no explanation and by definition cannot be given explanation. Ultimacy is a given, encountered in the religious culture, beyond human explanation.

This comparison between religious culture and what could now be called everyday or secular culture indicates the complexity of social life. In the first instance human beings have access to a variable number of cultural systems. Perhaps they may live their life within the one culture, being aware of that single possibility for human order. The one culture could be both religious and secular. Perhaps they have access to several and so they can choose. The result may be a choice of one with rejection of others, a dual system in which the individual oscillates from one to another or a hybrid system in which the individual selects elements from two or more to form a personal cultural system. For our present purposes the complexity becomes more obvious in our own environment when there is access to many religious systems. The secular culture has become disengaged from the religious culture. Each have their separate existence,

---

[23] Geertz, *op. cit.*, pp. 100-101.

with lines of demarcation more or less firmly laid down. A variety of forms of interaction is therefore possible.

Whether consciously or intuitively Strong had perceived that the Christian churches of his own day had moved in this direction. He desperately wanted to bring religious culture into the sphere of everyday activity, to lessen the gulf between everyday and religious cultures. He perceived that this could be done only by dismantling the church institutions, the constructed 'world' wherein religious culture was confined. Religion and the everyday culture had to occupy a common 'world'. Thus, Badger writes of Strong's thought:

> Religion, he thought, was bound up with the whole of life and not only and not even most importantly with that aspect of it deemed to be 'spiritual'. The activity of the church, its whole point and mission, was directed to the world. It was a means and not an end. It was not a piece of machinery, miraculously devised to 'save souls'; its business was to forward the Kingdom of God on earth, to stand over against the world in judgement and to point always to the enduring values of the Gospel, to preach freedom, justice, peace, charity, compassion, reconciliation and by its example to point to what these values actually meant in the day-to-day circumstances of life. The church was not to say, 'Believe this', but 'Do this' and its work and purpose was to be seen in the light of a critical appraisal of the main drift and tenor of the New Testament and not in an arbitrarily selected series of texts from a supposedly infallible book. Religion, he insisted, again and again, was primarily a recognition of a new relationship between man and God declared by Jesus—that of Sonship—and a recognition, therefore, of a new relationship between man and man, that of brotherhood. The only essential and significant work and task of the religious man, and especially of the Christian, was that of creating here and now a community founded upon the spirit of the Gospel of Jesus Christ. All else was secondary and of little account.[24]

Awareness of a variety of religious cultures at once raises the issue of relativism.[25] Obviously there are differences and disagreements between rival religious symbol systems. Disagreements can be in belief symbols and in practical symbols. Some of the disagreements can be relegated to historical differences of opinion: Jesus died on the cross (Christianity) as against Jesus did not actually die on the cross (Islam). Historical evidence could reconcile such disagreements but they are not of vital importance in comparing rival cultural systems. Other disagreements, on the surface more substantial, are really quasi-historical: reincarnation is possible (Hinduism); reincarnation is impossible (Judaism). It is possible to con-

---

[24] Badger, p. 231.
[25] On this issue of relativism see J. Hick, 'On Grading Religions,' *Religious Studies* 17 (1981), pp. 451-467; 'On Conflicting Religious Truth Claims,' *ibid.*, 19 (1983), pp. 485-491; R. Trigg, 'Religion and the Threat of Relativism,' *ibid.*, pp. 297-310.

ceive a historical test that would substantiate one or other side of the argument. Once again the disagreement does not touch the essence of the symbol system. It is interesting, and predictable, that Strong disengaged his Christian belief from any such historical proof or even any philosophical underpinning. Christianity was a way of life, to be lived out without the benefit of logical certitude. Badger writes:

> He held that the evidences for Christianity and the arguments in favour of religion and theism generally fell short of proof and were not finally convincing. He believed that attempts to found religious faith on 'evidences' were mistaken. Philosophical enquiry, he thought, did indicate that at the least Christian faith was not irrational or unreasonable and that the 'given' of experience contained within itself indications of a reality which, so to speak, underlay and conditioned experience. But he was far from being dogmatic about his philosophical views and held that philosophical and scientific enquiry must be pursued rigorously and for its own sake, without any regard to the possible consequences for orthodox belief. He always kept an open mind about the possibility that the unbeliever, the complete sceptic, could be right and the Christian thinker wrong. Faith was neither demonstrable nor provable. Its essence lay in the fact that it was a kind of answer to a demand or an invitation which appeared to come from beyond the sensory world and from beyond the self.[26]

Where religious cultures do differ substantially is in their ways of conceiving and relating to Ultimacy. The conception and the mode of relationship has been determined by unique life experiences and unique historical events. Ultimacy could thereby take the variant forms of Yahweh, Allah, Nirvana, the Dreaming. Strong was fascinated by this variety of religious cultures, not questions of historical disagreement.

At this point a significant distinction needs to be drawn between Ultimacy in itself and Ultimacy as humanly conceived within a particular religious group. Ultimacy in itself is the ultimate order of things. It is neither capable of validation nor disproof. It is a reality beyond the human order but it becomes part of human awareness in terms of sets of concepts which structure cognitive consciousness. Ultimacy as humanly conceived will be as unique as the experience of the founding group and the unique experiences of others who, by tradition, will affect the religious culture.

If the differentiation of religious cultures is dependent upon variant, human conceptions of Ultimacy the observer of religions can take up several stances. The first would be exclusivism, the view that one particular religious culture is alone valid, possessing the only valid conception of Ultimacy and the only legitimate mode of contacting that form of Ultimacy. The second would be inclusivism, the view that one religious culture is certainly valid and true but that other religious cultures may share, partially and perhaps inadequately, the truth of the one valid

---

[26] Badger, pp. 231-232.

culture. Thirdly, there is pluralism. Pluralism would maintain that all religious cultures that do enjoy or have enjoyed currency are true.[27] They all embody variant perceptions of Ultimacy and variant systems of contacting Ultimacy. They are incommensurable and no value judgement can be passed on them. Choice between one and another would be dependent on an individual's life circumstances, prior enculturation and some degree of personal choice.

The Reverend Charles Strong was remarkable because, in the midst of a world that was strongly exclusivist, he was an inclusivist who, at times, passed beyond the inclusivist limits into pluralism. The pluralism with which he dallied in his Religious Science Club would not have been completely relativist. It could be compared to the more general stance of those who hold humans to be genetically determined in their response capacities, which capacities are subsequently activated by specific human cultures. Likewise, in the religious situation, a capacity for ultimate order could be variously activated by a variety of religious cultures. To his colleagues he appeared, understandably, as a heretic. The Australian Church was basically an inclusivist group that Strong would have liked to see progress along the path towards pluralism. He was caught between his own advanced ideas and the more limited vision of his constituency.

In hindsight, then, it seems most appropriate that of the many projects to which the funds of the Australian Church, upon its disbandment, could have been applied, it was decided that they should be channelled into the sympathetic promotion of the study of world religions, other than Christianity, in an Australian context. At that stage, during the 1950s, the Australian academic world was particularly bereft of scholarly direction in the study of religion. Australian public life had suffered from sectarian strife and tertiary education did not want to be embroiled in the issue. Even the scholarly study of religion was eschewed. The provisions of the Charles Strong Memorial Trust laid down that one of the principal uses of its funds should be the availability for academic circuits of visiting scholars and lecturers in world religions and religious philosophies.

In the intervening years the Australian situation has changed dramatically.[28] Universities and Colleges of Advanced Education have fostered the academic study of religion. Charles Strong Memorial lecturers tend to meet with more informed audiences, undergraduate and graduate students formed in the discipline. The lectures that now follow

---

[27] The pluralist stance does not deprive a religion of all objectivity. Ultimacy in itself can still be objective, a real order existing in things.

[28] V. Hayes, 'Religions and Religion Studies in Australia,' *Bulletin of the Center for the Study of World Religions*, Harvard University, Fall 1983.

in this volume have been selected on the basis of their academic worth and their topical variety. They treat of the phenomenon of religion from various aspects and from within various traditions. They are an ongoing monument to Charles Strong, a person of vision and courage who grasped the elusive reality of religion in a world of real people.

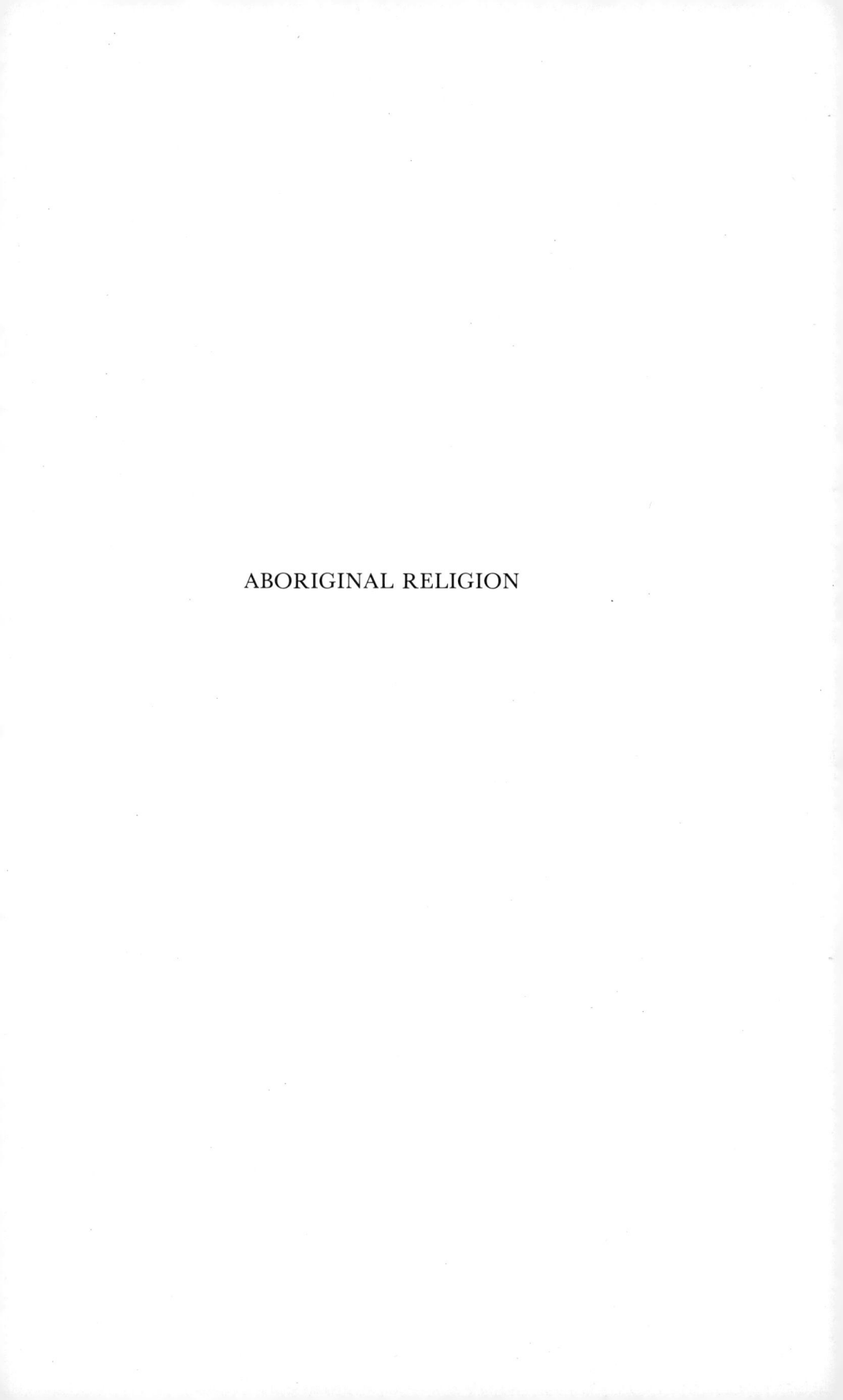

ABORIGINAL RELIGION

W. E. H. STANNER

SOME ASPECTS OF ABORIGINAL RELIGION

I

There may still be some who question the rightness of including Aboriginal beliefs, acts and objects within the scholarly scope of Comparative Religion. In this Lecture I will contend that all the intellectual requirements can be, and long have been, amply satisfied.

If, for the purpose, I adopt William James's dictum[1] — that the word 'religion' cannot stand for any single principle or essence, but is rather a collective name — it will not be in deference to the sceptics, but rather in acknowledgment of two things: the Aboriginal materials are too various and subtle for our present stage of professional insight, and we cannot yet make powerful general statements on a continental scale. I will therefore aim only at a broadly informative sketch.

If Aboriginal culture had an architectonic idea I would say that it was a belief that all living people, clan by clan, or lineage by lineage, were linked patrilineally with ancestral beings by inherent and imperishable bonds through territories and totems which were either the handiwork or parts of the continuing being of the ancestors themselves. This belief was held in faith, not as an 'official truth' or dogma, but as part of a body of patent truth about the universe that no one in his right mind would have thought of trying to bring to the bar of proof. The faith was self-authenticating. The very existence of the clans or clan-like groups, the physical features of the countryside, the world of animate and inanimate things, were held to make the truth, as received, visible. Even the somewhat abstract categories into which some people were grouped — the sections, subsections and moieties (which took us a good hundred years to begin to understand) — were thought corroborative. Customs, usages, even the fact of language and dialect were taken to be evidential: after all, who but the ancestral beings had taught men the ways of living and speaking? Songs, stories, dances, mimes and rites of high solemnity, deep secrecy, and sometimes of holy status, gave powerful buttress. As far as we know, there was no impulse, and no one tried, to break out from the vast circularity of these reasonings. Yet there was a dynamism at work, to which I will draw attention from time to time.

My main purpose is to discuss the tetrad already mentioned — living people, their countries, their totems and their ancestors — together with the inherent and imperishable bonds between them, and the philosophical ground on which the related entities alone have full meaning. I will hope that by so doing I may throw some further light on a religious outlook which, in the words of my good friend the late Fr. E. A. Worms, "penetrates all facets of Aboriginal life and has little to fear from distinctions which are both abstract and disunitive and which we, with our philosophic education, often make".[2]

Some years ago I tried to sum up in about half a dozen propositions the understanding I then had of Aboriginal religion. There is nothing in them that I now want to unsay. But there is much that I could wish to have said better, so as to bring out the strength and beauty of the outlook I was trying to express. Since I have been led to believe that the subject is rather unfamiliar to many who are present, it may be useful for me to go through the propositions once again, amending them slightly as I do.

1. The Aborigines universally believed that ancestral beings had left a world full of signs of their beneficent intent towards the men they had also brought into being. The wisdom about living given to men, cherished by traditional experience, could interpret these outward and visible signs as saying that men's lives had to follow a perennial pattern and, if they did so, men could live always under an assurance of providence.
2. The human person, compound of body and several spiritual principles or elements, had value in himself and for others, and there were spirits who cared.
3. The main religious cults were concerned to renew and conserve life, including the life-force that kept animating the world in which men subsisted and with which they were bonded in body, soul and spirit.
4. The material part of life, and of man himself, was under spiritual authority, and the souls of the dead shared in maintaining the authority and the providence over them.
5. The core of religious practice was to bring the life of a man under a discipline that required him to understand the sacred tradition of his group and to conform his life to the pattern ordained by that tradition.
6. The underlying philosophy of the religion was one of assent to the received terms of life; that is to say, it inculcated a strong disposition to accept life as a mixture of good with bad, of joy with suffering, but to celebrate it notwithstanding.
7. The major cults inculcated a sense of mystery by symbolisms pointing to ultimate or metaphysical realities which were thought to show themselves by signs.

I added that these propositions, if true, were evidence that the Aborigines "had taken, indeed, had gone far beyond, the longest and most difficult step towards the formation of a truly religious outlook" in that "they had found in the world about them what they took to be signs of intent toward men, and they had transformed those signs into *assurances* of life under mystical nurture. Their symbolic observances towards the signs, in rites of several kinds, were in essence acts of faith towards the ground of that assurance".[4]

By and large, these statements still seem to me true, in a general sense, of the Australian scene taken widely, although I am the first to admit that they have been dated and by-passed by much recent thought and writing on the more esoteric aspects of myths, particularly their hidden logic and semantic structures. But each of my statements, and every idea in them, needs a sort of concordance, before that kind of analysis is possible. Let me illustrate the point by reference to the first sentence of the first proposition: "the Aborigines universally believed that ancestral beings had left a world full of signs of their beneficent intent intent towards the men they had also brought into being". I will draw the material of a sketch from the published works[5] of an Adelaide scholar whose primacy is acknowledged, and who has put in his debt every person who is interested in the Aborigines and in their unique religion — T. G. H. Strehlow.

It would seem from Professor Strehlow's writings that some of the Aranda-speaking peoples of central Australia could be said to have believed there were three domains of the primordial world: the sky, the surface of the earth, and the within of the earth.

In the sky were a nameless Father and his wives and children. He and his sons were emu-footed, his womenfolk dog-footed. All were young and sempiternal, there being no death. They were self-existent, undescended from anyone. Father ('Great Father', Strehlow calls him) had reddish skin and shining blond hair; his sons were strong and comely, his daughters full-bosomed and beautiful, his wives with the grace of young girls. They lived to themselves, self-sufficiently, in a land perennially green, free from drought, and full of trees, fruits, flowers and birds, but no other animals. The Milky Way was a river flowing through the sky, its course bordered by stars, which were the sky-beings' camp fires. Their glow threw a dim light on the surface of the earth. But the sky-beings had no interest in the earth or its beings, and had no power over them.

The terrestrial domain was dark, being sunless, and moonless, lacking even an Evening Star. It was also cold, featureless and desolate, without plants or animals. But there was a sort of life upon it in the form of innumerable diminutive beings, somewhat human-like but barely foetal, and clumped together at many places. They were immobile and helpless; their fingers and toes were webbed together; and each had nose, eyes and mouth closed. They were alive but unable to develop, age, decay or die.

In the third, the subterrestrial, domain there was veritable human-kind, in the form of a great many mature persons of both sexes. While being truly human they were also superhuman, or at least more than human in that, intermixed with their essential humanity, were animal, plant and other vital life-principles and capacities. These beings, in the words of Professor Strehlow, had been "born out of their own eternity". They lay under the surface of the earth, as they always had, deeply asleep.

Spontaneously, they awoke and, of their own will, broke through to the surface. As they did so, the sun rose and brought light and warmth. The sometime sleepers now revealed, or assumed, a fourfold distribution. One group had the forms of animals but thought and acted like human beings. A second looked like perfectly formed human beings but had inward affinities with species of animals and could change at will into them. A third was human in form but had plant affinities: they fed exclusively upon the affine species but did not — could not — take on the form. A fourth group, the smallest, were human in form with neither the animal nor plant affinities.

All the sometime sleepers were like men and women of today in that they had similar thoughts, strivings and feelings, could be hurt and suffer pain, could age and in a certain physical sense die although a part of them, a second soul, could not die. Otherwise they were free of the limitations, restrictions and inhibitions that affect today's men and women. Some of them acted violently, cruelly and unfairly but not always with impunity. Some came to downfall from having tried to do so: the good and the bad in living were beginning to define themselves.

Perhaps the greatest difference of the awakened sleepers was a truly superhuman creative capacity and/or energy which enabled them to work marvels that men now cannot emulate. They wandered widely working such marvels. Some went to help the protean earth-beings. They cut the huddled clusters into distinct individuals, freeing them from their physical disabilities, separating the sexes, and teaching them the arts of living as true men and women in the changed world now being brought about by other wakened sleepers, who were in their several ways bringing about all the distinctive features of the earth, indeed, of the cosmos.

At length the superhumans wearied. Some went into the earth; others turned into sacred objects, or into hills, rocks, trees, water-holes and other things, and resumed their deep sleep. Some went into the sky where, unlike the celestial beings, they remained interested in the affairs and able to affect men's lives on earth. The sun, moon and planets now became set upon their courses. Every place at which the sleepers had emerged, or made camp, or had performed a prodigy, or returned to sleep, even the tracks they had made as they wandered, became charged forever with their being, and with the powers or principles they possessed, and were marked eternally by tjurunga or other symbols and signs. Before the final disappearance from the visible plane, they composed songs, stories and ceremonies now used to commemorate what had happened. The rights to such property, corporeal and incorporeal, were bequeathed to persons or groups according to an immutable plan of descent or attribution. The heavy secrets of replenishing the world from each such place, by annual, seasonal or occasional rites, with the life-giving powers ordained for it, went each to its proper custodian, or a plan as immutable and as sacrosanct.

When all this had been done, in the words of our authority, "the world of labour, pain and death that men and women have known ever since, came into being".[6]

Now, this is not a word-by-word translation of any particular myth. It is an arrangement and a paraphrase of elements occurring in a number of myths which could be widely paralleled and in one form or another were possibly universal in Australia. Together they make a ground of understanding against which one must seek an insight into the Aboriginal *Weltanschauung,* while avoiding the errors of the conventional wisdom of cap, gown and cloth of the past. One can but marvel that scholars of the highest distinction should have been able to see in such myths, but a short time ago, only 'dark stories' (Tylor), a sort of disease of language, 'the dark shadow that language throws upon thought' (Max Müller), or 'strange stories, not to say absurd and incomprehensible' (Lévy-Bruhl). One might marvel rather more at the judgment expressed in a worthy text published for the Society for Promoting Christian Knowledge at about the same time: that Aboriginal "mental capacity does not admit of their grasping the higher truths of pure religion".[7]

Let us look briefly at the idea, the structure and the composition of a totality of three domains against the background of these examples of rationalist and Christian *superbia.* A schema of overworld, underworld and a tween-domain is not a novelty in mythology. One might say almost the same of an equation of overworld with the ideal, the underworld with the causative, and the tween-domain with actuality. Perhaps, again, the Aboriginal idiom is not all that remarkable in having made the 'underworld', or the 'underneath', or the 'inside' the locus of spontaneity and energy, and of creative, disturbing and other like forces in human affairs. But it does seem to me a work of imagination and of intellectual force to have made the 'inside' or 'underneath' the symbol of sleep. It is also frequently an Aboriginal metaphor of 'secrecy' or 'privacy' and perhaps even of 'sacredness' too. To have gone on to make dreaming, as the activity of sleep, into the master-symbol to which the whole corpus of Aboriginal religious life vibrated, was in my opinion still more impressive. The Dreaming, as activity, is represented as a continuing highway between ancestral superman and living man, between the life-givers and the life, the countries, the totems and totem-places they gave to living men, between subliminal reality and immediate reality, and between the There-and-Then of the beginnings of all things and relevances and the Here-and-Now of their continuations. On this material alone it seems to me that a sufficient answer could be given to the Christian critic I have quoted, and to the other writer whom *he* quoted approvingly as referring to a race "intellectually, as physically . . . poor and weak . . . ignorant beyond comparison . . . abjectly subject to terror, yet have not acquired a mythology, nor any one general superstition".[8]

Now, I have no wish, in correcting old misunderstandings, to go to the other extreme, but I am not alone in finding beauty, gravity and insight in much of the material I am discussing. May I perhaps go a little farther, and suggest that in the doctrine I have been summarizing there is an implicit theory of something very like the unconscious? That is, a theory that elemental forces, antecedent to the formation of the mature human being in society, operate below the level of the waking or conscious mind by continuing perennially through sleep and dream, as major determinants of conscious human conduct.

We are, remember, a society of book-worms. The absence of an Aboriginal tradition of literacy has enabled us to patronize a people whose languages are now revealing to professional linguists a semantic subtlety, a conceptual richness, and a categorial quiddity that in the next five or ten years will bring about a Copernican change in our understanding of Aboriginal culture and, incidentally, in our self-perception of what we did from 1788 onward. Pending that time, let us consider what the doctrine of three domains seems to 'say' through its imagery, including its spatial imagery.

It depicts the sky-beings as other than men (because they walk on animal feet, do not die, and so on) but not as wholly other (because of so many human attributes). It depicts them as high above the earth, far removed from it, and thus transcending it, exemplifying social life, idealized and unconditioned, as it might be in freedom from limits. It depicts them as self-existent beings, beginningless, underived from anyone, and self-responsible; beings who are and were "from everlasting"; beings who are as and where they were "before the hills in order stood or earth received her frame." So the conception deepens to one of transcendent and eternal beings, other than men but not wholly other, living an unconditioned life, but characterized by disinterest in true men and an absence of power over them.

The imagery, again often spatial and perhaps somewhat less ambiguous in a temporal sense, depicts the earth-beings who were to become true men as having been less than men but as having had a beginning as men at a point in time. They were made into men by a power beyond themselves; this theme becomes wholly explicit in the initiation rites: no boy 'becomes' a man; other men 'make' him a man. The assertions in the myths seem to say that the inert earth-beings did not become, like their transformers, greater than men, but were transposed from one modality to another, though still ultimately dependent on the transforming power. The change was from an inactive and potential modality to an active and kinetic modality. The imagery together with the

* assertions seem to say that life was actualized for such beings in come sense in division and strife, and under restraint and limit, not in the conditions of constancy and ideality of the sky-beings. Nor, because of their mortal element, were they to be ever-existing and never-changing in anything like the same sense.

The imagery depicting the earth-sleepers is more complex than I can condense suitably. It seems to me profoundly suggestive. Their spatial locus suggests immanence rather than transcendence. A philosopher or theologian of Aboriginal religion would have much to contemplate in that difference. The earth-sleepers were like the sky-beings in having been 'self-existent', other than men but not wholly other, though in a different sense. They were unlike the sky-
* beings in having been 'self-existent', other than men but not wholly other,
* though in a different sense. They were unlike the sky-beings in having true human feelings, interest in and (by attribution) compassion for earth-beings,
* and in having a mortal or quasi-moral property mystifyingly linked with their ever-existing and never-ending properties, which are theirs — though in a strange modality — since, when they came on earth, they developed and distributed multiple self-differences which persisted inexhaustibly everywhere, yet their identities and powers remained as before.

I would suggest that, with a minimum of attribution, sufficient resonances come from such data to encourage us to believe that we are beginning to know what the Aborigines are talking about. Let me then go forward to talk about six ideas which, whoever else may have had them, in my opinion are also authentically Aboriginal, and had a major place in their religious outlook.

a. All Aboriginal myths postulated that some sort of entity *pre*-existed independently *before* the cosmos was transformed into the system and the state in which it now exists (at least until we Europeans came like meteorites). Nowhere in the myths was there any suggestion of that extraordinary idea of a creation *ex nihilo*. To Aborigines something always was; the something had an arrangement or at least a structure; in some sense, it involved both space and time; but no one, as far as our good knowledge goes, seems to have seen as problematical or intellectually interesting how the pre-existent entity or its division into three had come to be as they were. It sufficed, that something was, with an implicit order amongst its given things; and that it was *re*ordered and *transformed* by posited means and agents so as to take on an explicit structure in which men had a determinate place.

b. The second idea was that power or energy was part of the primordial scene. The Aboriginal conception, at least inferentially, appears to have encompassed both the ideas of potential and of kinetic power, inasmuch as it was a basic postulate that the capacity of potential or applied power in things and places (including drawings, paintings, spells, songs) was there for release by the 'right' people. Hence, of course, the enormous and unshakeable attachment of the 'right men' to their ancestral 'countries'.

c. A third idea, much more difficult to express, was that the power itself, and the right to use it, were both speciated and individuated. Any and every kangaroo-man, if that is the totemic group we are speaking about, having the right ritual, which might take many years to acquire, could release from the sacred site the life-essence stored and potential there, so as to become kinetic in the form of actual kangaroos, not just this or that particular kangaroo but all and any kangaroos of that particular kind that were, are or may be. This seems to me to mean that the Aboriginal world was one of plural identities and a world of universals also.

d. But — and this was the fourth great idea — the world was, or was made, one of determinate relationships in which the relevance of anything to anything else was established. The sometime sleepers had linked the earth-beings as men everlastingly with themselves and with some at least of the sky-beings. They had put the three domains on a common framework and network of historical, substantial, spiritual and mystical ties. By 'historical' I refer to the supposedly unbroken lines of descent from the first true men through named persons known to have lived as men 'in history'. By 'substantial' I refer to the supposition that the country of each descent group, and its waters and food, had from the beginning given soul and body to clansmen, and had from the beginning been the last repository of their bones or ashes, and the everlasting home of their souls. By 'spiritual' I refer to the belief that at least one of the several elements of which, in Aboriginal thought, the 'person' is compound, connected him to clansmen through some incorporal entity with everything in the country which was 'his'. By 'mystical' I again draw on William James: I refer to "a state of consciousness which seems to deepen and enlarge the ontological sense of life", not as a "mere reproach, to throw at any opinion which we regard as vague and vast and sentimental, and without a base in fact or logic".[9]

e. A fifth idea was that the human will has always played a decisive part in men's affairs. The earth-sleepers irrupted on to earth of their own will and returned to sleep of their own will. Spirit-children impregnate women (or find pregnant women) and malignant spirits intervene in men's lives of their own will. All the myths make much of the fact of private will and of the conduct that may be said to express it — from stubbornness and indifference to egotism, pride, jealousy, cruelty, deceit and treachery.

f. A sixth idea had to do with the founding drama of the cosmology. A great event occurred with calamitous consequences of the 'forever after' kind. The particular event may be represented as an error, foolish or culpable, inexplicable or left unexplained. It usually concerns death, how it became a necessity needlessly, or at least with some kind of option foregone. The clear suggestion is that men were not meant to die.

Now, I do not think it could reasonably be said that I have imposed these viewpoints on the material. I have tried to avoid attribution, though whether I have wholly succeeded may be in question. I put them forward as being at the least implicit postulates of the religious outlook, contributing towards what Feibleman, the philosopher, might have called the 'implicit dominant ontology', or ethos.[10] It seems to me no inconsiderable feat of mind to have conceived of an independently pre-existing entity transformed into a world of relevances, and therefore into a moral system, by a cosmic force immanent in men but somehow still transcendent over them. Given the physical conditions of life, the tenets concerning death, and the somewhat anarchic polity, it seems to me a psychological achievement of a high order to have developed an art of life so strongly characterized by humour and jollity. These things, together with the confidence in their power to survive, the practise of a life-long discipline of body and mind as a mark of their valuation of man both as flesh and as spirit, and the repetitive celebration — no less joyous a word will do — of the continuance of their way of life, seem to me to argue powerfully for a re-assessment of some of our past depreciation.

VI.

I have felt that I could safely assume in such a gathering a good deal of general knowledge of Aboriginal society, in particular of the wider structure resting on and connecting the small, localized descent-groups (the 'clans' or 'patrilineages' I have referred to). It is plainly impossible for me even to summarize the scene made by thousands of such small groups, each possessing its own territory, its own idiosyncratic heritage of stories, songs, sacred places and ceremonies, and each a focus of order within a wider structure of variable social intercourse. There is much about this "wider structure in which society and external nature are brought together and a system of organized relations established, in myth and ritual, between human beings and natural species or phenomena" that, for full appreciation, needs more general information than I have any right to assume. All I can hope to do is to make some side-long gestures as I turn now to a second important field. I shall consider the subject of ritual to try to discover whether it could help to clarify what was 'religious' in the content of the Aboriginal *Weltanschauung*.

There are immediate difficulties. At present there is no agreed nomenclature for the different kinds of ritual and no agreed classification. What precisely do we intend to denote by 'initiation' or 'totemism' or 'increase' rites? Many efforts are being made to think things out again. Some of Eliade's (and mine) have been described as "an enterprise which seems to consist partly at least of translating the native idiom of thought into the technical language of metaphysics and theology".[11] The critic seemed to feel that he was not tinkering with the 'native idiom of thought' in proceeding to discuss the subject of 'totemic myth' as "the relation of the individual to the object-world, and libidinal cathexis as the defence used by human beings to bear the deprivation of object-loss or separation".[12] The languages of positivist philosophy and psycho-analytics are not less 'technical' and may do as much violence in 'translating the native idiom' as any specialist language. What, essentially, I and some others are trying to do is to weaken the ethnicity of our approach, including the Christian approach, so as to be able to accommodate Aboriginal perceptions of life and world, and their ultimate concerns with both.

For a long time scholars have tended to see the major rituals as in four groups: (1) 'commemorative' or 'historical' rites, (2) 'increase' rites, (3) 'initiation' rites, and (4) death and mortuary rites. The list pleases no one, for several reasons. In some sense, all the rites have a historical and a commemorative implication. As Meggitt has pointed out the so-called 'increase' rites are ill-named: their purpose is to maintain the supplies of natural species at their usual level, to support the normal order of nature, not to increase it. Both Elkin and Berndt would, I think, give the concept of 'initiation' a somewhat more restricted application than I do, in order — as I read them — to enhance the fact that some senior rites are much more 'revelatory' than 'initiatory' in purpose. They, and others, also are persuaded that we should recognize a special class of initiatory rites as 'fertility cults', such as the Kunapipi cult, which has attained an extraordinarily wide distribution. And are not death and mortuary rites in some sense 'initiations' also? There are also some residual forms of behaviour that are hard to know where to put e.g. some forms of magic, and meetings of very senior men to anoint, repair and contemplate sacred objects. The material is surprisingly rich and complex, with scores if not hundreds of locality-patterns. The 'dynamism' to which I referred earlier was very much at work here. Just as the rock-paintings may by 'over-painting' show a long temporal sequence of art-styles, so we are certain now that there have been historical changes of ritual-styles, over an unknown but possibly very long span of time. Professor Berndt recently made a courageous attempt to put the facts of the whole continent into perspective. He set up tentatively four main regional patterns, with intermediate and transitional forms. But after what might have been 40,000 years of development it is now difficult to isolate patterns which are mutually exclusive for significant defining properties. We should go on with the task and profit from his painstaking and exhaustive approach since there is certainly no Australianist who knows the material better than Berndt.

It is common ground to all anthropologists, I would imagine, that all rites of the kinds mentioned were concerned in one way or another with the most precious good of all, life itself, and more particularly with the continuance of life; and that the rites had a natural distribution along the course of the life-cycle of males. There was also an explicit comprehension that the continuance of life depended upon a power or powers external to men and beyond them. One is tempted to say that the rites were 'religious' in the measure in which, implicitly or explicitly, they acknowledged that dependence.

The historical or commemorative rites were consciously concerned to honour the particular ancestral life-givers of this or that clan or clan-like group, such as the father-son couple of subsections of tribes like the Waramunga. They did so often though not necessarily at the very places, now held to be deeply sacred, where the ancestors were credited with having emerged from the earth, or returned to it, leaving sacred tokens of their presence or passage. The ceremonies might be most spectacular and devout, including the drawing of blood, and using unstintingly the full treasury of song, story, mime, dance and icon, including the making of superb group-paintings.

The 'increase' or maintenance rites were consciously concerned to ensure the normal flow of the kinds of life specific to each of the sacred places reputed to have been endowed with the life-potential of that totemic species. The ceremonies might be again spectacularly beautiful and devout, or merely notional, but always were a way of venerating the totemic ancestors and the site.

The classical initiation rites were consciously concerned to induct males by stages into the fellowship of the most senior men who understood the religious mysteries in part or in whole. The ultimate purpose was to ensure the passage to and retention by the rightful persons of the knowledge required for the continuance of life. These rites have sometimes been referred to as age-grading ceremonies, but in my opinion this is something of a misnomer because, although the novices who went through a rite on a particular occasion were roughly of the same age, were sometimes known by a common term, and were closely bonded by the experience, they were graded by age only in a secondary way: what really graded them was their degree of religious knowledge.

I should interpolate here that the oldest and most knowledgeable ritualists might spend long periods, without any novices or postulants being present, reverently handling and contemplating the sacra. They were consciously concerned to nurture, revere, protect and preserve the physical embodiments or tokens of the persons and/or powers of ancestral beings, and with the exegesis of their import for living men.

The last group of rites — at death and later at burial — were consciously concerned with two tasks: to enable the ghost of a dying or dead clansman to be quit of earthly ties, and to shepherd his immortal soul towards and into the place within his clan-country where his bones could lie at peace, and whence (the doctrine varied a great deal) his or an equivalent spirit might again animate a human host.

It is clear from this cursory survey that all the major rites can be related functionally to the life-cycle of a person, a clan-member, except to the fact of birth; that is a puzzle in itself. Aboriginal attention centred on the fact of conception, or at least the proof of pregnancy. It is also clear that study is reaching a point at which it may be as important to push inquiry intensively as extensively. The task of continental inquiry, including the broad comparison of regional cults like the Kunapipi, the Djuṅggawon, and the Jabaduruwa, to name three only, is obviously a fascinating one and I can well understand yielding to it. But I prefer to ask questions of a sharper kind. In what way, if at all, does the ground so far covered bring us nearer a grasp of what was specifically 'religious' about the rites mentioned?

VI.

The material seems to establish beyond question that the Aborigines acknowledged that men's lives were under a power or force beyond themselves; that they venerated the places where such power or force was believed to concentrate; that they imposed a self-discipline to maintain a received tradition relating to the provenance and care of such power; and that part of the discipline was to maintain what might be called a 'religious economy'. The elements of belief and action were in a sense an 'address' to the givers of life. There was no element of direct petition, so that to speak of 'prayer' would be to go too far, just as it would be to speak of 'worship'. But I agree that we are dealing with lives of religious devotion.

I have probably said enough of the first two matters — the recognition of dependence on powers beyond themselves, and the veneration of the places where the powers are present or represented. Let me say something further of the two others — the initiatory ordeals and the religious economy.

Everyone has heard about the tossings of boys in the air, the smoking and toasting over fires, the head-biting, the physical beatings, the tooth evulsion, the cicatrization, the circumcision, the subincision, and so on. They have often been made to appear as bizarre savageries; indeed, I have been most surprised to learn that there are still suggestions of mere cruelty and bloodlust as the bases of such practices. These acts always had a social context and observed certain public conditions. A boy or youth about to be initiated was set apart from all that was mundane and ordinary: in a sense, he was made 'sacred' for the occasion. He was brought to the forefront of community attention, and for weeks or months became the cynosure of all eyes and thoughts. During that time, and on successive initiatory occasions, he was put in the care of guardians or instructors, whose task it was to prepare him and bring him in safety, well-being and good heart to his ordeal. At every stage he had close at hand comfort, encouragement, sustenance and protection while undergoing the isolation, privation, discipline, anxiety, fear and pain — quite often extreme fear and excruciating pain — that were his lot. A theory of 'callousness' and 'deliberate cruelty' is quite inconsistent with these and other concomitant facts. A boy, to my knowledge, was never circumcised by his own father, brother, or grandfather. The surgery was done by a member of another clan, who could operate with more detachment. I was told that no father could bear to inflict such pain on his own son. I saw fathers and brothers, distracted by grief, abuse and throw spears towards the operators. The rite of subincision differs. I did not myself see it but I was told that men of a man's own clan might join with others in performing the first operation, but that men were commonly seized by a sort of ecstasy to enlarge their own subincisions to draw blood for a ritual purpose. These facts are also recorded.

I suggest that in all this there was a spectrum. At one extreme, physical ordeals were *imposed* on boys and youths as preparative tests and as sanctifying acts. At the other end, men of some religious standing were *invited* to submit to ordeals as meritorious acts of asceticism and self-mortification. We are not entitled to overlook the differences. To the best of my knowledge, many men shrank from the agony of subincision and from the further ordeal — a worse agony, if possible — of having one or two finger nails torn out to make religious merit great enough to fit a man to make new sacra. But others accepted and passed the test — their religious status and repute were higher. So it is pretty clear that the spectrum had about it something of a *gradient* too: it measured degree of devotion to the self-disciplinary demands of the religious life. It would be more consistent with the evidence of the actual content and context of the rites to say that pain was inflicted, not from mere cruelty or blood-lust, but in a sorrowful public duty towards religious novices or postulants, and from ecstatic motives amongst the older and more devout. Men who cut *their own* arm-veins to pour blood on novices or on sacred objects and places, or lacerated *their own* sex-organs for similar purposes, were surely not affected by 'blood-lust': they were making an offer and gift of one of the symbols of life — at their own cost — to the novice or to whatever symbol was the recipient.

Now, to the fourth point — what I called 'the religious economy'. I have led my remarks to a point which in my opinion offers to students a true subject of comparative religion, one susceptible of detached scientific study: the analysis of Aboriginal ritual for a comparison of the liturgical formularies used throughout Australia. I have argued that there is no justification in the evidence we possess for dealing in concepts of 'prayer', 'worship', 'sin', 'guilt', 'grace', 'salvation' and so on, but there is a half-explicit concept of men co-operating ritually with unseen powers at holy places and on high occasions, to further a life-pattern believed to have been ordained by its founders, and of doing so under an assurance of a continuing flow of benefits. Some of the rites we have been considering plainly had a liturgical character, in that they were organized works of public — as distinct from private — duty, deference and even reverence towards, and of faith in, an otherworldly provenance of human well-being.

It has been said that "the living heart of the Christian Church"[13] can be found in its liturgy, and that "an exchange of prayers and graces is the very substance of the liturgical life".[14] In this minimal and aphoristic form one can perhaps see what might be called "the Christian economy of salvation", the salvation of souls being the supreme benefit of the exchange. The Aboriginal 'economy' was one under which souls were kept in circulation from clan-country to clan-country through clansman after clansman, the continuance of The Dreaming being the supreme benefit obtained through liturgical acts of dutiful observance.

The conception I have formed can be put simply. There were two data to which Aboriginal life conformed: a cosmic datum and a social datum. Under the cosmology a soul, which could never die, entered a human being. Under the same cosmology soul and human host were linked indissolubly until the host died. During life, body and soul were kept together by developmental and integrative rites necessitated by the social datum. To do so was the chief religious art of life. As a man grew up, was initiated, and assumed all the duties and privileges of a full man, his spiritual development was attained by religious disciplines at great personal cost. The cost expressed the value of what was gained. When death came, a man's undying soul and his bones or ashes completed the cycle by returning to his 'bone and soul country'. Under this religious system human society and cosmos were made and kept co-relative.

I have remarked elsewhere[15] that only a blindness of the mind's eye prevented Europeans in the past from seeing that "the ritual uses of water, blood, earth and other substances, in combination with words, gestures, chants, songs and dances, all having for the Aborigines a compelling quality" were not "mere barbarisms" but had a sacramental quality. I went on to add that "one doubts if anywhere could be found more vivid illustrations of a belief in spiritual power laying hold of material things and ennobling them under a timeless purpose in which men feel they have a place". Obviously, one has to look beyond the symbols to what is symbolized; behind the spoken images of myth, the acted images and gestures of rite, and the graven or painted images of art, to what they stand for; beyond the chrism of blood and ochre to what they point to, within the Aboriginal *Weltanschauung.*

During the lead-up to the Yirrkala land case I was present when the old man Mathaman, who had dared to sue Her Majesty and the Nabalco Company, was preparing to die. The 'right men' painted on his chest, with ochre and blood, the design that pointed beyond itself to things sacred and mystical to his clan. The industrial and commercial world made by the Commonwealth and Nabalco was roaring all around but if ever a man died at peace with The Dreaming, in spite of the ruin overtaking his people, it was Mathaman.

VII.

I turn now to my last topic: the new-found interest in the 'philosophy' of Aboriginal religious thought and life. The misgivings expressed by the late Fr. Worms about looking at the Aboriginal data through Western philosophical spectacles are of course not new. Durkheim made a general criticism many years ago. He said that all philosophers since Socrates had become used to relating reality to a combination of concepts in the belief that they were explaining life by reducing it to a system of abstract, logically related ideas. What they saw, he said, was only the general framework in which things are related, not the vitality that makes things move. To live, he said, is not to think, but to act. The train of our ideas is a reflection of the events which we experience.

The criticism was renewed recently by a young American sociologist[16], who referred also to "an implicit component of Western anthropocentrism in most philosophical systems" constructed by Western philosophers. This had led to a "culture-bound" philosophy that "talks about man, his nature and artifacts without adequate empirical foundations". The result is "a product of the philosophical experience of Western civilization" made up of "constructs abstracted from notions of men taken *in vacuo*". He closed his argument with the statement: "to consider man apart from his social setting is to leave a gap in all philosophical generalizations concerning man and human knowledge".

I have no great confidence in my ability to clarify the discussion of this difficult topic but it is obviously of much import for the subject of this Lecture. Let me say then that the great difficulty which I see involves the distinction, radical separation, even in certain circumstances opposition, between 'subject' and 'object'. The postulate that 'out there', external to and independent of the knowing or experiencing 'subject', is a 'reality' concerning which the subject forms 'objective knowledge' excluding all 'subjectivity', is simply incongruent with Aboriginal mentality in certain situations of life. When an Aboriginal identifies, say, his clan-totem and its sacred site, he is not 'pointing' to 'something' which is 'out there' and 'external' to him, but 'not him': he is identifying a part of his inwardness as a human being, a part of the plan of his life in society, a condition of his placement and activity in a manifold of existence in a cosmic scheme. We have to do what we can to try to 'see' the Aboriginal's intersubjective reality, made up of facts known to everyone in his community, and upheld by them as public, objective, true and valid, not just for him, or just for him for the moment, but for everyone, everywhere, at all times. According to the Aboriginal theory of 'reality', living and dead, human beings and animal beings, persons and things, persons and environment, can and do compenetrate each other. I meant as much by my earlier remark that between the elements of the tetrad there were, in Aboriginal understanding, historical, substantial, essential and mystical links that were inherent and imperishable. Our categories are too Procrustean, our abstractions too dry and spare, our intellectual habits too dessicated for the material we have to handle. Yet with care and patience something may be achieved.

It is appropriate that the first serious essay[17] should have come from A. P. Elkin, for long the ranking Australianist, whose insight into Aboriginal mentality and culture has ripened over half a century. I offer my comments with the most full respect.

He begins by pointing out how much Aboriginal thought takes for granted — the ultimate origins of the world, the earth, the sky, the sea, and life itself. The heroic personages now regarded as 'totemic ancestors' are believed to have made the world, not by a reaction *ex nihilo,* but by what he describes as "a transformation and a revealing of what already exists". That "transformation" and "revealing", he says, still happen in every religious ritual e.g. in initiation rites. He says that what is made available to the novice in such rites is "the essence of the non-appearing", which he likens to the Kantian *noumena,* which are intellectual or intuited things. He likens it also to the Ionians' *physis,* the principle or *Arche* of all things, "the sustaining ground of man and his universe". Thus, for Elkin, The Dreaming is in cosmogonical terms "the ever-present, unseen ground of being — of existence".

From cosmogony he passes to cosmology. The cosmos is The Dreaming as it appears in phenomena. It is the universal ground of every particular, unlimited by space or time.

Elkin appears to wish to show Aboriginal thinkers as having wrestled with most of the perennial philosophical problems: the one and the many, the particular and the universal, time and duration, the conditioned and the conditioning, and so on. In order to do so he draws on parallels with some of the pre-Socratic philosophers (e.g. Thales and Heraclitus), some of the moderns (Leibnitz, Kant and Bergson) and even finds some analogies in Hindu thought. Some of the propositions that emerge are that "man and natural species and phenomena are considered parts of one and the same social, moral and psychological order or structural system", which is very reminiscent of Radcliffe-Brown's view; that "man and all that exists not only have a common source in The Dreaming but also constitute a personalized system"; and that that is why "contingencies can be interpreted and met, and even forestalled, through behaviour of a ritualized or formal pattern".

He then goes on to consider some questions of epistemology: the Aboriginal categories of causation, time, space, number and — perhaps a little strangely — property. I have no time to go into details but will indicate only his main observations.

As to causation, Elkin appears to embed the discussion in the context of 'personalized system' already mentioned. I believe he means by this that some events put into operation by personal, spiritistic and magical activities by ritual, were countered by the same means. He seems to say that what we call 'cause' was the facilitation by ritual means of invisible noumena to become visible. An illustration was the use of totemic ritual to release the life-principle from totemic sites. Probably I have not understood this part of the exposition, but it seems to be Elkin's opinion that Aboriginal thinkers had not conceived of cause as "a linkage of preceding events together with the total context of situations" but thought instead of "personal and spiritistic and magical causes, seen or unseen, nearby or at a distance".

As to time, Elkin accepts that the Aboriginal does "recognize a past as distinct from the immediacy of today" but it is not a past that stretches very far back — at the most two or three generations — and "it is not a past that is gone forever". Elkin explains that under this conception "man and natural phenomena do not exist *now,* and events do not happen *now,* as a result of a chain of events extending back to a long-past period — a 'Dreamtime' — a beginning. They exist and they happen because that Dreamtime is also here and now. It is The Dreaming, the condition or ground of existence". He draws a formidably difficult picture in explanation. It is a picture of time, not as "a horizontal line extending back horizontally through a series of pasts but rather of a vertical line in which *the* past underlies and is within the present". It is an argument, as I understand it, that time was not a feature of the Aboriginal cosmos; that 'chronological distance' did not exist for them; and that all existence cycled, being replenished from The Dreaming, which was inexhaustible.

It seems to me that Elkin is saying that time for the Aborigines was not 'real' or 'objective'; not quantitative in being a measure of change; not a relationship such as that between past, present and future as we understand them; not any kind of entity, but essentially a psychological experience. By implication he goes farther: these are not his words, but time for an Aboriginal does not 'fly like an arrow'; again these are not his words, but time for an Aboriginal 'flies like a boomerang'; it curves and returns upon itself. With a sort of cosmic courtesy, it cycles and, because of that, it allows what to us are asymmetrical and irreversible temporal relations to become for Aborigines non-temporal and mutually compenetrative between past and present. It is therefore of no significance that Aborigines may seem ahistorical in outlook, and remember nothing farther away than the great-grandfather's day: the cosmos, as it were, remembers for them. The world of any Aboriginal community is saturated with memorial signs of things on the remembering of which human life depends. So that, for Elkin, The Dreaming as the condition or ground of existence, is timeless and cannot receive any change, which may help to explain the discovered tendency of Aboriginal society to accept only those new things that will fit the forms of permanence.

Elkin handles the Aboriginal categories of space and number in somewhat similar fashion. In essence, he regards the absence of measuring and numbering by units in linear order as "a striking, if not the basic, difference in the epistemological concepts of Western and Aboriginal thought". I will leave that very large proposition as stated, and to move on to his, to me, rather strange proposition that Aborigines were 'owned' by the territory which, in ordinary speech, we would say they 'owned'. He repeats the proposition in a number of ways: a man's country 'knew' him and gave him 'sustenance and life'; what we call 'possessions' or 'things' — the ground itself, symbolic sites, totems, totem places — are not 'things' but "sacramental means through which man identifies himself with, and participates in, The Dreaming".

Now, having written much about 'The Dreaming', and, in a sense having invented it, in that I was the first to write about it with a capital T and a capital D, I should perhaps be the last to say so, but The Dreaming is coming in for a lot of attributions that I think it should accept only under advisement. There is, for example, a distinctly zoological undertone to the idea of any person being 'owned' by a tract of country. This notion has entered into Australian law, at least as an obiter dicta, as an outcome of Mr Justice Blackburn's judgment in the Yirrkala land case, in which he used certain words to the effect that the members of certain clans were owned by the clan lands.

Having admitted — superfluously — as you will have noted, that I am no philosopher, I now admit, in supererogation, that I am no lawyer, but at the same time I insist that there is something wrong at the heart of this proposition. I argue that a 'property' relation is a direct relation between a person and an object only in an elliptical way. It is a relation between persons *in respect* of an object: and this is vastly different. It is at the least a triadic, not a dyadic relation. What we see in the Aboriginal world is a relationship between the members of a patrilineal local clan, or similar group, jointly and the whole world of other persons, single, joint, or common: a relationship expressed as a claim of right, with well-understood 'incidents', in respect of a finite territory, and all its symbols. It approximates to a covenanted relationship, entered into by, and multilaterally agreed to amongst, the ancestral founders of Aboriginal society, and raised by religious tradition to sacramental status. To speak of land 'knowing' or 'owning' anyone is to me a reversion to animatism.

I spoke earlier of the anthropological criticisms of the post-Socratic Western philosophical tradition. But even if we turn to the pre-Socratics we need to remember that they were already "the heirs of a mature civilization and culture and to some extent (were) reactionaries against it. They revolted against the mythological, imaginative view of the universe and its origin, and endeavoured in a scientific, free and unprejudiced spirit to answer the problem in a rational way".[18] There is clearly a risk of enormous anachronism even if we attempt no more than to look for similarities between their anti-mythological thought and the pre-philosophic thought we imagine we can intuit or deduce from Aboriginal religious thought and practice. Moreover, one is entitled to ask whether even the earliest Greek philosophers, from the very nature of their known interests, are likely to be helpful. They were in a sense physical philosophers, trying to discern a common hidden structure behind the outward appearance of the physical world. Their imagery was material, and so was their nomination of the substance common to all corporeal change — water, fire, air, and 'the boundless' — as the material principle of things. I would think that, if we accuse the Aborigines of philosophy, we cannot justly accuse them of hylozoism, of attributing life to matter, as did the Ionians. Nor, as I understand them, did the Aborigines puzzle over movement and change like the Greeks, or pursue knowledge of the cosmos for its own sake. I can see no evidence that they had conceived of an *Arche,* a material principle of all things, although their symbolism of water, air, fire and — dare I say? — the boundless Dreaming is well known to be richly developed. But it seems to me to be following a false scent to pore over the Aboriginal data looking for hints of a search for unity of substance in all material diversity, or for a hidden structure of reality behind physical diversity, or for a search for knowledge for its own sake. And lastly, I doubt if it could rightly be said that the Aborigines were, like the pre-Socratics, "captivated by 'movement' in the widest sense of the word: movement in the heavens, in the coming-to-be and passing-away of things of experience, in the incessant change of human life, individual and political".[19]

Now, I do not deny the value even of distant analogy, but here are four good reasons for caution until whatever analogies we draw with Western philosophical thought are deepened and refined. There are other difficulties too, the greatest being the absence of a literate tradition, the fact that there was nothing to suggest the growth of a self-conscious intellectual detachment towards the myths — no Hesiod or Homer to winnow and organize the raw material, and, last but not least, except for a few specialists, our abysmal ignorance of the deeper semantics of Aboriginal languages, including the secret languages often used by ritualists.

But here I withdraw a pace or two. In their own way the Aborigines did try to catch hold of a hidden structure of things. I wrote elsewhere that they seemed fascinated almost to the point of obsession with "vitality, fertility and growth", and that

". . . vitalistic things obtruded throughout the myths and rites — water, blood, fat, hair, excrements, the sex organs, semen, sexuality in all its phases, the quickening in the womb, child-spirits, mystical impregnation and reincarnation; the development of the body from birth to death, the transitions of the human spirit from before organic assumption until after physical dissolution; apparently animated phenomena such as green leaves rain and the seasons, lightning, whirlwinds, shooting stars and the heavenly bodies; or things of unexplained origin, unusual appearance and giant size . . ."[20]

FOOTNOTES

1. William James, *The Essential Writings*, Edited by Bruce Wiltshire, 1971, p.221.
2. E. A. Worms, 'Religion' in *Australian Aboriginal Studies*, 1963, p.231.
3. W. E. H. Stanner, 'Religion, Totemism and Symbolism' in *Aboriginal Man in Australia*, 1965, p.213.
4. *ibid.* p.215.
5. T. G. H. Strehlow, Aranda Traditions, 1947; 'Personal Monototemism in a Polytotemic Community', in *Sonderdruck aus Festschrift fur Ad. E. Jensen.* 1964.
6. *ibid.* p.729.
7. Charles H. Eden, *The Fifth Continent*, S.P.C.K. 1877, pp.69-70.
8. *ibid.*
9. William James, *op.cit.* p.241.
10. James Feibleman, *The Theory of Human Culture*, 1946.
11. L. R. Hiatt, Introduction to *Australian Aboriginal Mythology*, 1976, p.10.
12. Hiatt, *ibid*, p.10. The quotation is from Roheim.
13. Anton Baumstark, *Comparative Liturgy*, 1958, p.1.
14. *ibid.*
15. Stanner, *loc.cit.* p.235.
16. Edward A. Tiryakian, *Sociologism and Existentialism*, 1962, p.3.
17. A. P. Elkin, 'Elements of Australian Aboriginal Philosophy', *Oceania*, Vol.XL, No. 2, Dec. 1969, pp.85-98.
18. Ignatius Brady, *A History of Ancient Philosophy*, p.31.
19. *ibid.* p.66.
20. Stanner, *loc.cit.* p.217.
21. *ibid.*

ADDENDA

Page 24, line 11: come *read* some
Page 24, line 22: should be deleted
Page 24, line 23: should be part-deleted from 'though' to 'sky-'
Page 24, line 25: quasi-moral *read* quasi-mortal
Page 27, last line on page: group-paintings *read* ground-paintings
Page 32, line 15: reaction *ex nihilo read* creation *ex nihilo*
Page 35, after line 29: *add* To say so is not to rediscover the Tylorian *anima* or Marrett's animatism. But it is a topic for another occasion

RONALD M. BERNDT

A PROFILE OF GOOD AND BAD IN AUSTRALIAN ABORIGINAL RELIGION

- I -

I am honoured to be asked to deliver the 1979 Charles Strong Memorial Lecture. My theme of 'good' and 'bad' in Aboriginal religion is one which is close to all theological thinking. It is also one which, I believe, was implicit in some of Strong's writings,[1] as one would expect it to be. Before I explore this issue, however, it is necessary to say something about Aboriginal religion in general terms so that my theme can be viewed in perspective.

Most of us have ideas about what constitutes religion, or *a* religion, even though we might be hesitant in articulating a definition which could fit a number of different religious orientations. Moreover, in view of the spate of material on Aboriginal society and culture emanating from varying sources, some of which may well be dubious, we might take the line of least resistance and read into what we hear about Aboriginal religion what we already know about our own or others.

That kind of approach is almost a time-honoured one. We like to clothe the strange or the unfamiliar with an identifiable mantle which provides an explanatory frame of reference in our own terms. Bringing alien things into our own experience and treating them in this way is a relatively common device. It enables us to rationalize them; and by finding basic similarities we can commence to use them, or express tolerance toward those who use them, or are of them. However, that process of transformation usually takes us a long way from their empirical reality and, in our particular case, from what Aboriginal religion means to traditionally-oriented people.

The search for meaning is central to systematic anthropological research; but methodological devices used in that process often remove it from the empirical situation. Consequently, the end product that tells us what particular religious phenomena mean to particular believers or practitioners can differ considerably from an explanation offered in more general terms. The process of interpretation can have its dangers. It can hide or, at best, overshadow what people have to say about their religion. To put this in another way, the understanding of Aboriginal religion has been greatly affected by theories *about* religion. That does not mean that interpretation is not a significant heuristic device. My much revered teacher, the late Professor A.P. Elkin, saw Aboriginal religion as concerning primarily the 'secret life of men'. Only grudgingly did he include women within the sacred dimension, and then only with particular limitations. In the third edition (1954) of his *Australian Aborigines* he wrote, of women, that 'they are in the "nave", and sometimes even in the "chancel" '.[2] Because he conceptually separated religion from everyday living and emphasized the idea of 'secrecy', his philosophical approach led him to think in mystical terms, a kind of oversanctification of belief and ritual. Elkin sought a methodological scheme in order to provide added meaning to his material on Aboriginal religion;[3] and that guided him toward paths which were vulnerable to criticism, as Stanner has quite rightly pointed out.[4]

Stanner himself, however, has not been immune to this. In his monograph 'On Aboriginal Religion',[5] it is clear that various theories of religion have influenced considerably his own thinking about Aboriginal religion. While I do not follow him in his delineation of ritual sacrifice in relation to initiation,[6] nor in his treatment of sacramentalism, his analysis of Murinbata religion was grounded in a firm belief in the continuous relevance of religion in everyday living.[7] He has probably influenced me, at least to some degree, in my own approach in *Australian Aboriginal Religion*[8] — of which he has been critical.

- II -

Elkin and myself have been the only two Australian anthropologists so far who, in writing about Aboriginal religion, have been able to draw on firsthand knowledge of a fairly wide range of Aboriginal societies. Most other studies (for example, those by Warner, Strehlow and Meggitt), including Stanner's, have focused on the religion of one particular Aboriginal society. It is well to remember that, traditionally, Aboriginal culture was not the same throughout the continent. Nor was there any central or federal authority. The picture was one of relatively independent socio-cultural constellations, that interacted only within a certain regional range. The members of such constellations were jealous of their own internal integrity and proud of their own unique identity: differences and contrasts between them were important in helping to define that identity. It was not strictly possible to speak of one Aboriginal religion. There were, rather, many Aboriginal religions. We can identify basic similarities — notably, in the organization of activities associated with ritual expressions; but differences between belief systems, in meaning and in symbolic interpretation, were quite crucial.

The social component, the social dimension of religion, must not be underestimated; but the question of mytho-ritual meaning is of fundamental significance. While religious knowledge was something which all members of a particular social group possessed in some degree, and was seen as being uniquely theirs, related to them and to them alone, some mytho-ritual complexes were much broader in perspective. Common threads of belief and practice did link or hold together large numbers of people belonging to different social units, although acknowledgement of similarity was not always made explicit. Even where it was, variation between one socio-cultural constellation and the next was expected and 'normal'. It is only in recent years, with the growing interest in establishing an overall Aboriginal identity, that attempts are being made to play down differences and to highlight common elements.

The lineaments of all Aboriginal religion, looked at from outside, in overview, were basically alike. They rested on a three-fold set of relationships: between human beings themselves; between human beings and nature; and between human beings and their deities. This was articulated through what has been called in translation 'the Dreaming', a concept which was and is a key to the eternal verities of human living. Variously expressed, it provided a charter for the whole pattern of human existence. It was manifested through mythic characters, often in human form but often with shape-changing propensities. Their actions shaped the land and the environment we know today. Some were responsible for creating human beings and natural species and for introducing particular social orders. Some were more circumscribed in their actions and/or more localized. They humanized the world — the world of their believers and adherents.

Their adventures and travels usually concluded in either of two ways. One was transformation or metamorphosis: they finally changed their physical shape, adopting the physical forms we can see them in now. *Or* they moved out of one particular area into another; and within a certain range, their paths provided lines of communication and shared ritual linkages between neighbouring groups. In either case, they left behind them an essential quality which we can call a sacred power. Thus they continue to live on eternally in spiritual form, and to influence the actions of human beings. They also left tangible expressions of themselves throughout the countryside. Such places contain something of their spiritual essence. They sanctify the land, and are often focal points for ritual action.

These mythic beings, then, are not only intimately associated with the land. They are part of it. They are also directly related to living Aborigines. This linkage exists mainly through the ability of mythic beings to change their shape. For example, a particular spirit is mythically manifested through a particular creature. In fact, all such creatures today are a reflection of different spirits, and all are believed to contain the essential essence of the Dreaming. There may also be other correlations through which that spiritual essence is conveyed. Through conception or birth, every Aboriginal person is believed to have a similar linkage. A mythic symbol, in the form of a creature or some associated manifestation, animates a foetus, bringing with it a life-force emanating from the Dreaming. This symbol, or 'totem' as it is sometimes called, serves as an agent, a manifestation of that bond. In doing so, it underlines the belief that he, or she, has the *same* spiritual quality as a particular mythic being, and is closely identified with that being. In some areas, he or she is regarded as a living representation of a particular mythic character. Aboriginal men and women are identified through the myths, and identify themselves within these. Human beings are regarded as being part of nature, bound to it by strong emotional ties, sharing a common life-force.

This view emphasizes the contemporary relevance of a *living* mythology which concerns everyday behaviour and thought. Mythology, whether or not it has a ritual expression or a ritual counterpart, is not so much a celebration of the past. It has to do with the present, and is a continuing force, adaptive to changing social circumstances. In brief, the structure of mythic events is believed to have been set once and for all at the very beginning of things, during the creative era. Those events have a continuing relevance to man. And mythic actions, shorn of their supernatural and magical elements, bear a close resemblance to those of traditionally-oriented Aborigines. Such myths are symbolic statements, believed to convey more than their bare story value. They are explanatory vehicles which are subject to interpretation. The events they portray provide guides to action, the good and the bad among them.

Traditional Aboriginal societies were examples of what have been called sacred societies. That is to say, religion was all-pervasive and permeated all aspects of social living. It is true that certain rituals or particular areas or sites were set apart, that access to them was restricted. Many of the great rituals, including their songs and the emblems which were used, were of a secret-sacred nature. There were rules governing the admission or exclusion of particular persons, both males and females. In general terms, the major religious rites were dominated by men, and women were more or less submissive supporters. Nevertheless, virtually everyone in a particular society was involved in some way. Aboriginal religion was marked, not so much by a visible demarcation between the sexes, as by complementarity between men and women. Socio-economic interdependence between men and women, whether young or old, made possible the holding of large ritual sequences. This did not invalidate or detract from the significance of the secret-sacred. Detailed religious knowledge was held by a selected few. Symbolic meanings and mytho-ritual interpretations were graded. There was scrupulous protection of emblems and other aspects from the uninitiated. Custodians of religious knowledge — the specialists, as it were — were fully-initiated older (not necessarily 'old') men. Nevertheless, the outlines of the great myths were known (*had* to be known) by all members of a particular society or group. Their more esoteric symbolic allusions, their more complex inner meanings, were the concern only of fully-initiated men.

Two points need to be made. One, Aboriginal religion concerned everyone within a community, in varying degrees. Two, Aboriginal religion in its mytho-ritual expression was intimately associated with everyday social living, with relations between the sexes, with the natural environment, and with food-collecting and hunting. And, *as* religion, it was concerned with the meaning of life, with the fundamental patterning of human existence, and with what we can call the moral universe.

- III -

There are several ways in which we may look at this 'moral universe'. I shall approach the matter through the internal content of particular myths. Not all can be treated in this way, but many of them can.

Statements are made about what happened in the creative era — in that dimension of the Dreaming. Through some action on the part of a mythic being, a direction is taken which changes subsequent events; it has not only mythic but also continuing-human implications. A simple example is one that tells how death came into the world. The reference is to *physical* death. There are many versions, from all over the continent. These are two very short ones.

In a Maung version from western Arnhem Land,[9] Moon man quarrels with Spotted Possum, or Spotted Cat, who is mortally wounded. As Possum lies dying he says: 'All the people who come after me ... will die forever!' Moon, however, replies: 'You should have let me speak first, because *I* won't die.' Because Possum spoke first, human beings die.

In a similar myth from north-eastern Arnhem Land,[10] Moon man lives with his sister, Dugong. Because she is in pain after being severely bitten by leeches, she decides to leave her human form (that is, to die) and become a dugong. Moon, however, does not want to die. He says he will go into the sky: that he will die, but will come back alive. His sister replies: 'When I die, I won't come back, and you can pick up my bones.' That is how death came into the world.

In a different context, Stanner,[11] on the basis of Murinbata mythology, writes of a 'wrongful turning of life'. There is 'the persistent suggestion', he says, 'of many myths that there has been some kind of "immemorial misdirection" in human affairs, and that living men are committed to its consequences'. His example is that of the mythic woman, Mutingga, who swallows several children. As a result, she is killed, her belly opened up and the children removed alive. In the discussion of this myth, which concerns the rite of *punj*, Stanner observes, among a number of things, that Mutingga should not have died. However, she had 'gone wrong', and it was her own fault. As a result, men now have the bullroarer which 'stands for' or is symbolic of her. A parallel should not be drawn between this sequence of events and the disobedience of Adam and Eve. In the case of Adam and Eve, a contract was made, and the breaking of that contract brought sin into the world. The original mythic picture as far as Aboriginal Australia is concerned is different.

The Mutingga example is roughly similar to the Mara version of the Kunapipi myth.[12]

Mumuna (the Mother), aided by her two daughters (the Mungamunga), entices men to their camp. During the night, when they are making love with the girls, she kills the men, then roasts them and swallows them whole. Afterwards she regurgitates them, expecting them to be revived by the bites of meat ants; but they are not. This performance is repeated again and again, until her daughters become worried about the death of so many men. In the meantime, however, relatives of the men have formed a search party and eventually discover what has been happening. Their leader, Eaglehawk, catches Mumuna in the act and kills her. Her death-cries enter every tree, and so does her blood. It is really the blood which contains the sound. Eaglehawk then cuts down a tree and makes a bullroarer. As he swings it, it 'turns into a *mumuna*'; its sound is that of the Mother as she died.

As with the Murinbata example,[13] the Gunwinggu-speaking people of western Arnhem Land have myths in which the death of a mythic being brings about a ritual 'advantage'.

In one case,[14] Lumaluma, the Whale, comes on two men incorrectly carrying out a sacred *maraiin* ritual. He is enraged at this, and frightens them away. Then he finds their *maraiin* emblems, which represent various natural species. He spears each of the emblems in turn, calling its name: each takes its animal shape and returns to its natural habitat. He gathers up some of the other objects he finds and goes back to his home camp. The people are angry, and plan to hold another *maraiin* ritual. Against the advice of his relatives, Lumaluma attends, and is speared. Before he dies, he reveals all of his own emblems and the appropriate ritual that goes with them. After that, he goes down to the sea and 'turns himself' into a whale.

The problem here is one of interpretation. Do such examples represent 'an immemorial misdirection', as Stanner has put it? In our own work on the Gunwinggu, we commented briefly on this issue.[15] While an 'immemorial misdirection' can easily be seen to be relevant to myths about death coming to man, it is not particularly apparent in the others. Gunwinggu-speakers would interpret such actions on the part of mythic beings as an exercise of 'free will'. Mythic beings, like human beings, can choose one course of action in contrast to another. The choice they make has consequences for themselves and for others, but does not necessarily commit them irrevocably. However, one consequence of the mythic action for human beings (as in the case of Mutiṅgga, Mumuna and Lumaluma) is ritual advantage. It results in the introduction of ritual which, supposedly, would not have come about without a wrong act taking place. Out of bad, comes something good. In the myth itself, no moral judgement is made: it is simply that this is the course of events which brings about ritual benefits — 'this is how it came about'. The comment by Stanner that Mutiṅgga 'went wrong' can well be regarded as her having made a wrong choice, that it was her own fault, and need not have been. Among the Gunwinggu, there are other examples which underline the aspect of 'destiny' or of 'fate': that certain events occur which are beyond the control of a mythic being and, presumably, beyond the control of man.

- IV -

Spirit characters most subject to this fatalistic complex are, in western Arnhem Land, called *djang* characters. Like the major mythic beings already mentioned, they move across the country and, in the process, they introduce changes in the local landscape and leave behind there supplies of natural species. The primary difference between them and the others is that they actually take a 'wrong turning', do something they should not have done and, importantly, recognize this. The suggestion is that, if only they had *known* that what they were doing would bring disaster on themselves and on others, they would have acted differently. Possession of that knowledge would have enabled them to make a choice between one course of action and another. However, the dice are loaded and, consequently, they are fated to 'go wrong' — nothing can be done about it, and they don't really resist their destiny!

At Gudjegbin, a spirit man killed a wallaby, and he and his wife prepared an oven in which to cook it. Unfortunately, they have made their oven on tabu-ed sandy ground. As the animal is cooking, its stomach bursts and the blood seeps into the sand. The noise and the smell of the blood attract two Rainbow Snakes (Ngalyod), who emerge from nearby rocks. They swallow the pair and then vomit them as rocks. The two characters in the story had 'made themselves wrong'.

In another example, an orphan living at Ilngir, near the mouth of Cooper's Creek, cried continually. His mother's sister, Inimbu, offered him different kinds of food to keep him quiet, but he refused every one. Ngalyod, the Rainbow Snake, was disturbed by his crying. She came across the country toward the camp where the noise was coming from. She made the ground shake and made flood waters rise, foaming. And the cold wind was so bitter that all the camp fires died. Eventually, she surrounded all the people camped there and swallowed them, including the orphan. In a sequel to this, other people, on hearing of this, followed up Ngalyod and speared her so that she vomited all of them, still alive.

Such myths are very detailed and there are many variations on this particular theme.

A common one is that an orphan is neglected, and not adequately fed. His brother is angry. To punish the whole camp, he deliberately breaks a tabued Ngalyod egg (sometimes a tabu-ed stone) secreted in a tree. Ngalyod makes her appearance, bringing with her an intensely cold wind which 'turns' all the people into rock at Ganyulaidjgandi:'they make themselves *djang*'. Something wrong had occurred; nothing could have been done to avert disaster.

And finally, among the many myths of this kind:

A man named Gawariwari lives on wild honey which he collects. Since he eats only this, and is always collecting honey from trees, one of his arms remains raised in an upright position. He moves across the country, putting honey into his basket. He comes to a place named Gugulgoidj. Everywhere he looks, there is honey. From a large tree, however, comes the loud buzzing of bees. There is something different here, he thinks, and his body starts to tingle. He begins to worry. 'What am I going to do?' he asks. 'Perhaps I have spoilt this honey?' A storm breaks, and with the rain comes Ngalyod. Gawariwari cries out: 'I have spoilt myself. I had better run to Gulbalga!' But he can do nothing to save himself, there are too many Ngalyod waiting to swallow him. So he 'turns himself' into a painting at Gulbalga rocks: he 'makes himself *djang*'.

The interpretation of such myths as these, which are part of the fabric of western Arnhem Land religion, requires the presentation of much more detail than I am able to include here. They are not typical of Aboriginal mythology as a whole and are quite distinctively Gunwinggu. Many characters set out in search of a country, a particular place (or a particular *kind* of place) where they are to become *djang*. They embark on their journey with that specific expectation — that they will be transformed, will put their spirits 'for ever', at their pre-defined destination. It is *within* that frame, and not outside it, that they take a course of action which leads to that dénouement. If and when they 'do wrong', or 'go wrong', it is within the context of an already-shaped destiny.

The interplay of free will blocked, and inevitable disaster, constitutes a cultural emphasis which points up an essential conflict in human values. But the myths are much more than this. They symbolize a fundamental dilemma of man. While not necessarily undermining man's essential harmony with nature, they nevertheless indicate the presence of hostile forces which are not easily placated and which can be aroused inadvertently.

Ngalyod, the Rainbow Snake, is a key cathartic figure. Ngalyod (or other equivalent names) may be referred to as male or female, may be represented in multiple form, and may or may not have children. As the 'good Mother', in this region, she is an expression of human and environmental fertility and the sponsor of ritual which concerns the well-being of the society and its members. In her 'bad Mother' manifestation, she is fear-inspiring, easily angered and quick to respond to real or supposed transgressions. She is a living symbol of the balance between 'goodness' and 'badness', and of the view that wrong actions on the part of human beings (whether or not they are intentional) are to be expected and will not or cannot necessarily be prevented. This theme is at the root of questions about the destiny of man. While warnings are apparent in the myths, which make explicit what disasters can befall human beings, these disasters are not easy to evade and the results are inevitable.

Even in the context of the *djang* myths, therefore, it is not a case of an 'immemorial misdirection'. Mythically, each *djang*-transformation or 'turning' (that is, becoming something else) is a creative act in the overall process of humanizing or spiritualizing the natural world. Many *djang* centres are species-renewal sites, activated through particular rites. Many, of course, are not, and exist as *self-perpetuating* species-renewal sites. In that sense, out of a perceived wrong act, good emerges.

- V -

This problem of 'good' and 'bad' was one that undoubtedly exercised the minds of Aborigines as they told their myths around camp fires or sang and danced them out on the ritual ground. Differences between good and bad actions were never in doubt. They were spelt out in considerable detail in the mythology which constituted the basis of their belief system, and were identified in everyday life.

When a north-eastern Arnhem Lander of the *dua* moiety dies, his or her spirit is taken by Bunbalama (the Paddle Maker) in his canoe out to sea in the direction of Bralgu, the land of the dead. He or she transfers to the back of a porpoise, and goes on to Bralgu. There a *bilgbilg,* masked plover, warns Gringbilma, who is on the look-out for newly arrived spirits. The newcomer is asked where he comes from and who his relatives are, and then passes on to meet two old women named Yambiyambi and Lialugidj. He is told to drink unclean water from a well. As he bends forward, they look at his nasal septum. If it has been pierced properly and can be seen through, he is told not to drink, but to continue on to where the other Bralgu spirits are living. If not, Yambiyambi hits him on the head with her conch shell and the new spirit is killed for ever: he cannot join the other Bralgu spirits and will not be reincarnated as a human being — he simply disappears entirely.

There are several variations on this theme, in this area and in others.

Among Gunwinggu speakers, for instance, a new spirit passes ill-intentioned guardians of the spirit world who attempt to do him harm. Escaping them, he continues on to the sea coast where he meets the Ferry Man, who takes him across by canoe to the land of the dead where he joins the other spirits. If the new spirit is a woman, the Ferry Man brings a new canoe, lifts her gently into it, and does not beat her as he does a male spirit.

In these accounts, a spirit of a newly dead person is not judged according to the good or bad behaviour of that person during his or her lifetime. The tests relate entirely to whether or not he or she had conformed with traditional custom, although there is preferential treatment for women in some cases. The journey to the land of the dead is supposedly fraught with difficulties which symbolize the vicissitudes experienced in life. On having reached the promised land, he or she joins the immortals, and may be reborn. This absence of accountability to mythic beings for what a person has or has not done during his or her lifetime, emphasizes a basic Aboriginal view toward such issues.

Aboriginal mythology is abundantly supplied with what can be described as 'good and bad examples'.[16] The question really is, how should we interpret these? If we accept the premise that myths are a kind of mirror of reality (although never an exact mirror), that they reflect to some degree contemporary living, and that they are symbolic statements about these things — then, we can make a little headway in interpreting them. Radcliffe-Brown once wrote about the cosmos being ruled by law, that men and women ought to observe the rules of behaviour — but that 'there are irregularities in human society and in nature'.[17] Stanner, speaking of myths, also suggested that they 'are a sort of statement about the whole reality, a declaration about the penalties of private will, and by implication a thesis on the spoiling of possible unity'.[18] I would agree with the first part of this, but not necessarily with the implication. It was with a different interpretation that I was concerned in my paper on 'Traditional morality as expressed through the medium of an Australian Aboriginal religion'.[19]

In brief, the 'irregularities of human society and in nature' constitute part of a total system and are written into it as part of the condition of social living. Consequently, they are *part of that unity*. Hiatt misunderstood this point when he wrote that 'If a myth merely describes the good and evil that people do, then either it is a charter for both good and evil or not a charter at all'.[20] The issue is not as simple as this. In the Western Desert, the great mytho-ritual religious cycle of the *dingari* expresses in its patterning a series of mythic incidents, commenting on the difficulties experienced in Desert living at both the social and environmental levels.[21] These conceptually provide two complementary orientations, in which particular circumstances are regarded as being good or bad, as the case may be. While the seasons remain good, people (mythic or otherwise) are able to achieve reasonable personal satisfaction. Bad seasons can bring hunger, thirst and even tragedy. In social living, breaches of the peace occur, which may be occasioned by fear, jealousy, quarrelling, trickery, theft, seduction, murder and so on. These infiltrate the ethical system as such. In this way, the *dingari* provides a yardstick against which both moral and immoral actions are conceived of as a natural condition of man. Each incident categorized as being bad, or immoral, is resolved in some way which permits a return to the *status quo*. The resolution may not at all times appear to be of a kind we would 'naturally' expect. After all, we are dealing with different assumptions about law and order and the moral universe. Nevertheless, an act adjudged 'bad' follows its own course, which is likely to bring disaster or punishment on the wrongdoer. That course of action is spelt out in the myth, and is not simply assumed or left unrecorded.

I shall give two examples, very much summarized:

(1) Ngadjinaulweru, an old man, makes a small boy, Mudila, carry a heavy load of boomerangs without giving him food. While he is out cutting more wood for boomerangs, Mudila obtains meat himself and cooks it. However, he eats this alone and hides the fire. Ngadjinaulweru returns hungry and cold. In the night, Mudila escapes with his fire. The old man tracks him down, but is tricked by the boy and drowns in a creek, where he remains. The boy goes into a hole, where he also remains. (These are their Dreaming sites, near a big hill on the Canning Stock Route.)

(2) Gadadjilga, a mythic lizard man, seduces a tabu-ed relative (one of the Ganabuda mythic women). In turn he is killed by the other Ganabuda women at Djawuldjawul soak, near Lake White.[22]

Such examples can be multiplied, within differing contexts and in relation to different reprehensible acts. What must be kept in mind is that such examples are mythically framed, are religious, and may be re-enacted in ritual. They reflect, as Stanner mentions, '... much of the "human-all-too-human" character of man'.[23]

Myth, as to some extent a reflection of reality — and Western Desert mythology mirrors this reasonably well — demonstrates this essential character of man. Moreover, because such myths belong to the Dreaming, as do all of those I have noted here, they are part of the sacred-past-in-the-present. In other words, these myths and the religious system into which they fit, concern issues relevant to the welfare of man. If we think of some of these as bizarre, or even as fantastic (as Hiatt seems to think some of them are[24]), that is not really the point. They are symbolic statements, sufficiently flexible to meet the demands of changing events within their own universe of experience. In another sense, they explore the vagaries of human thought, which is not necessarily systematic at all times and does not always identify the implications of specific acts.

In such a body of mythology, relevant to a particular religious expression such as the *dingari,* we are presented with a moral system which portrays the actions of mythic beings who are themselves deities. The lesson driven home is that wrong-doing brings its own punishment in this life, *not* in the next. In the Bralgu case, where a new spirit is finally 'killed' if his or her nasal septum is not pierced, this is not punishment for doing wrong to others. He or she is being punished for not conforming with the cultural norm. In ordinary circumstances, everyone *would* have their nasal septums pierced, so that the situation is in a sense unreal. The myths I have just discussed are more down-to-earth. What they are saying is that there are things which can and do happen in the ordinary process of social living. They may be good or they may be bad, and they happened to mythic beings; it is therefore likely they will happen to human beings. They are part of an inevitable and irreversible frame of existence — when bad actions affect, harmfully, other persons, some form of punishment is bound to result. The good is conceived as co-existing with the bad.

Supernatural intervention is not really envisaged — except in the case of specific ritual infringements, where sanctions are imposed, through human agents. Generally, a deity does not intervene in the affairs of man unless induced to do so. People themselves must take some initiative, or make some move. Ritual activity is the normal channel through which man communicates with his deities. Intrusion into a tabu area, or contravening some rule directly associated with a mythic being, automatically triggers off a ritual response, which arouses the deity. In the *djang* examples, we saw that cooking on sandy ground, breaking a Rainbow's egg, repeated crying on the part of a child, and so on, can bring — or summon — the Rainbow Snake. The breaking of a tabu is in itself a kind of ritual, in reverse, which brings about what can be called divine punishment.

In ordinary circumstances, human beings must work quite hard to gain a livelihood directly from their environment. But, in Aboriginal belief, this kind of hard work is not enough. For the seasons to come and go in an orderly fashion, for the species to be regularly renewed, ritual must be performed. Human beings must play their part. The three-sided relationship I mentioned before, between people and natural environment and deities, was seen as one of interdependence, of working in conjunction with one another; but it called for a concerted effort on the part of human beings. I use the word 'conjunction' in this context, rather than 'harmony', for a particular reason. It is not so much that Aboriginal creative beings made people in their own image (or *vice versa*) — although many of them did so, as in the case of the great Gadjari, the Djanggau (Djanggawul) and Waramurungoindju, to mention only three. Remember that Aborigines in many areas, particularly in the Western Desert,[25] through birth or conception, have within them a part of, or are manifestations of, particular mythic beings.

There is, however, a basic dilemma here — not necessarily seen as such by those Aborigines involved in traditional situations. On one hand, myths purport to show a range of possible mythic *and* human action. Superficially, a range of choices is presented for inspection. It is not so much the 'good' which is emphasized. That is taken for granted. But the 'bad' receives much more attention — as it should, because through that device its inevitable, harmful repercussions are highlighted. On the other hand, there is the question of destiny, which removes free choice, or severely limits it. Once someone has taken a 'wrong turning', the process is irreversible. *Djang* myths demonstrate this aspect. So, in a sense, do those from the Western Desert where wrong actions speak for themselves. The dilemma is not resolved by saying, as do these myths, that good and bad acts are part of the natural order of living. Or, is it saying quite simply and unequivocally that human beings are innately fallible? One point, however, enhances the view that the moral order of Aboriginal man consists of a mixture of both good and bad *because* this is also the state of nature, of which man is an integral part.

'Evil' is, on the whole, too strong a word for the kind of concept we have here. 'Bad' is more appropriate. As we have seen, good and bad were not polarized as two sharply opposed forces, or entities. Perhaps such a stark crystallization of opposites, a confrontation of two monolithic concepts or symbolic figures, would not have suited Aboriginal perspectives. That approach possibly sits better in the framework of a religion which emphasizes a single supreme deity, or a struggle for supremacy between two key deities. In this respect, some people have hesitated to use the term deity for the supernatural beings, even the main creative beings, of Aboriginal religions; but I do not want to go into the matter of terminology here. They have enough of the attributes of beings usually called deities, in their activities *and,* particularly, in the attitudes of believers toward them, to warrant that label.

It is not that Aborigines did not recognize two-fold contrasts and oppositions. Their social structures are built up almost on a basis of such divisions, and not only the two-fold moiety categorizations that were (and still are) fundamental in so many areas. Structural analysis of Aboriginal myths is an especially intriguing and absorbing field of study because of its contrasting features. The point is that in all these fields there is a complex intermeshing or cross-cutting of contrasts, of opposites and oppositions and mediators. There seems to be no room for a massive confrontation which would subsume or override or discourage mediation. Or, to change the analogy, in myth there is not a continuing struggle between the forces of good and the forces of evil, or between good forces supporting God and bad forces aligned with the Devil. In religious statements, in myth, as in social structure, the contrasts are not cumulative. The picture is more muted. The 'essence' of good and bad is there, but the drama is not presented in terms of a pre-defined moral formula. Just as people traditionally, in their socio-economic activities, had to contribute a fair amount of work and not wait for others to do it, so they did not get all of their myth-interpretations ready-made. Something was left to *them,* to put the implications together in the course of their *own* lives.

- VI -

It is the intimate relationship between human beings and their natural environment which distinguishes Aboriginal religion from so many others. Aboriginal religion was, and is, concerned with physical and spiritual survival. These imperatives are enunciated within the mythological context of the Dreaming; and they pervade all aspects of social living. Aboriginal religion is a total way of life; and the transcendental is viewed as a necessary component, inseparable from ordinary living.[26]

While myths are receptive to change, and can be variously interpreted as the occasion demands, they also reflect specific circumstances relating to Aboriginal traditional social living and, as I have said, are deeply rooted in the natural environment. Not only are the deities '*of* the land', a land which they moulded and humanized. Many of them have the potential to take other shapes — perhaps human, perhaps animal, bird and so on. The land is a living and tangible expression of their presence within it; and they are represented and symbolized by virtually everything within it. Aboriginal people were traditionally in harmony with this view, identifying personally within that patterning, identifying with their gods in either their good or their bad manifestations.

In such circumstances, the changes which have been wrought by alien intrusion were more than merely damaging in socio-personal terms. They were a deliberate and thoughtless erosion of the Aborigines' emotional and affective life, an erosion which was even more far-reachingly significant to their welfare than the senseless killings and maltreatment which have marked the greater part of their contact with Europeans. Missionaries, who were on the scene from the earliest period of European settlement, were mostly ignorant of the tenets of Aboriginal religion. Unfortunately, many have remained so. In a sense, they were blinded by their own religion, just as Aborigines were. Any attempt at rapprochement led only so far. With Aborigines, it was not simply a matter of changing their belief system. It meant (or would have meant) changing virtually every aspect of their very being. However, since all religions have a measure of commonality, it would conceivably have been possible to establish a unity of interest, whereby Aboriginal religious views could have been taken into account. This happened only rather late in the day. By ignoring Aboriginal religion, earlier missionaries undermined the essential ingredients of religiosity which were there, and in doing so hastened the downhill plunge toward increasing secularization. A parallel to that course can perhaps be found in the fatalistic idea of a 'wrong turning' which led to inevitable destruction — except that, as far as the *djang* are concerned, the context was different, and so were the results.

The tide was stemmed to some extent, but not for all Aborigines. Many socio-cultural systems were totally destroyed — often along with all or most of their members. Nevertheless, in a number of other areas the mytho-ritual orientations continue to exist, although mostly in a modified or reconstructed form.

There are a few, very few examples where genuine attempts were made by Aborigines themselves to combine both Aboriginal and Christian elements. The Elcho Island adjustment movement, in north-eastern Arnhem Land, is a case in point,[27] where a memorial composed of sacred emblems was erected. Among them was one emblem, primarily concerned with local mythology, which had at its apex a Christian cross. I shall not attempt to discuss this innovative approach here, except to say that it was mainly politico-religious and symbolized possibilities which were unfulfilled, and which received a considerable set-back in the development of bauxite mining on the Gove peninsula. Another marked innovation was the introduction of two large panels in the Yirrkalla Methodist church.[28] These depicted incidents from the great *dua* and *yiridja* moiety mythic epics of north-eastern Arnhem Land. However, the abiding presence of these deities (manifested through the paintings) played no part in the church service as such: they simply became part of the local congregation.

The background to both of these examples was the favourable climate of Mission opinion. The Methodist Overseas Mission, on all its stations along the Arnhem Land coast, had a policy or an ideal of 'keeping what's best in the Aboriginal culture'. Not all of the individual missionaries were equally enthusiastic about this, and there were difficulties in translating it into practice. But it made a place for Aboriginal *culture* in the new regime, in suggesting that the Aboriginal creative beings were equivalent (in one respect) to the prophets of the Old Testament, who preceded the coming of Christ and the changes and revelations that came with Him. This Mission view also made a place for Aboriginal *people* of the past: the argument went that they could not be condemned to hell because they had died before the Christian message came to them. The enlightened Methodist approach was in marked contrast to that of some other Christian missions working among Aborigines, even until quite recently.

Even more destructive of Aboriginal religion was alienation of the land. In some regions, as in the Western Desert and eastern Arnhem Land, Aborigines had more opportunity to continue their normal associations with their own territories. Of course, this was not always the case. Inroads were made and continue to be made in varying directions that tend to undermine traditional religion, even in its present, modified forms. The increasing presence of Europeans and of mining is perhaps the most conspicuous and devastating in this respect. Nevertheless, even when Aborigines came into mission settlements they did not lose sight of their own country, and their emotional attachment toward this did not diminish. Recent movements toward decentralization (in regard to the 'homeland' movements, as they are called) offer opportunities to take up at least some of the threads which in the immediate past have frayed or become slack. Some threads have, however, been entirely broken. In the pastoral areas of the north, in the Northern Territory and in the Kimberleys, traditional religion has certainly not remained intact. But a fair amount has survived, to serve as a refuge to which its adherents could, and still can, escape from the exigencies of an unsympathetic and demanding situation which remained entirely outside their control.

The picture of contemporary traditional Aboriginal religion, in areas where it is still a living reality, is one of a people's reliance on its basic tenets and adherence to its local manifestations. The mythological content remains structurally unimpaired, except for the omission of particular repertoires which are not handed on owing to inherent difficulties of oral transmission in the new situation. Belief remains relatively firm. The word 'relatively' is crucial here, because far-reaching changes have occurred in interpretation and symbolic allusion. Mainly, these changes have been brought about through two developments.

One is an upsurge of interest, not just in finding Aboriginal identity, but in strengthening and ratifying it. Real socio-personal identity, as we have seen, rests in the Dreaming. We could therefore expect religious expressions to receive some attention, and even some refurbishing. The other source of pressure toward change is the recent interest in land rights claims. Some Aborigines see in these an opportunity, not only to regain their own home lands, but also to revivify their religion. A great deal has been made of the political aspects of this struggle, but it really goes much deeper. Possession of land means in effect a continued commitment to traditional religion, whatever form that may take in such changed circumstances. It means, too, a measure of emotional security. These two aspects dominate Aboriginal opinion today.

Both these emphases have led either to an enhancement or to a revival of religious activity. They have led also, as I have already indicated, to many changes. In the Western Desert, for instance, there is a strengthening and a widening of the sphere categorized as being secret-sacred. Some of these changes concern aspects which were traditionally much more flexible. To take one point, the exclusion of women is more apparent today than it was previously. This is also the case with certain rituals, and the emblems and designs used in them. Many of these a few years ago were ordinarily sacred, or open-sacred; now they are regarded as *secret*-sacred.

The theme of exclusion-inclusion has always been a marked feature of Aboriginal ritual life. In my view, this has militated against its more adaptive potentialities. That aside, the strengthening of the secret-sacred dimension is also a device through which 'outsiders' may be excluded and Aboriginality enhanced. In contrast to this is an example from north-eastern Arnhem Land. While retaining sections of the secret-sacred, religious leaders there have relaxed some of the rules of restriction so that parts of the most important rituals may be performed publicly. As a consequence of this, overall religious commitment has been immeasurably widened.[29] In the Kimberley region of Western Australia, religious revival has taken the direction of encouraging large initiatory meetings which attract members of surrounding communities as well as others from far distant places.

Land, and what it means in socio-personal terms, continue to remain significant. When land is alienated, its natural resources depleted, its physiographic features destroyed, this irrevocably harms not only the *trappings* of belief but, without doubt, traditional religion as such.

In a film produced in 1978, *Walya Ngamardiki — the Land, My Mother*, the creative Mother Waramurungoindju of western Arnhem Land is represented in the shape of a young Aboriginal woman. This imagery brings together three elements: land, symbols, and human figure — specifically, a female human figure. One message it conveys is the importance of the land for Aboriginal people, not only now but for future generations (the young, potentially-fertile-mother aspect). The other is the mythic substantiation of land

— not simply a generalized relevance, but a specific and a direct local one. Land rights submissions to the Northern and Central Land Councils in the Northern Territory are framed, at one level, in terms of hereditary occupation by particular Aborigines in regard to particular stretches of country. At another and more fundamental level, ownership and possession of land are emphasized through mythic and ritual affiliation. It is myth, sometimes with associated ritual, sometimes in the form of what Stanner has called 'riteless myths', which provides the charter of ownership and constitutes its deeds of possession.

Thus the deities themselves are brought into the harsh light of a court of law, and paraded for the public scrutiny of unbelievers. While their role has changed in recent years, it has not changed in relation to their own land. They continue to justify and to substantiate the rights of their human representatives to hold that land.

Traditionally, of course, there were never any doubts concerning who held that land, in the name or names of the mythic beings. Land was taken for granted. While ownership was thrown into doubt from earliest European settlement, there was no doubt among the Aborigines themselves. The fact that some of these lands are being legally recovered today, simply fulfils the promise of the eternal Dreaming.

Current developments emphasize the fact that Aboriginal religion is vitally concerned with all aspects of social living. Metaphorically, the deities need to display themselves in the service of man and of themselves: that their 'presence' should be sought, and found necessary, in a mundane court of law is not incongruous.

However, we have seen that mythic beings were not, and are not necessarily all-powerful. In many cases, as their mythology reveals, they were and are just as vulnerable to disadvantageous circumstances as are their human counterparts, beset by the forces of good and bad as all of us are. Circumstances were and are often beyond their control, as they are beyond ours. The 'human, all too human' quality of the deities underlines the fallibility of them and of man. The good does not necessarily triumph. The bad may well do so — since, after all, it is part of man's expectation of living.

There are converse parallels we might make, too, concerning the powerful and catastrophic personality of one side of the great Ngalyod, the Rainbow Snake of western Arnhem Land. Those parallels no doubt have been made by Aborigines themselves and will continue to be made — but I shall not spell them out here.

In spite of that, in the face of overwhelming vicissitudes experienced by Aborigines throughout this continent, and wherever Aboriginal religion prevails, the deities, so many Aborigines still believe, will continue to live spiritually.

Provided faith sustains them, Aborigines may win out in this life, *not* necessarily in the next. But the trend toward secularization is not a figment of the imagination. It is a reality, a powerful reality, facing all Aborigines today, as it faces us. Could it be that Stanner's 'immemorial misdirection' has already taken place?

FOOTNOTES

1. C. R. Badger, *The Reverend Charles Strong and the Australian Church* (Melbourne: Abacada Press, 1971).
2. A. P. Elkin, *The Australian Aborigines* (Sydney: Angus and Robertson, 1938/1974) 213.
3. A. P. Elkin, "Elements of Australian Aboriginal Philosophy", *Oceania* 40, no. 2 (1969).
4. W. E. H. Stanner, "Some Aspects of Aboriginal Religion." *Charles Strong Memorial Trust Lecture* (Melbourne: Australian and New Zealand Society for Theological Studies, 1976) 31-34.
5. W. E. H. Stanner, "On Aboriginal Religion", *Oceania* 30, nos. 2 and 4, 31, nos. 2 and 4, 32, no. 2, (1959-61).
6. W. E. H. Stanner, "On Aboriginal Religion, I. The lineaments of sacrifice", *Oceania* 30, no. 2 (1959) 109-10.
7. W. E. H. Stanner, "On Aboriginal Religion, II. Sacramentalism, rite and myth", *Oceania* 30, no. 4 (1960) 278.
8. R. M. Berndt, *Australian Aboriginal Religion* (Four fascicles; Leiden: Brill, 1974).
9. R. M. and C. H. Berndt, *The World of the First Australians* (1st ed., 1964; Sydney, Ure Smith, 1977) 397.
10. R. M. Berndt, "A Wonguri-Mandjikai song cycle of the Moon-Bone", *Oceania* 19, no. 1 (1948) 19-20.
11. "On Aboriginal Religion, II. Sacramentalism, rite and myth", 260-65.
12. R. M. Berndt, *Kunapipi* (Melbourne: Cheshire, 1951) 149-52.
13. W. E. H. Stanner, "On Aboriginal Religion, II. Sacramentalism, rite and myth", 265.
14. R. M. and C. H. Berndt, *Man, Land and Myth in North Australia: the Gunwinggu People* (Sydney: Ure Smith, 1970) 121-22.
15. *Ibid.*, 229-33.
16. *Ibid.*, 27-29.
17. A. R. Radcliffe-Brown, *Structure and Function in Primitive Society* (London: Cohen and West, 1952) 166.
18. "On Aboriginal Religion, II. Sacramentalism, rite and myth", 266.
19. R. M. Berndt, "Traditional morality as expressed through the medium of an Australian Aboriginal religion" in *Australian Aboriginal Anthropology* (ed. R. M. Berndt; Perth: University of Western Australia, for the Australian Institute of Aboriginal Studies, Canberra, 1970) 216-47.
20. L. R. Hiatt, ed., *Australian Aboriginal Mythology* (Canberra: Australian Institute of Aboriginal Studies, 1975) 6-7.
21. R. M. Berndt, "Traditional morality".
22. *Ibid.*, 224-25; *idem*, "The Walmadjeri-Gugadja" in *Hunters and Gatherers Today* (ed. M. G. Bicchieri; New York: Holt, Rinehart and Winston, 1972) 207-09.
23. "Religion, totemism, and symbolism" in *Aboriginal Man in Australia* (ed. R. M. Berndt and C. H. Berndt; Sydney: Angus and Robertson, 1965) 218.
24. *Australian Aboriginal Mythology*, 7.
25. R. M. Berndt, *Australian Aboriginal Religion*, fasc. 1, 10.
26. *Ibid.*, fasc. 4, 28.
27. R. M. Berndt, *An Adjustment Movement in Arnhem Land* (Cahiers de l'Homme; Paris and The Hague: Mouton, 1962).
28. A. E. Wells, *This their Dreaming* (St. Lucia: University of Queensland, 1971).
29. R. M. Berndt, "Looking back into the present: a changing panorama in eastern Arnhem Land", *Anthropological Forum* 4, no. 3 (1978-79).

DIANE BELL

ABORIGINAL WOMEN AND THE RELIGIOUS EXPERIENCE*

In giving the Charles Strong Memorial Trust Inaugural Lecture in 1976, Professor Stanner[1] discussed what he called the "tetrad" of Aboriginal Religion: living people, their countries, their totems and their ancestors. With the elegance and insight characteristic of Stanner's writing on religion, he contended that although there may still be some who question the rightness of including Aboriginal beliefs, acts and objects within the scholarly scope of Comparative Religion, the intellectual requirements can be, and long ago have been, amply satisfied. It was a theme to which he had turned in 1962 in his essay "Religion, Totemism and Symbolism"[2], and one which, for my topic, "Aboriginal Women and the Religious Experience", is particularly apposite.

Reading Stanner had been one of the delights of my undergraduate career. His Boyer Lectures, "After the Dreaming"[3], set me thinking about the nature of Aboriginal society; his monograph, On Aboriginal Religion[4], directed my attention to the beauty, complexity and sheer poetry of Aboriginal belief systems; his portrait of "Durmugam: a Nangiomeri"[5] brought to the arid wastes of anthropological theory, the intimacy and immediacy of the lives of the people who become the basis of our studies. But it was not until 1976, when I took up a postgraduate scholarship at the Australian National University, where Stanner was Emeritus Professor, that I met him. I sought his advice on the project I was about to undertake in Central Australia: a study of Aboriginal women's ritual life. While at that stage my understanding necessarily was derived from the classic desert ethnographies of Spencer and Gillen, Meggitt, Munn and Strehlow,[6] my questions were generated by my intuition that a feminist critique could lead to deeper understandings of Aboriginal women's lives and Aboriginal sociey, just as feminist social scientists had shown was possible in other societies.[7] According to desert ethnographers, Aboriginal women were deemed to be of lesser cultural importance than men, but then, from other sources, I knew that desert women had a separate and secret ritual life.[8] How, I wondered, did women perceive their role? Did they endorse a derogatory self-image or did they nurture a more sustaining one? Did they merely submit to male authority or did they have an authority base of their own? Were men the only guardians of religious Law, or did women, too, share in that body of culturally valued knowledge?

Many saw me as an angry young woman, but Stanner smiled conspiratorially and, with reference to his Daly River material, said, "You know I always checked my work with one old lady". He tugged my long hair and added, "That won't last long". It was not the problem of caring for long hair to which he referred but rather the Aboriginal practice of cutting one's hair on the death of close relatives. Because I wanted to work on ritual he knew I would need to participate in the ceremonial life of women and that, in so doing, I might well be drawn into a mourning ceremony. For 18 months I lived in an Aboriginal community,[9] where I was incorporated in the kinship system and, as a classificatory mother, sister and mother-in-law to various young men, participated in their initiations; where as an older woman with two children — a son who was seen to be nearing the age of initiation and a daughter approaching marriageable age — I was admitted into the ritual world of women and participated in many women's ceremonies. When I returned to Canberra I was able to discuss my ethnographic understandings of desert society with Stanner anew. We argued long and furiously. On some issues there was no resolution: our fieldwork experience was undertaken in such different regions and under such different circumstances.

Then, in 1981, as anthropologist to the newly formed Aboriginal Sacred Sites Protection Authority in Darwin,[10] I had the opportunity to work with women of the Daly River and to participate in a closed and secret women's ceremony. Although I could not discuss the content of the rite with Stanner, I desperately wanted to explore with him the implications of the structure of the ceremony and my analysis of its import, for his analysis of women's role and status. But Stanner died in October 1981. I was working on the Daly River Land Claim[11] with people who had known him. We heard the news as we swam at the crossing where he had forded the river decades before.

Let me then, by way of tribute to the "old man" — a term of respect in Aboriginal Society — develop, with reference to Aboriginal women and approaches to the study of their religious beliefs and practices, the theme of his earlier essay and lecture. Beginning with Tylor's observation that "a once-established opinion, however delusive, can hold its own from age to age" Stanner[12] traced the gradual awakening of scholars to the intricacies of Aboriginal religion. If, he argued, we looked beyond the symbol to the symbolized, we would find that the end of Aboriginal religion was, in Confucian terms, "to unite hearts and establish order".[13] However, Stanner pointed out, the myopia of early observers had restricted the study of religion. Of people such as David Collins, the Reverend J.D. Woods, Bishop Salvado, A.A.C. Le Souëf, all of whom held, in one form or another, that Aborigines were devoid of religious susceptibilities, Stanner[14] wrote:

> It should not be supposed that they lacked information, learning or humanism. For the most part they were knowledgeable, serious-minded men ... but they were very sure of their vision. They were genuinely unable to see, let alone credit, the facts that have convinced modern anthropologists that Aborigines are a deeply religious people. That blindness is an important part of our study. It profoundly affected European conduct towards Aborigines.

A host of skilled ethnographers[15] have done much to correct the faulty vision: shafts of bright light have illuminated important aspects of Aboriginal religion such as totemism, dreaming and cultural symbolism; regional cults and initiation practices. But when we look for expositions of Aboriginal women and their religious life we find not "that blindness" but a blinkered approach which none-the-less has ramifications for "European conduct towards Aborigines". Like the observers of yore, we find a surety of vision when it comes to Aboriginal women's place in society. It would seem that before Aboriginal women's religious life can be recognized, women themselves must first be reinstated as full members of their society. It is as if the white male observers' perception of older Aboriginal women as physically unattractive, has prevented any consideration of their cultural worth. One of the earliest observations is from Péron, a member of Baudin's expedition of 1801-1804, who was repelled by the ugliness of Aboriginal woman. He wrote:

> She was uncommonly lean and scraggy, and her breasts hung down almost to her thighs. The most extreme dirtiness added to her natural deformity.[16]

This response persists. Hart and Pilling[17] write of older Tiwi women as "ancient hags". Yet it is these women who are the repositories of knowledge, who in their own domain, the single women's camp, an area taboo to men, discuss important ritual concerns. Meggitt[18] characterizes these camps as "hot beds of gossip".

Unchallanged by the argument that the impact of changes wrought by the shift from a hunter-gatherer mode of subsistence to a sedentary lifestyle on missions, settlements, cattle stations and in the towns, may have implications for women's status,[19] male dominance is presented as a timeless, enduring reality. Unshaken by the work of Hamilton and Goodale[20] on women's important role in marriage arrangements, we still read of women as the pawns in the games of the male polygynous gerontocracy.[21] Unmoved by the in-depth studies of Phyllis Kaberry[22] in the Kimberleys in the 1930's; Catherine Berndt[23] in South Australia, Western Australia and the Northern Territory from the 1940's onwards, and Jane Goodale[24] with Tiwi on Melville Island in the 1950's, in all of whose work there is ample documentation of the religious character of women's ceremonies, the concept of Aboriginal woman as the profane and excluded persists. Feared for her life-giving powers and constrained by a hearth-centric worldview; the substance of symbols but never the creator of her own social reality; Aboriginal woman's views are dismissed as peripheral to an understanding of Aboriginal society.

In 1937, in introducing his reader to the totemic beliefs and practices of Murngin of north-east Arnhemland, Lloyd Warner[25] wrote of women, "Little sacred progress is made during her lifetime". In a similar mode but 35 years later, Ken Maddock[26] generalized that:

... men's cults, despite their secret core, require the active participation of the community at large ... [and] express broad cohesive and impersonal themes such as fertility and continuity of nature, the regularity of society and the creation of the world. Women's cults are centred upon narrow, divisive and personal interests such as love-magic and female reactions to physiological crises. It is in keeping with the generality of male-dominated religion that men's cults are enacted on a greater scale and with more elaborate symbolism than the women's.

Bern,[27] in basic agreement with Maddock and Warner, stated "Aboriginal religion is, par excellence, the business of men". He has argued that although there exists the potential for women "to construct a counter consciousness to challenge the mature male ideological and political hegemony",[28] women's own autonomous religious life is not one of these contexts because the relevance of women's rituals is for them alone.

On the basis of fieldwork spanning six years, mostly in Central Australian communities with Warlpiri, Warumungu, Alywarra, Kaytej, Warlmanpa and Anmatjirra speakers, but also in communities close to those in which Warner, Bern and Maddock worked in the Roper River area and Arnhemland,[29] I would paint a quite different picture of women's religious life.

My documentation and analysis of women's world suggests that in ritual women emphasize their role as nurturers of people, land and relationships. Their responsibility to maintain harmoniously this complex of relationships between the living and the land is manifest in the intertwining of the ritual foci of health and emotional management. Through their *yawulyu*** (land based ceremonies) they nurture land, through their health and curing rituals they resolve conflict and restore social harmony and through *yilpinji* (love rituals) they manage emotions. In *yilpinji*, as in their health-oriented *yawulyu*, women seek to resolve and to explore the conflicts and tensions which beset their communities. In centres of population concentration where Aborigines now live, jealous fights, accusations of infidelity and illicit affairs occur on a scale impossible a century ago when people lived in small mobile bands. Thus today, women's role in the domain of emotional management is, like their role in the maintenance of health and harmony, truly awesome.[30]

In women's rituals the major themes of land, love and health fuse in the nurturance motif which encapsulates the growing up of people and land and the maintenance of the complex of land/people relationships. When women hold aloft their sacred boards on which are painted ideational maps of their country; when they dance hands cupped upwards, they state their intention and responsibility to grow up country and kin. To Aboriginal women, as the living descendants of the Dreamtime, the physical acts of giving birth and of lactation are important but are considered to be one individual moment in a much larger design. Their wide-ranging and broadly-based concept of nurturance is modelled on the Dreamtime experience, itself one all-creative force. When women rub their bodies with fat in preparation for the application of body designs which, like the boards, symbolically encode information about sites, dreamings and estates; when they retrace in song and dance the travels of the mythological heroes, they become as the ancestors themselves. Through ritual re-enactment women establish direct contact with the past, make manifest its meaning and thereby shape their worlds. The past is encapsulated in the present: the present permeates the past.

Variously discussed in terms of the Dreamtime, or Dreaming, Aboriginal religion for desert people is the moral code which informs and unites all life under one Law, the *jukurrpa*. It was in the Dreamtime that the code was made known by the ancestral beings whose tracks criss-crossed the land. The ancestral activity gave form and meaning to the land for the maintenance of which, living men and women, as the direct descendants of the *jukurrpa*, are today responsible.

The body of knowledge and beliefs about the ancestral travels is shared jointly as a sacred trust by men and women, each of whom has distinct responsibilities for the ritual maintenance of this heritage. Both have sacred boards, both know songs and paint designs which encode the knowledge of the Dreamtime. How each sex then fleshes out this common core of beliefs and knowledge is dependent upon their perception of their role and their contribution to society. Men's roles and perceptions have been well documented: women's are rather less well known.

The structuring principles of women's rituals, their content and focus on the maintenance of social harmony, link the ritual worlds of men and women. In both sets of rituals there is celebration of the central values of the society. Women and men alike trace their descent from the Dreamtime through two distinct lines of descent. From one's father and father's father a person has the rights and responsibilities of *kirda*; through one's mother and mother's father those of *kurdungurlu*. From one's mother's mother one also enjoys a special relationship to what is called one's *jaja* (granny) country. Other interests in land are stated in terms of conception dreamings, residence, marriage, place of death and burial. Through these overlapping and interlocking modes of expressing how one is "of the land" Central Australian men and women locate themselves within the ancestral design. In ceremony, visits to country and decision-making, the complementarity and interdependence of men's and women's worlds are evident.

As we move further north the terms of course change. In the Roper River area one speaks of *minirringki*, *jungkayi* and *dalyin* but the multiplicity of ways of tracing a relationship to land remains a salient feature of the culture. For the benefit of those who may be unfamiliar with the disputes concerning local and social organization and land tenure systems in Australia, let me explain. Woman's relationship to land and to the ancestors is often explained as derivative of her relationship to someone else, for example, her husband or her father, but not as the mirror image of the male system. In the literature there has also been a stress on patrilineal descent as the basis of group membership. However, evidence forthcoming in land claims where Aboriginal witnesses provide direct statements concerning land, supports the position I have outlined here.[31]

Under the Law men and women have distinctive roles to play and each has recourse to certain checks and balances in social, economic and ritual domains, which ensure that

Alywarra women, wearing design for their country, Erulja, give evidence in the Alywarra and Anmatjirra Claim to the Utopia pastoral lease. 1979. © Bell 1979.

neither sex can enjoy unrivalled supremacy over the other. Men and women alike are dedicated to observing the Law which orders their lives into complementary but distinct fields of action and thought: in separation lies the basis of a common association that underwrites domains of existence. Men stress their creative power, women their role as nurturers, but each is united in their common purposes — the maintenance of their society in accordance with the Dreamtime Law. Ritual allows both men and women to demonstrate their commitment to the long-established code of the Dreaming in a manner which is peculiarly male or female.

Ceremonies may be classified as those staged by women which are secret and closed to men; those in which men and women participate and those staged by men which are closed and secret to women. Most analyses begin from within the latter. If, however, we begin from within woman's ceremonial world and explore her ritual domain, we find that women see their lives as underwritten by their independence and autonomy of action. These self-evaluations are not easily dismissed for they are legitimated by women's direct access to the *jukurrpa*. A further symbol of women's independence is the *jilimi*, or single women's camp, which has as its residential core the older and respected ritual leaders and their dependent female relatives. During the day it is the focal point of women's activities, during the evenings it provides a refuge. Like the women's ceremonial ground this area is taboo to men.

Obviously if women held they were independent while men insisted that women were subservient and the male claims were backed in terms of their control over women's domain, then we could suggest that women were not facing the harsh reality of life and that they were using ritual as an escape mechanism. I have found this line of analysis hard to sustain because, in my experience, women's ceremonies are respected by men. In the rituals jointly staged by men and women where interdependence is apparent, each brings to bear the knowledge that he or she is the proud descendant of a jointly shared spiritual heritage. Finally, in the rituals associated with male initiation, an occasion when male control of women is said to be writ large, women engage in key decision-making which affects both ritual procedure and the aftermath of initiation. Furthermore, while men are engaged in their initiation business at their ceremonial ground, women are similarly engaged in ceremonies at their ground.[32] These rituals celebrate their ongoing role as nurturer of people, relationships and land. When we focus on the world of men and treat women's rituals as a subset, we blur the playing out of independence and interdependence of the sexes in the spiritual domain.

In ritual the Law is made known in a highly stylized and emotionally charged manner: the separation of the sexes, so evident in daily activities, reaches its zenith. Ritual activity may therefore be considered as an important barometer of male-female relations, for it provides, as it were, an arena in which the values of the society are writ large, where the sex division of labour is starkly drawn and explored by the participants. In ritual I found both men and women clearly stating their perception of their role, their relationship to the opposite sex and their relationshp to the Dreamtime whence all legitimate authority and power once flowed. However, while women and men today, as in the past, maintain separate spheres of interaction, the evaluations of their respective roles and their opportunities to achieve status have altered fundamentally during a century of white intrusion into Central Australia.

How then are we to balance my statements concerning women's religious experience with those which cast women as outsiders? How are we to find a way of analysing male and female domains which does not distort women's contribution to the maintenance of religious values in Aboriginal society? Questions concerning religion are inexorably tied to those concerning gender values and women's role and status in Aboriginal society. To probe one is to find answers to the other. Let us then examine the factors which have distorted our vision of women in Aboriginal society.

At the most obvious level, because of the sex segregated nature of Aboriginal society, it is extremely inappropriate (and in terms of in-depth fieldwork unproductive) to attempt to work equally with men and women. Usually one is identified with members of one's own sex and is able to move freely within that sphere. It follows that women can most easily be studied by another woman, but funding more female fieldworkers will not necessarily ensure that women's perceptions are explored. There have been women in the field, for example Ursula McConnel and Nancy Munr.,[33] both of whom worked on Aboriginal religion but neither of whom found women to be critical to their study.

Fortunately for my study, women considered my position agreeable for one who sought ritual instruction. As a divorced woman in receipt of a government pension (pensioners are important people in Aboriginal communities) I was in a similar position to the ritual bosses with whom I worked: I was economically and emotionally independent of men. Aboriginal women often worry that white women, if allowed access to their secrets, might discuss the same with their husbands, but I was classified as a widow and considered to be safe. Further, the social status I enjoyed by virtue of my two outgoing and energetic children, allowed me access to the world of adult women. Ritual knowledge resides with the older women who, once freed from the immediate responsibilities of child care, devote their time and energies to upholding and transmitting their spiritual heritage to successive generations.

At another level, if we step back from the field situation, we find that the theoretical preoccupations, research design and the nature of the discipline in Australia have all conspired to relegate women to a position of marginality within Aboriginal society and within the discipline. Let me explain. Aboriginal society was not systematically studied until two Oxford scholars, Baldwin Spencer and W.E. Roth, began their scientific work in Australia during the late nineteenth century. Hitherto data had been drawn from the casual observations of early explorers and settlers. Well-educated professional men who dabbled in anthropology collated and compiled this information. Even when detailed research began, the methodology was more of an armchair variety where speculation abounds: intensive participant-observation fieldwork which may have highlighted women's activies, and which has come to characterize the practice of anthropology, was not undertaken. Once again, let me draw a parallel with Stanner's theme. Although he was writing of religion as a male prerogative, his observation applied equally well to studies of women.

> Contemporary study is weakened by the fact that there is so much bias in the old printed record. One cannot turn very hopefully to it for test or confirmation of new insights. For so much of the information was the product of minds caught up with special pleading of one kind or another.[34]

Of course Spencer and Roth were men of the Victorian era and their own model of femininity is evident in their notes and in their published work. It was a model wherein their own social order was the epitome of all civilization, a characteristic of which was the domestication of female sexuality.[35] All other sexual values and sexual orders were held to be primitive, lacking the hallmark of civilization. Such an analysis obviously has attractions because fifty years later Evans-Pritchard[36] was still extolling the virtues of Victorian womanhood as a standard against which to measure the position of women in other societies. It is little wonder then that the independent and, to the Victorian eye, wilful ways of Aboriginal woman, received scant recognition in the ethnological debates. In behaving in such an untamed fashion she was merely demonstrating her uncivilized and uncultured primitiveness.

Australian anthropology bears very much the stamp of British anthropology. The founder and first Professor of Anthropology in Sydney, Radcliffe-Brown, was a student of Rivers and influenced by Durkheim. For these men, women's opinions, values and activities were not critical to an understanding of society. No matter how stridently or positively women asserted that they shared the spiritual heritage of their society, they remained mute or socially disruptive in analyses based on the Durkheimian sacred-profane dichotomy.

In summary then, the tendency has been for male fieldworkers to study male institutions and subsequently to offer analyses which purport to examine the totality of Aboriginal society. Evaluation of female institutions has too often been based on male informants' opinions, refracted through the eyes of male ethnographers and explained by means of the concepts of male-oriented anthropology. Thus statements concerning the role and status of women are formulated within a context of a public male ideology, which means that only rarely can they be reconciled with the behavioural patterns of Aboriginal women in their society.

Why have practitioners felt so secure with this approach? I suggest we delve deeper and look at the way in which male-female relations have been conceptualized. This aspect of the problem has been tackled from within three different frameworks, each of which has generated different questions and thus produced different answers. The first, which I call "Man Equals Culture", is the most consistently worked out and certainly the most popular. The second, an Anthropology of Women Approach, presents an ethnographic challenge to the first, but may be easily dismissed or subsumed. The third, which I call "Towards a Feminist Perspective", is the only real challenge to the first. It brings to bear on the problem of women the burgeoning corpus of feminist scholarship, but so far it has produced more questions than answers.

These three organizational frameworks are akin to Kuhn's[37] notion of "a paradigm" which predicts a problem or set of related problems that the community of practitioners then sets out to resolve. But, as Kuhn makes clear, one cannot move easily from within one version of the paradigm to work within another, as to do so involves something of the magnitude of a Gestalt switch. Although the various practitioners of one paradigm may use the same vocabulary, the conceptual baggage which adheres to a term varies radically between paradigms. For example, if religion is defined as the sacred domain controlled by men, then it is difficult to document the activities of women as anything other than profane. However, if religion is defined in terms of a commonly held set of values, beliefs and practices, both men and women may then be depicted as sharing in religious experiences.

Within the "Man Equals Culture" paradigm, the problem has been to find a suitable characterization of woman's role and status in terms of her lack of control over her own life. Armed with a diverse theoretical weaponry, such as Marxian class analysis, Levi-Straussian structuralism and Durkheimian dualism, the practitioners have sought to explain women's secondary position in terms of economic markers, in the realm of symbolism, social organization and kinship. I have already discussed Warner, Maddock and Bern but not Geza Róheim, who undertook fieldwork in Central Australia in 1927 and wrote specifically of Aboriginal women.

Women, Róheim contended, had no religion, no corporate ceremonial life, only magic. Róheim[38] asked two important questions of woman:

1) What sort of person is she?
2) What are her work, her plays, her interest in everyday life, her passions, anxieties and pleasures?

His study was restricted by the form of these questions and by his Freudian approach. Róheim's particular version of the psychoanalytic approach, although crude, has provided insights which have been refined and were popular again in the 1970's.

Shulamith Firestone[39] has argued that, in the Victorian era, Freudianism was a more palatable doctrine than feminism because it supported the *status quo* and the integrity of the family. Women who did not conform were simply deviants. It is tempting to run the same argument in the 1970's, when feminism poses a threat to male hegemony in many domains and seeks more wide-ranging concessions than simply the right to vote. In a similar vein, Stanner suggests we may find a link between the blindness of which he writes and the struggle over ritualism within the Christian church between the years 1850 and 1920.[40]

Perhaps the most sophisticated and well worked analysis of the adherents to the "Man Equals Culture" paradigm is a symbolic analysis of Nancy Munn.[41] Like Róheim, Munn takes the male-female opposition to be a fundamental starting point in any analysis of Aboriginal society, but Munn's concern is with the socio-cultural order, whereas Róheim's is with the individual psyche. As a woman, Munn certainly had access to the world of women but her focus is the ritual symbolism of men and her valued informants male, because in Nancy Munn's analysis men control the keys to cosmic order.

From within the second paradigm the practitioners, such as Kaberry, Berndt and Goodale, begin with the assumption that women also have rights, opinions and values and that these are not exactly coincidental with those of the men. This type of research makes a chink in the doctrine of male dominance. It becomes apparent that it is not as complete as we once thought; nevertheless, as long as we insert certain qualifications, the model will more or less suffice and the data on women will illuminate the institutions of marriage, kinship, social structure etc.

For example, in her extremely detailed and rich portrait of Aboriginal women, Phyllis Kaberry[42] was able to challenge several of Róheim's grosser misconceptions about the function of women's religious life; to offer a counter to Warner's assertion that women make little sacred progress; and finally, to depict Aboriginal woman as:

> A complex social personality having her own prerogatives, duties, problems, beliefs, rituals and points of view, making the adjustments that the social, local and totemic organizations require of her and at the same time exercising a certain freedom of choice in matters affecting her own interests and desires.[43]

Yet, many of Kaberry's most important observations concerning the nature of women's ceremonies have not been fully explored. Kaberry's[44] critically important observation that men represent the uninitiated at women's ceremonies remains buried beneath a pile of studies of secret male cults, totemism and kinship which assume that the male view is the only important perspective. We could suggest that supported by Elkin "to tackle through women the problems of kinship, totemism, social organization in general and the religion", Phillis Kaberry found her answers in those anthropological ways of looking at the world and of other cultures which were developed by men of the structural-functional school. Men were located at the centre of social action in such approaches.

Catherine Berndt, who has undertaken fieldwork in many different parts of Aboriginal Australia, has proposed a model of the relationship between the sexes in terms of domestic, economic and religious domains within which the links of marriage and descent and the relations of dominance and authority are articulated.[45] This organizational device allows Berndt to discuss the inter-penetration of the spheres of male and female action. Berndt[46] emphasizes woman's importance as an economic producer and the brakes which women may thus apply to male ritual activity. A questionmark remains though in respect of the relationship between male and female ritual domains.

Jane Goodale[47] claims that her work is mainly descriptive and limited to the Tiwi, but comparison with mainland Aboriginal studies is enlightening. The nature of Goodale's debate with Hart and Pilling over marriage arrangements is reminiscent of Kaberry's challenges to Warner and Róheim. Both Kaberry and Goodale went into the field to study women, both worked mainly with women informants and stressed women's importance, equality in some fields and near equality in others in their depiction of women's role and status.

Like Kaberry, Goodale chose to organize her data within a life-cycle framework which, while providing a sympathetic portrait of women's lives, allows one to sidestep certain critical issues concerning the way in which men evaluate women's activities. Goodale however does tackle this problem in her final chapter where she sets out the differences between male and female worldviews. Tiwi women are unusual in that they are initiated at the same ceremonies as are the males, pass through the same formal procedures and are not excluded at any stage during the ceremony. But Tiwi women, like the women of Kaberry's study, are substantially economically independent, while being ritually dependent. Goodale[48] states:

> Opportunities for males to express their individual qualities, and thereby gain prestige, appear to be more obvious and variable than those granted to females ... Women are not expected to be innovators or creators — they do not even create "life".

The women who have published in-depth studies of women have been, I suggest, constrained by the theoretical perspectives developed to focus on men as the leading and most interesting social actors. There was little impetus from within Australia to develop frameworks within which women were deemed of anthropological interest as social actors. While Elkin was encouraging women to document the lives of Aboriginal women, male fieldworkers who thanked "my wife who collected material from the women" were laying the foundations for future research in Australia.

Like Kaberry's portrait of Aboriginal women, which concludes with questions concerning the nature of the relationship between men's and women's ceremonies, so with Berndt and Goodale. There are questions yet to be asked, answers yet to be given. The lack of dynamic models for analysing women's activities is a handicap. The Durkheimian yoke of women's profanity and the structural functionalist equilibrium model wherein women are wives, mothers and sisters, weigh heavily on female oriented research in Australia.

We then come to the third paradigm, that of feminist social scientists, who question the origins and mechanisms of the all-pervasive and hitherto persuasive cultural dogma of male dominance. Perhaps, they suggest, it is not an enduring, timeless constant which regulates male-female in Aboriginal society. As yet this framework has produced more questions than answers and in the Kuhnian sense we are still at the stage of having too many anomalies to be satisfied with earlier paradigms but not yet a sufficiently elegant structure within which to analyse our new data. The old paradigm is under threat and an anthropology of women is not a satisfying alternative.

Stanner[49] spoke of "mystery mongering", and cautioned that we need not only to shake off the "narrow scholarly preoccupations", but we need also "to grub out the roots": also sound advice for a study of women's lives. In seeking a clearer vision, I suggest we need to explore the possibility that qualitative changes in the relation between the sexes may have occurred during the past century. We cannot begin with a static model of male-female; we know too little of the women's lives, past and present, to argue for male dominance as an enduring, timeless reality. We need to be clear regarding the nature of woman's contribution to her society, her rights and responsibilities, before we endorse one particular model of male-female as an accurate gloss on gender relations. The recognition that male-female relations are not rigidly fixed and that women may develop their own power base, leads us to an analysis of the power differentials in Aboriginal society. Feminists have indicated important areas of enquiry but the extreme separation of the sexes in desert society represents an analytic challenge which I suggest is best met in the first instance by increasing our ethnographic understanding of women's domain.

Isobel White,[50] in an exploration of sexual antagonism as symbolized in the male myths of Central Australia, argues that the values celebrated are those of a male-dominated society. Men, White contends, see women as sex objects. Turning to her own fieldwork material from South Australia, she proposes that women see men as sexual conquerors to whom they submit, but not without a show of resistance. While I endorse White's analysis of Central Australian myths as exploring unresolved tensions inherent in male-female relations in Aboriginal society, I suggest that she has articulated a male value system which is not necessarily endorsed by women in Central Australia. The extreme separation of the sexes in everyday life in the desert is a phenomenon which myths also explore. It is therefore all the more important to examine women's myths from this area before endorsing one sex as controlling a mythological charter of values for all members of the society. I would suggest that in their myths women argue for the extreme flexibility of gender relations. The tension is not resolved, even in the myths.[51]

Writing of male-female tensions in the eastern portion of the Western Desert of South Australia, Annette Hamilton[52] has suggested that women's secret ritual life represented a serious challenge to "consolidation of male dominance", not because of any "coherent ideological opposition expressed within it", but because its "mode of organization provides a structural impediment". Underlying the contrast between the sexes Hamilton[53] argues there is:

> A well developed organization that can best be understood as a dual society ... I suggest that these two systems are, in the Western Desert as a whole, in a situation of dynamic disequilibrium whereby the male domain is intruding into the women's through ritual transformations and through the strengthening of male links between generations as a result of changes in the system of kinship and marriage.

Hamilton argues that at the time of the arrival of whites, the whole of the Western Desert cultural area was in a state of transition. She suggests possible trajectories along which transformations can be traced and concludes that "patrilineal descent has transcended the previous form of symbolic ancestor-based descent".[54] It is in the shattering of the ritually maintained nexus of land as resource and land as spiritual essence that I have located a shift from female autonomy to male control, from an independent producer to one dependent on social security.[55] Thus while Hamilton and I are concerned to explore the changing nature of the relations between the sexes from an historical perspective, we have focussed from rather differing conceptions of time and place and upon different institutions and sets of relationships.

To infiltrate women's autonomous ritual world in the Western Desert men need to undermine the mother/daughter tie because endogomous generation moieties organize ritual life. However ritual organization in Central Australia emphasizes the relation of person to place in terms of two distinct and complementary lines of descent — one through the father's patriline (*kirda*) and the other through the mother's patriline (*kurdungurlu*). Furthermore, Central Australian women have a wide range of ritual items which symbolize their relation to land and the *jukurrpa*.

Population-intensive settlement life has allowed women to consolidate these relationships and to forge, through ritual, new links with other women. But, while women today have increased opportunities to stage rituals, the range of rituals is restricted and women's independence eroded. Increased ritual activity has therefore not necessarily been accompanied by an increase in women's overall status.[56] We need to look to the way in which male and female roles are construed within the wider society of Central Australia in order to understand shifts in the locus of ritual power. Then we can argue that women's ability to stage closed sex-specific rituals constitutes a continuing and potent element of gender relations in Central Australia.

For Central Australia I have argued that men's and women's ritual worlds draw on a common spiritual heritage and that women's contribution to the religious life is not subsumed by the male practice. What then of other ethnographic areas? What of the regional cults of Kunapipi and Yabaduruwa? We have in the studies of Maddock, Bern,

Elkin and Berndt,[57] fine-grain ethnographic descriptions and analyses of male-controlled activities. Women, we read, are necessary but their role is supportive: they cook; they are drawn to the verge of knowing men's secrets but their own participation is limited.[58] But what of women's own ceremonies? None of the above has suggested the possibility that women may have regional cults.[59]

In July 1981 I was able to record and participate in a *jarada*, a closed women's ceremony held at Nutwood Downs (in the Roper River area) which women from far-flung communities attended.[60] In song and dance, in gesture and design, the assembled women celebrated the travels of the *Munga Munga* ancestral women who pioneered the country from Tennant Creek to Arnhemland. They scattered across the Barkly Tablelands; they travelled from Macarthur River and from the junction of the Wilton and Roper Rivers to a site on Hodgson River and thence to Nutwood Downs, where their tracks divide, one following the "road" to Alice Springs, the other to a site on Brunette Downs. The *Munga Munga* assumed different forms, met with, crossed over, absorbed and transformed the essence of other ancestors; their influence infused country with the spiritual essence of women.

In the *Munga Munga* ceremony I saw (and was later able to discuss on several occasions with women who had participated), it was apparent in song and dance that they were retracing the extensive travels of the *Munga Munga*. In this way they provided a graphic representation of the links forged between groups in the Dreamtime. Within the context of this overarching responsibility for the Dreaming, women also stated their responsibility for particular tracts of land and emphasized certain themes and, as with Central Australian women, emotional management and health were the principal ones.

At one level women gave form to a generalized notion of their responsibility for land, its dreamings and sites, in expressions such as "we must hold up that country", "not lose him", but at another level the ceremony allowed certain divisions of labour for responsibility for country to be played out. (Those who traced their relationship from their father and father's father as *minirringki* and from their mother and mother's father as *jungkayi*, and from their mother's mother as *dalyin*, each had a particular role). In the dancing the women marked out the extent of the country of each language group.

Unfortunately I cannot go into details here but suffice it to say that in the *Munga Munga* ceremony women demonstrated their rights and responsibilities in land in both a generalized and particularistic fashion. Men were rigidly excluded from the ceremony but at the conclusion of the activity on the women's ground, they entered the main camp where the men had been sitting quietly. A gift exchange between men and women then took place. In this way the interdependence of men and women's worlds was celebrated. More work is necessary on the *Munga Munga* cult before we can discuss women's ceremonies in the area as dealing with "personal reactions to physiological stress". More work is necessary to show the structural continuities from desert to the riverine regions.

In Central Australia women celebrate their relation to land in *yawulyu* which focus on specific sites and dreamings. As we move further north, *yilpinji* is often equated with *jarada*. Elements of *yawulyu* have been incorporated in some *jarada* ceremonies in the riverine areas (for example in the Victoria River Downs region) but the distinguishing feature of *jarada* in the Roper River region remains the universality and pervasiveness of the *Munga Munga* in providing the mythological charter for all women's ceremonial activity. This includes women's participation in men's ceremonies.

In his lecture, Stanner[61] set out the positive characteristics of Aboriginal religion all of which stressed male practices and beliefs. However, I would suggest that this summary could have been generated by a study of the ceremonial life of women. But Stanner was very sure of his vision. He wrote:

Almost universally the evaluation of women was low in respect of their personal as distinct from their functional worth. They were usually held in low regard ritually, too, but not in all circumstances. Their blood-making and child-giving powers were thought both mysterious and dangerous, but there was nothing elevated in their sex or marriage.[62]

While there *are* wide-ranging regional variations in the organization, thematic emphasis and form of women's ceremonies, as a guide to future research let me, in conclusion, generalize concerning the structure concerning women's religious life and consequences for approaches to this study.

1. Women trace their rights and responsibilities for the maintenance of their religious heritage to the past in diverse ways. In each region women's ritual roles appear to be the structural equivalents of men's. However we need to undertake regional studies before attempting wider generalization.

2. In secret rituals which are closed to men, women celebrate their relations to the land, its sites and its dreamings. In ritual their lives and those of the ancestors fuse. Their focus on health, emotional management, resolution of conflict, benefits the whole of society, not just women.

3. In women's ceremonies the dominant theme is that of woman the nurturer. The mode of expressing this varies from the symbolic representations in the desert to the more direct physical representations in the lush north.

4. Analysis of women's role and status and gender values must be within a framework which allows for the dynamic intertwining of the sexual politics of Aboriginal society and the impact of social change.

5. Studies of women's ritual life are best undertaken by women fieldworkers who are accepted by Aboriginal women. "Don't send girls on a woman's errand", older women have told me. Studies should also be by women who respect the Aboriginal women's code of secrecy.

6. Certain information concerning Aboriginal women's ritual lives is communicated through ceremonial activity. It is therefore necessary to observe and if possible to participate in ceremonies if one is to gain access to women's understanding of their religious life. Women do not verbalize their intense and complex spiritual attachment to land and to the ancestors, but rather answer questions concerning the *jukurrpa* in action.

"Is women's liberation really relevant to Aboriginal society?" I am often asked. "Aren't you imposing your ideas on another value system?" This would be true if I were working with the western women's concept of liberation, but in different societies, different issues are stressed. The desire of feminists in white Australian society to break down sex-role stereotyping to achieve social equality by men was viewed by my Aboriginal women friends as yet another cross which white women had to bear. They often sympathized with the lot of the white wife and mother. "Poor thing, stuck inside all day, like a prisoner", they would comment. For themselves they sought to have their distinctively female contribution to their society recognized and accorded the value which it had in the past when they were critical to group survival. The role they wished to see recognized was not one of dependence or subjugation as wives and mothers, but a role of independence, responsibilty, dignity and authority wherein they were enhanced as women, as members of their society, as daughters of the dreaming. It is this which I take to be the basis of "liberation" in their society.

Within the context of Aboriginal society the maintenance of male-female relations entailed an ongoing dialogue based on an interplay and exchange between the sexes. This allowed women to participate actively in the construction of the cultural evaluations of their role in their society. But today, as members of a colonial frontier society, Aboriginal women no longer participate so predominantly in this process. The loss of land over which to forage constitutes more than an economic loss for it is from the land that Aboriginal people draw not only their livelihood but also their very being. Today women are constrained and defined by the male dominated frontier society as the female sex, a necessarily dependent sex. No longer are women treated solely as members of Aboriginal society. The interrelations between the sexes are thus no longer shaped first by the set of male-female relations of Aboriginal society but also by the new forces of the wider colonial society.

In Northern Australian the incoming whites have brought new ideas and resources. These have been differently exploited by Aboriginal men and women. Women were disadvantaged from the onset because the male bias of frontier society immediately relegated them to the role of domestic worker or sex object. Men have been able to take real political advantage of certain aspects of frontier society, while Aboriginal women have been seen by whites as peripheral to the political process.[63] Women's separateness has come to mean their exclusion from the white male dominated domains whence new sources of power and influence now flow. There was no place within the colonial order for the independent Aboriginal woman who, once deprived of her land, quickly became dependent on rations and social security.

In land claim hearings Aboriginal women are speaking of their spiritual heritage, of their rights and responsibilties in land. The impact is profound. As one witness, Mollie Nungarrayi,[64] said in the Kaytej, Warlpiri and Warlmanpa land claim:

> My father was *kurdungurlu* for that place. It was his to look after. He looked after the two places, Waake and Wakulpu and then I lost him; he passed away. Now it is up to me looking after my own country, Jarra Jarra and also Waake and Wakulpu. As my father could not go on to that country so from when I was a young girl I kept on doing the *yawulyu* [women's ceremonies], looking after the country ... My sisters, Mona and Nancy, they are looking after that country too ... we do that *yawulyu* for Wakulpu all the time ... for fruit ... so it will grow up well so that we can make it green so that we hold the Law forever. My father instructed me to hold it always this way so I go on holding *yawulyu* for that country. Sometimes we dance, man and woman together. For Wakulpu. So we can "catch him up", "hold him up".

Perhaps the Reverend Charles Strong[65] may have championed these women had he been aware of the nature of their values. Certainly his view that religion should be regarded as the spirit of life rather than a formal theological creed, would have been intelligible to Aboriginal women.

FOOTNOTES

* *I am grateful to McPhee Gribble, Melbourne, publishers of Bell, Diane *Daughters of the Dreaming* (forthcoming) for permission to reprint material.

**Throughout I have used the orthography of the Warlpiri bilingual programme Yuendumu, N.T. With the exception of the terms from the Roper River, all other terms are in Warlpiri and are well known throughout Central Australia.

1. Stanner, W.E.H., "Some Aspects of Aboriginal Religion", reprinted from Colloquium Journal of the A.N.Z.S.T.S., Melbourne, 1976:1.
2. Stanner, W.E.H., "Religion, Totemism and Symbolism", 1962 in *White Man Got No Dreaming*, Stanner, W.E.H. Canberra, A.N.U. Press, 1979:106-143.
3. Stanner, W.E.H., "After the Dreaming", 1968, *ibid.*, 198-248.

4. Stanner, W.E.H., *On Aboriginal Religion*, Oceania Monographs, No. 11, University of Sydney, 1966.
5. Stanner, W.E.H., "Durmugam: A Nangiomeri", 1959; Stanner op. cit., 1979:67-105.
6. Spencer, Baldwin and F.J. Gillen, *The Native Tribes of Central Australia*, London, McMillan, 1899; Meggitt, M.J., *Desert People*, Sydney, Angus & Robertson, 1972; Strehlow, T.G.H., *Songs of Central Australia*, Sydney, Angus & Robertson, 1971; Munn, Nancy D., *Warlbiri Iconogrpahy*, Ithaca and London, Cornell University Press, 1973.
7. See Rosaldo, Michelle and Louise Lamphere, *Woman, Culture and Society*, Standford, Stanford University Press; Leacock, Eleanor, "Women's Status in Egalitarian Society: Implications for Social Evolution", *Current Anthropology*, 1978(19)2, 247-255.
8. Berndt, C.H., "Women's Changing Ceremonies in Northern Australia", *L'Homme*, 1950, 1, 1-87; Ellis, Catherine J., "The Role of the Ethnomusicologist in the Study of Andaringa Women's Ceremonies", *Miscellanea Musicologica: Adelaide Studies of Musicology*, 1970, 5, 76-212; White, Isobel, M., "Sexual Conquest and Submission in Aboriginal Myths", *Australia Aboriginal Mythology*, Hiatt, L.R. (ed.), Canberra, A.I.A.S., 1975:123-142.
9. From August 1976 to January 1978, I undertook fieldwork at Warrabri, 375 km north of Alice Springs, Northern Territory. At that time it was a government settlement but with the passage of the *Aboriginal Land Rights (N.T.) Act*, 1976, it has become Aboriginal land (see below, note 11). In 1977 it was home to approximately 700 Aborigines (Warlpiri, Warumungu, Alywarra, Kaytej) and 70 whites.
10. This authority is a statutory body established under Northern Territory legislation, the *Sacred Sites Act*, 1978, which is reciprocal legislation to the Federal Land Rights Act. In 1981 I was employed to respond to requests from Aborigines for site protection, throughout the Northern Territory.
11. Under the *Aboriginal Land Rights (N.T.) Act*, 1976, Aborigines may bring claims to unaliented Crown land or land in which all interests other than those held by the Crown are held by or on behalf of Aborigines. Certain reserve lands, described in Schedules 1, 2 and 3, were also made Aboriginal land. Title to successfully claimed land is held by a Land Trust established for that purpose. Anthropologists assist in the preparation, hearing and assessing of evidence brought on behalf of the traditional owners. In the Daly River claim, I was engaged by the Northern Land Council, to prepare a submission regarding Women's interests in the claim area. See Bell, Diane, "Daly River (Malak Malak) Land Claim: Women's Interests", (Exhibit 8) Darwin, Northern Lanc Council, 1981:1-33.
12. Stanner, W.E.H., op. cit., 1979:106.
13. ibid., 143.
14. ibid., 108.
15. Elkin, A.P., "Studies in Australian Totemism", *Oceania*, 1933, 4, 113-131; Warner, W.L., *A Black Civilization*, New York, Harper, 1937; McConnel, Ursula, *Myths of Mungkan*, Melbourne, M.U.P., 1957; Berndt, R.M., *Kunapipi*, Melbourne, 1951; Strehlow, op. cit., Munn, op. cit.
16. Péron, M.F., *A Voyage of Discovery to the Southern Hemisphere*, London, 1809:67-68.
17. Hart, C.W.M. and Arnold R. Pilling, *The Tiwi of North Australia*, New York, Holt Rinehart & Winston, 1960:14.
18. Meggitt, op. cit., 236.
19. Hamilton, Annette, "Aboriginal Women: The Means of Production", *The Other Half*, Mercer, Jan (ed.), Harmondsworth, Penguin, 1975:167-179; Barwick, Diane E., "And the Lubras are Ladies Now", *Women's Role in Aboriginal Society*, Gale, Fay (ed.), Canberra, A.I.A.S., 1970:31-38; Reay, Marie, "Aboriginal and White Australian Family Structure: An Inquiry Into Assimilation Trends", *Sociological Review*, n.s., 1963, 11(1), 19-47; Bell, Diane, "Desert Politics: Choices in the 'Marriage Market'", *Women and Colonization*, Etienne, Mona and Eleanor Leacock (eds), New York, Praeger, 1980:239-269.
20. Hamilton, Annette, "The Role of Women in Aboriginal Marriage Arrangements", *Women's Role in Aboriginal Society*, Gale, Fay (ed.), Canberra, A.I.A.S., 1970:17-20; Goodale, Jane, C., *Tiwi Wives*, Seattle, University of Washington Press, 1971; see also Bell, op. cit., 1980.
21. Hiatt, L.R., *Kinship and Conflict*, Canberra, A.N.U. Press, 1965.
22. Kaberry, Phyllis M., *Aboriginal Women, Sacred and Profane*, London, Routledge, 1939.
23. Berndt, C.H., op. cit., 1960; "Women and the 'Secret Life'", *Aboriginal Man in Australia*, Berndt, Ronald M. and Catherine H. Berndt (eds), Sydney, Angus & Robertson, 1965:236-282; "Digging Sticks and Spears, or, the Two-Sex Model", in Gale, op. cit., 1970:39-48.
24. Goodale, op. cit.
25. Warner, op. cit., 6.
26. Maddock, Kenneth, *The Australian Aborigines: A Portrait of Their Society*, London, Allen Lane, 1972:155.
27. Bern, John, "Politics in the Conduct of a Secret Male Ceremony", *Journal of Anthropological Research*, 1979a, 35(1), 47.
28. Bern, John, "Ideology and Domination", *Oceania*, 1979b, L, 2, 129.
29. In my work as consultant to Central Land Council, Northern Land Council, the Aboriginal Land Commissioner and in various projects concerning land rights, site registration and law reform, I have been able to complement and extend my original fieldwork (see above, note 9). See Bell, Diane and Pam Ditton, *Law: the Old and New*, Canberra, Aboriginal History, 1980. Other information is in submissions to land claim hearings and reports to the Aboriginal Sacred Sites Protection Authority (see above, note 10).
30. See Bell, Diane, *Daughters of the Dreaming*, Melbourne, McPhee Garibble, forthcoming.
31. See Bell, Diane, "Statement to the Kaytej, Warlpiri and Warlmanpa Land Claim", Exhibit 48, 1982a; Maddock, Kenneth, *Anthropology, Law and the Definition of Australian Aboriginal Rights to Land*, Nijmegen, 1980.
32. See Bell, op. cit., forthcoming.
33. McConnel, op. cit.; Munn, op. cit.

34. Stanner, op. city., 1979:123.
35. Fee, Elizabeth, "The Sexual Politics of Victorian Social Anthropology", *Clio's Consciousness Raised*, Hartmann, Mary S. and Lois Banner (eds), New York, Harper & Row, 1974:101.
36. Evans-Pritchard, E.E., *The Position of Women in Primitive Societies and Other Essays in Social Anthropology*, London, Faber & Faber, 1965:37-58.
37. Kuhn, Thomas S., *The Structure of Scientific Revolutions*, Chicago, University of Chicago Press (Second Edition), 1970:43ff.
38. Róheim, Geza, "Women and Their Life in Central Australia", *R.A.I.J.*, 1933, 63, 207-265.
39. Firestone, Shulamith, *The Dialectic of Sex*, Great Britain, Jonathan Cape, 1971:46-72.
40. Stanner, op. cit., 1979:108-109.
41. Munn, op. cit.
42. Kaberry, op. cit., 188-189.
43. ibid., ix.
44. ibid., 221.
45. Berndt, op. cit., 1970.
46. ibid., 41.
47. Goodale, op. cit., xxiii. See also Rohrlich-Leavitt, Rudy, Barbara Sykes and Elizabeth Weatherford, "Aboriginal Woman, Male and Female Anthropological Perspectives", in *Toward an Anthropology of Women*, Reiter, Rayna (ed.), N.Y., Monthly Review Press, 1975:110-126.
48. ibid., 337-338.
49. Stanner, op. cit., 1979:136.
50. White, op. cit., 1975:136.
* 51. Bell, op. cit., forthcoming.
52. Hamilton, Annette, "Dual Social Systems: Technology, Labour and Women's Secret Rites in the Eastern Western Desert of Australia", unpublished ms., 1978, 17p.
53. Hamilton, Annette, "Timeless Transformations, Women, Men and History in the Australian Western Desert", unpublished Ph.D. thesis, University of Sydney, 1979:xxi.
54. ibid., 78-79.
* 55. Bell, op. cit., forthcoming.
56. ibid.
57. See Elkin, A.P., "The Yaduduruwa", *Oceania*, 1961, 31, 166-209; Berndt, R.M., op. cit., 1951; Maddock, K., "The Jabuduruwa", unpublished Ph.D. thesis, University of Sydney, 1969; Bern, op. cit., 1979a & b.
58. Bern, ibid., 1979a:418-419.
59. See Berndt, C.H., op. cit., 1950:30-39, for a discussion of *Munga-Munga* in the Victorian River Downs area and suggestion that *Munga-Munga* came from the Roper River area.
* 60. Bell, Diane, "In the Tracks of the *munga-Munga*", submission to the Cox River Land Claim, Darwin, Northern Lanc Council, 1982b.
61. Stanner, op. cit., 1976:20ff.
62. Stanner, op. cit., 1979:118.
63. See Bell and Ditton, op cit.
64. Transcript of Evidence, *Aboriginal Land Rights (N.T.) Act*, 1976, re Kaytej, Warlpiri and Warlmanpa claim, 1981:191. (I have edited out the questions of counsel so that only the answers of the witnesses remain in the text).
65. *The Australian Encyclopaedia*, Vol. 5, Sydney, The Grolier Society of Australia, 3rd edition, 1977; see also Badger, C.R., *The Reverend Charles Strong and the Australian Church*, Melbourne, Abacada Press, 1971.

ADDENDA

Page 12, line 37: discuss *read* dismiss
Page 13, line 7: concerning *read* of
Page 14, note 1: publishers *read* for permission to reprint material from (forthcoming) *read* 1983
Page 15, note 11: Lanc *read* Lan
Page 15, note 32: forthcoming *read* 1983
Page 16, note 51: forthcoming *read* 1983
Page 16, note 55: forthcoming *read* 1983
Page 16, note 60: munga-Munga *read* unga-Munga
   Lanc *read* Lan

EASTERN RELIGIONS

JOSEPH KITAGAWA

SOME REFLECTIONS ON THE JAPANESE WORLD OF MEANING

It is indeed a great privilege for me to be asked to deliver the Charles Strong Memorial Lecture in Australian universities. I have chosen to discuss on this occasion the major characteristics of the early Japanese "world of meaning" for two reasons. Firstly, while I was trained to be a historian of religions and not a Japanologist, it has been my concern to approach Japanese religion and culture from the perspective of *Religions-wissenschaft,* a field more commonly known as the History of Religions or the Comparative Study of Religions. Secondly, it seems relevant for people in Australia, a nation destined to play an important role in the Pacific Community, to learn more about the religious and cultural traits of early Japan which have been preserved to a significant degree to the present day by the Japanese people.

Sir George B. Sansom once wrote: "Few countries have been more copiously described than Japan, and perhaps few have been less thoroughly understood".[1] His observation is particularly applicable to the religious and cultural life of the Japanese. No less an interpreter of Japan than Lafcadio Hearn stated in his diary that he experienced a "delightful confusion" when he first visited Buddhist temples and Shintō shrines in Japan, "for there are no immediately discernible laws of construction or decoration: each building seems to have a fantastic prettiness of its own; nothing is exactly like anything else, and all is bewilderingly novel".[2] Moreover, it is far easier to describe a temple or a shrine than to understand the ethos, mood and inner texture of Japanese religions and culture.

It goes without saying that any attempt to understand Japanese religions and culture is naturally conditioned by one's perspective. For example, a student of Buddhism, with justification, will stress the decisive influence which Buddhism has exerted on all aspects of Japanese life. On the other hand, a student of Shintō, again with justification, will tend to hold that Buddhism, Confucianism, and other religious and cultural traditions have been assimilated into an overall framework provided by Shintō. A student of art will view religious and cultural life in Japan from yet another perspective, quite justly holding that in Japan religion is art and art is religion. Thus, he will see the religious and cultural development of Japan primarily as an ever-changing work of art, with each new epoch emerging out of the creative fusion of the old and new.

Enlightening and important though these perspectives are, I would like to approach Japanese religions and culture from another standpoint, that is, by reflecting on some of the basic

---

1 George B. Sansom, "Foreword", *Japan—Past and Present* by Edwin O. Reischauer (Alfred A. Knopf, New York, 1953), p. vii.
2 Henry Goodman (ed.), *The Selected Writings of Lafcadio Hearn* (The Citadel Press, New York, 1949), p. 400.

characteristics of the "world of meaning" of the early Japanese. In this respect, my own perspective is based on the simple premise that every individual, and every culture and people, lives not only in a geographical, physical world but also in what we might call a "world of meaning". Some are more self-conscious than others about the mental and psychic processes involved in the ordering of diverse experiences and meanings that comprise the mystery of life. In that memorable account, entitled *Teacher* by Helen Keller, we are told how Annie Sullivan began to teach the deaf and blind child.

> She began at once spelling into Helen's hand, suiting the word to the action, the action to the word, and the child responded by imitating the finger motions like a bright, inquisitive animal. . . . [One day], while Annie Sullivan pumped water over her hand it came to the child in a flash that water, wherever it was found, was water, and that the finger motions she had just felt on her palm meant water and nothing else. In that thrilling moment she found the key to her kingdom. Everything had a name and she had a way to learn the names.[3]

This, to be sure, is an extreme example, but it is something like a slow motion film, and it makes clear the process whereby each one of us emerges from that phase of life Helen Keller called "a phantom living in a world that is no-world". To put it another way, to be fully human means to be able to shape one's own structure of meaning, through association and imagination, education and effort, with regard to the things we observe and experience. In large measure our "world of meaning" stems from what has been handed down to us, and thus, either consciously or unconsciously, our world of meaning approximates the world-view implicit in our cultural and religious traditions. Furthermore, the world of meaning thus created exerts a decisive influence in patterning our behaviour, beliefs and goals of life. This is another way of saying that our individual sensory perception, our mental and psychic reactions are guided into habitual channels by our corporate cultural experience. It is difficult enough to understand the extent and breadth of this pattern of interpretation in our own lives, but it is a far more difficult problem for us to appreciate the depth of the "world of meaning" of other peoples who have been moulded by different kinds of historical, religious and cultural experiences.

If I may speak personally, I have experienced serious difficulties in teaching religions of Asia in my History of Religions classes to American students. My constant problem is how to present the subtle and often illusive *geist,* styles and attitudes of Eastern religions using a Western language which is inclined to be logical, precise and systematic. To be sure, not all Westerners are logical and precise, and there have been many intuitive thinkers and mystics in the West. But by and large the Westerner's mind-set has been conditioned to a critical and systematic form by the

---

3 Helen Keller, *Teacher: Anne Sullivan Macy* (Doubleday, Garden City, 1955), "Introduction" by Nella Braddy Henney, pp. 11-12.

strong cultural emphasis on reason. There is much truth in Betty Heimann's observation that the profound gulf between East and West is epitomized by a word "system" (*systema*), which implies "putting together" or "com-position" in a rational order. The underlying assumption here is that "the human mind thinks 'systematically', prescribes the order of research, the selection, disposition and composition of ideas". On the other hand, the Easterner's mind-set is accustomed to be more intuitive and appreciative— "to look, to contemplate, to be receptive—but in no degree implying any idea of regulating the facts of Nature".[4] We might keep this helpful insight in mind as we explore the basic characteristics of the early Japanese "world of meaning".

THE SEAMLESSNESS OF THE EARLY JAPANESE "WORLD OF MEANING"

I am always struck by the way most Westerners use the two terms—"reality" and "illusion"—as sharply demarcated opposites. "Reality", so Webster tells us, refers to the "state, character, quality, or fact of being real, existent . . .", or "an actual person, event, or the like; an accomplished fact", implying thus that "reality" is "that which is not imagination or fiction—that which has objective existence". In sharp contrast to "reality", "illusion" is defined as "an unreal or misleading image presented to the vision's deceptive appearance", or "a perception which fails to give the true character of an object perceived". Such a sharp dichotomy between reality and illusion in the West has tended to place art, music, literature, poetry, myths and religion into a broad and ambiguous category of "imagination", situated somewhere between reality and illusion. In this respect it is significant to note that the early Japanese world of meaning was "seamless", that is, it affirmed a basic continuity between reality and illusion, between facts and fantasies, and between consciousness and dream. We might even say that for the early Japanese illusion was one facet of reality.

The seamlessness of the early Japanese world of meaning is evident in the ancient myths concerning a three-dimensional universe—the Plain of High Heaven (*Takama-no-hara*), the Manifest World (*Utsushi-yo*) and the Nether World (*Yomotsu-kuni*). Here, it must be pointed out that the mythical accounts portray these three realms as almost interchangeable, in that certain gods and heroes move back and forth freely between the Plain of High Heaven and the Nether World and/or the Manifest World. Accordingly, in the view of the early Japanese the mythical world and the natural world interpenetrated one another to the extent that human activities were explained and sanctioned in terms of what gods, ancestors and heroes did in the sacred past.

---

4 Betty Heimann, *Indian and Western Philosophy: A Study in Contrasts* (George Allen & Unwin Ltd., London, 1937), pp. 27-28.

KAMI, SPIRITS AND MIKO

Among all the ambiguous and untranslatable words in the Japanese religious vocabulary, the most confusing is the term *kami,* which etymologically means "high", "superior", or "sacred". Semantically, it is usually used as an appellation of all beings that are awesome and worthy of reverence, including good as well as evil beings. There is every reason to believe that the early Japanese found *kami* everywhere—in the heavens, in the air, in the forests, in the rocks, in the streams, in animals and in human beings. It would be misleading, however, to consider the religion of the ancient Japanese, which came to be known as Shintō (the Way of the Kami), simply as polytheism or nature worship. While it certainly accepted the plurality of the *kami* as separate beings, its fundamental affirmation was considerably broader and stressed the sacrality of the total cosmos. That is to say, it was felt that within nature all beings, including those which we now call inanimate, share and participate in the common *kami* (sacred) nature. It is also worth noting that the *kami* of the mythical accounts were given human traits, while the princes and heroes were often characterized as *kami* in human form. Animals, too, were regarded as having *kami*-human characteristics. There is no indication, however, that the *kami* had any of the supramundane qualities usually ascribed to the deity in the Judeo-Christian and Islamic traditions.

According to early Shintō, all beings were endowed with spirits or souls, called *tama* or *mono.* It was widely held that the spirit or soul could leave the body of a person or an animal on certain occasions, and special rites were thus performed to prevent the soul from leaving the body. Other rites were practised to console the spirits of the dead. The spirits of *kami* and/or animals were believed to be capable of "possessing" men and women. In fact, one of the earliest features of Japanese religion was the existence of the shamanic diviner (*miko, ichiko* or *monomochi*), who in the state of *kami*-possession performed healing, fortune-telling, or transmission of messages from the spirit. Another important feature of early Shintō was the belief in "spirits residing in words" (*koto-dama*). According to this doctrine, beautiful words, when correctly pronounced, were held to bring about good, whereas ugly words or words incorrectly uttered were believed to cause evil. This was particularly true of words or speeches addressed to the *kami.*

The spirit of the deceased was believed to depart to the other- or eternal-world (*toko-yo*), often equated with a mountain or island beyond the sea, but at the time of the harvest and the new year the spirits of the ancestors were expected to return from the eternal-world as "sacred visitors" (*marebito*) in order to receive the homage of their descendants.[5] It was also believed that those

---

5 See Hori Ichiro. *Folk Religion in Japan: Continuity and Change,* ed. by J. M. Kitagawa and A. L. Miller (The University of Chicago Press, 1968), pp. 153-54.

spirits of the dead which had not been properly consoled, and the spirits of those who had been murdered or killed by accident would come as ghosts to haunt the ungrateful descendants or the guilty ones. Sometimes the unhappy ghosts would communicate their complaints by means of the shamanic diviner (*miko*), but in other instances they might appear in dreams, communicating their wishes and complaints directly to the individuals concerned. In this respect, the dream was taken seriously by the early Japanese as a direct link between two interpenetrating realms of existence, the world of the living and the world of the dead.

It may be worth repeating that for the early Japanese the "world", though comprised of various facets, divisions and realms, was nevertheless a one-dimensional monistic universe. The Plain of High Heaven, the Manifest World, and the Nether World, as recorded in mythical accounts, were almost interchangeable. There were no rigid lines of demarcation between the domains of *kami*, human beings, animals and plants. Even the gulf between the world of the living and the world of the dead was blurred by the frequent movement of spirits and ghosts and by other channels of communication between the two realms, such as oracles, fortune-telling and divination. In other words, the world of early Shintō had a unitary meaning-structure, based upon the *kami* nature pervading the entire universe, which was essentially a "sacred community of living beings" all endowed with spirits or souls.

LIFE AS POETRY

One of the most important sources for our understanding of the early Japanese attitude toward life and the world is an anthology of poems entitled the *Collection of Myriad Leaves* (*Manyō-shū*). While it was compiled in the eighth century A.D., nearly two centuries after the introduction of Sino-Korean civilization and Buddhism into Japan, almost all the gods whom the *Manyō* poets sang, or who fed their lyric inspiration, were *kami* of the indigenous Shintō tradition.[6]

Many of the *Manyō* verses reflect the poet's childlike enchantment with the four seasons. "In the meadow full of yellow roses / Violets have blossomed forth with spring rain." Or, "As I see the messenger walking on the fallen leaves / I think of the time when I first met my beloved."[7] Many poets were captivated by the rivers, mountains and seas of the Japanese landscape. The *Manyō* poets were just as spontaneous in responding to various human situations as they were in their response to the poignant beauty and wonder of the four seasons and the landscape. They were not inhibited in expressing tender passions of love, or the gentle

6 The Nippon Gakujutsu Shinkōkai (tr.), *The Manyōshū* (Columbia University Press, New York, 1965), p. xxxviii.
7 *The Great Asian Religions: An Anthology*, compl. by **Wing-tsit Chan**, Isma'il R. al Faruqi, Joseph M. Kitagawa and **P. T. Raju** (The Macmillan Co., New York, 1969), pp. 238-39.

throbbing of hearts as they bade farewell to friends or in time of grief, and through it all, they took for granted that there existed a continuity and correspondence between the capriciousness of human life and the swift change of the seasons. Even then, what motivated the *Manyō* poets was not speculation on the theme of life's uncertainty, but the spontaneous and sympathetic response of the heart to the rhythm of human life and the world of nature. For the early Japanese life had elements of sorrow, tragedy, trial and tribulation, yet the meaning of life and all its ambiguities were authenticated in terms of the givenness of the world of nature. Basically, they affirmed life in this phenomenal existence as essentially good (*yoshi*) and beautiful (*uruwashi*), in spite of or even because of its transitoriness. Significantly, "good" and "beautiful" were almost synonymous, so that the Chinese term *shan* (good or virtuous) was translated by the Japanese expression *uruwashi* (beautiful).[8]

The one-dimensional monistic world of meaning of the early Japanese also implied acceptance of the continuity between the "original" and the "natural", as it were, so that they did not look for another order of meaning behind the phenomenal, natural world. That is to say, this world was not seen as a "fallen" state of a more ideal order of existence. The *natural* world, according to the early Japanese, was the *original* world, which was in itself good and beautiful. Thus, in the early Japanese context, even the term *tsumi*, which later took on the moral connotations of "sin", meant simply "defilement", "lack of beauty", or "something dirty", which could be washed away by ablution or lustration.

There is much truth in Langdon Warner's observation that Shintō, from its early days, has been the artist's way of life. "Natural forces are the very subject matter for those who produce artifacts from raw materials or who hunt and fish and farm. Thus Shintō taught . . . how such forces are controlled and these formulas have been embedded in Shintō liturgies."[9] This does not mean that Shintō has been *only* or even primarily the artist's way of life. Nevertheless, Shintō did teach succeeding generations of Japanese that the world of nature is something good and beautiful and that men and women have every reason to be thankful for its existence. Indeed, as Muraoka succinctly points out, the early Japanese outlook "on life and the world was essentially one of unsophisticated optimism . . . [To them], there could be no better world than this world . . . Nature was good and natural laws were moral laws".[10] Living as they did in such a simple, yet all-embracing world of meaning, the early Japanese took it for granted that there existed no discontinuity between art and reli-

---

8   Muraoka Tsunetsugu, *Studies in Shintō Thought*, trans. by Delmer M. Brown and James T. Araki (Ministry of Education, Tokyo, 1964), p. 58.

9   Langdon Warner, *The Enduring Art of Japan* (Harvard University Press, Cambridge, 1952), p. 18.

gion, song and prayer, dance and cult, consciousness and dream, reality and illusion. It is no accident that this sensitive awareness of the continuum between man and nature was expressed in poetic verse. After all, not only did they write poems but they viewed life itself as poetry as well.

Fortunately or unfortunately, such a simple unitary meaning structure could not be sustained when Japan came under the impact of Chinese, or more strictly speaking Sino-Korean civilization and Buddhism. Yet, what is fascinating is the fact that during the relatively short period between the sixth and eighth centuries when this encounter occurred, the Japanese world of meaning was able to appropriate many features of the Continental civilizations without losing its own basic structure. Furthermore, the basic principles which shaped the development of government, religion and art in this period have remained operative during the subsequent periods of Japanese history until our own time. Let us, therefore, discuss the highlights of the encounter of early Japan with Chinese civilization and Buddhism.

SYMBOLS AND REALITY

The penetration of Chinese civilization and Buddhism during the fifth and sixth centuries A.D. brought about not only a series of social, cultural and political changes in Japan, but also a variety of new ways of giving ordering or meaning to the experience of the Japanese. Chief among these were two universal principles: *Tao,* the underlying principle of the Confucian socio-political order, and *Dharma,* the eternal principle underlying the Buddhist notion of reality. We may recall that the early Japanese were inclined to accept the givenness of life and the world with poetic sensitivities. They did not lack rationality and they were aware of the meaning of things which they saw and experienced, but they did not reflect upon the meaning of meanings. Following their encounter with Chinese civilization and Buddhism, however, the Japanese became aware that there might be meanings beyond the realm of their immediate experiences, and that different levels of reality could exist. For example, they were introduced to the cosmological speculation of the Yin-Yang School, based on the two complementary principles (*yin* and *yang*), the five elements (metal, wood, water, fire, and earth), and the orderly rotation of these principles and elements in the formation of nature, man and seasons. These concepts were appropriated by the Japanese into their native Shintō, which hitherto had lacked cosmological theories. The Japanese also learned from Taoism and Confucianism respectively, the cosmic significance of a natural order and a socio-political order, and further, that Confucian ethics, political theory, legal and educational institutions were based on the universal principle of *Tao* (*michi* in Japanese). Numerous kinds of divination and witchcraft, palmistry and fortune-telling were also

10 Muraoka, *op. cit.,* p. 59.

introduced from China, and the influence of astrologers and sorcerers was strongly felt in all walks of Japanese life. Meanwhile, the Japanese learned from Buddhism to become aware of an ultimate reality, explicated in terms of *Dharma* (*hō* in Japanese), which exists behind and beneath the transitoriness of phenomenal experience.

As might be expected, the impact of Chinese civilization and Buddhism was strongly felt in various aspects of the social and cultural life of the Japanese. In the course of time, the Japanese world of meaning, which was earlier characterized as a one-dimensional, undifferentiated monistic universe, was destined to become multi-dimensional and more compartmentalized. Such a change in their world of meaning was influenced by, and at the same time authenticated the gradual departmentalization and stratification of Japanese culture and society. In this situation, the link between the internal world of meaning and the external world of culture and society came to be understood in "symbolic" terms.

This is not the occasion to discuss theories of symbolism, except to state that all human activities involve some form of symbols and that the early Japanese were no exception in this respect. In the main, however, the early Japanese, who regarded everything in the universe as a manifestation of *kami* were never self-conscious about the "process of symbolization" because they participated so naturally and fully in such a process. Only when they encountered Chinese civilization and Buddhism did the Japanese realize the significance of new symbols, particularly of the Chinese "script" and the Buddhist "image". It was through these that the Japanese were able to participate, though perhaps only vicariously, in the historic experiences of the Chinese and the Buddhists who created these symbols. And it was by adopting the Chinese script for their written words, and by appropriating the Buddhist images as visual representations for their understanding of the Sacred, that the Japanese world of meaning was able to absorb important features of difficult foreign civilizations and religions.

THE CHINESE SCRIPT

We can readliy understand that the task of adopting the Chinese script, with its highly developed pictographs, ideographs and phonetic compounds, to match Japanese words was a complex and painful one. Initially, Chinese civilization infiltrated Japan through Korean and Chinese immigrants who settled in Japan, and whose services as instructors, interpreters, scribes and artists were sought after by the imperial court. Shortly thereafter some of the Japanese intelligentsia learned the use of literary Chinese, which was used for writing the historical and official records of the court. One system used Chinese characters but read them in Japanese,[11] and

---

[11] The complexity of this system, which was used in the *Kojiki* (Records of Ancient Matters), is such that "the modern reader of the *Kojiki* . . . has a sort of bilingual puzzle which he must decipher as he goes along". See Donald L. Philippi (tr.), *Kojiki* (University of Tokyo Press, 1968), p. 28.

another system utilized Chinese characters only for their sound value, disregarding their lexical meaning, in order to express Japanese sounds. This system was called the *Manyō-gana* (a form of syllabary used in the *Manyō-shū* or *Collection of Myriad Leaves*), the forerunner of the *hiragana* and *katakana,* the two syllabaries which have been used until the present time.

I might mention in passing that those who grew up in Japan can testify how difficult it is to master the use of Chinese script to express Japanese words. But, given the geographical and historical situations of early Japan, we can readily see that knowledge of written Chinese provided the only channel by which the Japanese might have access to the immensely rich civilization of China. Given this mode of access, though, Chinese civilization could serve as a resource and a model for Japan, which had barely grown out of the state of pre-history.

Chinese influence not only gave impetus to the development of the Japanese language, but also provided those Japanese poets and writers who had mastered literary Chinese with another medium in which to express themselves. Ironically, mastery of Chinese often did not include the ability to speak the language orally, so that most of the officials and students who were sent to China had to depend on interpreters. Nevertheless, the Chinese "script" served as an important "symbol" of Chinese civilization, which was not only more advanced than that of Japan, but also commanded a greater authority as a result of its claim to be grounded in the universal principle, *Tao*. It was largely due to the prestige of Confucianism as the guiding ideology of the Chinese empire that Japanese society which heretofore had been based on primitive communal rules and authority, was so quickly influenced by Confucian ethical principles, Confucian social and political theories, and Confucian-inspired legal and educational systems. Although the traditional paternalistic authoritarianism was retained, interpersonal relationships came to be regulated in terms of such typically Confucian concepts as filial piety, veneration of ancestors, and reciprocity of rights and obligations between superiors and inferiors. Thus, the stratification of Japanese society was closely linked to the extension of the scope and expansion of the horizon of the Japanese world of meaning which took place through participation in the historic experience of the Chinese through the medium of the Chinese script, or the written language.

THE BUDDHA'S IMAGE

As to the official introduction of Buddhism into Japan, the chroniclers agree that it was during the sixth century A.D. when the King of Paekche, Korea, presented to the Japanese court the image of Sākyamuni Buddha, along with scriptures and ceremonial articles as well as priests, representing the Three Treasures of Buddhism, i.e., Buddha (image), *Dharma* (scriptures), and *Saṁgha* (priests). We must remind ourselves in this connection that early Shintō, because of its affirmation that all things were potentially if not actually hierophanies or manifestations of *kami* (the Sacred), never developed representations of *kami* in anthropomorphic form, even though it had a rich variety of ritual acts, sacred dances, purification rites, and the like. Nor did early Shintō acknowledge the qualitative superiority of certain manifestations of *kami* over others. In sharp contrast to early Shintō, the Buddhism which reached Japan was a highly developed religion with comprehensive philosophical and doctrinal systems codified in voluminous scriptures, elaborate ecclesiastical structures, colourful rituals, and accompanied by splendid art and architecture, all of which made profound impressions on the Japanese. Moreover, as Anesaki astutely observes, the Japanese learned for the first time from Buddhism that "there was a deity or superman who looked after the welfare and salvation of all beings . . . The people saw, to their astonishment and admiration, the figure of a divine being represented in beauty and adored by means of elaborate rituals".[12] Indeed, to the early Japanese the symbolization of the divinity or the Sacred in a human-like image or statue was a new revelation, which had far-reaching effects in the subsequent development of Japanese religion.

The expansion of Buddhism during the two centuries following its introduction was greatly aided by its use of statues, art and architecture. Without these "symbols", the Japanese would have found it difficult to incorporate the profound spiritual insights of historic Buddhism into their own world of meaning. Conversely, these symbols, seen through the mental "prism" of the Japanese, came to have a new mode of meaning which was unique to the Japanese. In this sense, we might paraphrase Spengler and say that what was accepted by the Japanese was not the *Dharma* or the Buddahood as symbolized in the images but rather the images (symbols) themselves "as disclosing to the native sensibility and understanding of the observer potential modes of his own creativeness".[13] Indeed, the accounts of the *Chronicles of Japan* (*Nihon-gi* or *Nihon-shoki*) vividly portray how the early Japanese, who had no tradition of visual representation of *kami* in anthropomorphic form, were initially befuddled yet attracted by the image of the Buddha, which was reputed to have the power to give merit and reward or curse people.

In a real sense, the Buddhist images did not alter the magico-religious sensibility of the early Japanese, but rather provided a symbolic form for them. For example, in the famous battle of A.D. 587 between the pro-Buddhist Soga Clan and the anti-Buddhist Mononobe Clan, an imperial prince later known as the Prince Regent Shōtoku (573-621) sided with the Soga. "He cut the lacquer tree and made images of the four heavenly guardian kings and then vowed, 'If you enable us to be victorious over our

---

12 Anesaki Masaharu, *History of Japanese Religion* (Kegan Paul, Trench, Trubner, Ltd., London, 1930), p. 54.
13 Oswald Spengler, *The Decline of the West* (Alfred Knopf, New York, 1932), Vol. II, 57.

enemy, I solemnly pledge to build a temple in honour of the Four Heavenly Guardians'." And, when the anti-Buddhist forces of the Mononobe Clan were defeated, the prince erected the Temple of the Four Heavenly Guardians (Shitennō-ji) in what is now Osaka. After the battle, during the administration of the Prince Regent Shōtoku a new page was turned in the history of Japan, politically, culturally and religiously.

As we reflect on the introduction of Buddhism to Japan, we share Sir Charles Eliot's observation that "though it was judged by the crude standard of its power to stop plague and though it triumphed as part of the [policies] of the Soga Clan, these accidents must not blind us to the fact that it came as the epitome of Indian and Chinese civilization and wrought a moral as well as intellectual revolution [in Japan]".[14] Let us now examine how such far-reaching and multi-dimensional changes took place in early Japan.

GOVERNMENT, RELIGION AND ART

The combined impact of Chinese civilization and Buddhism, exemplified by the Chinese script and the Buddhist image respectively, was destined to leave a lasting imprint on aspects of Japanese culture and society. Indeed, the fact that political administration (*matsuri-goto*), religious cults (*matsuri*), and cultural activities, especially art, came to be thought of as interrelated but nonetheless separate dimensions of life indicates the extent to which the seamlessness of the early Japanese world of meaning was transformed under the influence of foreign perspectives on life and the world. Nevertheless, we also find the persistent impulse of the Japanese to re-homologize and to maintain the connection between various dimensions of life, especially that between political administration and religion, as well as that between religion and art. Parenthetically, it might be mentioned that the effort of the Japanese to unify various aspects of culture and society was greatly aided by Confucian inspiration during the seventh century A.D., followed by the Buddhist inspiration during the eighth century A.D. or the Nara period.

(i) GOVERNMENT

It may be worth noting that the introduction of Buddhism to Japan in the mid-sixth century A.D. was motivated not only by the piety of the King of Paekche but also by his desire to secure Japan's military assistance in his struggle against the rival kingdom of Silla. Significantly, the split among ministers of the Japanese court between pro-Buddhist and anti-Buddhist factions coincided with the split between pro-Paekche and pro-Silla factions. It was with the support of the victorious Soga clan, which was pro-Paekche and pro-Buddhist, that the Prince Regent Shōtoku

---

14 Sir Charles Eliot, *Japanese Buddhism* (Barnes & Noble, New York, 1959), p. 202.

attempted to establish a centralized government administration, following the example of the Sui dynasty which had unified China in A.D. 589. Prince Shōtoku himself was a pious Buddhist, but his policies represented an ingenious attempt to harmonize Buddhist and Confucian traditions with the native Shintō tradition. Accordingly, Shōtoku exalted the throne and urged the veneration of the Buddha's Law (*Dharma*), but he also maintained that the basic principle of government administration was "propriety" (*li* in Chinese; *rei* in Japanese) as taught in the Confucian tradition. Thus he proclaimed:

> The ministers and officials should abide by propriety, which is the principle of governing the people. . . . Only when the ministers abide by propriety, the hierarchical ranks will not be disrupted, and when the people abide by propriety, the nation will be governed peacefully by its own accord.[15]

Prince Shōtoku and his advisers were aware of the magnitude of the task involved in establishing a government according to the principle of propriety. Realizing that the projected centralized government would require formal codes of law and trained bureaucrats, Shōtoku sent a number of talented young scholars and monks to China for study. Unfortunately, most of Shōtoku's reform measures remained unfulfilled at the time of his death in A.D. 622. It was not until A.D. 645 that the "Edict of Reform" was promulgated with the aim of consolidating the centralized structure of the government by initiating such "Sinified" measures as land distribution, collection of revenues and the taking of a census. Also, the government depended on those who had studied in China for the compilation of written law. Significantly, those penal codes (*ritsu; lü* in Chinese) and civil statutes (*ryō; ling* in Chinese), which were appropriated from the Chinese legal systems, were issued as the will of the emperor, who came to be regarded as the "manifest *kami*". The government structure which thus developed in the second half of the seventh century is referred to as the "Imperial rescript (*ritsu-ryō*) state".

It is evident that the seventh century reformers, starting with Prince Shōtoku, were greatly inspired by the Confucian principle of propriety. At the same time their natural inclination was to homologize Confucian, Buddhist and Shintō traditions into a multi-value system, which was, in effect, a more sophisticated and extended form of the seamless world of meaning of the early Japanese. Once such a multi-value system was established as the framework for a centralized nation with the throne at its apex, it provided the paradigm for the political structure of Japan until the present century.

(ii) RELIGION

We have already discussed how early Shintō, which was not a unified system and lacked coherent theology, metaphysics, liturgics, ethics and ecclesiology, was destined to be influenced by the Ying-Yang School, Taoism, Confucianism and Buddhism, all of

---

15 See *Great Asian Religions: An Anthology*, p. 253.

which had sophisticated philosophies, doctrines and cults. Nevertheless, in the development of Japanese culture, Shintō left its lasting mark because of its aesthetic temperament and its inclination to view everything as part of one continuum. Moreover, Shintō played a decisive role in the development of the multi-value system by providing several factors that contributed to the basic political framework which was established. Chief among these were myths of the solar ancestry of the imperial clan and of the divine origin of the nation, and the notion of the unity of religion and political aspects of life (*saisei-itchi*).

During the seventh and eighth centuries the rapid expansion of Buddhism and the growing stratification of the Buddhist hierarchy and ecclesiastical structure stimulated a similar development in Shintō. By the turn of the eighth century, the Office of Shintō or *Kami* Affairs was placed side by side with the Great Council of the State. While such a development testifies to the great prestige accorded to Shintō, it also implies that Shintō was now under the control of the centralized bureaucracy of the government.

As for Buddhism, its initial success was no doubt due largely to support received from the powerful Soga clan. But soon Buddhism secured the patronage of the imperial court and came to be treated as the state religion. It was the pious Prince Regent Shōtoku who proclaimed:

> You should sincerely venerate the Three Treasures, namely, the Buddha, Buddha's Law (*Dharma*), and the Buddhist Order (*Saṁgha*), which are the final refuge of [all creatures] and have indeed been venerated by everyone at every age. There are only a few in this world who are by nature bad, and even they can be corrected if they be properly taught about the Three Treasures.[16]

The influence of Buddhism, however, was confined more or less to the court and aristocratic circles during the seventh century A.D. Even then Buddhism contributed to the one-dimensional world of meaning of the Japanese the notion of past, present and future and the moral law of cause and effect which runs through them. Buddhism also introduced the concept of meritorious deeds, such as copying the scripture, presenting Buddhist images and building temples, storing one's merit for the healing of the sick or for the repose of the deceased ancestors.

With the establishment of the capital city of Nara early in the eighth century, Buddhism gained power, prestige and influence. The imperial court began to build state-supported Buddhist temples in the provinces as well as the national cathedral in the capital city. One emperor even went so far as to call himself publicly "the slave of the Three Treasures". Encouraged by royal favour, six orthodox schools of Buddhism were officially recognized. On the other hand, the activities of Buddhist clerics were strictly controlled by the "Law Governing Monks and Nuns (*Sōni-ryō*)",[17] which made Buddhism effectively subservient to the authority of the government.

16 *Ibid.*, p. 252.
17 See *ibid.*, pp. 258-59.

Three indigenous Buddhist movements first appeared during the eighth century. The first was the "Nature Wisdom School", which attracted many monks dissatisfied with traditional monastic disciplines in the mountains and forests. Following the indigenous Japanese affirmation that the "natural" is the "original", those who belonged to this school were convinced that the world of nature was the manifestation of *Dharma* and that the direct path to *Dharma* through nature was superior to the traditional monastic path. The second was the development of shamanistic, folk Buddhism, which combined Shintō, Buddhist and folk religious elements. The leaders of this movement, called *ubasoku* (un-ordained priests) or holy men, advocated a simple path of salvation for the masses, disregarding the teachings and practice of orthodox Buddhism. The third movement tended toward a Shintō-Buddhist amalgamation, which encouraged not only the practice of building Shintō shrines within Buddhist temples and Buddhist chapels attached to Shintō shrines, but also promoted the popular notion that the original nature of the Shintō *kami* was the Buddha.

The development of these movements show clearly how Japanese Buddhists interpreted and appropriated the historic tradition of Buddhism in terms of their own particular religious experiences, and in this process then developed new forms of Buddhist tradition more relevant and congenial to the Japanese world of meaning.

(iii) ART

One of the striking aspects of cultural development in Japan during the sixth, seventh and eighth centuries was the fact that the aesthetic impulse of the Japanese responded so enthusiastically to the beauty, elegance and refinement of Buddhist art and architecture. These, in turn, found a direct passage to the inner fabric of the Japanese world of meaning. In the words of Langdon Warner: "Buddhist temples were erected, Buddhist bronzes cast, priests' robes woven, and holy pictures painted all in foreign style, but it was all done by artists who invoked native Shintō spirits of timber, fire, metal, loom and pigment".[18]

The process of homologization of Shintō and Buddhist traditions of aesthetics was so intricate that those of us who are un-initiated in iconography can say very little on the subject. We might, however, more profitably discuss the impact which the interpenetration between Shintō and Buddhist aesthetics had on the world of meaning of the Japanese. I have already mentioned that early Shintō did not depend on visual and plastic religious art forms as representations of the Sacred. Shintō also was inclined to accept the world, which was beautiful and transitory, as both real and illusory. In short, the early Japanese did not develop a symbolic way of thinking, because they made no distinction

18 Warner, *op. cit.,* p. 19.

between the visible and the real, or between the form and the structure of meaning which it represents.

When Buddhism was introduced in the mid-sixth century, the Japanese did not view the image of the Buddha as a symbol or an ideational representation of a different order of meaning, because to them the "form" itself was real. Soon, however, the Japanese began to distinguish between form and meaning, or between the statue and the Buddhahood it symbolizes. Even then the Japanese never lost the sense of a magical aura in their dealing with images of the Buddhas, Bodhisattvas and saints.

In dealing with the development of art in Japan between the sixth and eighth centuries, I find Sierksma's distinction between ritual art and religious art very helpful. According to him, ritual art implies that its sole or primary meaning is that of religious act, e.g., ritual dance, gesture, music, or that of religious expression, e.g. images, visual symbols, painting and architecture. On the other hand, in religious art the meaning of art as ritual act or expression remains, but it also provokes and allows the artist scope for his own artistic creativity.[19] Sierksma's categories help us to appreciate the changing ethos of Japanese art from that of ritual art to one of religious art during a relatively short span of the two centuries mentioned above.

It is interesting to note that those figures of Buddhas and Bodhisattvas which survive from the sixth and early seventh century, signify the ethos of ritual art, expressing as they do the universality and eternity of *Dharma*. Soon, as Katō Shūichi points out, the change took place from the universal, supramundane towards a model in nature: "this shift away from the abstract and towards the figurative became decisive around the end of the seventh or beginning of the eighth century . . ."[20] With this shift, "ritual art" changed into "religious art" during the eighth century (Nara period). The change in the ethos of Japanese art, from the "ritual art" of the sixth and seventh centuries to the "religious art" of the eighth century, reflects the process of *rapprochement* between Shintō and Buddhist aesthetic traditions. In the subsequent periods of Japanese history the combination of these two traditions continued to develop creative forms of art and iconography.

In closing, we might reiterate once again that it was Chinese civilization and Buddhism which contributed to Japan the meaning of "symbolism" and "symbolization" in religion. This in turn greatly expanded the scope and enriched the quality of the Japanese "world of meaning" without, however, obliterating its enduring characteristics, particularly its sensitivity to the seamlessness of all aspects of life and the world, ranging from "reality" to "illusion".

19 F. Sierksma, *The Gods As We Shape Them* (Routledge & Kegan Paul, London, 1960), p. 49.
20 Katō Shūichi, *Form, Style, Tradition* (University of California Press, Berkeley, 1971), p. 90.

LIU TS'UN-YAN

THE ESSENCE OF TAOISM

Its Philosophical, Historical and Religious Aspects

In the study of Taoism, we should make some distinction between the substance of what is known as philosophical Taoism, and what is religious Taoism, although in later generations, because of the activities of the Taoist priests, these two have been intermingled, and merged, to some extent, for their religious interest.[1] To speak of someone who is philosophically a Taoist would mean his attitude towards life is Taoistic: he may be a public servant but loves and enjoys the life of a hermit at a scenic spot on holidays; he prefers retreat to argument, or to competition, and so forth, while his religious affiliation may be unknown. He may be atheistic, he may be a Buddhist, he may be a Christian, and of course he may be a real religious Taoist and a member of a certain non-ecclesiastic Taoist assembly, but we simply do not know. It is for a similar reason, and against a similar background, that a scroll of Chinese landscape painting may be described as full of Taoist spirit, although we are certain that the painter himself is agnostic.

Taoism as a religion did not develop earlier than the first part of the second century A.D. It flourished during the periods of T'ang (618-907), Northern Sung (960-1126) and Ming (1368-1644). It was rooted in China, but its influence was felt in Japan, Korea, Vietnam and some parts of Southeast Asia. In a word, all the countries whose peoples were using the Chinese written language as a part of their cultural inheritance inherited also Taoism, though Taoism may not have been the only belief for them. In early Japanese myths there are the heavenly *kami* and the earthly *kami*, the distinction being very similar to that between a celestial immortal and an earthly immortal in Taoist records of Han times. Needless to say, the last part of the word, *Shinto*, is in fact the Chinese word, *Tao*, the key-word for Taoism, meaning "the Way". In the 1952 edition of St John's Gospel, we have: "In the beginning was the Word, and the Word was with God, and the Word was God". In the Chinese version, if the first line of this were translated back, it would read, "In the beginning was the Tao".

To the Chinese etymologists as well as to the Chinese mind, the *Tao* is the way, and is an indication of the purpose of life. Confucius (551-479 B.C.), a great thinker and educator, spoke also about the purpose of life, therefore he also spoke of the *Tao*. In the Chinese language, the word, *tao*, or "the way", is not necessarily a sacred word, as the word, Word (capital letter), in the Holy Bible. Each and every pre-Ch'in philosopher who lived during the Warring States period (403-221 B.C.) spoke of his *tao*, a common word for the

Confucianist, the Legalist, the Sophist in China, in short, the way of the principle for everyone. However, it was the early Taoist thinkers, such as Lao-tzu and Chuang-tzu, who distinguished themselves and were honoured by people of later generations as the Taoist thinkers par excellence, or *Tao-chia*, the thinkers of the Taoist School.

From the very beginning the man who was known as Lao-tzu to people of later generations, and as Lao Tan (the Long-eared Master) to his immediate followers, was a mystery, if not a myth, in the history of Chinese philosophy. He was a scholar from the State of Ch'u, whose territory had extended far beyond the limit as one of the feudal states during the early sixth century B.C. to present-day Honan, where Lao-tzu was born. As a Keeper of the Royal Archives in the Imperial Household of Chou, also in Honan, now functioning under pressure and in reduced circumstances, Lao-tzu was said to have met Confucius at the latter's request in 525 B.C. at the capital of Chou, Loyang. After the interview, Confucius's impression of the senior scholar, told to his disciples according to Ssu-ma Ch'ien's *Records of the Grand Historiographer*, was: "I know that birds can fly, fishes can swim, and animals can run. But the runner may be snared, the swimmer hooked, and the flyer shot by a corded arrow. But here is the dragon — how does it mount on the wind and the clouds, and rise to heaven? I do not know. Today I have seen Lao-tzu, and I venture to compare him to the dragon". (Ch.63)[2] Mind you, this is the Chinese dragon, which is beneficent, and wingless, and is not the same as the fire-breathing fabulous monster found in Egyptian religion, Greek mythology, or in the tales of the near eastern world.

The text of the *Tao-te ching*, also known as the *Lao-tzu*, as it is traditionally ascribed to him, is probably an anthology of wise sayings compiled sometime in the fourth century B.C. Living in a time of constant contention and chaos, the sad experiences of killing and ravages of war made Lao-tzu's teaching of meekness and retreat as a philosophy of life like water in the desert for those who had suffered, forgetting almost completely that under his morals there were the cynical remarks and the craftiness of an old rogue.[3] Language of mystical illumination is still abundant as far as his crisp and rhymed words based upon ontological and metaphysical speculations are concerned. Thus he maintains:

What cannot be seen is called evanescent;
What cannot be heard is called rarefied;
What cannot be touched is called minute.
These three cannot be fathomed
And so they are confused and looked upon as one.
Its upper part is not dazzling;
Its lower part is not obscure.
Dimly visible, it cannot be named
And returns to that which is without substance.
This is called the shape that has no shape,
The image that is without substance.
This is called indistinct and shadowy.
Go up to it and you will not see its head;
Follow behind it and you will not see its rear.
Hold fast to the way of antiquity
In order to keep in control the realm of today.
The ability to know the beginning of antiquity
Is called the thread running through the way. (Ch.xiv)[4]

In less esoteric language than the above-quoted, Lao-tzu says that he had three treasures. They are Compassion, Frugality, and Not daring to take the lead in the empire. "Being compassionate", he says, "one could afford to be courageous; being frugal one could afford to be liberal; not daring to take the lead in the empire one could afford to be the head of the officials". (Ch.lxvii)[5] In another place he likens the Way to water, and says:

"Highest good is like water. Because water excels in benefiting the myriad things without contending with them and settles where none would like to be, it comes close to the Way". (Ch.viii)[6]

Unless the meagre historical accounts available to us are completely legendary, the Taoist thinker, Chuang-tzu, flourished at least two hundred and fifty years after Lao-tzu, although in his books, particularly the so-called *Outer Chapters* and the *Miscellaneous Chapters*, the name of Lao-tzu and the teachings of the *Tao* and *Te* (the Way and Virtue), are often mentioned. In the Third Chapter of the *Chuang-tzu*, the death of Lao-tan is narrated to illustrate a Taoist explanation of life,[7] though the information gathered from other records indicates very clearly that, seeing the decay of the dynasty, Lao-tzu left it and went westward to Han-ku Pass where, at the earnest request of the Keeper of the Pass, he wrote a work in two books (i.e., the *Tao-te ching*), and then he departed, and it is not known where he went in the end.[8] Generally speaking, Chuang-tzu may be described as an honest expounder of Lao-tzu's philosophy. Though in his own writings he indulges in hyperbole constantly, there are many places where passages cited from *Lao-tzu* are elaborated. However, in his theory on *Ch'i-wu* or the Adjustment of Controversies, Chuang-tzu brings out more systematically his own views. In this chapter, the voices of controversialists of the time are compared by him to the noise issuing from the crevices in the enormous trees where a gale passes by. Although two opposite views may be controversial, Chuang-tzu believed that each of them contains both a right and a wrong. The trouble is that neither is patient enough to be paired with the right half. Whoever understands this, Chuang-tzu says, understands the pivot of the Way.[9]

In both the works, *Lao-tzu* and *Chuang-tzu*, the words, *ti* (to mean Heavenly Lord) and *kuei-shen* (ghosts and deities), appear quite naturally in the passages, and ancestor-worshipping and sacrifice-offerings are also mentioned. But such terms, as well as the description of their functioning, are common stock found even in the Confucian texts, as rites and rituals were most important for the maintenance of law and order in a feudal society. However, there are still a number of things which were unique to the Taoist School, and it was from the fragmentary depiction of such practices that the religious Taoist priests of later times saw a chance to use them to their advantage. May I here cite a few instances:

Lao-tzu often compared the completeness or wholeness of the Way to the body of an infant child. Therefore he says: "One who possesses virtue in abundance is comparable to a new born babe: . . . Its bones are weak and its sinews supple yet its hold is firm. It does not know of the union of male and female yet its male member will stir: this is because its virility is at its height". (Ch.lv)[10] At this point Lao-tzu also questions us: "When carrying on your head your perplexed bodily soul can you embrace in your arm the One and not let go? In concentrating your breath can you become as supple as a babe?" (Ch.x)[11] This is probably the first appearance of breath-control we may ever find in a Chinese classical text. To supplement this, anyway to echo the same tone, is the chapter entitled The Great Master of the *Chuang-tzu* (ch.6):

> The True men of old did not dream when they slept, had no anxiety when they awoke, and did not care that their food should be pleasant. Their breathing came deep and silently. The breathing of the true man comes [even] from his heels, while men generally breathe [only] from their throats.[12]

Elaborating this further, in Ingrained Ideas, Chapter XV of the *Chuang-tzu*, we read:

> Blowing and breathing with open mouth; inhaling and exhaling the breath; expelling the old breath and taking in new; making the [climbing] movements like a bear, and stretching and twisting [the neck] like a bird; — all this simply shows the desire for longevity. This is what the scholars who manipulate their breath, and the men who nourish the body and wish to live as long as Peng Tsu, are fond of.[13]

Peng Tsu is the fictitious long-lived old man whose recorded age is over eight hundred years, very similar to that of Seth, or Enoch, or Methuselah, if not Adam himself, in Genesis.

Breath-control is a kind of physical exercise, and the inhaling and exhaling of the breath (or *ch'i*) must pass through a vein, or veins. The important vein in this connection is the *tu* vein parallel to the spine on our backs. One line describing this is included in the third chapter of the *Chuang-tzu*, but this point is often missed in the earlier translations, when the study of acupuncture was not yet quite known to the West. For in every acupuncture diagram this vein is clearly marked.

In the book, *Lao-tzu*, there are also some mystical descriptions which may be read, or misread, as something mysteriously related to the action of sex. Like the many other passages, these are written in rhyme:

... Is not the space between heaven and earth like a bellows?
It is empty without being exhausted:
The more it works the more comes out.
Much speech leads inevitably to silence.
Better to hold fast to the void. (Ch.v)[14]
The spirit of the valley never dies.
This is called the mysterious female.
The gateway of the mysterious female
Is called the root of heaven and earth.
Dimly visible, it seems as if it were there,
Yet use will never drain it. (Ch.vi)[15]

These are the lines the Taoist priests were to make use of to elevate their sexual rites, the games of Dragons and Tigers.

Charms and talismans are very important for the Taoist priests. None of them are found in the pre-Ch'in (i.e., before 221 B.C.) Taoist works. However, in the *Lao-tzu* again we read:

I have heard it said that one who excels in safe-guarding his own life does not meet with rhinoceros or tigers when travelling on land nor is he touched by weapons when charging into an army. (Ch.1)[16]

Probably picking up some inspiration from this passage, the writer of the chapter, Autumn Floods, in the *Chuang-tzu* remarks:

This does not mean that he is indifferent to these things; it means that he discriminates between where he may safely rest and where he will be in peril; that he is tranquil equally in calamity and happiness; that he is careful what he avoids and what he approaches; — so that nothing can injure him. (Ch.17)[17]

Well this is fair enough and common sense. However, because of the line found in the *Lao-tzu*, there is a particular charm named "Lao-tzu's Talisman for Ascent to Mountains" and another charm "To Avoid Encountering a Tiger or a Wolf in the Hills" included in the *Pao-p'u tzu* (Ch.17),[18] a genuine Taoist work of the fourth century written by Ko Hung (283-343?), a great Taoist priest and alchemist.

Before the formal establishment of religious Taoism sometime not later than the late second century A.D., there were para-Taoistic activities which had been rampant since the time of the Warring States. Indigenous worship was being monopolised by local priests known collectively as *fang-shih*, whose heterogeneous beliefs involved even shamanism and witchcraft. Inhabitants along the coastline of Po-hai and the Yellow Sea often saw mirages, and the many kinds of atmospheric optical illusions which compelled their active imaginations to believe that, on the distant sea, there were three Isles of Blest, where immortals lived and elixir was produced. On more than one occasion the *fang-shih* of nearby regions were sent to investigate and bring back some efficacious drugs on order of Emperor Shih-huang, the first unifier of China. The invention of the Five [Cosmic] Elements by the scholars of the Yin and Yang School and the absorption of some apocryphal interpretations of the *Book of Changes* influenced by them into orthodox Confucianism also increased the chance of Taoist penetration, since for a considerable period of time the formation of the guidelines for the government of the Former Han was very firmly in the hands of philosophical Taoist sympathisers. I have already cited some passages from the *Chuang-tzu*. Allow me to cite once more, to illustrate the change of time, without actually changing the *dramatis personae*. In *Chuang-tzu*, there is a story about the legendary emperor, Huang-ti, who was said to have been given an audience by a Taoist sage, Kuang-ch'eng tzu, another legendary figure (Ch.11), and the ascension of Huang-ti to heaven is also recorded (Ch.6). These are more imaginary than factual. However, during the second century A.D., thanks to the Taoist priests or their predecessors, the worship of Huang-Lao Chün had become so popular that an imperial edict from Huan-ti (r. 147-167 A.D.), himself a pious devotee of the Huang-Lao cult, ordered that, with two exceptions, all the temples of other cults were considered heterodox and to be destroyed, while the Huang-Lao itself had safely found a special niche in the temple of the palace.[19] It may still be ambiguous for us to determine who this Huang-Lao Chün (the Lord Huang-Lao) was, as it could mean a single Lord, or it could also mean Huang-ti and Lao-tzu, two separate deities. But one single fact is established beyond doubt: it was religious Taoism.

As a religion, Taoism has always been popular with the general populace, either in the cities or the countryside. To suit the taste and the educational level of the people in an agrarian society, in which probably more than seventy percent of the population was unable to read or write, the precepts of the Way were made to appeal only to the ears. For many years the *Five-thousand Characters of the Lao-tzu* (Lao-tzu wu-ch'ien-wen) was used for promulgating purposes, because it was short, divided into approximately eight-one chapters, and was rhymed. It was easy to remember, even for illiterates, after it was chanted many times, but its abstruse content, though often lending some lustre to the literary status of the followers who read it, would in fact defy the long-term attempt to popularize the cult. To remedy this, sometime before 166 A.D. an even more popular perhaps slightly vulgar, Taoist scripture named *T'ai-p'ing ching* (The Classic of Great Peace) was being circulated, and used partly in the service of a cult called the T'ai-p'ing Tao, led by its priests, Kan Chi (also written Yü Chi), Kung Ch'ung, and others. Chang Chüeh, one of the leaders of the Yellow Turban rebellion, which broke out in 184 and spread over several provinces, was also a member of this cult. The dynastic history, *Hou-Han shu*, records that: "Chang Chüeh worshipped the Huang-Lao Tao, and claimed himself the Great Master of Worthy, and took disciples. He made those who had sinned kneel down and confess their faults. He used charms and holy water to treat illness, and when the sick ones got better they believed him. On account of the success of his preaching he sent eight disciples to travel in the four directions of the empire, to preach his 'fine' doctrines. In over ten years they gained influence among several hundred thousand people by hood-winking, and were able to join them together for action in the eight provinces". (Ch.101)[20]

Only part of the *T'ai-p'ing ching*, originally claimed to have been compiled in 170 chapters, is preserved. Even these surviving chapters are sometimes incomplete. The language and grammar is plain, but it contains a lot of vulgar expressions and jargon known perhaps only to contemporaries and the initiated. But for this reason, the historical authenticity of the text has never been questioned. A general survey of the remnant shows that it advocates the union of the three realms, Heaven, Earth and Man, and the harmony brought about by such a union would induce the Atmosphere of the Great Peace to come, which will bring prosperity to the country. As an idealistic, equalitarian text for preaching, this scripture maintains filial piety, loyalty and obedience are three important virtues one should observe. The organized society revealed in the text gives its reader the impression that it speaks about both a government and a Taoist church, which could be meant to be one, and in one place the plan for an army is also touched upon. As a sort of functionary arrangement for the organization, the term Six Divisions has been introduced, which could be the origin of the Eight Divisions actually organized by Chang Chüeh during the rebellion. Many passages in the text are dialogues between a Celestial Master (*t'ien-shih*) and his six disciples. The name for the site of a church is called *ching* (or a place of quietude), a name which was followed by the T'ien-shih Tao (Celestial Master Cult), which was active in Szechwan.[21]

In the text, severe criticism of the Han government is found in Ch.86. While the people were suffering from oppression and distress, it says their voice could never reach the ruler. People are also advised not to indulge in "digging the earth" (Ch.45),[22] implying that too many new buildings were erected by the rich and privileged class at the time. When one dies, the text believes that "his spirit is also gone after he breathes his last breath" (Ch.42),[23] but there are other places where the existence of a soul is admitted and inquisitions for the wicked in the nether world are also described. Many Taoist devices in the making, such as wearing charms and swallowing talismans, concentration of the mind for introspection, and conservation of sperm, are mentioned, and during the cultivation, the possibility of trials, conducted by spirits and deities, is alluded to. The attitude towards women, as described in this text, is slightly biased. It maintains that a man should keep two women as wives, because too many girls were killed by their families when they were born. The Celestial Master was someone who really understands love. He advises us: "Of all the good-living and pleasant creatures in the world there is nothing better than a fine young lady whom one may take as his match and have her bear his male-seed" (Ch.46)[24]

The T'ien-shih Tao or the Celestial Master Cult was active in Szechwan at about the same time that the Yellow Turban revolt was rampant. The cult was said to have been started earlier by a man named Chang Ling (d. between 157 and 178), who was a native of Northern Kiangsu, but settled down later in Szechwan and made himself known there as the Celestial Master of the cult, which was also called the Cult of Five Pecks of Rice, being named after the measures of rice the church took from each of its members or patients after recovery as a contribution. The cult was further developed under Chang Lu (fl. 190-220), Ling's grandson, who lorded it over some parts of Szechwan and Shensi for nearly thirty years, until his surrender to Ts'ao Ts'ao in 215. Chang Lu's Taoist theocratic state was established in Han-chung. Personally he studied Taoism under Chang Hsui, another contender at the time, whom he killed and whose followers he took over.[25] The patriarchate of the church was hereditary. As the genealogy of the family was interrupted and a large part of it can never be clearly proved authentic, the present scion of the family, who still holds an ecclesiastical title in Taiwan, is able to claim an accurate genealogical record back to the early eleventh century only. Chang Ling, the alleged founder of this cult, is, however, remembered by a commentary on the *Lao-tzu* he wrote, a fragmentary copy of which is preserved in the Tunhuang collection at the British Museum (S 6825).[26] Chang Lu, Ling's grandson, is remembered not only by the formal organization of a Taoist church which he helped to institutionalize, but also by a range of policies of social welfare which he administered, including free rice and meat and the food provided by the state in public hostels for travellers.[27]

The damage caused to the country by the various revolts and disturbances during the later second century was serious, and among the rebels, though most of them might have been compelled to take the law into their own hands, there were many charlatans and opportunists, like Chang chüeh and others, who were severely condemned by Ko Hung, author of the *Pao-p'u tzu*, I mentioned before. In Chapter Nine of his work, Ko Hung writes:

In the past, persons like Chang Chüeh, Liu Ken, Wang Hsin and Li Shen sometimes claimed to be a thousand years old, and had made use of some minor tricks to deceive the ignorant and unite the multitude. Neither did they advance the practice of longevity, nor did they help to cure illness and disperse evil calamities. Instead they formed wicked leagues and started rebellions, which in the end brought their own deaths. In the course of disturbances, they killed many righteous men, and deceived the masses for the purpose of accumulating wealth. Their treasures were mountain-high, and they were richer than kings and dukes. They led an extravagant and lascivious life . . .[28]

Ko Hung's life was that of a pure religious Taoist, as indicated by his own style of Pao-p'u (embracing simplicity). His grand-uncle, Ko Hsüan, was a very well-known Taoist at the time of the Three Kingdoms, but Hung benefited more from his own master, Cheng Yin, whose appearance and mode of life described by Ko Hung in his book may be of some interest to us uninitiated. When Ko Hung was a novice, Master Cheng Yin was already over eighty. Ko Hung says:

His grey hair turned black in a few years' time, and his complexion was fine and pleasant. He was still able to draw a crossbow and shoot a hundred paces. He walked several hundred *li* every day, and could drink two large containers (*tou*) of wine without becoming intoxicated. Whenever he climbed mountains, his physical movement was light and agile. He mounted precipitous cliffs with such speed that many younger persons were unable to catch up with him. He ate and drank like everyone; I never saw him avoid cereals. Huang Chang was another disciple who was senior to me. He advised me that once when Master Cheng returned to Ditch-digging Shore from Yü-chang of Kiangsi, the boat encountered a strong wind. It was also rumoured that there were bandits ahead. So his fellow-travellers urged Master Cheng to stay till another group of travellers arrived, but then everyone was worried because of a shortage of grain. Master Cheng gave his portion of grain to others, and stopped eating for fifty days without feeling hungry. People simply didn't see him doing anything, and were simply amazed that he was able to do so. He could write in very tiny characters by lamplight, much finer than a younger person. He understood music and could play the lute. When at leisure and surrounded by several attendants and musicians, he gave replies to their questions without interrupting the tune, while watching the performances of others, pointing out their good points and errors with minute precision. (Ch.19)[29]

In order to nourish life, Ko Hung informs us that there were four schools besides alchemy. These are: nourishing life by the healthy exercises of sex, technically known as *fang-chung*, or chamber-art; nourishing it by breath-control, known as *t'u-na* (inhaling and exhaling); nourishing by physical exercises, known as *tao-yin*, or calisthenics (bending and stretching of the limbs); and nourishing by medicines, known as *ts'ao-mu*, or herbs and drugs. I shall discuss each of them except physical exercise, as this is now common knowledge.

The study of the chamber-art began much earlier than the time of Ko Hung. A large part of its study is related to personal hygiene, taboos and even superstitions, and all of them may be explained satisfactorily in terms of either natural sciences or social sciences. Sexual techniques are also included, though not necessarily all very practical, but this is common with similar works produced by people of different races, and at different times. However, there was the unique theory, and presumably also the practice, of "gathering more *yin* to nurture the *yang*", recorded very frequently in Taoist works of Sung and Ming times, which has the *Pao-p'u tzu* as one of its very early sources for serious investigation. Ko Hung records:

The methods for the practice of the chamber-art are specially studied by scholars of more than ten schools. Some are for the remedy of ailments arising from over work, some are for the healing of various illnesses, some are for gathering more *yin* to nurture the *yang*, and some are for protracting life and augmenting longevity. The essential thing for all these lies in the reversing of one's sperm flow and directing it upwards to replenish the brain. However, details of this are transmitted by the True Men mouth to mouth, and they have never been consigned to paper. Though one may have the chance of tasting famous medicines for prolonging one's years, one is still unable to accomplish the aim, because of lack of the essential knowledge. Since not everyone is able to give up intercourse completely, by avoiding normal coitus intentionally, one is sure to suffer from melancholia, depression and other morbid conditions, resulting in further diseases, which may cut short one's life. On the other hand, over-indulgence will also affect one's life-span. . . . It is a pity that many small-minded Taoist priests are still over enthusiastic about such an art, taking it as a sure way to immortality, instead of studying the Golden Pill. (ch.8)[30]

The item on breath-control may be more interesting to both the physiologist and the layman. The purpose of practising this is, in the main, still for the attainment of longevity. In Chapter 68, Biographies of the Oracles Prosphesying on Tortoise-shells, of *Records of the Grand Historiographer*, the exceedingly long life normally enjoyed by a tortoise is vividly illustrated by the followed instance:

In the South there was an old man who had used a tortoise to support a foot of his bed. After twenty more years the old man died, and his bed was removed. The tortoise was found still alive. Tortoises are able to make their breath circulate.

This chapter was actually written by a Ch'u Shao-sun, also a Former Han scholar who lived about fifty years later than Ssu-ma Ch'ien, as this part of Ssu-ma Ch'ien's original work had been lost. Nevertheless, this traditional belief in the Chinese context is substantiated by another story found in the *Pao-p'u tzu*:

The late Mr Ch'en Chung-kung (Ch'en Shih, *Hou-Han shu*, 92) of Ying-ch'uan, the Magistrate of T'ai-ch'iu, was an honest scholar. In his *Notes on Strange Happenings I Have Heard*, he writes that someone from the same district as he, named Chang Kuang-ting, once fled the district with family at the time of confusion. He had a daughter aged four who could not walk fast or wade the streams, and it was difficult for him to carry her. He planned to abandon her, and then she would have to die of hunger. But he didn't wish her body to lie uncovered on the road. It happened that, at the entrance to the village, there was an old grave, the top of whose mound had already been opened up. So he sat his daughter in a huge basket and lowered her down into the tomb by a rope, where he left her some dried rice and drink sufficient for her to last a few months, and left. After three years, when the crisis was over, he returned home, and wished to gather the bones of his daughter and bury her properly. When he and his wife went down there, surprisingly they found that their daughter was sitting in the tomb. She still recognized her parents and was very pleased. At first her parents were rather scared, believing that they might have seen her ghost. Only when they reached her did they realize that she was a living being. When asked where she got supplies when her provisions were gone, she said that at first she was terribly hungry and didn't know what to do. Then she saw a creature she could not name in the corner, and it was stretching its neck and swallowing its breath. The sight of it was very strange to her, and since she had nothing to do, she tried to imitate its movement, and gradually she became less and less hungry . . . Amazed by her story, the father sought the creature in question and found that it was a huge tortoise. (Ch.3)[31]

Breath-control is also known as *t'ai-hsi* — breathing like a foetus in its mother's womb. Imitating the swallowing of breath of a tortoise or not, Ko Hung informs us that:

When one has successfully practised the circulating of breath without inhaling and exhaling through one's nose and mouth, like a foetus in its mother's womb, one has already achieved the Way. At the first stage of practising such an exercise, one has to hold the breath in the nose and count from one to a hundred and twenty, then let it out through the mouth. In both exhaling and inhaling, it would be better if the breaths are kept so light that one cannot even hear the sound of their movement oneself, and the exhalations are fewer than the inhalations. A test for this is to put a wild goose feather on the nose and mouth when the breath is coming out and, if the feather remains stationary, this is evidence of success. Gradually the counting should be increased to a thousand before the breath is released. When this is achieved, an aged person will become younger day by day. Exercises should be carried out during the hours that the breath is active (or alive, *sheng*), not during the hours it is dead (*ssu*). A day has twelve *shih* (or double-hours). During the six *shih* from midnight to midday the breath is known to be active, but during the six *shih* from midday to midnight, it is dead, and it is useless for one to do breath circulation exercises at this time. (Ch.8)[32]

In the original text of the *Pao-p'u tzu*, the word for breath is not the ordinary character *ch'i*, but a specially coined one, consisting of a radical of four dots indicating fire with another invented character, *chi*, meaning choked in eating, over it. This Taoist-invented new character is also pronounced *ch'i*, meaning breath, but this breath, according to their interpretation, is the Primordial *Ch'i*, which comes from the Great Nature or macrocosm, while the ordinary breath, or *ch'i*, inhaled and exhaled, since one is born through the mechanism of a human body, is from an epitome of the universe, or microcosm. Metaphysically speaking, the Primordial *Ch'i* is the *hsien-t'ien chih-ch'i* (the *ch'i* existing even before the creation), alleged to have been borne out by the text in the *Lao-tzu*, "There is a thing confusedly formed, born before heaven and earth". (Ch.xxv) Only the breath of a foetus in a womb could resemble this, because it is the *ch'i* of the unborn though in a microcosm. However, when a baby is born, the remnant Primordial *Ch'i* in its body is intermingled with the ordinary breath which it breathes, and it starts to diminish, though it has not completely disappeared, even in an adult. The Taoist attempt here is to recollect as much as possible one's Primordial *Ch'i* through forced exercises to revive partially the primordial environment in miniature, so that one's life-span may be protracted, and one's youthfulness, hopefully regenerated.

The distinction between the time for active breath and that for the dead breath is of great interest. About a hundred years before Ko Hung there was a Taoist alchemist, Wei Po-yan (fl. 147-167), who had written a cryptic work entitled *Tallying The Ideas of Taoist Cultivation with the Book of Changes* (Chou-yi ts'an-t'ung-ch'i), which was, even in Ko Hung's time, regarded as an authority on Chinese alchemy, but has been utilized since the tenth century as a treasure-book for the interpretation of the theory of chamber-art, applying methods of breath-control, and similar devices. Han scholars, including Wei, had picked up twelve hexagrams from the 64 hexagrams in the *Book of Changes* and called them the Twelve Sovereign Hexagrams. The choice was made so ingeniously that in its arrangement the first six hexagrams are in an increasing order from the hexagram, *fu*, which has only one line of *yang* at its bottom, to the hexagram, *ch'ien*, which has *yang* for all its six lines. Now when the force of *yang* has reached its zenith, it is followed by another series of six in a decreasing order from the hexagram, *kou*, which has only one *yin* line at its bottom, to the growth of pure *yin* in the hexagram, *k'un*, which is pure *yin*, having all six lines *yin* in its composition. According to this tradition, agreed upon in both the Taoist and the Confucian apocryphal texts, the double-hours between 11 p.m. and 1 a.m. (or *tzu-shih*), represented by the hexagram, *fu*, is the time that the active breath of *yang* begins to grow. 11 p.m. is also the time the Taoist cultivators, having learned by experience, claim that, if I may quote *Lao-tzu*, the "male member will stir".[33]

Speaking of nourishing by medicine, we should never forget the profound knowledge of medical herbs the Taoist priests possessed, for collecting herbs in the hills and mountains was a part of their profession. Several prototypes of the Chinese *Materia Medica* began to be compiled roughly at this time, and Ko Hung himself was the author of a medical work, which is still preserved, entitled *Prescriptions Close at Hand* (Chou-hou pei-chi-fang).[34] Though nothing is more thrilling than the findings in alchemy to which Ko Hung devoted more than one chapter in his Taoist work, the purpose for the advancement of Chinese alchemy at the time was somehow different from its Western counterparts advocated by the metallurgical workers and promoters of the Hellenistic culture of Alexandria in that, besides the common ground of transmutation, in which the Chinese didn't quite succeed to the extent the Taoists normally boasted, they did succeed in adding medicine to mercury and other metals and procured something like Paracelsus did for iatrochemistry in the sixteenth century for curing illnesses. If those metallic medicines found in the Chinese *Materia Medica*, or *Pen Ts'ao*, were still useful for modern research, the following passage quoted from the *Pao-p'u tzu*, containing a number of herbs and plants proved to be efficacious in his time, are equally familiar to the Chinese ears today:

> The set prescriptions of *Li-chung* and *Ssu-shun* dococtions are suitable to cure cholera; the coltsfoot (*Petasites japonicus*) and aster are used to counter spasms of coughing; eulalia and male fern are vermifuges; ligusticum and peony are to ease acute stomach pain; *Gendarussa vulgaris* and angelica are carminatives; calamus and dried ginger stop arthritis and rheumatism; dodder and Phelipea are tonics; ipecac and seeds of *Sisymbrium* dispel mucus; root of bryony (*Trichosanthes kirilowii*) and *Coptis japonica* cure diabetes; *Aenophora* and licorice are antiseptics; aloes and *yi-je* help to cure wounds; and ephedra (*Ephedra vulgaris*) and Justicia are to reduce fever. (Ch.5)[35]

Because of the agrarian nature of religious Taoism in its initial stage, seditious elements slipped in, and in the long and complex political history of China, there has been a train of popular uprisings prompted by the expectations of messianic saviours, directly or indirectly involving the Taoist cult. Even so, the originally primitive teaching of the Celestial Master Cult or its ramifications had been spreading out very successfully in Shantung, Kiangsu and Chekiang, and when it came to the Eastern Chin (317-418), during a time of political instability and social disintegration, many high officials and intellectuals had joined in such worshipping groups as pious members of the Way. Ko Hung was originally a Confucian scholar and an army officer, and he and his grand-nephew, Ko Ch'ao-fu, helped to circulate the Taoist scripture, *Ling-pao ching*, which was probably invented by Ko Hung's grand-uncle.[36] Another scripture, the *San-huang wen*, compiled by the Taoist, Po Ho, of the Three Kingdoms period, was being promulgated by Pao Ching, Ko Hung's father-in-law, who was a governor in Kwangtung. But they were not members of the T'ien-shih cult.

Another group of scholars who assisted in the promotion of Taoist scriptures were the Hsü brothers, and Yang Hsi (330-386). The Hsü brothers were Hsü Mai (300-348, *Chin-shu*, 80) and Hsü Mi (305-373), and at a later stage, their work was continued by Mi's youngest son, Hsü Hui (340-370), and grandson, Huang-min (362-429). The centre of their activities was Mt Mao, in the district of Chü-jung, where Ko Hung was born. Before Yang Hsi's time there had been a woman named Wei Hua-ts'un (251-334), who was a sorceress or female medium, claiming to have been possessed by dieties who descended from heaven to offer her the scripture, *Shang-ch'ing ta-tung chen-ching*, and other texts. These scriptures were passed on, in 365, to Yang Hsi probably through planchette, the parapsychological practice of providing a sand-board and a wooden Chinese brush held by two people, who could write out the message on the board when a spirit or spirits appeared. Yang Hsi, being a well-known calligrapher, was said to have jotted down the words in 'clerical script' (*li-shu*), which were copied and transcribed by the Hsüs. It is also believed that this group of scholars, known members of the Shang-ch'ing Sect, named after the scripture they preached, also helped the development of drawing charms, as well as contributing considerably to the aesthetic aspects of Chinese calligraphy.[37]

Another Taoist scholar of interest is Lu Hsiu-ching (406-477). He was a descendant of the hereditary gentry south of the Yangtze during the Three Kingdoms period, but preferred to lead the life of a Taoist recluse, and visited many sacred mountains in the south before he was summoned to Nanking, by the Liu-Sung Emperor Wen, to expound the doctrines at the court, in 450. He was the famous collector and editor of a large number of Taoist scriptures, compiled by Taoist priests and sympathisers, which were available at that time. In 471, he presented to the court a Catalogue of Taoist Texts he compiled, alleged to have consisted of 1,228 hand-written scrolls. There seems to be some exaggeration, but this was the first catalogue of its kind ever made. In the Catalogue, Taoist titles are classified into three categories, the *Tung-chen* (literally, a thorough understanding of truth), the *Tung-hsüan* (a thorough understanding of profundity) and the *Tung-shen* (a thorough understanding of spirituality). Although there were additional divisions made for catalogues compiled in later generations, these basic classifications were still retained in the great *Taoist Tripitaka* (Tao-tsang) of over five thousand three hundred *chüan*, which was completed in 1445 and published in a concertina format.[38]

Not all the works in Lu's list are still extant, but there have been suspicions, even some confirmations, that the Taoist priests plagiarised material from Buddhist sources to enrich the contents of the Taoist works and to compete with their ideological antagonists. For instance, it is known that the *T'ai-shang ling-pao yüan-yang miao-ching* (Tao-tsang, 168) is a plagiarised version of the 13th chapter of the *Nirvāna sūtra*, and the 8th chapter of the *Tung-hsüan ling-pao t'ai-shang chen-jen wen-chi ching* (Tao-tsang, 758) is taken from the 7th chapter of the *Lotus Sūtra*, and so on. Even a certain portion of the famous *Chen-kao* (Declarations of the Perfected, Tao-tsang, 637-40), the work of the Taoist master, T'ao Hung-ching (456-536) was found by Chu Hsi (1130-1200) to be identical with the Buddhist *Sūtra of Forty-two Chapters*, which had probably been translated into Chinese in the middle of the second century.

With the discoveries of later scholarship, the contributions of T'ao Hung-ching to a more fully developed and firmly established religious Taoism seem to have become less attractive than it would have been for a modern investigator, but apparently it was not the case with his contemporaries and other Taoist followers before our time. T'ao's greatness lies in that he benefited greatly by the labour of his predecessors and he, being the last, was able to make a better judgment. T'ao served as a minor official at the end of the declining Ch'i dynasty, then relinquished his post and went to Mt Mao to study Taoist scriptures, talismans and verbal formulae for producing elixirs under Sun Yu-yüeh, a disciple of Lu Hsiu-ching. It was said that T'ao had procured some manuscripts of Yang Hsi and the Hsü brothers, which he incorporated into his *Declarations of the Perfected*, a draft version of which he inherited from an earlier scholar, Ku Huan (d. c.485). In this ecclesiastical work, T'ao describes many different levels and ranks of the deities in the Taoistic pantheon, institutions, geographical distributions of sacred lands, and admonitions given by the deities and their revelations to Yang. T'ao was a great connoisseur of calligraphy. His literary collection contained his correspondence with Emperor Wu, the founder of the Liang dynasty, who usurped the throne in 502, discussing the authenticity of some of the writings of the great calligrapher, Wang Hsi-chih (300-348). The emperor, though a known pious Buddhist, was said to have shown special favour to Hung-ching, and often discussed affairs with him. For this reason Hung-ching was also known as the "prime minister in the mountains".

As a Taoist, T'ao Hung-ching began to cherish the worship of the Yüan-shih T'ien-tsun (the Celestial-honoured Primordial), a Taoist invention equivalent to the Buddha in the Buddhist belief. At Mt Mao he conducted several laboratory experiments with formulae for elixir without success, but he regrettably attributed this to their failure to obtain some of the necessary ingredients produced only in North China, then ruled by non-Chinese dynasties. However, his commentary on the earlier version of the Chinese *Materia Medica*, often cited in later writings, was a real contribution to pharmacology.[39]

The tremendous efforts T'ao Hung-ching made in the South for the consolidation of religious Taoism were very similar to the endeavours of K'ou Ch'ien-chih (d.448), who had devoted himself to the renovation of Taoist worship in the North. K'ou was the Celestial Master of a reformed Taoist theocracy in Northern Wei, north of the Yellow River, who had the enthusiastic support not only of Minister Ts-ui Hao (381-450), but also of the nomadic Toba ruler, Emperor T'ai-wu (r.424-52), who in 440 assumed a reign-title with a very strong Taoist flavour, "the Perfect Ruler of Great Peace" (T'ai-p'ing chen-chün, 440-450). K'ou came from a family of Northern gentry. He had a good relationship with the Chinese high officials at the court, and at least one of his religious teachers knew also about Buddhism. The Conservatism of the Northern gentry preferred religious Taoism to Buddhism, which was foreign, but they didn't seem to be very happy with some of the degenerated developments of the Celestial Master Cult, which practised erotic attachment in a form of sexual rite called "union of the vital breaths" (nan-nü ho-ch'i), and the institution of a religious body regularly collecting rice levies from its members to the detriment of the proper revenue of the government met also with their disapproval. The above constitutes the main reasons suggested for the renovation of Taoist worship within the huge territories of Northern Wei. Measures for reform were adopted and successfully carried out for at least two decades, including a short period of persecution of the Buddhist clergy, a campaign which went against K'ou's free-will. Before K'ou Ch'ien-chih went to the court in 424, he claimed that he had been given spiritual audience on two separate occasions by Lao-tzu and another deity who called himself Li P'u-wen, and was Lao-tzu's great-great-grandson. The revelations were made to him on the sacred Mt Sung in Honan, and from them he received the New Code of Precepts and other directives, which he presented to the court for purification of the doctrine.[40] A large part of the Code is still preserved in the *Taoist Tripitaka*.[41] With fundamental texts, talismans, methods for self-cultivation, alchemy and magic, statuettes and images, legends and biographies, liturgies, pennants and other paraphernalia, and organized if divergent church institutions, all well provided and speedily developed, religious Taoism had grown far beyond its earlier size and stature.

From the reunification of China in Sui-T'ang times to the end of Ming, there are still more than one thousand years for us to cover, excluding the last three hundred years. Both time and research will prevent me from going into more detail than presenting to you some of the salient aspects of the ever-growing Taoist activities during these periods, which actually affected the Chinese community and the life of the Chinese people. There are at least four things which, I believe, account for what Taoism is now:

The first important thing we should bear in mind is the patronage of the rulers, Chinese and foreign as well, which Taoist activities enjoyed through the long course of Chinese history. We have learned in Chinese history that there were several persecutions of the Buddhist clergy, but such a thing never happened to the Taoists. Instead Taoism enjoyed the highest respect of most of the emperors of the T'ang dynasty,[42] and some of whom were suspected of having died of elixir poisoning, and many of the philosophical Taoists of ancient times were also deified at that time. Two emperors of Northern Sung, Chen-tsung and Hui-tsung, were known to have been infatuated with Taoist worship to the extent of obsessions. Chen-tsung was said to have been urged by political gain, for he wanted to use Taoistic tricks of make-believe to impress the Khitan invaders, from whom he suffered humiliation and defeats on the frontier, but Hui-tsung, a great expert in Chinese literature and art himself, actually produced two commentaries on Taoist works, one of them being the *Lao-tzu*.[43] Several of the Ming emperors not only loved alchemy and methods of cultivation, but also were lax enough in administration to appoint some of their favourite Taoist priests to positions of court ministers.[44] Following in the footsteps of the Toba rulers of the Northern Wei in the fifth century, the Taoist patriarch, Ch'iu Ch'u-chi (1148-1227), was given an audience by Chingis Khan in Samarkand in 1222. Though this could have been a mere gesture of acquiescence on the part of the conqueror to allow the newly-developed Ch'üan-chen Sect to continue its services, it has eventually helped to aggrandize Taoist activities in North China since that time. The White-cloud Monastery built in Chin-Yüan times in the Western suburbs of Peking as the centre of the Ch'üan-chen Sect is still intact.[45]

The second important thing affecting, but not hindering the Taoist movement is the tendency of amalgamation of the Three Teachings. Of the three, Confucianism has never been a religion, but Buddhism and Taoism were at loggerheads with each other for quite some time between the third and the sixth centuries. The conflict between the Buddhists and the Taoists was mainly ideological, and in those polemic battles, the Taoists, being inferior in theories to the Mahāyana approach, sometimes resorted to producing apocryphal works claiming that the westward journey of Lao-tzu was actually a visit he paid to India, where he taught Buddha the dazzling *dharma*. The Confucianists' refutation of the Two Teachings was more institutional than religious, for both the Buddhist monks and the Taoist priests failed to pay tax and never did labouring service required of the people by the government.

Conflicting and controversial as it might sound, as early as the fourth century, many of the Buddhist treatises written by both Chinese and foreign monks showed that their authors must have had the Neo-Taoist jargon used by the scholars of "Pure-talks" at their fingertips. When a scholar who lived in the late sixth century was asked how he regarded the three schools of teaching, "he answered, 'Buddhism can be compared to the sun; Taoism to the moon; and Confucianism to the Five Planets'", and the questioner could not press him further.[46] From the Northern Chou till the end of T'ang, court debates on the Three Teachings were very popular. In T'ang times the debate was customarily held on the emperor's birthday — it was more an official rite than a chance for vehement argumentation, and in the end a courteous and plausible compromise was always reached. According to some Buddhist records, sometimes the Taoist high-priests were openly humiliated, but these are only Buddhist records.

Taoism itself is particularly susceptible to the idea of amalgamation, as from its inception it had the propensity to assimilate rather than to exclude. In the religious hierarchical society, the Jade Emperor, who is the ruler in heaven, was evolved from the Great Unique One (T'ai-yi) of the second century B.C., who in turn was evolved from the even earlier Lord on High (Shang-ti). The jurisdiction of the Jade Emperor closely resembles that of the temporal bureaucracy. Superimposed on him are the Three Pure Ones, represented by the triumvirate of the Celestial-honoured Primordial, the Supreme Old-sovereign (Lao-tzu) and a third god, which are simple plagiarisms of the Buddhist *trikāya*. Other gods or lesser deities Taoism owes to Buddhism are numerous, including the King of Hell (Yama), the Dragon-kings of the Four Seas (nāgas), Mother of the Dipper (Chandi), and last but not least, the God of Wealth (Vaiśravaṇa). Nearly all the layers of heaven found in Buddhist literature have their Taoist equivalents, and a general name, *Ta-lo* Heaven, which sounds Chinese, is suspected to have been Zoroastrian or Persian.[47] The legends of the Eight Immortals have special attraction in Chinese fiction and drama. Amongst them, the most active immortal, Lü Tung-pin, may have some Nestorian connections.[48] Gods from many cults, and historical figures, in particular warriors, have also been elevated into the Taoist pantheon. Theriomorphic gods of Hindu origin have been incorporated. The Way is all pervasive. As the Indian incarnate god, Krishna, claimed, "Whatever god a man worships, it is I who answer the prayer".[49] To the Taoist priests, if Chandi, the Mother Goddess, could be sinicized, surely Krishna would also be.

The third important thing is the emergence of the Internal Pill, which was evolved from both the ancient idea of ascension and the longtime practice of the alchemic experiments in the quest of the elixir, or the External Pill.

While the External Pill is materialistic, the Internal one is both physical and metaphysical, as a part of its process can be experienced by only the initiated practitioner, or those who are in the know. In Ko Hung's writings and other Taoist texts cited before, the methods of breath-control have been described, though not in detail, and in those writings the jargon used for alchemy, though symbolic and obscure, is not mixed with the descriptions for other types of cultivation. However, from the eighth century on, the study of the breath-exercise was developed at a very high speed, and when it came to the Sung dynasty (960-1126, 1127-1276), a formal Internal Pill School, using many of the cryptic words normally used for alchemy, was fully established. This School is also known as the Southern School of Taoism, while the Ch'üan-chen, which laid greater stress on the moral side and was active in Peking and North China, is the Northern School.

The cultivation of the Internal Pill is another method, besides elixir, for the individual spirit to be mystically identified with the Absolute. The basic study is to learn, by regulated breathing, to kindle the *ch'i*, which has the lower navel (the lower cinnabar-field) as its base, to pass through the *tu* vein parallel to the spine, with the coccyx (*wei-lü*), the course between the kidneys (*chia-chi*) and occiput (*yü-chen*) as the three check-points, before it reaches the brain (ni-wan, a transliteration for *nirvāṇa*). The *ch'i* then descends down the face, passing through the *jen* vein on the front of the body parallel to the trunk, to return to the cinnabar-field where it came from, and completing this microcosmic cycle once. This is called "laying the foundation".

Another preparatory exercise in this process is to regulate the trigram, *li*, which is fire of passion in the heart, and the trigram, *k'an*, the water in the lower abdomen. Using breath-control, the fire above is driven down into the water below, and the water below is brought up and evaporated to achieve a mental equilibrium. In exercising this, the sperm of the body will gradually be evolved into *ch'i*, which in due course will again be evolved into spirit, or *shen*.

When the above has been practised for months under supervision, the practitioner is at the advanced stage to be qualified to learn how to circulate his *ch'i* from the heels through the *tu* vein to the brain, thence it comes down through the *jen* vein to return through the solar plexus (*huang-t'ing*) to the lower cinnabar-field. The solar plexus is the middle cinnabar-field, and the brain, the upper. The ascending breath through the *tu* vein is pure, but the descending one through the *jen* vein is corrupt, and should be transmuted and cleansed. A sign of hope for success is evidenced by the producing of sweet fluid resembling nectar in the mouth, and by the appearance of a golden light from the solar plexus, which is the purified primordial *ch'i* to be united with the white light of the prenatal spirit emitted between the eyebrows (cavernous plexus). The union of them will accelerate the expected breakthrough, when the sacred foetus will leap out through an aperture on the top of the head and appear in the air.[50]

I have some suspicion that the theory and practice of the Internal Pill might have been influenced, even partially, by Tāntric Buddhism, which was known to the Chinese before the eighth century.[51] In the Haṭha Yoga, which rose probably in the eleventh century, the dormant divine potency, *kuṇḍalinī*, is the great magical Śakti or power residing at the base of the spine, which is to be driven upward by the concentration of *citta*, activated by controlled breathing. A vein (or nerve, *nāḍī*), known as *suṣumṇā*, links the *kuṇḍalinī* through the back-bone with the centre of supreme power, *sahasrāra*, at the top of the head, by means of six *cakras* (wheels).[52] It is interesting to note that, in both teachings, the lower plexus is female, and the upper is male. The three cinnabar-fields might be a simplified version of the six wheels.

The last thing I wish to mention is the very deep influence of religious Taoism on the minds of the Sung-Ming scholars who were, on the surface, Neo-Confucianists. In those days all scholars had to sit for the state examinations, and the Taoist-invented God of Literature (Wen-ch'ang), who was supposed to manipulate their failure or success naturally earned their highest respect. A popular tract entitled *The Silent Way of Recompense* (Yin-chih wen) was alleged to have been compiled by this god himself. This and a sister work, *The Treatise on Influence and Response Delivered by the Supreme-high* (T'ai-shang kan-ying-p'ien), were two popular tracts, hundreds of thousands of copies of which had been printed for chanting like religious formulae. Besides this, there was the practice of entering the *Columns of Merits and Demerits* as a daily routine. It is a para-Taoist device for scholars to keep a record for self-discipline and confessions. Many of them also refrained from eating beef, even from childhood, not because of the worship of the sacred cow (Mother Earth), but because it was prohibited in some of these popular tracts for ethical enlightenment.[53]

Without the predilection of a modern man, I believe Taoism is a religion in the sense that it has its worship, its precepts and right beliefs, and its adherents participating in religious services. As a religion, it may not be as great as Mahāyāna Buddhism or Christianity, but it isn't narrow, and it has its own pursuits. Its dreams for elixir or for liberation and sublimation of self is actually a perennial struggle of human beings against Nature, and against Man's own environment. In this connection Taoism is extremely universal, and its social impact requires much attention from scholars of cultural anthropology, sociology, psychology and other related disciplines. But its borrowed philosophy from the ancient Taoists and the experiences of individual men gained in solitude are more individualistic. Therefore, if you are helping somebody to do charity work at a fete, you are a Taoist. If you watch birds or walk in the bush, you are a Taoist too.

FOOTNOTES

1. Michel Strickmann says in "On the Alchemy of T'ao Hung-ching", in Holmes Welch & Anna Seidel (ed.), *Facets of Taoism*, Yale, 1979, p.165: "though the early Taoists spoke of high antiquity, of the Yellow Emperor, Yü the Great and the famous immortals of the Chou dynasty, and though they used the *Lao-tzu* for their own purposes, the social history of Taoism begins with the founding of the Way of the Celestial Master in the second century A.D." This is very true.
2. Cf. D.C. Lau, *Lao Tzu Tao Te Ching* (Penguin Classics), 1972, p.8; James Legge, *The Texts of Taoism* (reprint from *The Sacred Books of the East*, Vol. XXXIX), Dover Publications, New York, 1962, pp.34-5.
3. Liu Ts'un-yan, *On the Art of Ruling a Big Country: Views of Three Chinese Emperors*, The 34th George Ernest Morrison Lecture in Ethnology, ANU Press, Canberra, 1974, p.3.
4. D.C. Lau, *op.cit.*, p.70.
5. D.C. Lau, *op.cit.*, p.129. Last sentence altered slightly at my discretion.
6. D.C. Lau, *op.cit.*, p.64.
7. Legge, *op.cit.*, p.201; James R. Ware, *The Sayings of Chuang Chou*, a Mentor Classic, New York, 1963, p.30.
8. Cf. Note 2.
9. Legge, *op.cit.*, p.183.
10. D.C. Lau, *op. cit.*, p.116.
11. Lau, *ibid.*, p.66. The ancient Chinese believed that man has two souls. Cf. Liu Ts'un-yan, *Buddhist and Taoist Influences on Chinese Novels*, Wiesbaden, 1962, pp.204-5.
12. Legge, *op.cit.*, p.238.
13. *Ibid.*, p.364.
14. Lau, *op.cit.*, p.61.
15. *Ibid.*, p.62.
16. *Ibid.*, p.111.
17. Legge, *op.cit.*, p.383.
18. *Tao-tsang* (The Taoist Tripitaka), 870/15b, 17a.
19. "Biography of Wang Huan" in *Hou-Han shu*, *Erh-shih wu-shih* ed., 106/228. The edict was probably issued in 165, in which year the emperor sent eunuchs to pay tributes to Lao-tzu's temple twice. See *ibid.*, 7/24-5.
20. "Biography of Huang-fu Sung" in *ibid.*, *Hou-Han shu*, 101/215; Rafe de Crespigny, *The Last of the Han*, Monograph 9, Centre of Oriental Studies, Australian National University, Canberra, 1969, p.7.
21. Wang Ming, *T'ai-p'ing ching ho'chiao*, Chung-hua, Peking, 1960; also *Tao-tsang*, 746-755. For the items in the text cited here, read Wang Ming, *op.cit.*, pp.710, 294-5, 229, 29, 129, 551 respectively. For other works on the *T'ai-p'ing ching*, read Ōbuchi Ninji, "Taiheikyō no shisō ni tsuite", *Tōyō-gakuhō*, 28:4, 1941, pp.145-68; Max Kaltenmark, "The Ideology of the T'ai-p'ing ching", in Holmes Welch & Anna Seidel (Ed.), *op.cit.*, pp.19-45.
22. Wang Ming, *op.cit.*, p.114.
23. *Ibid.*, p.96.
24. *Ibid.*, p.127.

25. See Liu Ai's *Record* (Chi) found in a footnote under the year A.D. 184, "Annals of Emperor Ling", *Hou-Han shu*, 8/26.
26. Jao Tsung-i, *Lao-tzu hsiang-erh-chu chiao-chien*, Hong Kong, 1956.
27. "Biography of Chang Lu" in *Wei-chih, San-kuo chih*, 8/28.
28. James R. Ware, *Alchemy, Medicine and Religion in the China of A.D.320, the Nei-P'ien of Ko Hung*, The MIT Press, Cambridge; Mass., 1966, p.156. Cf. also T.L. Davis & Ch'en Kuo-fu, "The Inner Chapters of Pao P'u-tzu", *Proceedings of Arts and Sciences*, LXXIV, Boston, 1940-42, pp.297-325.
29. Ware, *Alchemy*, pp.310-11.
30. *Ibid.*, pp.140-41, with some alterations at my discretion.
31. *Ibid.*, p.57.
32. *Ibid.*, p.139. Read also Henri Maspero, "Les procédés de 'Nourrir le principe vital', dans la religion taoïste ancienne", in *Le Taoïsme et les religions chinoises*, Gallimard, Paris, 1971, pp.497 ff.
33. Lu-ch'iang Wu and T.L. Davis, "An Ancient Chinese Treatise on Alchemy Entitled Ts'an T'ung Ch'i", *Isis*, XVIII, 1932, pp.240-41; O.S. Johnson, *A Study of Chinese Alchemy*, Shanghai, 1928, p.133; A. Waley, "Notes on Chinese Alchemy", *BSOAS*, VI, 1, 1930, pp.1-24.
34. *Tao-tsang*, 1013-1015.
35. Ware, *Alchemy*, pp.103-4; alterations are made at my discretion.
36. Ōbuchi Ninji, "On Ku Ling Pao Ching", *Acta Asiatica*, 27, Tokyo, 1974, pp.35-36.
37. Ch'en Yin-k'o, "T'ien-shih-tao yü pin-hai-yü chih kuan-hsi", *CYYCY*, 3:4, 1934, reprinted in *Ch'en Yin-k'o hsien-sheng wen-shih lun-chi*, Vol.I, Hong Kong, 1971, pp.175-9; R.A. Stein, "Un example de relations entre Taoïsme et religion populaire", in *Fukui kakase shōju kinen toyō bunka ronshū*, Tokyo, 1969, pp.79-90.
38. Liu Ts'un-yan, "The Compilation and Historical Value of the *Tao-tsang*", in Donald Leslie, Colin Mackerras & Wang Gungwu (ed.), *Essays on the Sources for Chinese History*, ANU Press, Canberra, 1973, pp.104-119.
39. Michel Strickmann, *op.cit.*, pp.123-92; Wang Ming, "On Tao Hongjing", *Shijie Zongjiao Yanjiu*, I, Peking, 1981, pp.10-21; also Ishii Masako, *Dōkyō gaku kenkyū*, Tokyo, 1980.
40. Richard B. Mather, "K'ou Ch'ien-chih and the Taoist Theocracy at the Northern Wei Court, 425-451", in *Facets of Taoism*, pp.103-22; Ch'en Yin-k'o, "Ts'ui Hao yü K'ou Ch'ien-chih", *Ling-nan hsüeh-pao*, II:1, 1950, pp.123-4; and Tsukamoto Zenryū, *Gisho shakurōshi no kenkyū*, Kyoto, 1961.
41. See Yang Lien-sheng, "Lao-chün yin-sung chieh-ching chiao-shih", *CYYCY*, 28: 1, 1956.
42. The T'ang rulers claimed that members of the royal family were descendants of Lao-tzu.
43. Liu, *On the Art of Ruling a Big Country*, p.7.
44. Liu Ts'un-yan, "The Penetration of Taoism into the Ming Neo-Confucianist Elite", in *Selected Papers from the Hall of Harmonious Wind*, E.J. Brill, Leiden, 1976, pp.96-111; "Pu Ming-shih ning-hsing Tao Chung-wen chuan", in *Ho-feng t'ang tu-shu-chi*, Vol.I, Lungmen, Hong Kong, 1977, pp.227-33.
45. A. Waley, *The Travels of An Alchemist: The journal of the Taoist Ch'ang-ch'un from China to the Hindukush at the Summons of Chingiz Khan*, London, 1931.
46. Liu, *Buddhist and Taoist Influences on Chinese Novels*, Vol.I, p.190.
47. Liu, "Traces of Zoroastrian and Manichaean Activities in Pre-T'ang China", *Selected Papers*, p.30.
48. Saeki Yoshirō, *Keikyō no kenkyū*, Tokyo, 1935 gives a detailed account of this speculation. For the legend of the Eight Immortals, read T.C. Lai, *The Eight Immortals*, Swindon, Hong Kong, 1972.
49. His words addressed to the hero, Arjuna, in Bhagavad Gītā, a bhakti text inserted into the Mahābhārata epic.
50. Read, for instance, Lu K'uan-yu (Charles Luk), *Taoist Yoga Alchemy and Immortality*, which is a translation of Chao Pi-ch'en (born 1860)'s *Hsin-ming fa-chüeh ming-chih*, Rider & Company, London, 1970.
51. Lin Li-kouang, "Puṇyodaya (Na-t'i), un propagateur du tantrisme en Chine et au Cambodge à l'époque de Hiuan-tsang" *JA*, CCXXVII/I, 1935, p.83 ff.; Chou Yi-liang, "Tantrism in Chinese", *HJAS*, VIII, 1945, pp.241-332; Shashi Bhusan Dasgupta, *An Introduction to Tantric Buddhism*, Calcutta, 1950, pp.163 ff.
52. Mircea Eliade, *Yoga: Immortality and Freedom* (transl. by Willard R. Trask), Pantheon, New York, 1958, p.234.
53. Liu, "Yüan Huang and His 'Four Admonitions'", *Selected Papers*, pp.232-256.

PETER BISHOP

TIBET IN ITS PLACE

For over 300 years a strange assortment of Europeans have made their way across the Himalayas, the Karakorams, and other mountain ranges which form the formidable boundaries of Tibet. These journeys began hesitatingly in the 17th century with the Portugese Jesuit Antonio d'Andrade. This almost forgotten visit was followed by that of the Jesuits Johann Gruber and Albert d'Orville from whom the first information on the capital Lhasa reached Europe. In the 18th century more monks reached Tibet — the Jesuits Ippolito Desideri and Manuel Freyre, and the Capuchin Francesco Orazio della Penna who in fact translated the classic Tibetan text by Tson-Kha-pa, the Lam-rim chen-mo, which systematizes the entire Buddhist teachings of Tibet. Britain's Bogle and Turner visited Tibet and established a firm connection with the Pachen Lama towards the close of the 18th century. They travelled on behalf of Warren Hastings and the British East India Company. Drawing upon this groundwork, European and particularly British interest in Tibet gained momentum throughout the 19th century and continued right into the 20th century.[1]

The 19th century is a chronicle of desperate attempts to enter Tibet and to reach Lhasa, attempts which scarcely diminished in intensity during the 20th century. These included explorers such as the Russian Prejevalsky who crossed the worst deserts in the world — the Takla Makan and Gobi, who journeyed through a terrible civil war, and across unimaginable bleak mountains in an effort to reach Lhasa only to be turned back near the border.[2] Few Europeans had seen Lhasa. The strange, isolated and eccentric Englishman Manning had somehow reached Lhasa in 1811, probably because of his idiosyncracies and his complete lack of interest in the capital city or even in Tibet.[3] It would be over 90 years before another Englishman followed.

In 1846 the French Lazarist priests Huc and Gabet stayed briefly in Lhasa.[4] These two, together with Manning, were the sole Europeans to visit this isolated capital during the whole of the 19th century. But this certainly was not through lack of trying. The Russian, Prejevalsky for example, set out across Siberia in 1879 with 23 camels loaded with 2½ hundredweight of sugar, 40 pounds of dried fruit, a crate of brandy and a crate of sherry. His party was armed with a formidable arsenal of rifles, revolvers, a hundred weight of powder, 9,000 rounds of ammunition and four hundred-weight of lead shot. His 'gifts for the natives' included tinted pictures of Russian actresses. An additional gift was some wild strawberry jam which Prejevalsky had bottled personally for the Dalai Lama. He boasted that if necessary he would bribe or shoot his way to Lhasa.[5]

In 1898 the Swede, Sven Hedin, after preparations which included cold baths, and naked plunges into snowdrifts to toughen himself, determined to make a dash into Tibet.[6] Disguising himself as a Siberian Lama he hoped that by travelling fast on horseback he would outpace the news of his entry and hence reach Lhasa before he could be stopped. He got within two days ride of his goal before being turned back. The solitary approach had also been unsuccessfully made earlier in 1892 by the Englishwoman Annie Taylor. She had struggled for 4½ months through a Tibetan winter before being turned back.[7] Disguise was commonly used in attempts to enter Tibet — William L. Moorcroft and Hyder Jung Hearsey were among the first to use it successfully, in 1812.[8] Madam Alexandre David-Neal was probably among the last when in 1923 at the age of 56, she walked 2,000 miles from China to Lhasa disguised as a Tibetan beggar.[9] The last years of the 19th century saw many desperate failures — The American Rockhill, the Frenchmen Grenard and Dutreuil de Rhins (who was killed), the English couple, Mr. and Mrs. Littledale, and the sad case of Dr. Susie Rijnhart who lost both her small son and her husband and still failed to reach Lhasa.

The most notable non-Europeans to enter Tibet were the 'pundits'. These were Indians trained in survey work, who carried compasses fixed to the top of their walking staves, notes hidden inside their prayer wheels and used beads on the rosary to count their paces and hence to measure the vast distances.[10] The first pundits, Nain Singh and Mani Singh set out in 1864 and, of course, their exploits were made famous by Kipling in his novel *Kim*. The last of these Indians to reach Lhasa as a clandestine British agent was Sarat Chandra Das in 1882 and terrible punishments were dealt to those Tibetans who had befriended him. The other famous non-European to reach Lhasa in the years prior to the Younghusband expedition was the Japanese monk Kawaguchi who in fact stayed for three years in Tibet disguised as a Chinese priest.

Finally in 1904 the mystically inclined Francis Younghusband fought his way to Lhasa as the political officer at the head of a column of several thousand soldiers, porters, yaks, bullocks, sheep and ponies.[11]

Of course, this singleminded and intense fascination with Tibet ebbed and flowed but it sustained itself for nearly 200 years through a great span of Western social change — from the dawning of the Victorian era right through to the present.

Travellers & Religious Studies

Philosophers have achieved remarkable results in the comprehension of Tibetan religious texts. Anthropologists have examined kinship, ritual and monastic organization. Psychologists have contributed to our understanding of Tibetan symbolic systems. Art historians have given us detailed iconographic studies from the immense canvas of Tibetan sacred art. What have travellers and explorers contributed to our understanding and appreciation of Tibetan religions?

In addition to sacred texts, art, ritual, and symbolic systems, there still remains untouched the 'feel' of a religious culture, its 'tone' and the sense of *place* associated with it. Accounts of travel and exploration have contributed to this sense of *place*, to the *genius locii* of Tibet. Over the past 200 years Tibet has been transformed from a vague and unknown geographical site into a definite *place* in the sacred landscape of Western imaginings.

In the Western dialogue with Tibetan Buddhism it is *Tibet* itself which has been, and continues to be, one of the first, great and central symbols. I wish to put the *Tibet* back into Tibetan Buddhism and to put less emphasis on the 'ism'.[12] What exactly *is* Tibet? How can we put Tibet in its place?

Place

A *place* is not an objective thing. A *location* only becomes a *place* when it is filled with subjective meanings. So Tibet as a place is not simply located 'out there' in some remote corner of the objective physical and geographical world, but also lies within the imagination of the traveller.[13]

This idea of the *place* of Tibet contributes to our understanding of Tibetan Buddhism, especially as it has spread its influence to the West. Tibet as a place was where the sensitive and complex nerve endings of European imaginative sensibility made a soulful contact and drew sustenance from this Eastern spiritual tradition. We see in a *place* what needs to be seen. We invest a location with meaning to give it a sense of place.

East-West studies have generally focused upon questions such as the nature of Eastern wisdom, the parallels between Eastern and Western philosophy, or how Eastern ideas can be used in the West as a series of advanced techniques in fields such as psychotherapy or quantum physics.[14]

But there is another strand of East-West studies which focuses upon the history of *how* the East has been *read* by the West, and what the East *means* to the West. This approach poses such questions as: under what conditions were the various Eastern cultures encountered by the West, and what was the 'operating table', the ground of meaning, the mythic or imaginative sub-stratum upon which the West established discourses concerning 'the East'. Such a perspective views concepts and ideas as being moved around upon an ocean of symbols.[15]

Place is a crucial image in this project. Places relate to memories and to the heart, their contours are shaped as much by fantasies and stories as by careful observation and knowledge. Heidegger conceived a place to be where mortals, gods, earth and sky could gather and where we mortals could 'dwell poetically on earth'.[16] Aristotle connected place with the image of a vessel. This should not be thought of as a merely passive container, but rather place provides its own boundaries, because it evokes a fascination — it is an affair of the heart.[17] Tibet became a landscape to which Western, soulful imaginings were drawn and which has sustained a deep fascination over the centuries.

It has been said that to be without a relationship to a place is to be in spiritual exile.[18]

In religious studies this intense sense of place has been investigated under the broad heading of sacred landscape and sacred space.[19] Sacred space has been defined in terms of its separation from the profane world, by the limited access accorded to it, by a sense of dread or fascination, as well as by a sense of order and power combined with ambiguity and paradox. Sacred places also seem to be located at the periphery of the social world.[20] As we shall see, Tibet easily fits such a description, in so far as the West is concerned.

Notions of sacred space and travel come together in the phenomenon of pilgrimage. Like travel accounts, pilgrimage has its landscapes, sacred places, sacred routes and its literature of guide books and individual accounts often written in a confessional style.[21] Victor Turner has emphasised the peripheral nature of pilgrimage geographically, culturally and imaginatively.[22]

I want to argue for a wider definition of pilgrimage or of sacred journey which will encompass exploration and travel. As with the more conventional pilgrimage, travel and exploration can convey a public sense of the sacred. Through the ceremony of travel the individual can be involved in a collective celebration, production and maintenance of the sacred and of the mythic.

One of the great problems with travel writing is that the imaginative aspect of place and landscape is frequently lost. In the search for the *authentic* Tibet or the *real* Tibetans, it is forgotten that travel does not so much discover worlds as create them. The gross physicality, the geographical locatability, of travel accounts should not blind us to their imaginative nature.

Sacred Geography

The relation between humanity and nature has frequently been viewed as implicitly spiritual.[23] Ideas such as humanity's place in the Great Chain of Being, or, later, in an evolutionary scheme, are theological as well as scientific ideas. Recently the ecological debate has entered at the centre of religious concern. In this debate, rightly or wrongly, the East has often been used as an exemplary model of a spiritual ecology.[24]

The ideas of John Ruskin, for example, span the most formative years of Britain's imaginings on Tibet and his influence was seminal. He wrote that the *essence* of a landscape lay beyond science and that landscapes had a deep symbolic meaning. To comprehend this essence one needed to see rather than observe, to develop a full engagement of self with the landscape. For Ruskin, beauty and God were almost synonymous, and the most sublime beauty lay in mountain landscapes.[25] His vision has been called a 'theocentric aesthetic'.

But ideas on landscape did not just support and influence the experiences of travellers in Tibet. These experiences in their turn, fed back and subtly modified the underlying attitudes towards landscape. Sometimes such an interaction is clear and direct. For example, Ruskin's ideas of beauty and the heart of landscape were carried on by the influential Francis Younghusband — explorer, soldier, political agent in charge of Britain's 1904 'invasion' of Tibet, President of the Royal Geographical Society and author of numerous books advocating a mystic, universal religious sensibility. Younghusband recounts how, after the treaty with Tibet had been signed at the Potala in Lhasa, after all the struggles, fighting, bloodshed, frustrations and diplomacy of the previous months, he 'went off alone to the mountainside'. He wrote, 'The scenery was in sympathy with my feelings ... I was insensibly suffused with an almost intoxicating sense of elation and good-will ... Never again could I think evil, or again be at enmity with any man ...

Such experiences are only too rare', he continued, 'Yet it is these few fleeting moments which are reality'. He concluded, 'that single hour on leaving Lhasa was worth all the rest of a lifetime.'[26]

The geographer Vaughan Cornish heard the middleaged Younghusband's lecture in 1920 and was profoundly influenced by his ideas on the beauty and transcendental power of landscape.[27] Cornish went on to establish firmly a geo-poetic perspective within cultural geography and is well known for his pioneering effort in creating national parks and wilderness areas. There is a quality in the attention currently given to the 'wilderness' today which contains elements of a religious attachment. Many use such parks as sanctuaries, as places for reverie and for a kind of prayer.[28] It is perhaps interesting to muse upon how that single mystic moment of Younghusband's in Tibet is echoed distantly in the national parks scattered around the Western world.

Geographical imaginings can hence provide us with access to the operating table upon which East-West studies rest. Indeed, it is an obvious but overlooked point that the very idea of East-West is geographical.[29] Tibet was associated with the fantasy of Central Asia and of *Tartary*. It was also a remote part of the *Orient*.[30]

The creation of the place, of the landscape of Tibet did not therefore occur in a vacuum. Even in the 18th century Britain was involved in ruminations about the 'East', and about its religions and customs. British culture also contained definite conceptions of geography, landscape, the picturesque, the sublime, the beautiful and the good. These conceptions constituted the imaginative arena from which Tibet, as a clear object of fascination, arose.[31]

Tibetan Religion As A Geographical Fantasy

Professor Huston Smith in his classic 1974 film on Tibetan Buddhism, *Requiem for a Faith*, commented that,[32] 'Tibet is more than a land, it is a religion'. Huston-Smith continued by saying that Tibet 'is a land so close to the sky that the natural inclination of her people is to pray'. This beautiful image should not blind us to the relationship between religion and landscape which is being expressed. At first it seems to be such an obvious connection as to be somehow an empirical fact. But this is not the case. It is part of the play of the imagination. To associate prayer, altitude and sky in such a way reveals much about the image of sacred places in the Judeo-Christian tradition and in the imaginative milieu of the West in the second half of the 20th century. Above all, such a conection between geography and religion is a consistent theme in the imaginations of the West about Tibetan Buddhism. For example, Christmas Humphreys in his very popular study on Buddhism, wrote:[33]

'The physical conditions of Tibet lend themselves to religious thinking. The great spaces, the height of the mountain ranges which surround them, the rarified air in a land which is largely over 16,000 feet, these and the silence where men are scarce and wild life is rarer still, all lend themselves to introverted thought,...'

A final example comes from Sir Charles Bell, the influential commentator on Tibet in the early years of this century and a close friend of the 13th Dalai Lama. He wrote:[34]

'Buddhism, of the type that has been formed in Tibet and Mongolia, flourishes characteristically in their great expanses...

The dry, cold pure air stimulates the intellect but isolation ... deprives the Tibetan of subjects on which to feed his brain. So his mind turns inwards and spends itself on religious contemplation, helped still further by the monotony of the life and the awe-inspiring scale on which Nature works'.

We find a specific fantasy of religious experience arising from these geographical imaginings: religion as an introverted, solitary and rarified activity.

Many Tibets

It would, of course, be quite wrong to reduce all of the discourses on Tibet into a single uniform fantasy. While I feel that there was an overall pattern to most of the imaginings on Tibet, there also existed within it, contradictions, tensions, and paradoxes. In fact there were, and are, *many* Tibets and some of the various imaginative discourses need to be isolated and identified at this point.

In the case of the British imagination and Tibet, three such imaginative contexts immediately spring to mind.

1. The imagination of imperialism, particularly in India, exerted its influence throughout the formative years of Britain's involvement with Tibet. Imperial rivalry, a sense of imperial destiny, the consolidation of the Empire through exploring, mapping and surveying, plus concerns of diplomacy and trade were uppermost in the imperial imagination.[35]
2. The imagination of exploration, which found one of its fullest flowerings in the 19th century, also dominated Britain's relationship to Tibet. Under the heading of exploration can be included adventurers and mountaineers, as well as scholars in the fields of geography, archeology, ethnology and the psychical and natural sciences. The Empire and its frontiers were a spur to investigation.[36] This was a time of great international rivalry in the fields of exploration and associated scientific discovery. This was a period when explorers, archeologists, ethnographers etc. were often greeted with enthusiastic acclaim both by the public and by scientific bodies.[37] Rivalry over various institute medals could become intense at times.[38]
3. Tibet and the East in general, seem to have long excited a fascination for certain Western mystics. The mystical imagination has formed a continuous thread in Britain's relationship with Tibet.

Tibet also lay at the intersection of three discourses, namely those concerning the relationship of the West (1) to nature, particularly to mountains and wildernesses; (2) to non-European cultures; and (3) to ideas of personal experience. These will be discussed as the paper progresses.

For the purposes of this paper, I wish to initially organize the vast amount of material by looking at three characteristics of Tibet as a sacred place — upwards, source and boundaries.

Tibet As A Sacred Place: Upwards

The position of Tibet atop the world's highest mountains is its single most important characteristic as a sacred landscape. One even has to go *up* just to imagine Tibet.

It is well known through the work of Eliade and others, that mountains have been viewed widely as an *axis mundi*, as the dwelling place of gods, as the meeting place between humans and gods.[39] The top of the mountain 'touches heaven and hence marks the highest point in the world'. The territory around the mountain is held to be spiritually the highest country. But traditionally these high places have been the dwelling place of both benevolent and malevolent supernatural beings. Hence humanity has long held an ambivalent attitude to such lofty regions.[40]

Beginning in the 18th century this ambivalence towards mountains began to undergo a profound change, particularly in the British imagination. In earlier times, mountains had often been referred to as blemishes, or even as warts, upon the surface of the globe. But within the romantic view and under the impact of the 'discovery' of the Alps by Rousseau, Saussaure, Wordsworth, Ruskin and others, mountains became unequivocally associated with a sense of the sublime and the beautiful.[41]

If the Alps were the inspiration for mountain mysticism then the Himalayas gradually became its cathedral. In 1869 Nina Mazuchelli was the first Western woman to see Mount Everest, and she commented,

'It was the dream of my childhood to see this nearest point of Heaven and Earth... As I stand in these vast solitudes I do so with bent knee and bowed head as becomes one who is in the *felt* presence of the Invisible'.[43]

However it was not until quite late in the 19th century that the Himalayas managed to rival the grip which the supposedly more picturesque Alps had over the British imagination.[44]

Even in Younghusband's accounts at the turn of the 20th century there are moments of ambivalence. He refers to the 'nightmare of the mountains'.[45]

Scarcely *any* trace of ambivalence is to be found in many subsequent accounts, including Marco Pallis' influential work of 1939 or that of Fosco Maraini in 1952. For example Maraini describes an episode when he is deep in a cloud covered valley, then:

'Glory and liberation this morning! For a moment the clouds lifted and after many days we saw the blue sky again, and there at an incredible height... we saw that divinely pure and unsubstantial thing, consisting only of shape and light, the sparkling pyramid of Kanchenjunga.'[46]

The Himalayas came into their own as the love of 'the wild picturesque' became supplemented in the 20th century by the increasingly widespread love of 'the wilderness'. In one of the most contemporary accounts, that by Peter Matthiesson in *The Snow Leopard*, this unequivocal worship of the highest mountain peaks reaches a new intensity. For him the Himalayas are directly associated with sublime feelings of pure insight, and the peak of spiritual wisdom and knowledge. They are almost direct proof that impermanence and death can be transcended. The use of the Himalayas by the Victorians for character building has become accentuated into the 20th century search for the self. Matthiesson writes:

'Then, four miles above these mud streets of the lowlands, at a point so high as to seem overhead, a luminous whiteness shone — the light of the snows. Glaciers loomed and vanished in the greys, and the sky parted, and the snow cone of Machhapuchare glistened like the spire of a higher kingdom'.[47]

Up in the mountains is 'clean air', 'the absence of sound', 'warmth and harmony' and 'whispers of a paradisical age'. Matthiesson comments that he wishes to 'penetrate the secrets of the mountains.'[48] The titles of many earlier accounts intimate his sentiments: viz. *'The Throne of the Gods, Peaks and Lamas,* and *Himalays — Abode of Light.'*[49]

We may well ask, what has happened to the ambivalence, to the interplay between the forces of light and darkness which characterized so many traditional imaginings on mountains? Where is the darkness of the sacred landscape? It is all too white, too silent, too pure, too rarified on the mountain peaks. There is too much light. Often in these accounts such darkness is left down below, in the valleys. Maraini, for example, in the 1950's wrote:[50]

'The valleys down below were hot and wet, full of a voracious, imperious or cunning, aggressive or insinuating vitality. Up here we are in a realm of ice and clarity, of ultimate and primordial purity... Down below night is even more alive than day... But up here the night is nothing but light and space... Time and matter seem no longer to exist. Hence here death immediately suggests eternity. Down below death is decomposition, a minor, unimportant phase in the cycle of living... Up here night has the solemn, crystalline dignity of the great truths; it is mind, God.'

More recently, Matthiesson on his trek to Dolpo on the Tibetan border described valleys as grim, full of decay, degeneration, corruption, impermanence, ignorance and confusion.[51] It reaches such an intensity that even the inhabitants of the valley are contaminated by their environment. Matthiesson compares the 'friendly and playful children' of the mountains with the 'grim Hindu children of the towns' and valleys. He dreaded the return to lowland life.[52] Such a bias towards the people of the hills as against those of the plains has a long history in British imaginings.[53] Often it is described in terms of the hill peoples' independence, individuality, openness and honesty. The women of the mountains are portrayed time and again as laughing, self-confident and assertive, while the men are portrayed in terms of 'manliness' and self sufficiency.[54] These are of course qualities which have appealed to Western fantasies. In Victorian times it was notions of virility and independence which were bestowed upon these mountain people, whereas now it is an all-pervading mystic harmony. The Tibetans, living on the *highest* mountains, become increasingly reified as we move from the 19th century to the present day.[55]

In addition to being imagined as *axis mundi*, as conduits to the gods, mountains are also related to images of overview, of control and protection. Tibet has often been called the 'roof' of the world — offering protection from the gods.[56] Madam Blavatsky and other early Theosophists imagined the Himalayan Masters as influencing and even controlling the spiritual destiny of humanity from their commanding heights.[57] Prejevalsky imagined Lhasa as the Rome of Asia, set high up and spreading its influence, control and power like a net over 250 million people from Ceylon to Japan.[58] I recently came across a 1950's children's novel in which Hitler escaped from Germany into Tibet with a band of S.S. Troops, and set up a battery of missiles armed with atomic warheads. From these unassailable heights he could rain terror on the rest of the world down below.[59] (He was defeated at the last moment.)

Darwinian evolution uses the metaphor of the *ascent/descent* of humanity. Occultists in the 19th century were quick to use this image in terms of spiritual evolution. The masters in Tibet were often viewed as the peak, the culmination of spiritual evolution.[60]

Source

In Matthiesson's account, Tibet is presented as the source of all the great rivers of Southern Asia, these 'fall from the highest country in the world'.[61] Rivers are rich symbols — holy, life giving, even metaphors for life itself.[62] The four greatest rivers in India have their origins in Tibet — the Indus, Sutlej, Ganges and Brahmaputra. The sources of these rivers are endowed with intense spiritual and mythic qualities. The search for these sources occupied the imagination of explorers and geographers for over 100 years.[63] Even though this quest was overshadowed in the popular imagination by the search for the source of the Nile, the 19th century seemed obsessed with the fantasy of the source of all great rivers.

The 19th century was also concerned with the image of origins or sources in more ways than simply those of rivers. The Hungarian Csoma de Koros, the first European to systematically study Tibetan language, arrived in Western Tibet about 1825. He was determined to find the origin of the Hungarian race and language, and was en route for Mongolia just north of Tibet.[64] This search by Csoma de Koros was also echoed in the concern with locating the origins of the Aryan race. The Himalayas and the regions of Central Asia just north of Tibet were all caught up in this search.[65]

Seemingly under the sway of evolutionism, the 19th century imagination was singlemindedly obsessed with origins: e.g. the *origin* of various human races, the *origin* of civilization and so on.[66] Tibet and the Himalayas occupied a unique place in this search. For example, Brian Hodgson during his long solitary sojourn in the Himalayas throughout a considerable portion of the 19th century wanted to classify and to establish the origins of various traditional peoples that he encountered. He considered the Himalayas to be a vast museum of races.[67]

Tibet has frequently been viewed as a source of spiritual and occult wisdom. Blavatsky, David-Neal, Evans-Wentz, and Govinda obviously lean in this direction due to their overwhelming spiritual concern. But such a sentiment is to be found throughout the literature of travel and exploration. Tibet has been called a storehouse of spiritual wisdom, a vast library, a tradition in deep freeze.[68] In Tibet, it has been argued, was preserved a kind of original religion, more pure, more essential, more in touch with the living source of all religious feelings than any other, the last living part of the original mystery traditions of the world.[69]

I think it is significant that in 1879 Prejevalsky on his Tibetan expedition discovered the original horse in the remoteness of Mongolian Central Asia. It was a species which had flourished in the Pleistocene period and which had survived in a region too remote for humanity to domesticate. He had discovered one of the wild strains from which our modern horse is a degenerate descendent in terms of toughness and fierceness.[70] Here was the answer to the riddle of the famous ponies of Genghis Khan and the Mongol armies. The Mongols obtained their mounts by domesticating half castes of these wild horses. They were the original, the archetypal source of vigour and life energy uncorrupted by civilization. What a powerful metaphor for the horse worshipping Victorians.

Frontiers

Heidegger wrote that 'a boundary is not that at which something stops but... is that from which something *begins*'. Maraini writes of Tibet's 'hungry horizon.'[71] The boundary, the frontier, the horizon. For a considerable portion of the last two centuries Tibet defined hundreds of miles of the northern frontier of the Indian Empire. For the British in India, Tibet was above all a frontier question. But the northern frontier, with Tibet and Afganistan, was never a merely administrative affair. The frontier was always a place for the imagination.

Lord Curzon, the flamboyant viceroy of India who masterminded the expeditionary force into Tibet, gave a lecture in 1906 entitled *Frontiers*. In it he spoke of the fascination with boundaries, the romance of frontiers, the kind of literature inspired by them, the type of 'manhood' fostered by them, even the effect upon national character of being engaged in expansionist frontier struggles. The expansion and struggles in the American West and its pivotal place in forming American culture was viewed by Curzon as being parallel to Britain's frontier struggles particularly to the North of India.[72]

He stressed rather enthusiastically to his audience that the frontiers of Empire continued to beckon.

In addition to being places where something *begins*, frontiers are also essential to a fantasy of *completion*. Empires have boundaries which are well marked, well established and firmly defended. Curzon warned that the Roman Empire collapsed because it could not maintain its boundaries. He wrote of 'silent men in clubs tracing lines upon unknown areas.' The frontier of Empire marks the boundary between the known and the unknown. Frontiers, Curzon wrote, were 'the razor's edge'.[73]

Tibet was inextricably caught up in this frontier imagination. It was imbued with a mixture of both the romance of the unknown and the defense of the known. In discussing the various types of frontier, Curzon emphazised:

'Backed as they are by the huge and lofty plateau of Tibet, the Himalayas are beyond doubt the most formidable natural frontier in the world.'[74]

Yet Tibet was also an unnatural frontier. The power, force and momentum of 19th century imperialism questioned the viability of even the Himalayas to act as an effective boundary. The fear of Russian supremacy in Tibet and in Central Asia, haunted imperial India. Britain's attitude was one of minimal interference. They wanted Tibet to remain static, unchanging, a buffer zone between them and the aggressively expansionist Russian Empire.

Protection is just one frontier activity, another is crossing them. Generations of Westerners were consumed by this fantasy with regard to Tibet. Tibet seemed to be a hermetically sealed vessel enclosed by vast walls of ice and stone, surrounded by inhospitable freezing deserts. The mountains encircling Tibet were called 'bastions' and 'ramparts.' Within its frontiers lay mystery.[75]

Eliade wrote of the spiritual *chaos* of unknown and unoccupied land. By occupying it, it is symbolically transformed into a cosmos, into a part of 'our world'.[76] Over the centuries Tibet has been increasingly occupied not just literally but by the Western imagination. From this standpoint Younghusband's invasion was perhaps a desperate attempt to bring the unknown city of Lhasa within the sphere of tangible Western imaginings.

In European imaginings, Tibet's frontiers had all the characteristics of the boundary of a *temenos*, a sacred space. Within such a space, time and history are suspended. Again and again we read Westerners commenting that Tibet was a society in deep freeze, left on the shelf, a museum. Rarely was any interest shown in Tibetan history, but mainly in its mythology, its reincarnations, its supposedly unchanging tradition.[77] Such a static, fixed, isolated view of Tibet is a gross exaggeration. Tibet has a colourful history, its institutions are not immemorial no matter what Westerners may say. Reincarnation, for example, as a state system emerged comparatively recently in *history*. It was the Western imagination which needed an unchanging Tibet, outside time and history.[78] How nicely this mystical fantasy dovetailed with the imperial demands discussed above.

Eliade writes of the passage across the threshold of sacred space.[79] For many explorers the crossing of the high passes over the mountain frontier of Tibet was like entering a new world. Giuseppe Tucci wrote that, 'To enter Tibet was not only to find oneself in another geographical world. After crossing the gap in space, one had the impression of having trailed many centuries backward in time.'[80] Huston-Smith commented that Tibet 'seemed not to belong to our Earth.'[81] Travel accounts have titles which imply this other worldliness such as, *Out of this World — Across the Himalayas to Tibet*, *To Lhasa and Beyond* and *Beyond the Himalayas*. Even the slightly dry but humourous Robert Byron was moved to write in 1933, of his entry into Tibet:

'here was a land where natural colouration, as we understand it, does not apply.'[82]

As the geographers, explorers and imperial surveyors charted the geographical regions of Tibet, they were at the same time establishing the contours of an imaginary landscape. They were plotting not just the physical routes into Tibet but also the routes between Tibet and the British imagination.[83]

Fascination

The idea of *place* does not consist simply of spacial vectors — origins, upwards, downwards, boundaries — it also involves the heart. In the case of Tibet this heart connection primarily manifested itself in terms of *fascination*. This is a very specific form of eros. Conquest, colonization, destruction or taming had virtually no place in the West's relationship with Tibet.

Marco Pallis has only to catch a glimpse of Tibet from afar, for it to summon up an intense yearning which eclipses even that felt for the mountains:

'But there was something else which... drew our gaze even more than that icy spire. To the left of it, through a distant gap in the mountains, we could just make out lines of rolling purple hills, that seemed to belong to another world, a world of austere calm,.... It was a corner of Tibet. My eyes rested on it with an intensity of longing ... Tibet is well guarded, as it should be.[84]

It is as if Pallis is a Dante catching a glimpse of his beloved Beatrice — a hem of her dress, or perhaps a shoe. Matthiesson never actually reaches Tibet but its presence, just above and beyond his immediate horizon, nourishes and sustains his fantasies. Tibet is like an enchanted place to Matthiesson which lures him ever deeper into the mountains.

Indeed, Tibet *is* Pallis' Beatrice, it is his anima, a symbol of his soul.[85] This is a different quality to the youthful longing expressed whilst gazing out over unknown horizons, or from the intense desire for spiritual authority and order. Both of these as we have seen have their place in the imaginings on Tibet. But the fascination is with appearances, with the *display* of the landscape, of the art, the architecture, the colours and the light.

The language of travel accounts is revealing. It has been observed for example, that in Robert Byron's 1933 book on Tibet, words like *strange*, *odd*, *uncanny*, *outlandish*, *astonishing*, and *unnatural* occur far more than in any of his other travel accounts.[86] The titles of Tibetan travel accounts abound with such words: e.g. *Tibet the Mysterious, In the Forbidden Land, Forbidden Journey, Secret Tibet, To Lhasa in Disguise, Lost World, Secrets of Tibet, Lhasa and Its Mysteries.*[87] Maraini describes the Tibetan mountain landscape as 'a beautiful, temperamental woman'.[88]

For much of this era of Tibetan exploration Western culture has been highly patriarchal. Travel and exploration, despite the exploits of a number of women, was a man's world. It emphasised all the characteristics considered to be desirable in a man. One could argue that the unconscious of this age, from the early 19th Century onwards, could be seen not only in the consulting rooms of Vienna and Zurich but also, strongly, in its geographical fantasies.

After Lhasa had finally been reached by a European, in the form of Younghusband and his British troops in 1904, the Viceroy of India wrote apologetically to the explorer Sven Hedin:[89]

'I am almost ashamed of having destroyed the virginity of the bride to whom you aspired, viz. Lhasa.

For Hedin it was sufficient reason to make him lose 'the longing that had possessed .... (him) to penetrate the Holy City' ...[90] Younghusband's entry into Lhasa, the unknown, the fascinating, the holy, the untouched, city, has been referred to as rape. An account written at the time of the Younghusband expedition had the title, — 'The Unveiling of Lhasa.'[91] Being the first to enter Lhasa, was an obsession with many of the explorers.[92]

The Legitimacy of the Traveller

The idea of place therefore includes the psychological attitude of the traveller, the particular route or style of travel adopted and above all the type of person who travels. Definite notions existed as to for whom, how and under what circumstances a journey to Tibet was valid. The most obvious quality of course was the restriction placed on women for most of this period, and the silencing or trivialization of many who actually did manage to make it.[93]

Other semi-invisible travellers into Tibet were the Indian pundits, already mentioned above. One of the pundits Nain Singh was even awarded a gold medal by the Royal Geographical after reaching Lhasa.[94] But there again, these non-Europeans did not *really* count. They were faithful surrogates for the British. Basically one had to be European to count in the quest for Lhasa. Even Prejevalsky's cossacks received scant recognition.

To descend from the aristocracy or at least to be an officer and a gentleman, was essential. Accounts of Himalayan exploration up until quite recently were descriptions of the world of the ruling class — the silence of the solitudes is frequently disturbed by the rattle of medals, titles, ranks and honours.

This raises an important issue which can only be touched upon here and which relates to the class structure of travel. Firstly there is the relationship between the image of Tibet being formed by the literate and educated middle classes and aristocracy in Britain and that which began to appear in the popular press late in the 19th century. Tibet in the popular imagination would also have received a boost through the oral accounts of returning soldiers after campaigning both in Tibet itself and on the frontier. Regimental histories provide a valuable source of information in this respect. The second issue relates to the power and influence of the Royal Geographical Society over the contours of Tibetan imaginings. From the middle of the 19th Century through to the middle years of the 20th Century the R.G.S. dominated the discourses concerned with exploration. I realize therefore that the term 'Western' imagination or 'British' imagination is imprecise.[95]

The one British traveller who did manage to reach Lhasa between 1800 and 1904, Manning in 1811, was ignored at the time and received little acknowledgement later. He was too eccentric to be taken seriously. Also, he did not write anything public about his experiences. Worst of all he insisted on going native and dressing in Chinese and Tibetan clothes.

Prejevalsky sneered at amateurs and virtually dismissed the French Lazarist priests, Huc and Gabet who reached Lhasa in 1846.[96] Mystics have always been viewed with suspicion and a recent author discounts Alexandra David-Neel's 'magical fantasy', Madam Blavatsky's 'thaumaturgical' accounts and those others who paint a picture of 'chimerical marvels'; he favours a down to earth, rational view, which he claims is 'nearer to the real Tibetans.'[97]

Younghusband, writing in 1937 of his remarkable solo journey as a young man in 1896 from Peking to India, commented that 'in those staid days youth received scant attention. Because such a journey was made by a young man it could not be of much importance. Only seasoned explorers of the Stanley type could make a journey of any value'.[98] (He was about 35 at the time — hardly a youth by today's standards).

The Underworld of Tibetan Travel

Prior to the first World War, there was never any suggestion that Tibet as a cultural entity was in danger. Even the fears of Russian or, more plausibly, of Chinese advances into Tibet were viewed as political threats to India and not as cultural threats to Tibet.

Tibet was a secure and unquestioned *place* in Western imaginings. Consequently the West felt free to express ambivalence about many aspects of Tibet. The mountains and deserts were not always viewed as sublime as I have discussed above, but were also considered to be hellish, even ugly.[99]

The British encountered in Tibet an almost Kafkaesque parody of their own formidable imperial bureaucracy. The Tibetan government seemed to have all the negative characteristics of bureaucracy — indescribably slow to operate, an unwillingness to make big decisions at regional level, an obscurity so profound that ignorance and timidity seemed to be the essential qualifications for belonging to it. There seemed to be an underworld of vicious punishments for those who either disobeyed rigid orders or who inadvertently showed individual initiative. Corruption seemed rampant and a total ignorance of international diplomacy existed. Younghusband could not decide whether the bureaucrats were evil or just stupid. In the British imagination, the imperial administration was one of the wonders of the World. It had its faults, to which Younghusband again alludes, but by comparison with the sinister machinations of Tibet it was exemplary.[100] It was almost as if Britain was faced with the shadow of its own bureaucratic imagination.

Lamas and priests in their role as 'church' or political administrators were also generally viewed with distaste. Their position seemed dictatorial, almost totalitarian in its fusion of blatant power and its absolute ideological and spiritual control.[101] To an era in which individual democratic freedom was increasingly becoming an exemplary idea, if not a practice, Tibetan lamaistic power was anathema. Many commentators were quick to distinguish between these bureaucratic monks and the ordinary people, for whom the feelings tended to be warm. A distinction was also made between the lamaistic organization and the religion of Buddhism itself.[102]

The general attitude towards Buddhism during this period varied enormously. Many, like Prejevalsky detested it.[103] For him it was a 'pretext to idleness, a religion that sapped vitality and hindered progress.' 'The mindless discipline, the untidiness and the filth of the lamas' community', was what he noticed, not the high level of scholarship achieved by a small elite. Hodgson, Younghusband and Waddell had respect for Buddhism but commented negatively on both the Tibetan version and the superstition of the general populace.[104] However, Bogle, Turner, Younghusband and Mazuchelli, for example, were all touched by some moments of sublime admiration for the spirituality of the Tibetans.[105]

Explorers and the like probably represented the extreme vanguard of an extroverted, aggressive, expansionist culture which valued above all else involvement in the world, individuality, earnestness, and will. To this cultural ideal of 'manliness', the extreme introversion and world denial of hermits, recluses, siddhas and lamas was seen as a form of madness. This total withdrawal from the world by ascetics was even discussed in the very first British account of Tibet, by Turner in 1800.[106] The idea of someone voluntarily walling themselves up in a cave for life exceeded the extroverted imagination of the British travellers. It was a strange encounter as a culture which valued extroversion met a culture exactly its opposite — one for whom heroes were solitary recluses.

Prior to the first World War we also encounter an ambivalence towards East-West relations. For a number of travellers, such as Prejevalsky, the West was rapidly becoming degenerate and the solitudes of Central Asia offered an escape.[107] But he certainly did not imagine the East as somehow saving the West in a spiritual sense. Hodgeson even writes of the role of the West in regenerating a sick and faded, but nevertheless ancient civilization such as India.[108]

From the 1920's onward a sense of doom appears on the horizon of travel accounts about Tibet and a profound shift occurred in the West's imaginative relationship to Tibet. Suddenly it seemed as if Tibet was in danger and needed protection. Marco Pallis' influential and popular work of the 1930's placed an almost desperate emphasis upon the undermining influence of Western things and ideas. He wrote:

'There is little room to turn; one ill-judged movement may cause a fall to the bottom. This is Tibet's danger ....'

This sense of danger to the ancient tradition of Tibet is a remarkable shift in the West's imaginings. Certainly the catastrophe of the war had something to do with it, but even more important were the Socialist revolutions in Russia and in China. Along with India these two countries made up the 'big three' of Tibet's international relations.

As the confidence in Tibet's future became eroded we find that the general attitude towards the culture loses its ambivalence. This gradual loss of ambivalence towards Tibetan culture by the West throughout the years of the 20th century bears a striking parallel to the transformation of Western imaginings on the Himalayan Mountains. As viewing the peaks became an unequivocal, sublime aesthetic experience, so the Tibetan culture became an examplary model of that ancient tradition now lost to the West.

By the 1950's the shift in imaginings on Tibet became even more pronounced. Even such poetic accounts as Maraini's, lack an ambivalent edge.[110] The proverbial dirt, filth and mess which looms so large in earlier accounts and which is tolerated or ignored in subsequent ones, almost becomes a virtue in some accounts of the 1950's.[111] We read little of the harsh forms of punishment or serfdom. The Kafkaesque theocratic government with its obscure larnaistic bureaucracy is actually considered as an exemplary organization. Andre Migot for example argued in 1955, that Tibet ranked as 'one of the best-governed countries in the world.'[112]

Even the Tibetan people became reified. In these subsequent accounts Tibet, the culture, the religion and even the people, rarely throw any shadows. Pallis calls Tibetans 'some of the happiest on the face of the earth.'[113] Matthiesson writing in the 1970's imbues *all* of his Sherpas (with their close relationship to Tibet), with a selflessness and with 'the wise calm of monks.' He reassures us that in his destination of Inner Dolpo, the people are of 'pure Tibetan stock.'[114] Generalizations about the Tibetans abound in most accounts of this period. There is a surfeit of happy, serene, laughing Tibetans. One almost longs for the infamous bandits which infested so much of Tibet to come galloping over the horizon.

From Pallis to Migot we are assured that 'there is no rivalry between the various sects of lamas', although Pallis a few sentences later *does* admit that occasionally there are broken skulls and blood is spilt. There seems to be an extraordinary attempt to squeeze the material into a constricting imaginative mould. Tibetans become exemplary creatures whereas in earlier accounts they were still complex and human. (Indeed for early travellers coming from central Asia the Tibetans were sometimes portrayed as being rather lazy, ineffectual, and weak as compared with the Mongolians.)[116] There is a sense of desperation about much imagining on Tibet in this post-war period. The dominant question was not how to protect traditional Tibet but rather how much time was left to it. The landscape of Tibet became a geography of hope and despair. In Matthiesson's case, for example, the higher he ascended in his ecstatic climb to the Tibetan frontier, the deeper he plunged into his dark memories of personal failure and death.[117]

I think it is significant that although the first report of the Yeti, the abominable snowman, by a European was by Hodgson in 1832 and the first sighting of apparent Yeti tracks was by Waddell in 1889, it was not until the 1930's that the Yeti story began to deeply affect the Western imagination. The previous lack of sightings or even of any real interest is curious given the popularity of the Himalayas with experienced big game hunters. Can we suppose that the Yeti, the primitive human ape, emerged in the 1930's to step into the shadow left vacant by the Tibetans who were becoming increasingly spiritualized in Western travel literature?[118]

The exile of the Tibetan tradition in the late 1950's was also our exile. As they descended from their mountain fastness, there were many Westerners who followed them into an exile from their fantasy landscape.

Tibet As A Sacred Site

There is scarcely room in this paper to discuss the place of Tibet and the Himalayas within the *overall* structure of the Western imagination. It has frequently been referred to as a utopia, a Shangri-la, a Lost Horizon. I have already touched upon its place in the imaginative theme of the West's spiritual regeneration by the East. I have also mentioned the place of Tibet as a nascent anima image in the West's discovery of the unconscious.

Hodgson wrote in 1849:
> 'I had been for several years a traveller in the Himalayas, before I could get rid of that tyranny of the senses which so strongly impresses all beholders of this stupendous scenery with the conviction that the mighty maze is quite without a plan.'[119]

Tibet and the Himalayas were a part of this search for an imaginative *coherence*, a plan. Max Muller subsequently praised Hodgson for producing a 'rational grammar' of the mountain chaos.[120] Hodgson applied the same energy to classifying the 'babel' of the hill tribes and fitting them into a scheme of cultural evolution. The age seemed obsessed with 'blank spots' on the map, with finding 'missing links' in terms of geography, zoology, ethnology, religions and so on.[121] They wanted a world in which everything fitted and had its place. Those images of mapping, of missing links, of blank spots, dominated the imagination of the era and the 'plan' seemed to be constantly in danger of being overwhelmed by the plenitude of new discoveries.

Tibet was also a vital link in the West's imaginative connection with memoria, with the past, with the ancients. It provided continuity with archaic tradition. It was a part of the gothic and mediaeval fantasy of the 19th century.[122] Time and again Tibetan architecture, culture and religion are called mediaeval. Never is such an historic association used in a negative sense but always with a nostalgia or longing. Tibet was the museum of a fantasized past.

Conclusion: A Poetics of Religious Studies

Maraini was a photographer with one of Professor Tucci's post-war expeditions. Whilst in Gantok in Sikkim the party was invited to dinner by the Maharajah. Maraini comments on the latter:[123]

> 'I could not take my eyes off him as he tackled his peas; it was an exquisite, microscopic struggle; something between a game of chess and the infinite pains of the miniaturist; something between a secret rite and a piece of court ceremonial. But now the struggle was over. The last pea, defeated and impaled on the fork, was raised to the royal lips, which opened delicately to receive it, as if about to give, or receive a kiss.'

So often the 'place' of Tibet is conceived in terms of *view*, of the sweeping vistas of countryside. The grandeur, the vast scale, the uncanny light and geological formations understandably dominate most accounts. But Maraini is also describing a Tibetan landscape. The title of his book *Secret Tibet*, refers to the small everydayness of Tibet which frequently eludes traveller's attention and hence remains 'secret'. Maraini's Tibet is a place which is no more and no less valid than any other — Hedin's heroic landscapes, Younghusband's enthusiastic blend of politics and mysticism, or David-Neel's Tibet of sublime mysteries and dark occult undertones. These other Tibets are, of course, more obvious and striking and perhaps Maraini would not have considered the pea episode worthy of attention if he had been the first to scale the Himalayas. But I like to think that he would have carried news of this 'discovery' back to the West irrespectively.

The theme of this conference is 'Are religious studies on the right track?' I am making a case for an imaginative or poetic track in religious studies. Such a track is one which sees the fantasy in all tracks, even its own. I am suggesting an imaginative, a poetic, archeology. The poetic track would seek not to gather the poetry of Tibet, but to study Tibet poetically. The poetic eye comes from the sideways glance which draws into the sphere of religious studies things which otherwise may be by-passed, things such as money, eating habits and landscapes. Certainly, the 'place' of a religion deserves our attention. The operating table which supports Western discourses about Tibetan Buddhism is as much to be found in odd corners, as in debates about its dogma and philosophy. I like to think that Prejevalsky's hand bottled strawberry jam for the Dalai Lama that he never met, the Pundit's maps hidden inside their prayer wheels, Younghusband's mystical experience outside of Lhasa, and Maraini's sideways glance at the Maharaja of Sikkhim eating peas, all have their place in religious studies and in the search for the West's relationship to Tibetan Buddhism.

References

1. For details and overviews of the early period of Western contact with Tibet see, G. Woodcock, *Into Tibet* (The Early British Explorers) London: Faber & Faber, 1971; F. de Filippi, *An Account of Tibet:* (The Travels of Ippolito Desideri of Pistoia S.J. 1712-1727), London: 1937.
   J. MacGregor, *Tibet — A Chronicle of Exploration*, London: R.K.P. 1970; C. Markham, *Narratives of the Mission of George Bogle to Tibet and of the Journey of Thomas Manning to Lhasa*, London: Trubner, 1879; I. De Rachewiltz, *Papal Envoys to the Great Khans*, London: Faber & Faber, 1971; G. Sandberg, *The Exploration of Tibet* (1904), Delhi: Cosmo Publications, 1973.
2. N. Prejevalski, *The Tangut Country and the Solitudes of Northern Tibet*, London: Sampson Low, Marston, Searle & Rivington, 1876; D. Rayfield, *The Dream of Lhasa*, London: Paul Elek, 1976.
3. Markham, op. cit.; Woodcock, op. cit.
4. M. Huc, *Travels in Tartary, Tibet and China 1844-5-6*, London: Kegan Paul, 1850.
5. Rayfield, op. cit. p. 115.
6. C. Allen, *A Mountain in Tibet*, London: Andre Deutsch, 1982, p. 194; S. Hedin, *My Life as an Explorer*, London: Cassell, 1926.

7. Allen, ibid, p. 199; L. Miller, *On Top of the World*, (Five Women Explorers in Tibet), London: Paddington Press, 1976, p. 57, 59, 63.
8. e.g. Allen, op. cit. p. 81.
9. Miller, op. cit.; A. David-Neel, *My Journey to Lhasa*, London: Heinemann, 1927.
10. see, Allen, op. cit. & G. Heaney, 'Rennell & The Surveyors of India', *Geographical Journal*, vol. 134, part 3, Sept. 1968.
11. F. Younghusband, *India and Tibet*, London: John Murray, 1910; P. Fleming, *Bayonets to Lhasa*, London: Hart-Davis, 1961; P. Mehra, *The Younghusband Expedition*, London: Asia Publishing, 1968.
12. It has been a common mistake by Westerners to reduce all Tibetan religious life to Buddhism. But Buddhism co-existed with Bon-po and with popular folk religions. See R. Stein, *Tibetan Civilization*, Stanford: Stanford University Press, 1972.
13. I am not touching uon the complex issue of tourism in this paper.
14. F. Capra, *The Tao of Physics*, London: Wildwood Home, 1975; A. Elkin, *Aboriginal Men of High Degree*, Queensland; University of Queensland Press, 1980, pp. 57-66; Anderson, *Open Secrets*. Harmondsworth: Penguin, 1980 pp. 5, 14-15, 19, 21, 118.
15. C. G. Jung was one of the first to point to this underlying psycho-cultural ground, with his warnings directed to Westerners unreflectively adopting Eastern ideas and practices. See for example his *Collected Works Vol. II*, London: Routledge & Kegan Paul, 1963. J. Campbell attempted an identification of specific mythological 'signatures' of the East and the West in *Masks of God* (Vols. 2 & 3), London: Souvenir Press, 1974. Henri Baudet in his study *Paradise on Earth*, (New Haven: Yale University Press, 1965) sketched in a few masterful strokes the history of European images of non-European peoples and countries. H. de Lubac documented the history of the West's specific encounter with Buddhism in *La Recontre du Bouddhisme et de l'Occident*, Paris: 1952. Most recently E. Said's *Orientalism* (New York: Vintage Books, 1979) has used the ideas of M. Foucault to attempt an analysis of the phenomenon of Orientalism in the Western imagination. The idea of 'operating table' comes from M. Foucault (*The Order of Things*, London: Tavistock, 1970).
16. M. Heidegger, *Poetry Language Thought*, New York: Harper & Row, 1975.
17. E. Casey, 'Getting Placed', *Spring 1982*, Dallas: Spring Publications, 1982, p. 17. The contemporary geographer Yi-Fu Tuan has coined the term 'topophilia' to describe the intense relationship between people and landscape. (Topophilla in *Man, Space and Environment*, ed. P. English & R. Mayfield, New York: O.U.P., 1972) See also G. Bachalard, *The Poetics of Space*, Boston: Beacon Press, 1969.
18. E. Relph, *Place and Placelessness*, London: Pion, 1976; M. Samuels, 'Existentialism and Human Geography', in *Humanistic Geography* ed. D. Ley & M. Samuels, London: Croom Helm, 1978; C. G. Jung, *Collected Works Vol. 16*, 'Mind and Earth', London: R.K.P., 1963.
19. e.g. M. Eliade, *The Sacred and the Profane*, New York: Harcourt, Brace & World, 1959; P. Fickler, 'Fundamental Questions in the Geography of Religions' in *Readings in Cultural Geography*, ed. P. Wagner & M. Mikesell, Chicago: University of Chicago Press, 1962; Yi-Fu Tuan 'Sacred Space', in *Dimensions of Human Geography*, ed. K. Butzer, Chicago: The University of Chicago Press, 1978. Of course not all imaginative space is *sacred* space.
20. Yi-Fu Tuan, ibid, p. 84-92.
21. M. Foucault draws attention to the importance of the secularization of the confessional style in *The History of Sexuality*, New York: Vintage Books, 1980.
22. V. Turner, 'The Center Out There: Pilgrim's Goal', *History of Religions*, Vol. 12, No. 3, Feb. 1973, p. 213.
23. e.g. E. Isaac, 'Religious Geography and the Geography of Religion' University of Colorado Studies, Series in Earth Sciences, No. 3, *Man and the Earth*, Boulder, 1965; P. Deffontaines, 'The Religious Factor in Human Geography', *Diogenes*, No. 2, Spring 1953; I. Barbour (ed.) *Earth Might Be Fair* (Reflections on Ethics, Religion and Ecology), New Jersey: Prentice-Hall, 1972.
24. see, D. Sopher, 'Geography and Religions', *Progress in Human Geography*, Vol. 5, No. 1, 1981 for references to this debate.
25. D. Cosgrove, 'John Ruskin and the Geographical Imagination', *The Geographical Review*, Vol. 69, No. 1, Jan. 1979, p. 44-46, 54.
26. Younghusband, *India and Tibet*, op. cit., pp. 326-7.
27. E. Gilbert, *British Pioneers in Geography*, Newton Abbot: David & Charles, 1972, pp. 227-256.
28. L. Graber, *Wilderness as Sacred Space*, Washington, D.C.: Association of American Geographers, 1976.
29. e.g. B. Gordon, 'Sacred Directions, Orientation and the Top of the Map', *History of Religions*, Vol. 10, No. 3, Feb. 1971.
30. Said, op. cit., p. 216.
31. e.g. Allen, op. cit. p. 15; Rayfield, op. cit. p. 50; F. Younghusband, *The Heart of a Continent* (1896), London: John Murray, 1937, pp. xi-xii.
32. Huston-Smith, *Requiem for a Faith*, 1974, A Hardey Production.
33. C. Humphreys, *Buddhism*, Harmondsworth: Penguin, 1974, p. 189, (my italics).
34. E. Bell. *The Religion of Tibet*, Oxford: O.U.P., 1931.
35. Allen, op. cit. p. 160 and Rayfield, op. cit. pp. 26-29, 43 both situate exploration within British and Russian imperialism respectively.
36. W. Hunter, *Life of Brian Houghton Hodgson*, London: John Murray, 1896, pp. 306-7.
37. e.g. Rayfield, op. cit. p. 53.
38. e.g. Hunter, op. cit., Allen, op. cit. p. 187 and Rayfield, ibid, pp. 15, 41, 85 document examples of public acclaim given to scholars and explorers of Tibet and the Himalayas.
39. e.g. Eliade op. cit. pp. 38, 39.

40. Hence the Mongolian custom of building cairns or 'obos' on mountain passes.
41. M. Nicolson, *Mountain Gloom and Mountain Glory*, Ithaca: Cornell University Press, 1959.
42. Allen, op. cit. pp. 98-9.
43. Miller, op. cit. pp. 17, 33.
44. e.g. Younghusband, *The Heart of a Continent*, op. cit. pp. 176-7, 180.
45. e.g. ibid, p. 215.
46. F. Maraini, *Secret Tibet*, London: Hutchinson, 1952, p. 42.
47. P. Matthiesson, *The Snow Leopard*, London: Picador, 1980, p. 16, J. Lester, 'Wrestling with the Self on Mount Everest,' *Journal of Humanistic Psychology*, Vol. 23, No. 2, Spring, 1983.
48. Matthiesson, ibid, pp. 26, 121-2.
49. A. Heim & Gansser, *The Throne of the Gods*, New York: MacMillan, 1939; M. Pallis, *Peaks and Lamas*, (1939), London: Cassell, 1946; N. Roerich, *Himalayas — Abode of Light*, New York: David Marlowe, 1947.
50. Maraini, op. cit., p. 46.
51. Matthiesson, op. cit. pp. 16, 21.
52. *Ibid.* pp. 29, 271.
53. e.g. Allen, op. cit. p. 64; A. Greenberger, *The British Image of India*, London: O.U.P., 1969, p. 133.
54. e.g. Pallis, op. cit. pp. 33-4, 99. For example the inward sloping walls of Tibetan architecture have consistently provoked admiration from male Westerner travellers. Maraini perhaps spoke for many when he wrote in 1952 that these sloping walls suggest 'a man standing with courageous and noble architecture...'
 Byron, op. cit. pp. 259, 273;
 Pallis, op. cit. p. 260;
 Maraini, op. cit. p. 191.
55. e.g. Matthiesson, op. cit., pp. 40-41.
56. e.g. Maraini, op. cit., p. 182.
57. C. Ryan, *H. P. Blavatsky and the Theosophical Movement*, Pasadena: Theosophical University Press, 1975.
58. Rayfield, op. cit. p. 111.
59. D. Duff, *On the World's Roof*, London: Abbey Rewards, (1950?); The connection between the theosophical fantasy of Himalayan Masters and the fantasy of Nazism has been made by L. Pauwels and J. Bergier 'Theosophy and Nazism', in *On the Margin of the Visible* ed. E. Tiryakian, New York: Wiley, 1974.
60. e.g. see, R. Fields, *How the Swans come to the Lake*. (A Narrative History of Buddhism in America), Boulder: Shambhala, 1981 pp. 147, 159; Younghusband, *Heart of a Continent*, op. cit. p. 229; T. Roszak, *Unfinished Animal*, New York: Harper & Row, 1977, pp. 115-151. See also J. Hillman 'Peaks and Vales' (in *On the Way to Self-Knowledge*, ed. J. Needleman & D. Lewis, New York: Knopf, 1976) for a succinct discussion of the associated imagery of peaks and spirituality.
61. Matthiesson, op. cit. p. 37.
62. Allen, op. cit.
63. e.g. see, Allen, ibid, pp. 15, 17, 68, 87, 106-7, 129, for a discussion of the intense efforts to find the source of Asian rivers in Tibet.
64. Pallis, op. cit. p. 66-7 discusses Csoma de Koros' quest; see also T. Duka, *The Life and Works of Alexander Csoma de Koros 1819-1849*, London: Trubner, 1885.
65. e.g. Hunter, op. cit. pp. 284-5; V. Childe, *The Aryans*. (A study of Indo-European Origins), London: Kegan Paul, Trench, Trubner & Co., 1926, pp. 94-137.
66. e.g. E. Chandler *The Unveiling of Lhasa*, London: Edward Arnold, 1905, p. 124; & G. Seaver, *Francis Younghusband*, London: John Murray, 1952, p. 24.
67. Hunter, op. cit., pp. 81, 284-5, 297.
68. e.g. W. Anderson, *Open Secrets*, Harmondsworth: Penguin, 1980, pp. 5, 274, 279, 286-7, 305, 308; Hunter, op. cit. pp. 262-5; Pallis, op. cit. pp. 395-8; Huston-Smith in his film, *Requiem for a Faith*; F. Hitching, *The World Atlas of Mysteries*, London: Pan, 1978, p. 240.
69. Huston-Smith, ibid; p. 5; Maraini, op. cit., pp. 75, 111; Fields, op. cit., pp. 98, 274, 286-7, 305, C. Wilson, *The Occult*, New York: Vintage Books, 1973, p. 172; L. Govinda, *The Way of the White Clouds*, London: Hutchinson, 1969, p. 13; Humphreys, op. cit., considers that Tibetan Buddhism is a mixture of the best *and* the worst in Buddhism.
70. Rayfield, op. cit., p. 116.
71. Casey, op. cit. p. 18; Maraini, op. cit. p. 183.
72. G. Curzon, *Frontiers*, (Romanes Lecture), Oxford: Clarendon Press, 1908, pp. 55-57.
73. *Ibid.*, p. 5.
74. *Ibid.*, p. 18.
75. e.g. Rayfield, op. cit. pp. 74-5, 80.
76. Eliade, op. cit. p. 31.
77. e.g. M. Goldstein complains of this 'chronic religious indigestion,' in his 'serfdom and mobility', *Journal of Asian Studies*, Vol. 30, 1970-71.
78. Hillman, op. cit. suggests that a certain kind of spirituality wants to be free of the limitations of time and place, and constantly seeks to transcend history. See also his discussions in *Puer Papers* ed. J. Hillman, Dallas: Spring Publications, 1979.
79. Eliade, op. cit., pp. 25-26.
80. G. Tucci, *Tibet*, London: Elek Books, 1967, p. 15.
81. See also Pallis, op. cit. p. 138 and the comments of Moorcroft and Hearsey quoted in Allen, op. cit. p. 85.
82. R. Byron, *First Russia: Then Tibet*, London: MacMillan, 1933; also see P. Millington, *To Lhasa At Last*, London: Smith, Elder & Co., 1905, pp. 33, 48-50, 118-119.

83. The direction from which Tibet was approached seemed to play a distinctive part in the overall imaginative process. For example to approach Tibet from India was to encounter a tremendous climatic, geographic, ethnographic and cultural contrast. But this was not the case when coming from the North. Mongolian culture, religion, climate and so forth do not form an abrupt discontinuity with Tibet. For Prejevalsky, Central Asia was almost an extension of the rapidly expanding and recently colonized regions of Russian Siberia. As he points out, to a Russian from Siberia, the intense cold of Tibet should be quite bareable. The routes from China would similarly have their imaginative tone and so on.
84. Pallis, op. cit. p. 138.
85. For a full discussion of the anima image see J. Hillman 'anima I' Spring 1973 & 'Anima II', Spring 1974. Dallas: Spring Publications.
86. P. Fussell, Abroad, New York: O.U.P., 1980, p. 92.
87. T. Holdich, Tibet the Mysterious, London: Alston Rivers, 1906; H. Landor, In the Forbidden Land, London: Heinemann, 1898; E. Maillart, Forbidden Journey, London: Heinemann, 1937; W. McGovern, To Lhasa in Disguise, London: Butterworth, 1924; A. de Riencourt, Lost World: Tibet, Key to Asia, London: Gollanz, 1950; G. Tucci & E. Ghersi, Secrets of Tibet, London: Blackie, 1935; L. Waddell, Lhasa and Its Mysteries, London: Murray, 1905.
88. Maraini, op. cit. p. 183.
89. Q. in Allen, op. cit., p. 201.
90. Ibid., p. 202.
91. E. Chandler, op. cit.
92. e.g. Prejevalsky in Rayfield, op. cit. & Hedin in Allen, op. cit.
93. see, D. Middleton, 'Some Victorian Lady Travellers' Geographical Journal Vol. 139, Part 1, Feb. 1973, in which she discusses the place of women travellers in the Royal Geographical Society; also Miller, op. cit. on 5 women explorers in Tibet; A. Blum in her account of the first all women's expedition to climb Annapurna gives some details of discrimination against women climbers and explorers (Annapurna: A Woman's Place, London: Granada, 1980). For an account of the first all woman expedition to the Himalayas, see M. Jackson & E. Stark, Tents in the Clouds, London: Travel Book Club, 1957.
94. see Allen op. cit. for a discussion of the pundits.
95. The Royal Geographical Society provided funding, information, a scholarly outlet, organization and above all, class and contacts.
96. Rayfield, op. cit. p. 131.
97. Woodcock, op. cit. pp. 21-2.
98. Younghusband, Heart of A Continent, op. cit., p. xi.
99. For example a sensational and grim account of Tibet such as that given by H. Savage Landor in 1898 would hardly be credible today except perhaps from inside China (A. Savage Landor, In the Forbidden Land, London: Heinemann, 1898).
100. see Younghusband, India and Tibet, op. cit. for a continual series of complaints about Tibetan bureaucracy. Hunter op. cit., writing in 1896 makes it quite clear that the British Indian bureaucracy is considered to be an examplary institution (p. 18); see also Chandler op. cit. p. 207.
101. e.g. Hunter ibid, p. 252 and the many comments in Younghusband, India and Tibet, op. cit.; Kawaguchi, op. cit. p. 422; Seaver, op. cit.; Chandler, op. cit.; where lamas are referred to as 'frauds' as 'incarnations of vice and corruption' and where their power is called, 'spiritual terrorism'.
102. e.g. Rayfield, op. cit. p. 138; Chandler, op. cit. p. 146.
103. Rayfield, ibid. pp. 48-9, 162.
104. e.g. Hunter, op. cit. pp. 251-4; Chandler, op. cit. p. 106.
105. e.g. Miller, op. cit. p. 43 on Mazuchelli.
106. S. Turner, An Account of an embassy to the Court of the Teshoo Lama in Tibet, London: 1806, pp. 171-2.
107. e.g. Rayfield, op. cit. pp. 49-50, 187.
108. e.g. Hunter, op. cit. p. 320.
109. Pallis, op. cit. pp. 380-1, 418, 422-3.
110. e.g. Maraini, op. cit. pp. 50-2.
111. e.g. Pallis, op. cit. pp. 331-2.
112. A. Migot, Tibetan Marches, London: Rupert Hart-Davis, 1960, p. 104.
113. Pallis, op. cit. pp. 255, 257-8, 230.
114. Matthiesson, op. cit. pp. 10, 177; Tucci, op. cit. p. 15.
115. Migot, op. cit. p. 104; Pallis, op. cit. pp. 257-8.
116. e.g. N. Roerich, Altai-Himalaya, London: Jarrolds, 1929; Rayfield, op. cit.; F. Ossendowski, Beasts, Men and Gods, Sydney: Cornstalk Publishing, 1926.
117. Matthieson, op. cit.
118. J. Napier, Big Foot, London: Abacus, 1976.
119. Q. in Hunter, op. cit. p. 286.
120. Ibid., p. 287.
121. see Allen, op. cit. pp. 68, 140-145, 149 for some details of the quest to find 'missing links', to 'close gaps' and to fill in 'blank spots' on the map; also see Hunter op. cit. p. 296 and Rayfield op. cit. pp. 89, 127 for further examples.
122. e.g. Maraini, op. cit. pp. 147-8 on the mediaeval comparison. See D. Lowenthal 'Past Time, Present Place: Landscape and Memory'. The Geographical Review, Vol. LXV, No. 1, January, 1975, for a discussion of place and memory.
123. Maraini, ibid. p. 47.

KLAUS KLOSTERMAIER

THE BODY OF GOD
Cosmos — Avatara — Image

Preliminary Remarks

I wish to begin my lecture by expressing my gratitude to the Charles Strong Memorial Foundation and its trustees who provided me with the opportunity to visit a number of universities and other educational institutions in Australia and New Zealand.

The Charles Strong Memorial Trust, established for the sympathetic study of world-religions, asked me to prepare a public lecture on a central theme of Hinduism, of interest also to a wider circle of non-Indianists. I do not have to enlarge on the problematics of all definitions of Hinduism and on the difficulty of selecting a topic representative of *the* Hindu tradition. I have chosen the theme THE BODY OF GOD. I believe it is central to the Hindu tradition. It has become the master-analogy especially of the Vaisnava tradition, theologically elaborated by the Śrīvaisnava *ācāryas*, amongst whom Rāmānuja is the greatest. I am not claiming that Vaisnavism is identical with the whole of Hinduism or that Rāmānuja's theology is the only Hindu-system worth looking into. I do believe, however, that Vaisnavism is an expression of main-stream Hindu tradition, with roots as ancient as that of any other, that it does incorporate much of what is common to traditional Hinduism, and that Rāmānuja represents a type of Hindu theology which in its major presuppositions would be more widely accepted by more Hindus than any other. Over and above, the body-of-God analogy could well provide the framework for a contemporary holistic understanding of the world and a meeting-ground for science and religion.

Introduction

It is a telling comment on the impoverishment of human imagination by a reduction of our understanding of the universe to an abstract mathematical schematism that Steven Weinberg, one of the leading physicists of our age, has to conclude an otherwise admirably lucid exposition of the present state of astrophysics and scientific cosmology by saying:

"The more the universe seems comprehensible,
the more it also seems pointless."[1]

Can we be so sure of our late 20th century way of seeing things that we can squarely accuse the universe as a whole of being pointless? Or could it be that the chosen scientific methodology does not allow us to see its point? Obviously the universe as a whole is not useful in the Baconian sense nor can its meaning be discovered through telescopes and cyclotrons. If the universe has a meaning as a whole it must be different from both utilitarian-pragmatic and abstract-mathematical points of view.

It may appear as a fairly eccentric enterprise to counter the opinion of a representative of the most advanced contemporary science by a reference to a possibly pre-historic Indian myth. If, however, we understand with Kim Malville, a widely respected contemporary astrophysicist, our science as our contemporary mythology (in the sense in which Plato understood myth) realizing that all its statements are metaphorical (and not representative of reality as such) we may have a common point after all.

I.

Someone who is exposed for the first time to the traditional Hindu concept of the universe as the Body of God must find it very strange indeed. Not only does it strike one as mythological and therefore 'unreal' in terms of a scientific description of the universe but also religiously inappropriate and incompatible with Biblical notions of God. However, untold generations of Hindus have found meaning and comfort in such an understanding of the world and some great thinkers in this tradition have developed it into a coherent world-view.

The Ṛg-Veda, the most ancient document of Hindu religion, refers to the *puruṣa*, the primeval cosmic being, as the source and origin not only of the physical universe but also of religion and the social order. Quite clearly everything in this world was perceived as bodily related to the divine source: the Body of God.

"The moon was born from his spirit, from his eye was born the sun ... from his navel arose the sky and from his head originated the heaven ..."[2]

So evident must have been this conception of the universe as the Body of God that based on it a convincing case could be made for the overriding importance of the institutional sacrifice and the division of society into the four varnas.

The *Brāhmaṇas* elaborated this vision and invested it with rich symbolism: the sacrifice as the symbolic re-enactment of the creation of the world reflects the Body of God in its varied detail. The Upaniṣads greatly exploited this idea and developed the parallelism of macrocosm-microcosm into a path of ultimate liberation. If the visible world is the body of the Supreme Spirit, the Supreme Spirit must be immanent in whatever there is:

It is

"That which is the hearing of the ear, the thought of the mind, the voice of speech, as also the breathing of the breath and the sight of the eye ..."[3]

Seeming paradox alone is able to capture the meaning of it:

"Heavenly, formless is the cosmic being: He is without and within, unborn, breathless, mindless, pure ... From him is produced breath, mind and all the senses, Space, wind, light, water, and earth, the supporter of all. Fire is his head, his eyes the moon and sun, the regions of space his ears, his voice the revealed Vedas, wind his breath; his heart the whole world ..."[4]

In a further systematic development of this idea, reminiscent of Pythagorean correspondences (especially striking is the use of the Pentad as basic pattern) the Taittirīya Upaniṣad classifies all entities in the material world and in the human individual in such a manner as to suggest a complete mirroring of the Body of God in the human body. Thus, whatever could be asserted of the World Soul can be said to apply to one's own soul too:

".. this Self of mine within the heart is smaller than a grain of rice, or a barley-corn, or a mustard-seed ... this self of mine within the heart is greater than the earth, greater than the atmosphere, greater than the sky, greater than these worlds ... containing all works, containing all desires ... encompassing this whole world ... this is the Self of mine within the heart, this is Brahman. Into him I shall enter on departing thence ..."[5]

While guided by a conception of the spirit-soul as reality proper, and engaged in the attempt to extricate this spirit-soul from its entrapments, the Upanisads know that the spirit-soul is intertwined with the visible universe, its body: In a final analysis all the worlds are "woven, warp and woof ... of the worlds of Brahman ... about which further questions cannot be asked."[6]

"He who, dwelling in all things, yet is other than all things, whom all things do not know, whose body all things are, who controls all things from within — He is your Self, the Inner Controller, the Immortal ... He is the unseen Seer, the unheard Hearer, the unthought Thinker, the ununderstood Understander. Other than He there is no seer. Other than He there is no Hearer. Other than He there is no thinker. Other than He there is no understander. He is your Self, the Inner Controller, the Immortal."[7]

These texts can easily be multiplied: they clearly evoke the image of the universe as the body of God and quite unequivocally identify the meaning of the universe with its soul. Hearing without a hearer is pointless; it is the interiority of the universe which provides its "point", not the relative proportion of one of its parts as compared with another.

For the Upaniṣads the ultimate reality, which is invisible, intangible, ineffable is present and accessible in the visible, tangible, effable as salt dissolved in a measure of water is present in it.

The Spirit-soul, although accessible only to those who have undergone a rigorous disciplining of mind and body, is nevertheless as much of the substance of the universe as matter is, which is apparently accessible to all.

The Bhagavadgītā restates and summarises a great deal of the Upaniṣadic teaching. It presupposes as well known the idea that the deity dwells in the universe as the soul dwells in the body. Over and above the expression of this by now traditional insight it offers in its famous eleventh chapter the grandiose vision of the viśvarūpa of Krsna-Visnu. Arjuna has received the oral instruction of Kṛṣṇa concerning his immanence-cum-transcendence and he has mentally understood it. What he now desires is to see with his own eyes the divinie form of the Cosmos-Creator. Kṛṣṇa promises that he would "see here today the whole universe summed up in [his] body."[8]

Seeing the divine form, and by implication seeing the world as God's body, requires a "supernatural eye": the "ordinary" eye cannot truly see reality, it grasps only the surface. With this "supernatural vision", a gift of the very same Deity whom he beholds, Arjuna can see the supreme and divine form of God exhibiting itself as "the whole universe, with its manifold divisions gathered together in one, in the body of the God of Gods".

In a powerful hymn Arjuna describes the body of God which evokes feelings of awe and of terror in him. Like the splendor of a thousand suns he shines forth — he, who is time, world-destroying. Arjuna praises him as "... the one who pervades the entire universe ... ". Arjuna is shaking with fear — he cannot stand to see the true nature of the God whose body is the universe.[9]

For his sake Kṛṣṇa assumes again the guise of the human being. What the Gītā adds to the Vedic-Vedāntic image of the body of God is an illumination of the meaning of history:

the body of God is not merely a static presence and unchanging support for physical existence, it is also a historic agent. History too is an aspect of the body of God — the successive manifestation of the concrete deity. This haunting vision of Viṣṇu viśvarūpa has influenced a great deal of Hindu theology through the ages.[10] It is a statement about the nature of the world as much as about the nature of God; it explains the importance of worshipping the material image of God through a variety of material substances and it lays out nature and history as ways to God.

Visions of the deity must have stood at the very beginning of Vaiṣṇavism as an organized religion — to obtain sakṣātkāra, a true vision of the Lord has remained the goal of Vaiṣṇava piety. Many an ecstatic and detailed description of God's body has flowed from such experiences.[11]

In our time there are many as yet, who claim to have had such visions of Kṛṣṇa and the very identity of their vision with the pictorial traditional representations is for them confirmation of the truth of the experience.

Hindu theologians, while commenting on texts like the one from the Bhagavadgītā, referred to above, have developed a systematic philosophy of the body of God. Thus Rāmānuja, writes in his commentary on the Bhagavadgītā:

"God has two prakṛtis: a lower and a higher one. The former is constituted by the physical world, the latter by the souls of living beings. All spiritual and non-spiritual things, whether effects or causes, constitute God's body and depend on God who is their soul."[12]

Rāmānuja is fond of the Upanisadic image, where the creation of the world is compared to the activity of the spider, who emits from his body the thread which he uses to build his net and then re-absorbs it. The universe, then, is God's body also in the sense that it owes its existence — materially as well as causally — entirely to Him.

"These entities ... depend on God, whose body they constitute. God himself, however, does not depend on them."[13]

Rāmānuja wishes to make it clear that the analogy between the relationship of the human body and the human soul cannot be pushed too far without distorting the meaning of the world as body of God.

"The relation of God to his body is not the same as that of the individual souls to their bodies. With the latter the bodies, though depending on the souls, serve some purpose for the sustenance of the souls within them. To God his body serves no purpose at all: it serves to nothing but his sport."[14]

In addition to this twofold nature, which forms the body of God, God himself has his own supernatural body, constituted by 'auspicious qualities peculiar to Him' on account of which the qualities of material nature (viz. sattvas, rajas, tamas) do not affect him.[15] Thus it can be explained that in spite of his eternity and his omni-presence, he is not known to the world,

"for the world is perplexed by the entities consisting of (material) qualities (guṇas), however small and transient they may be, which are the material objects to be experienced by means of body and senses in accordance with their previous karman".[16]

The paradox of men not knowing a God whose very body they constitute and who is their creator and their support is explained by Rāmānuja with a reference to

"God's māyā, which consists of guṇas and which, being created by the sporting god, [which] is difficult for anyone to know. This absolutely real māyā causes the proper form of God to be obscured and one's own being to be thought of as the only fit object of experience. So being perplexed by God's *māyā* the whole world is ignorant of God whose real being is boundless bliss. Only those who resort to God relinquish *māyā* and worship Him alone."[17]

Only those persons, who have this true knowledge of God can perceive the world as God's body, ensouled by brahman; all others perceive the world as a multitude of independent objects in a fragmented and fragmentary vision.

Rāmānuja is not propounding a new doctrine: he re-articulates age-old popular beliefs. He builds up his case with reference to Vedas, Smṛtis, Śāstras and Purāṇas. His frequent references to purāṇic literature demonstrate his conscious linking up with tradition and his affirmation of this. The Viṣṇu-purāṇa, accepted by Rāmānuja as well as by most other Vaiṣṇavas as revealed scripture, contains a beautiful hymn incorporating the very same ideas.

"Homage to you, O lotus-eyed, homage to you, O Supreme Being! Homage to you, the soul of all worlds ... Homage to you who created the universe as Brāhma, who supports it as Viṣṇu and who destroys it as Rudra at the end of times ... Of devas and raksas, ... men and beasts ... earth, water, fire, ether and air, ... sound and touch ... intellect and self, time and the qualities of primeval matter, you are the underlying reality. You are the universe, O changeless one! Knowledge and ignorance, truth and untruth, poison as well as nectar you are. ... The great universe before us is your mighty form, a smaller form of yours in this world of ours. Still smaller forms of yours are the different kinds of beings and what is called their inner self is an exceedingly subtle form of yours. Homage without end to that Bhagavān Vasudeva, whom no one transcends but who transcends all."[18]

The Bhāgavata-purāṇa, again accepted as scripture by a great many Hindus — and today perhaps the most widely read of the Purāṇas — contains an account of the creation of the universe which links, limb by limb, the body of God with the material universe. This description is utilized to explain a form of Yoga in which the devotee enters, quite literally, into the body of God and thus comes to a direct experience of the deity.

As Śuka describes the process to King Parikṣit:

"Having acquired steadiness of seat and control of one's breath, and having conquered attachment and subdued one's senses, one should fix one's mind on the material form of the Lord, by force of one's reason. That is his cosmic or universal form, the grossest of the gross, wherein is seen this phenomenal universe in its past, present and future form. The Lord who tenants this cosmic body with its seven sheaths as the Virāt Puruṣa — He alone is the object of concentration.
The knowers of truth describe Him thus: Patala constitutes the soles of his feet, Rasatala the hinder and front parts of his feet. Mahatala corresponds to the ankles of the Creator of the universe and Talātala the shanks of the Virāt Puruṣa. Sutala represents the knees of the cosmic being, while Vitala and Atala form his thighs. The earth's surface corresponds to his loins, Bhuvarloka his navel. Indra's heaven forms his breast, Maharloka his neck, Janaloka his face. Tapoloka is recognized as the brow of the Primal Person and Satyaloka as the heads of the thousand-headed Lord. It is said that the gods from Indra downwards represent his arms. The cardinal points his ears, and sound his auditory sense. Nasatya and Dasra are the nostrils of the Supreme, odour his olfactory sense and flaming fire his mouth. The sky constitutes his eyes, the sun his sense of sight and day and night form the eyelids of the Cosmic Being. The abode of Brahma represents the play of his eyebrows, water his palate and taste his tongue. They declare the Vedas as the crown of his head; Yama constitutes his grinding teeth and the various forms of personal affection his other teeth. The *māyā* which deludes men represents his smile and the unending process of creation his sidelong glances. Bashfulness forms his upper lip and greed the lower. Piety constitutes his

(right) breast and the path of unrighteousness his back. Prajapati represents his penis and Mitra and Varuna his testicles. The oceans form the cavity of his abdomen and the mountains the systems of his bones. The rivers constitute his arteries and veins, and the trees the hair on the person of the Cosmic Being. The air is his breath, time represents his movement and the uninterrupted action of the three guṇas his activity. The wise recognize the clouds as his hair and twilight as the raiment. They declare the Unmanifest (Primal Matter) as his heart and the moon his mind, the seat of all passions. They speak of Mahat tattva as the power of understanding and Rudra as the Ego of the universal spirit. The horse, the mule, the camel and the elephant represent his nails, while the deer and all other animals abide in his hips and loins. The birds are his wonderful workmanship, the first Manu represents his intellect and man his abode. The Gandharvas, the Vidyādharas, the Caraṇas and the Āpsaras represent the reminiscences of His melody and the demon hosts his virility. The Brahman represents the mouth, the Kṣatriya his arms, the Vaiṣya the thighs and the Śudra the feet of that mighty being."[19]

The purpose of this Yoga is to see God in all and all in God, to realize that there is nothing but God in this universe. Apparently the God-Universe theme was so important that shortly afterwards, in a description of the process of creation, it is repeated. In the second, evolutionary-dynamic account, the same comparisons or identifications of aspects of the universe with God's Body are made as in the first, cosmographic-static. The Universe is creatively related to Him — the various entities derive their properties from the various parts of God's body from which they derive. The mountains derive their hardness from God's bones, the rivers their structure from God's arteries. This second account too is concluded by the statement, which provides the rationale for such mediations:

"There is nothing in this creation, whether existing as a cause or an effect, which is other than the Lord."[20]

While the Vaiṣṇavas have made the idea of the Body of God the central truth of their faith, it is not absent from the thought of the Advaitins either, who adhere to the idea that ultimately brahman is formless and as such bodiless.

Since it is a centra Upanisadic idea Advaitins could not ignore it. Thus, Madhavācārya explains in his *Pañcadaśī*:

"Śruti says that the Lord abides in the intellect and has the intellect as his body; but the intellect does not know him; it is itself controlled by him. As threads pervade a piece of cloth and constitute its fabric, (upadāna), so the Inner Ruler, pervading the whole universe, is the material cause of the universe. Just as the threads are subtler than the cloth, and the fibres of the threads are subtler than the threads themselves, even so, where this progress from the subtle to the subtler stops there do we meet the Inner Ruler. Being minuter than the minute, the inmost being is not subject to perception; but by reason and by śruti his existence is ascertained. As a piece of cloth is said to be the body of the threads which become the cloth, so when he has become the universe it is described as His body."[21]

Pañcarātra as adopted by Śrīvaisnavism speaks of five different levels of God's bodily presence: in his highest form as *parabrahman* he is all but unknowable by humans and inaccessible to them directly. In his four *vyuhas* he creates vehicles of mediation, further particularized and concretized in the *vibhavas*, commonly known as *avatāras*, 'descents' of the deity into an organism of either animal or man. The deity descends even further —into the heart of each human being as its *antaryāmin* or Inner Ruler and eventually into a material image as the *ārca-avatāra*.[22] This progressive self-diffusion of the divine essence takes place for the sake of gathering in again all things unto the Godhead.

It is impossible to determine the origin of the idea of *avatāra*: some scholars see its roots already in the Ṛgveda, others would have it develop under Buddhist or even Christian influence. In those classical works like the Bhagavadgītā which exhibit the fully developed idea of *avatāras* and provide a theoretical framework for it we are told:

"whenever *dharma* is threatened to be extinguished by *adharma* [the deity] descends into a [human] body to redeem the just and to punish the unjust".[23]

In a paradoxical sense the deity really enters history in an unreal body. The 'unreality of the body' is a theological postulate to explain that the descent of God is not conditioned by karma. The reality of God's embodiment in history is the presupposition for the truth of God's revelation through his *avatāras*: the sum total of the successive descents — the last descent coinciding with the end of the world — transforms the whole of history into a *Heilsgeschichte*. Time as body of god has its existential meaning, too. As T. Varadachari writes:

"These exploits of God (viz. in the *avatāra*) are concrete events and not general qualities, and have relevance for man. The reality of God is always not in an idealisation but in the actual impact of God in the life of man. The Puranas provide the fullest evidence of God's constant participation in man's life."[24]

Some texts say that the number of *avatāras* is infinite; others have lists of 36 or 22 *avatāras*. The most widely accepted number is that of ten: *daśāvatāra* has become a standard expression and a standard image. They range through all the four *yugas* of the present *kalpa*. Rāma and Kṛṣṇa are the two most popular *avatāras* — each associated with a large body of sacred lore.

As the *Adhyātma Rāmāyana* declares: "The Lord of Janakī, who is intelligence itself, and being requested by the devas to remove the afflictions of the world, though immutable, took the illusory form of a man and was apparently born in the solar dynasty. After attaining to fame eternal, he again took up his real nature as brahman."[25]

The most important among Visṇu's *avatāras* is undoubtedly Kṛṣṇa, the black one, also called *syama*. For his worshippers he is not an *avatāra* in the usual sense but *svayam bhagavān*, the Lord himself. For Vaiṣṇavas Kṛṣṇa is not only a local manifestation of the deity, but of universal importance for the entire period of history up to the end of times.

Hinduism in its classical phase visualized the deity as divine couple. Viṣṇu is never without his consort, Śrī, as Śiva is never without Pārvatī.

"This Śrī, the Mother of the Universe, is eternal and knows no separation from Viṣṇu. Even as Viṣṇu is all-pervading, she is all-pervading."[26]

Also the historic presence of Kṛṣṇa as Viṣṇu is accompanied by the contemporary presence of Rādhā as Śrī. Sexuality as an essential aspect of bodyliness characterizes also the Hindu deity. In numerous texts creation is described in terms of sexual procreation — the creator assuming male and female forms of various species and thus setting off the life-cycles of living beings. Many purāṇic tales emphasize sexual matters and some of the most ubiquitous symbols of Hindu religion have sexual associations. Tantricism, which gained such prominence in Hinduism from the 8th century onwards and which has in its turn influenced the mainstream *sampradāyas* and their literatures, quite often preaches and practices a path in which the creative and destructive power of sexuality is central. Thus also many of the most popular myths about the Kṛṣṇa-avatāra have a frankly erotic-sexual character and a quite important school of religious thought and practice associated with the name Caitanya fully developed the central motive of the relation between Krsna and his favourite *gopī* Rādhā. In it the beauty of Kṛṣṇa is extolled, for whose sake the married women of Braja left their homes and for whose love they pined. In many beautiful poems[27] and in countless enchanting miniature-paintings[28] the love between Kṛṣṇa and Rādhā is celebrated — in the manner of the Song of Songs of the Bible earthly bodily love is taken to be the most perfect analogy of the love-relationship between God and the soul. Mīrabāi, the famous princess, who rejected earthly love for the sake of love of Kṛṣṇa and who, according to a local tradition, never died but was bodily absorbed into an image of Kṛṣṇa, vividly describes her experience in this manner:

> I make love with Śrī Hari, and have shorn all relationship with others.
> I play the game of love with Him, as the acrobat plays his pranks.
> This however displeased the king, who rushed to kill me as I started on my journey to the saints.
> Having failed in his attempt, he tried a cup of poison to do away with me.
> Willingly I partook of the poison, but by the Grace of the lord it was turned into nectar.
> Bashfulness has no place in this path, just as one who goes out to dance should not feel shy.
> Subduing my mind, and careless of applause and condemnation I proceeded to play the game of love to my Lord.
> The king assembled all the relations and tried to stop me On my spiritual way.
> But heedless of all obstructions I proceeded in the strength of my Omnipotent Lord, who saved me from all onslaughts.[29]

In many ways the embodied God has influenced and directed the history of mankind: saving his devotees, destroying their enemies, as King and Lawgiver, as sage and as warrior, participating in battles and captivating the hearts of people by his charm and beauty. In his final embodiment, as Kalki, he will bring about the end of human history as well.[30]

* If anything characterizes Hinduism over against all other religions, it is the worship of images: countless images in temples and in homes, of precious metals and of cheap materials, large and small, artistically perfect and childishly crude, receive daily worship from hundreds of millions of people. The Indian word for image is *mūrti*: *mūrti* means embodiment, bodily presence. God is physically present in his *mūrti*: he makes himself available to his devotees and dispenses his grace in that form too. As the Arthapañcaka has it:

> "Although omniscient, he appears unknowing;
> although pure spirit, he appears as a body;
> although Himself the Lord, he appears to be at the mercy of men
> although all-powerful he appears to be without power
> although perfectly free from wants, he seems to be in need,
> although the protector of all, he seems helpless;
> although invisible, he becomes visibly manifest;
> although unfathomable, he seems tangible."

There are voluminous manuals which set out the detail of worship of God's image-body: but whether done with elaborate pomp in a huge temple or with a minimum of circumstance in a modest home, the basic faith is the same. For the sake of making himself most easily accessible to all people, the Lord descends into a material image and makes himself dependent on people's care. They lovingly dress him, feed him, put him to rest; they worship him, direct their prayers to him and sing and dance before him. Many are the stories which report how the Lord truly appeared from within his image either to confirm the faith of a believer or to counfound an unbeliever. The conviction that the *murti* is a true embodiment of God attracts millions of Hindus daily to have *darsan* of the deity in the temple and has given many in times of persecution the courage to bring the image to * safety. Proudly the visitor to the Visvanath temple in Benares, the most sacred if not the most conspicuous of the numerous sanctuaries, is told the story of the spiriting away of the main-*lingam* before the Muslim invaders and its triumphal return in safer times.

To provide a palace for the Lord, who has taken his abode in an image, Hindus throughout the centuries have built temples, large and small. Hindu temple architecture is among the most celebrated in the world — temples like those at Madurai, Khajuraho, Bhubbanesvar or Halebid (to mention some at random) have been studied and admired by many Western scholars and architects. The manuals which guided the builders of these edifices make it clear that the temple had to be planned from the *purusa-mandala* and was meant to be a replica of the cosmos, an image of time as well as of eternity, another way in which the divine embodies itself. The guiding principle of the sculptor who formed an image as well as of the architect who built a temple (very often one and the same person: the master-architect had the privilege to produce the main sculptures) was to prepare a suitable body for the deity out of stone and wood, brick and mortar, metals and precious stones. The fact that in order to do so they had to follow strict rules did not necessarily inhibit their artistic creativity. It made their art more easily accessible to the laymen who were familiar with the basic theology of their traditions. Majestic Viṣṇu with the royal insignia in his four arms, dynamic Śiva dancing the dance of creation and of destruction, gentle Śrī blessing the devotee — are all easily recognizable in their images throughout the centuries. The artistic rendering of God's body must reflect something of the unchangingness of God's own nature.

Avatāras and *mūrtis* are associated with specific places and regions which acquire themselves the status of 'body of God'. Thus the region around Mathurā is not only Kṛṣṇa's holy land — sanctified through his historical as well as his continued presence — it is Kṛṣṇa's own body. The *brajyātra*, the *parikramas* of either one of the holy places or the entire region, are more than pilgrimages in the usual sense, they are a communication with God's body. As an expression of this belief the journey has to be undertaken barefoot.

The conviction that every medium can become Body of God is guiding the belief that besides the 'gross' body of the material universe the deity also assumes the subtle body of *śabda*: words, sounds, mantras. That in one way or other Scripture is an 'embodiment' of the deity is fairly wide-spread Hindu conviction. Over and above that, Tantric Hinduism associates with the combination of certain letters and syllables a variety of Bodies of God (and/or the Goddess) distinguished through colour, attributes, functions. The practitioner of Tantricism believes that by pronouncing these secret mantras while touching various parts of his body, he can bring about a special bodily presence of God.

That the deity is seen as a dynamic living presence is nowhere more clearly demonstrated than in Indian classical music, dance and drama. The dancer/actor, while performing, not only 'acts' the part of the deity — he or she *is* the deity: people offer worship to them as embodiments of God. It is not by accident that the sacred dance has been cultivated especially in Śaivism, since Śaivism always emphasized the dynamic aspect of the deity. The famous Śiva Nātarāja image is the most complete representation of Śaiva Siddhānta theology — it comes to life in the dancer, who, after suitable preparation and invocation, is dancing the dance of creation and destruction.

While many images are works of true artists, their aesthetic quality is not of primary importance; the purpose of the image-maker is to provide a body for God so that he may dwell among men.

II.

Let us now sketch out some of the implications of this body-of-God view of the world of things and of humans, first in the language of Rāmānuja, then in the language of contemporary Western thought.

Rāmānuja, following the tradition outlined above, describes the relationship between the Supreme and the universe of physical entities and individual selves as *ātma-śarīra-bhāva*: soul-body-relationship. This central analogy has three implications:

adhāra-adheya-bhāva: support-supported relationship
niyantr-nyāmya-bhāva: controller-controlled relationship
Śesa-śesin-bhāva: subsidiary-principal relationship.[31]

From these fundamental relations Rāmānuja derives his definition of *ātman* (soul) as characterized by being support, controller, principal entity; *śarīra* (body) as characterized by being supported, controlled, subsidiary. Rāmānuja has anticipated many objections against his *ātma-śarīra-bhāva* and in answering these he provided deep insight into the meaning of his master-analogy.

1. An ontological problem:

How can the Supreme Being be creator and creature at one and the same time? Rāmānuja offers first a collection of scriptural passages exhibiting the affirmation of Viṣṇu's immanence in all beings, concluding:

> "From both the Vedas and the word of sages emerges the following teaching: the Supreme Brahman is the self of all. The sentient and non-sentient beings constitute its body. The body is an entity and has being only by virtue of its being the mode (*prakāra*) of the soul of which it is the body."[32]

The idea of the Lord being the *prakārin* and everything else being his *prakāra* is spelled out in greater detail:

> "Brahman itself is the effect as it exists having for its mode the configurations consisting of *prakṛti*, *jīvas*, *mahat*, *ahāmkara*, *tanmātra*, elements, senses and the products of these, the cosmic sphere of Brahmā made up of the fourteen worlds and the varied forms of beings like gods, men, animals and plants."[33]

Turning the argument around he declares, on the strength of his hermeneutic principle of *samānādhikāraṇya*, that

> "*prakṛti* denotes *īśvara*, who is the inner self of *prakṛti* and has *prakṛti* as its mode. The term *puruṣa* also denotes *īśvara* who is the inner self of the *puruṣa* and has *puruṣa* as his mode".[34]

2. A moral and ethical problem:

If god is the inner self of all *jīvas*, how can one impute good and evil actions to humans? Shall we not have to say that God is cruel and vicious, since we observe cruelty and vice in this world?

Rāmānuja insists on free will as a god-given faculty of humans:

> "The supreme being endows all sentient beings with the power of thought and the power of action ... He abides as the fundamental *śesin* (principal entity) of all ... The individual engages in action and abstains from action by his own free will. The supreme Being, witnessing his activity, remains unconcerned."[35]

Rāmānuja emphasizes, however, an active role of God in his capacity as *śesin*:

> "If an individual by himself is engaged in the pursuit of what is most in accordance with the will of God, God being pleased with him, confers upon him a propitious (*kalyāna*) disposition of will and intellect and actuates him in the right direction.... If an individual is pursuing what is most contrary to the divine will, the Lord gives him a cruel bent of intellect and will and actuates him to proceed along cruel lines."[36]

Must we then call God cruel? Rāmānuja says:

> "The ascription of particularity and cruelty to Brahman is repudiated on the ground of the beginninglessness of the individual selves and the responsibility of their *karma* for the inequalities and sufferings of individuals."[37]

Rāmānuja shows a further dimension of the *ātma-sarīra-bhāva* in the following:

> "The question would arise as to how he, free from evil and change and abounding in auspicious excellences could be one with the world which is tied up with evil (*heya*). The position is explained in the text itself: 'He is the soul of all beings. He has the universe as his form as he is imperishable. ... Through Viṣṇu, the supreme Brahman is imperishable, there is nothing contradictory in his being one with the universe in the sense of having it as his body. The distinctive characteristics of the body and soul remain unmodified."[38]

3. A practical-spiritual problem:

Absolute and unconditional freedom had been the aim of India's spiritual quest since the time of the Upaniṣads, passionately pursued on all levels. Rāmānuja's idea of an eternal service of God met with the objection that 'service is a dog's life', as a popular maxim expressed it. Rāmānuja takes up the challenge and in the process develops one of the most profound insights into the relationship between God and soul.

> "The statement 'all dependence is painful' simply means that dependence on anything or anyone other than the supreme being is painful because there is no relationship of the principal entity and the subsidiary entity between anyone other than Brahman and oneself. 'Service is a dog's life' also means that service of one who is unworthy of service is a dog's life. Scripture says that the only one that ought to be served by all who are enlightened about the fundamental nature of the self, is the highest *puruṣa*: 'He is to be served by people in all stages of life. He alone is to be served by all.'"[39]

4. A problem of *karma* and divine independence:

All *samsāric* existence is governed by *karma*: the very fact of the coming into this world as well as the qualities of body and mind are — according to ageold, fairly universal Hindu tradition — proof of the all-embracing power of karma. Freedom from karma in all its forms, freedom from rebirth has been the main objective of the path taught by the Upaniṣads. Does the acceptance of a body in the world not taint the supreme being with karma? Would an embodied saviour-God not be himself in need of salvation? To counter such objections Rāmānuja insists on the free will of God and the non-physical character of the body of such a divine descent:

> "This supreme Viṣṇu descends by his own choice into the created world and becomes one among the dependent creatures ... This descent among the creatures on the status of equality with them is for making himself accessible to them in order to facilitate their coming to him for support ..."

And:

> "Brahma and the other *jīvas* being subject to karma are compelled to take birth in physical bodies, structures compounded by physical elements, in accordance with their karma. This is inevitable for them even if they were unwilling to be reincarnated ... But in the case of the Lord, whose will perfectly fulfills itself, and who is the controller of all, there is no evil birth of this nature. On the contrary, by his own desire, in his own supremely holy form, he takes many births among gods, men etc. for the purpose of effecting the good of the world (*jagadupakārāya*)."[40]

The supreme is related to human history not by way of a karmic involvement but by way of 'fulfilling' (pūranam) it:

> The supreme Lord did become the younger brother of Indra, thereby fulfilling the realm of the gods. He voluntarily descended to the mundane world and became the son of Dasaratha, thereby fulfilling the dynasty of the solar kings. The same Lord took birth in Vasudeva's household voluntarily for removing the burden on earth, thereby fulfilling the lunar dynasty."[41]

Rāmānuja takes care to note that this self-involvement of the Divine history is

> "to be understood in terms of the descent of the cause into the realm of the effects, as a matter of voluntary ingression, in pure sport, for fulfilling its own effect-series and to accomplish the good of the world."[42]

As Eric Lott has rightly remarked:

> "The point [of lilā-vibhuti] is not that the Lord regards his creative activity as playful sport and therefore mere amusement and of little account. Its primary intention is to show how activity is possible without there being some unfulfilled need that the agent or the action is determined by."[43]

The relationship of śarīra-śarīrin, śesa-śesin, is unique. The ātma-śarīra analogy is a genuine analogy: it obtains 'in some way' throughout the world but in reality only at the level of God and the universe. It is of crucial importance to maintain the analogy and not succumb to objectifying or subjectifying the supreme vis-á-vis the universe. The point of the analogy is that it comprises both subject (mind) and object (matter) and also transcends this duality. As Rāmānuja says:

> "Brahman exists as the inner ruler of the non-sentient realm of 'the objects of experience (bhogya) and of the individual self, the 'experiencer' (bhoktr). Brahman exists in its own intrinsic form radiant with its own infinite perfections."[44]

Objectivation and subjectivation have a basis in the 'lower' and 'higher' prakṛti of the Lord but they are not the central truth of physical or historical reality — the meaning of the universe and of its history lies in God's own transcendent form. Rāmānuja is not deterred by the logical paradoxes involved in the ātama-sarira-bhāva, paradoxes which made Śankara declare objectivity (materiality) — on logical grounds — as false, illusory, non-existent from the standpoint of brahman. The atma-sarira-bhava saves the appearances (salvat phenomena) in a quite literal sense by declaring them as real manifestations of the body of God.

Its resolution of the object-subject dichotomy into a unity of a higher order makes it appealing to us moderns, especially to some physicists who have come to realise the untenability of the Cartesian dichotomy which splits the world into res extensa and res cogitans. This in turn produced the split between the 'objective sciences' dealing with matter and its properties and the 'humanities' that were left to indulge in subjective views of consciousness in literature and art. The modern Western analytic mind has not only split the universe into an 'objective' and a 'subjective' part — it also split the 'objective world' (for many of our contemporaries the only reality) into smaller and smaller fragments in the belief that the smallest fragments would be 'the building-blocks of reality' who would explain the rest, if found.

Traditional Indian thought, although distinguishing between dharma and dharmin, visaya and visayin, śarīra and śarīrin, never transferred this epistemological distinction into an ontological dichotomy. As Rāmānuja has shown, one of the implictions of the ātma-śarīra-bhāva is the inseparable linkage between them (aprthaksiddhi), the mutuality of object and subject. Nature (prakṛti — material nature) too has an interiority — without understanding it, it cannot be understood. In the same way in which objectivity and subjectivity are intertwined in the human person, the total reality of nature cannot exhaust itself in objectivity alone.

The beginning of modern science is associated with the successful objectivation of nature, (nature = matter), which evoked as its counterpart the complete subjectivation of history, philosophy and art. Operating for several centuries along Cartesian lines we have pushed the objectivation of nature so far as to realize that it has intrinsic limits: the observer is part of his observation, theories guide our experiments. Equally we have pushed subjectivity so far as to be forced to recognize objective limits to the understanding of ourselves and our human history: the world is part of ourselves and material circumstances unmistakably shape history, too.

The solution of the dilemma obviously does not lie in a 'subjective natural science' or an 'objective history'. We are becoming aware again of 'wholeness' as a quality of reality which comprises objective as well as subjective features and transcends them both. As the physicist-philosopher C.F.V. Weizsaecker expressed it:

"In quantum-theory an object can be divided into partial objects but does not consist of them. This can be seen in the fact that it permits various, conceptually incompatible divisions (technically: various divisions of the Hilbert-space: Einstein-Rosen-Podolsky paradox). It is a whole which does not consist of parts but is losing its wholeness when divided up into parts; thus an atom is not a system consisting of nucleus and electrons but one can only find nucleus and electrons if one destroys the atom ... if we try to think the whole universe as quantum-theoretical object, the universe 'is' not the multiplicity of objects in it, but it divides into the multiplicity for the multiplying-objectivating views."[45]

Even closer to the śarīra-śarīri-bhava comes, in my opinion, the statement of the eminent physicist David Bohm:

"We are led to propose ... that the more comprehensive deeper and more inward actuality is neither mind nor body but rather a yet higher-dimensional actuality which is their common ground and which is of a nature beyond both. Each of these is then only a relatively independent subtotality and it is implied that this relative independence derives from the higher-dimensional ground in which mind and body are ultimately one (rather as we find that the relative independence of the manifest order derives from the ground of the implicate order) ... In this higher-dimensional ground the implicate order prevails. Thus within this ground, WHAT IS, is movement which is represented in thought as the co-presence of many phases of the implicate order ... So we do not say that mind and body causally affect each other, but rather that the movements of both are the outcome of related projections of a common higher-dimensional ground. The fundamental law, then, is that of the immense multidimensional ground, and the projections from this ground determine whatever time-orders there may be."[46]

One cannot, of course, positively verify or falsify the idea that the cosmos is the body of God. That would amount to a contradiction in terms. Nor can one expect a mathematical formula of it — this would presuppose a successful objectivation of the analogy, again against the very essence of the ātma-śarīra-bhāva.

However, the analogy can serve as heuristic device to accommodte the modern quest to see reality again as a whole, differentiated by internal relations on separate hierarchical levels. And as for the 'point' of the universe as a whole (as well as for humn life as a whole): perhaps the only plausible meaning is a religious one (although not necessrily a sectarian, dogmatic, denominational articulation of it). How else should we define religion but as the humanly most satisfactory answer to the question: What is the meaning of it all?

Possibly the ātman-śarīra-bahāva is as good a metaphor as any to give meaning to both science and religion, to make sense of the world and what is beyond it. Its further specification as *adhāra-adheya-bhāva, niyantṛi-niyāmya-bhāva* and *seṣa-seṣin-bhāva* could possibly serve as heuristic frame for quite specific holistic scientific investigations.

Let me at this point introduce a diagram to show how I see the *ātma-śarīra-bhāva* relating to, and offering a corrective of, our predominant dichotomised Western thinking.

The abstract essence of this view can be expressed as an *onto-logic*: the *śarīra-śarīri-bhāva* is not a dialectic of mind and body, matter and spirit. Nor is it a theory of complementarity of mind and matter. It is not a theory of matter or a theory of consciousness nor a combination of both. It is an understanding of reality from within. Western attempts to grasp the wholeness of reality over and above multiplicity have been largely in terms of dialectics and complementarity of mind and matter, struggling against the law of contradiction, seemingly so fundamental to all thinking, that its violation came to be considered as the original sin of Oriental Thought.

It was recognized, of course, by quite many that there is, in nature, a circular causality and a mutuality of cause and effect which could not be expressed in linear logic. Thus C.F.V. Weizsaecker pleaded on the ground, that considering the nature of our real world with its "dependence of real things on one another, which often close in a circle" one should "round the circle of natural sciences and humanities to come to a more adequate conception of the world in which we live".[47]

D. Bohm, committed as he is to a holistic view, leaves no doubt about the difficulty to express it and to rediscover it in our own terms. Thus he writes:

"It is ... impossible to go back to a state of wholeness that may have been present before the split between East and West developed (if only because we know little, if anything, about this state). Rather, what is needed is to learn afresh, to observe and to discover for ourselves the meaning of wholeness. Of course, we have to be cognisant of the teachings of the past, both Western and Eastern, but to imitate these teachings or to try to conform to them would have little value. ... For ... to develop new insights into fragmentation and wholeness, requires a creative work even more difficult than that needed to make fundamental new discoveries in science or great and original works of art."[48]

Conclusion

The progress of modern science, first greeted as the new and final enlightenment and liberation of mankind, and associated with a quasi-religious enthusiasm, has led to widespread fear among non-scientists and to resignation among many scientists. To quote Steven Weinberg again:

"If there is no solace in the fruits of our research, there is at least some consolation in research itself. Men and women are not content to comfort themselves with tales of gods or giants, or to confine their thoughts to the daily affairs of life; they also build telescopes and satellites and accelerators and sit at their desks for endless hours working out the meaning of the data they gather. The effort to understand the universe is one of the very few things that lifts human life a little above the level of farce and gives it some of the grace of tragedy."[49]

No doubt, it makes a difference whether we do science or whether we content ourselves with tales of gods and giants. It also makes a difference whether we do science for science's sake or whether we become through it more conscious of a reality of which we and the universe are part, and which is greater than both.

The *ātma-śarīra-bhāva* is, in the end, not a mere tale about gods and giants but a path to discover the depth-structure of the universe and become one with it. As Eric Lott has expressed it:

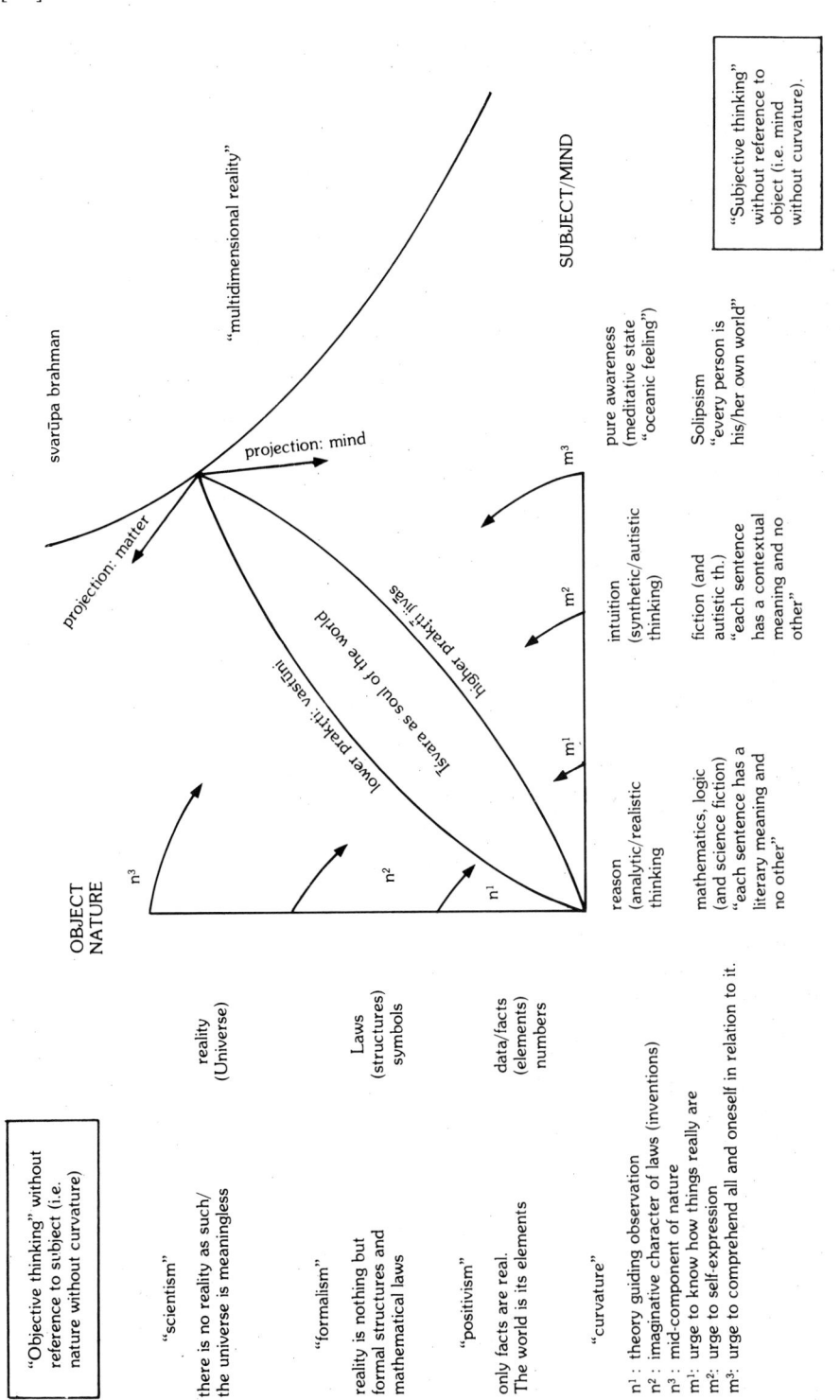

BODY OF GOD

"Objective thinking" without reference to subject (i.e. nature without curvature)

"Subjective thinking" without reference to object (i.e. mind without curvature).

svarūpa brahman

"multidimensional reality"

projection: matter
projection: mind

lower prakṛti: vastuni
Iśvara as soul of the world
higher prakṛti: jīvas

OBJECT / NATURE

SUBJECT/MIND

n^3
n^2
n^1

m^3
m^2
m^1

reality (Universe)

Laws (structures) symbols

data/facts (elements) numbers

reason (analytic/realistic thinking)

mathematics, logic (and science fiction) "each sentence has a literary meaning and no other"

intuition (synthetic/autistic thinking)

fiction (and autistic th.) "each sentence has a contextual meaning and no other"

pure awareness (meditative state "oceanic feeling")

Solipsism "every person is his/her own world"

"scientism"
there is no reality as such/ the universe is meaningless

"formalism"
reality is nothing but formal structures and mathematical laws

"positivism"
only facts are real. The world is its elements

"curvature"

n^1: theory guiding observation
n^2: imaginative character of laws (inventions)
n^3: mid-component of nature
m^1: urge to know how things really are
m^2: urge to self-expression
m^3: urge to comprehend all and oneself in relation to it.

*

"Within the śarīra-śarīri framework, the sadhana as well as the goal are integrated into the system as a whole. The mukti process becomes a realization of intrinsic inseparability, the mumukṣus's gradual growth in the very qualities characterizing the inner self .. becomes a movement towards the soul's Center of Being."[50]

The universe, viewed as God's Body, makes sense of its parts as related to a whole. It also allows us to find meaning in individual and collective history as the increasing involvement of the deity in creation. It provides purpose and value to language and art, it provides guidelines for our dealing with nature and fellow-humans. It gives concreteness to the idea of God and sacredness to the visible universe.

All these implications can be developed in many directions. Let me return, however, to its central meaning which is religious.

The first and foremost endeavour of genuine religion is not the study of nature, or history or art for their own sakes, but the knowledge of the transcendent. Its interest in the body is secondary to its interest in the soul. If the universe and everything in it is understood as body, as subsidiary to, controlled by, and dependent from its soul, the religious quest cannot find its fulfilment unless it reaches this soul, the heart of the world. It is the *visio beatifica* which stands at the end of the road of religion and in its reflected light the world and mankind's path through it receive illumination. Let me conclude with Rāmānuja's vision of the body of God, no longer seen in a mirror and through analogies but face to face:

"... splendour of a thousand suns .. serene beauty of the blue lotus, just opening in the morning-sun, symmetry and perfect proportion, harmony beyond words, loveliness filling all existence to overflowing, fragrance permeating the whole universe, eternal youthfulness, majesty enveloping all worlds looking down on us with compassion, love and sweetness, supreme atman, supreme brahman, Nārāyana."[51]

FOOTNOTES

1. Steven Weinberg, *The First Three Minutes: A modern view of the origin of the universe*, Bantam Books, p. 144.
2. ṚgVeda X, 90, 13 and 14.
3. *Kena Upaniṣad*, I, 2-3 (Translation S. Radhakrishnan).
4. *Muṇḍaka Upanisad* II, 1, 2-4.
5. *Chāṇḍogya Upaniṣad* III, 16, 2-4.
6. *Bṛhadāryanyaka Upaniṣad* III, 6.
7. *Ibid.*, III, 7, 15 ff.
8. *Bhagavadgītā* XI, 7.
9. *Ibid.*, vv. 15-31.
10. Vaiṣṇavisn seems to preserve here a pre-sectarian conception, also reflected in some schools of Śaivism, Śāktism and even Advaita Vedanta.
11. One of the most famous such descriptions in contained in Ramanuja's *Śaranāgati-gadya*.
12. Rāmānuja, *Gītabhāṣya* Ch. 7, 4 ff (J. van Buitenen's translation).
13. *Ibid.*, section 12.
14. *Ibid.*
15. Śrīnivāsadāsa, *Yatindramatadipika* Avatara 7.
16. *Gītābhāṣya* 7, 13.
17. *Ibid.*, section 14.
18. *Viṣṇupurāṇam* I, 19, 64 ff.
19. *Bhāgavatapurāṇam* II, 1, 23 ff.
20. *Ibid.*, II, 5-6.
21. *Pañcādaśi* V, 164 ff.
22. Cf. M. Yamunacharya, *Rāmānuja's Teachings in His Own Words*, Bhavan's Book University No. 111, pp. 80 ff.
23. *Bhagavadgītā* IV, 7 f.
24. *Alvars of India*, Bombay, 1956, p. xiv.
25. *Adhyātmata Rāmāyaṇa*, Bālakanda I, 1.
26. *Viṣṇupurāṇam* I, 8, 17.
27. The most celebrated in Jayadeva's *Gītāgovinda*.
28. Some good examples are contained in *Khangra Paintings of the Bhāgavata Purāna*.
29. Translation (and text) in Bankey Bihari, *Bhakta Mīrā*, Bhavan's Book University No. 81, p. 99 (158) (my own amendments).
30. A separate Purāṇa is devoted to Kalki, containing prophecies about the end of the world.
31. Rāmānuja *Vedārtha-Samgraha*, No. 95.
32. V.S. No. 81.
33. V.S. No. 87.
34. V.S. No. 92.
35. V.S. No. 124.
36. *Ibid.*
37. V.S. No. 89.
38. V.S. No. 161.
39. V.S. No. 250.
40. V.S. No. 162 and 163.
41. V.S. No. 149.
42. *Ibid.*
43. E. Lott, *Śrī Rāmānuja's Śarīra-Sarīrī-Bhāva* in: *Studies in Rāmānuja*, Madras, 1980, p. 35.
44. V.S. No. 121.
45. C.F.V. Weizsaecker — Gopi Krishna "Biologische Basis Religiöser Erfahrung," Weilheim, 1971, p. 42.
46. D. Bohm, *Woleness and the implicate Order*, p. 211.
47. *The History of Nature*, University of Chicage Press, p. 5 f.
48. D. Bohm, *op.cit.* p. 24.
49. cf. note 1.
50. E. Lott, *op.cit.* p. 36.
51. *Ibid.*, p. 39.
52. V.S. No. 220, extracts.

ADDENDA

Page 6, line 30: centra *read* central
Page 6, line 44: vyuhas *read* vyūhas
Page 7, line 16: Puranas *read* Purāṇas
Page 7, line 27: Visnu's *read* Viṣṇu's
Page 7, line 46: Krsna *read* Kṛṣṇa
Page 8, line 24: religious *read* religions
Page 8, line 49: Visvanath *read* Viśvanāth
Page 9, line 3: Khajuraho *read* Khājurāho
Page 9, line 4: Bhubbanesvar *read* Bhubbaneśvar
Page 9, line 6: purusa-mandala *read* puruṣa-maṇḍala
Page 10, line 3: Śesa-śesin *read* Śeṣa-śeṣin
Page 10. line 25: prakrti *read* prakṛti
Page 10, line 34: śesin *read* śeṣin
Page 10, line 37: śesin *read* śeṣin
Page 10, line 39: (kalyāna) *read* (kalyāṇa)
Page 11, line 5: ātma-sarīra *read* ātma-śarīra
Page 11, line 9: Through *read* Though
Page 12, line 2: (pūranam) *read* (pūraṇam)
Page 12, line 5: Dasaratha *read* Daśaratha
Page 12, line 18: śesa-śesin *read* śeṣa-śeṣin
Page 12, line 24: (bhoktr) *read* (bhoktṛ)
Page 12, line 29: ātama-sarīra-bhāva *read* ātma-śarīra-bhāva
Page 12, line 31: atma-sarira-bhava *read* ātma-śarīra-bhāva
Page 13, line 45: hunm *read* human
Page 13, line 49: ātman-śarīra-bahāva *read* ātman-śarīra-bhāva
Page 14, line 1: śeṣa-śeṣin *read* sesa-sesin
Page 15, legend to n[3]: mid-component *read* mind-component
Page 16, line 1: sadhana *read* sādhana
Page 16, line 25: atman *read* ātman; Nārāyana *read* Nārāyaṇa
Page 17, note 6: Bṛhadānyanyaka *read* Bṛhadananyaka
Page 17, line 10: Vaiṣnavisn *read* Vaiṣṇavis; Vedanta *read* Vedānta
Page 17, note 15: Yatindramatadipika Avatara *read* Yatīndramatadīpika Avatāra
Page 17, note 21: Pañcādaśi *read* Pañcádaśī
Page 17, note 46: Woleness and the implicate *read* Wholeness and the Implicate
Page 17, note 47: Chicage *read* Chicago
Page 10, line 25: prakrti *read* prakṛti

WESTERN RELIGIONS

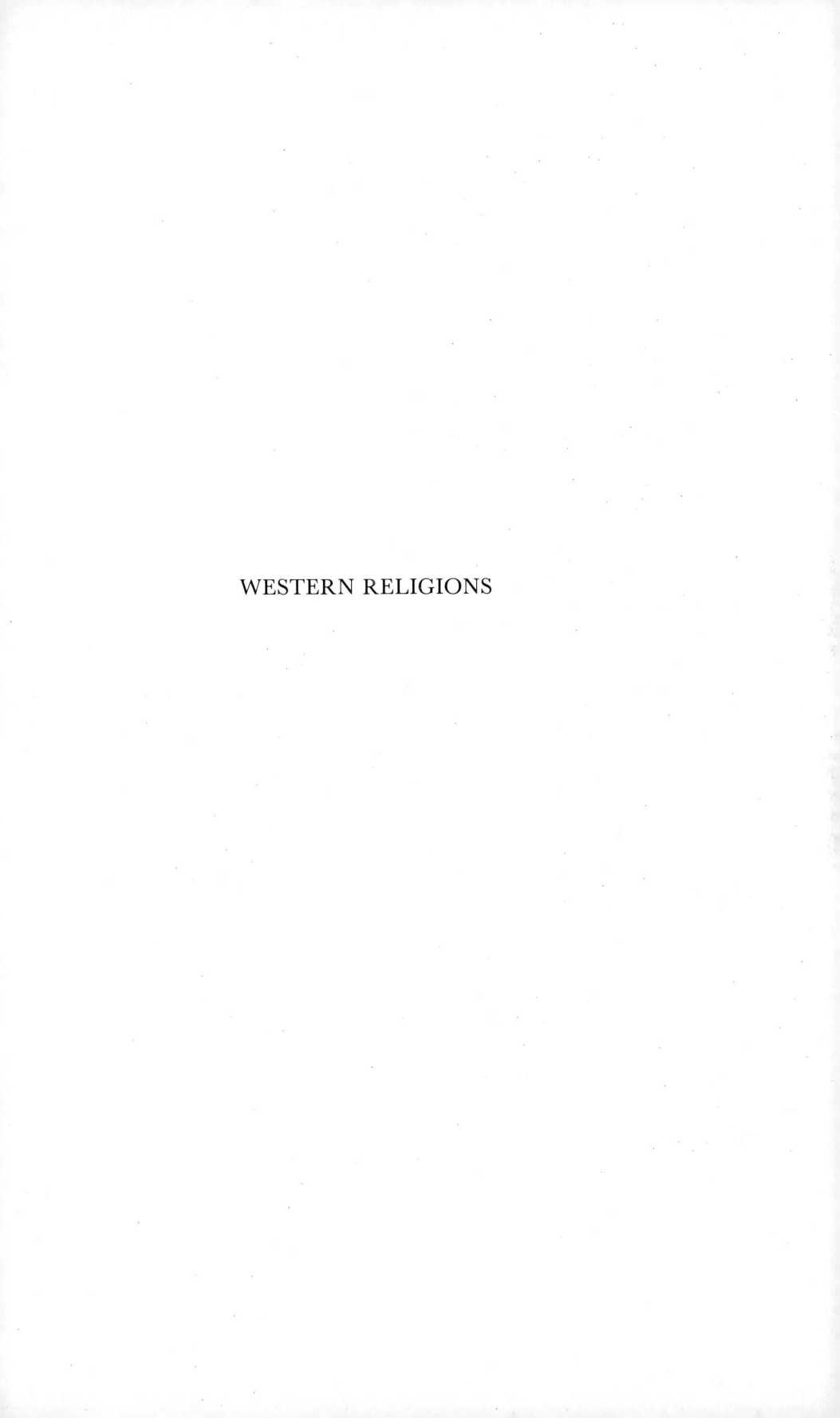

A. H. JOHNS

MOSES IN THE QUR'AN

Finite and Infinite Dimensions of Prophecy

"Miriam, the prophetess, Aaron's sister, took up a timbrel, and all the women followed her with timbrels, dancing. And Miriam led them in the refrain:
Sing of Yahweh: he has covered himself with glory,
horse and rider he has thrown into the sea."[1]

This song of Moses celebrates one of the great scenes in world religious literature: the escape of the Israelites from Egypt, and the drowning in the sea of Pharaoh and the Egyptians who were pursuing them. It marks a central point in the career of Moses, flanked on the one hand by his encounter with the burning bush, and on the other by the giving of the Law on Mt. Sinai. It is a scene that has a crucial role in salvation history as perceived in the traditions of Judaism, Christianity and Islam.

For Judaism, the commemoration of the Passover, the prelude to the escape of the chosen people from Egypt marks the first month of the year, an event to be celebrated annually until the Messiah comes; for Christians the crossing of the Red Sea represents the passage from death to life, signifying dying to sin and rising to grace, and an image of the resurrection. For Muslims it is one of the proofs of God's power in overwhelming those who reject his messengers. He chose Moses to be the great law-giver and ruler of his people and spoke to him, establishing a covenant that was to endure until the time of the final revelation to be made to Muhammad.

Each of these traditions has developed and elaborated its vision of Moses in line with its own pattern of development. In the Muslim tradition he became a model of sanctity, privileged above all others, apart from Muhammad, by God's speaking to him; an example of heroic holiness that reached the threshold of God himself.

It is prudent to be sceptical of the significance of word or verse frequency counts, but the fact that in the Qur'an there are 93 verses relating to Jesus, 131 to Noah, 235 to Abraham, and by comparison an overwhelming 502 to Moses,[2] gives us an approximate idea of how central the role of Moses is in the tradition that for Muslims was to find its apogee in the vocation of Muhammad, and how Moses was the figure that the Qur'an presented to Muhammad above all others as the supreme model of saviour and ruler of a community, the man chosen to present both knowledge of the one God, and a divinely revealed system of law, known in the Judaic and Christian traditions as the 10 commandments.

David Daiches remarks that 'the religious experience ... Moses first underwent alone with his flock of sheep in the wilderness of Midian was a genuine experience undergone by the man who remoulded the religious consciousness of his people, and in doing so made possible the history of both Judaism and Christianity'.[3] The words are thrilling, sublime to both Jew and Christian alike. But how could Daiches have overlooked the role of Moses in

Islam, as the first Muslim of his time in the Islamic design of salvation hisory, and as the greatest role model that the Qur'an presents to Muhammad, or the significance that Moses has in the Muslim tradition? A significance that Muhammad and the Qur'an attest time and again.

A superficial reader of the Qur'an, particularly one who has to rely on a translation, may not realize how important Moses is in the message of the Book. This is, in part, because of the character and internal organisation of the Qur'an, in part because non-Muslims often find it difficult to appreciate how seriously Muhammad took his predecessors, and their importance in his message. To grasp this it is necessary to perceive how he shared in their consciousness of their vocation, and how he re-lived the challenges they faced as challenges that he had to face. It was as such that they were known in the Muslim community; and members of this community in different degrees and at different levels responded to the Qur'anic accounts of them. They saw and see them as the architects of a universalistic salvation history.

Indeed, in the Qur'an, they are presented with such immediacy that they create in the imagination of the faithful a desire to set them in a broader framework, elaborating details which even if they go beyond the information given by the Qur'an, or beyond the facts that can be given a time and place by historians, present a human dimension to these culture heroes, generating an important literary genre of story-telling. Of these, the most famous is Joseph. His relations with Zulaikha have been interpreted in stories in moral, romantic and mystical senses. His magnanimity to his brothers is a model for Muhammad; and the comfort that comes to his grieving father Jacob for the loss of his son is a solace for all who grieve.

Never let it be forgotten that the figures of his predecessors presented in the Qur'an were real people to Muhammad, and that in sayings attributed to him he spoke of them as his brothers, whose actions and whose judgements he revered and imitated.

The heart of the Qur'an is not easily accessible to the non-Muslim. It is full of echoes and resonances which react upon, reflect and reinforce one another. Thus to see the Book as it presents itself, a study of verses, words, and names selected from a concordance without a grasp of the whole in which these individual references are set is not sufficient. It is only on the basis of a response to the book as a whole that the repetitions, rewordings, rephrasings of its central themes can be understood as integral parts of the whole book and are not simply failures of inspiration — or as has been said of von Karajan's successive recordings of Beethoven's symphonies, another attempt to get it right!

The Qur'an has to be taken on its own terms: whether accepted, as by the Muslim, rejected, or seen simply as a mysterious refraction of the light of the jewel that is Abraham. Torrey, who seems to have had a kind of love-hate relationship with the Qur'an sometimes comes up with phrases that are magically ambivalent: he speaks of 'the kaleidoscope constantly turning, the thought leaping from one subject to another', and of the 'ever-turning wheel of the Qur'an'.[4] If on the one hand these appear to be mechanistic images, yet on the other, they suggest an infinity of aspects.

References to Moses occur throughout the Qur'an. And if one regards the chronology of revelation as proposed by such scholars as Noeldeke, Bell and Blachere[5] as a rough guide, one can see references to Moses and his authority from the very earliest chapters to be revealed, increasing in frequency and detail towards the end of the Meccan period, culminating in splendidly dramatic accounts of two great encounters with God: in the burning bush where Moses receives his commission to warn Pharaoh, and on Mt. Sinai, when he is given the Law. In the Medinan period, we see more fully developed, Moses' experience with his recalcitrant followers as a model for Muhammad's own debates with the Jews who refused to accept his message, his role, or his authority. These perspectives are not mutually exclusive; all reveal aspects of the role of Moses. It does not matter whether one takes them in sequence or simply as aspects of a single event — and commentators, philosophers and mystics have done both.

The accounts of Moses in the Qur'an, then, focus on the two occasions on which Moses speaks to God: at the burning bush, and on Mt. Sinai.

A vivid presentation of the first is given in Sura 20, Ta Ha.

9. Have you heard the story of Moses,?
10. Of when he saw a fire
    And said to his family
    'Stay here!
    Indeed, I see a fire.
    Perhaps I can bring you a brand
    from it, or by the light
    of the Fire find guidance'.
11. When he approached it,
    A voice called: 'Moses!
12. I, indeed I am your Lord
    So take off both your sandals.
    You are in the sacred valley of Tuwa
13. I have chosen you, so listen to what is to be revealed to you:
14. I, truly, I am God
    There is no God, but I
    So worship me, and perform
    the prayer, so that you will remember me.
15. The Hour is coming; it is
    soon to be revealed, then every soul will be recompensed for
    what it has done.
16. Do not let yourself be hindered from [believing in] it by those
    who do not believe in it, and follow their passions and do
    evil.
17. Moses! what is that in your right hand?
18. He replied: 'It is my staff. I support myself on it, I use it to pull down branches for my sheep. There are other uses too I have for it'.
19. God said: 'Moses, cast it down'.
20. So he threw it down, and behold, it was a writhing snake.
21. God said: 'Take hold of it, do not fear, we will return it to its former shape.
22. Now, place your hand into your armpit, then draw it out, a brilliant white, without it suffering any harm as another sign,
23. so that we may show you the greatest of our signs.
24. Go to Pharaoh: He is acting arrogantly'.
25. Moses replied: 'My Lord, ease my breast,
26. make my task lighter for me;
27. loosen the knot upon my tongue
28. that they may understand my words.
29. Give me from my family one to support me,
30. Aaron my brother.
31. Through him, strenthen my loins
32. and make him my partner in this task,
33. so that we may praise you much,
34. and remember you often'.

....

God grants Moses his requests, and re-assures him, reminding him how on three earlier occasions he had shown his love for him, and formed him for himself, for example:

38. 'When we told your mother what we told her:
39. "Place him in a wooden box,
    and place the box in the Nile;
    then let the Nile cast it on the shore; and

39. our enemy and his enemy take it",
and I gave you love from myself, so that you might be formed under my care.
40. Then, when your sister was walking, she said:
'Shall I take you to one who will take charge of him'?
So we returned you to your mother to sooth her eye, and put an end to her grief.
Then you killed a man, and we saved you from affliction, and set you trials to endure.
Then you passed some years among the people of Midian.
Then, Moses, you came to the appointed time
41. and I fashioned you for myself.
42. Go, you and your brother, with my signs, and do not slacken in remembering me.
Go to Pharaoh, for he is arrogant, and speak to him gently.
Perhaps he will reflect, and fear me'.

Further details of the narrative are elaborated in Sura 28 (al Qasas), in verses which emphasize the love and concern of Moses' mother for him; assuring her that she will indeed suckle him (for in suckling him her role as a mother is fully realized); if she fears for him (for Pharaoh is having slain all the male children of the Israelites, and letting the female ones live) then she should place him in a box in the Nile, and neither fear nor grieve on his account, for God promises her:

7. 'We will restore him to you, and make him one of our messengers'.

In verse 9, Pharaoh's wife urges her husband not to slay him, assuring him that the child will be a 'soothing of the eye' both to herself and to him, persuading him to adopt him as a son.

Then the scene shifts to the grieving mother who almost reveals the assurance that God has given her about her son, and would have done so had God not strengthened her heart so that she should be a true believer. She tells her daughter, Moses' older sister:

11. 'Follow him'. So she watched him from a distance, (the Egyptians) were not aware of this.

There is a shift of scene again, and it is told how Moses refused to accept any wet nurse offered to him. It was then that his sister, un-recognized as such by any of Pharaoh's court officers, offered to take him to someone who would look after him, and thus returns him to his mother to take her breast. Thus she learns that the promise of God is true (v. 13).

This Sura also gives a full account of the third occasion on which God had shown his kindness to Moses.

The scenes shift rapidly. Moses is a young adult. He comes into the city when it is deserted, and finds two men fighting: one of his own people, an Israelite, and the other an Egyptian. The Israelite asks for help. Moses, traditionally a strong, swarthy man responds, strikes the Egyptian, and kills him (v. 15).

He is overwhelmed by shock and grief at what he has done, (v. 17) and prays for pardon, for he knows that God is the Pardoner, the Merciful. The following day he is still in the city, fearful for what may befall him, looking anxiously around him. The same Israelite as the day before is engaged in a fight, and again asks for help. Moses is prepared to help, but the man that is the enemy of them both brings him to his senses:

19. Are you going to kill me as you killed a man yesterday?
Are you bent on being a tyrant, and not one of the righteous?

At that moment a man comes running from the farthest part of the city to warn him to flee (v. 20). Moses flees, and prays for God to guide him. He finds his way to Midian and comes to a spring where men are watering their flocks. Standing at one side are two women, who are reticently waiting until the men have finished (v. 21-22).

24. He watered their flock for them, then withdrew to the shadow, and said (in prayer):
'My Lord, I am deeply in need of the good that you have given me'.

25. One of the two women approached him modestly, and said:
'my father invites you (to his home) to reward you for watering our sheep for us'.

Moses returns to the house. One of the daughters suggests to her father Shuᶜaib, the Jethro of Exodus, that he employ him. He does so, and marries him to one of them, with as a bride price, a pledge to work for him for eight or ten years (v. 26).

When the term is complete, Moses leaves with his wife to return to his homeland (Egypt). It is on this journey that he encounters the burning bush, and the account in this Sura i.e. 28 in part mirrors, in part creates new dimensions or perspectives to that given in Sura 20, Ta Ha.

For our purposes there is no need to go into the details of Moses' confrontation with Pharaoh, the manifestation of the two signs of the staff becoming a serpent, or his dark swarthy hand turning a brilliant white. Nor is there a need to tell of the defeat of Pharaoh's magicians, their acceptance of the faith of Moses, and their crucifixion.

After enduring the plagues of flood, locusts, lice, frogs and blood, Pharaoh allows the Israelites to leave Egypt. In Sura 7 (al-Aᶜraf) verses 134-137, the sequence of events is swiftly told: 'when the plague fell upon them, the Egyptians said: pray for us to your Lord to fulfill the promise he made to you. If he removes this plague from us, we will believe in you, and send the Israelites with you. But when we removed the plague from them for a certain time, they went back on their word. So we took vengeance upon them, and drowned them in the sea, for they had said our signs were lies, and had ignored them. And we made those who had been down-trodden to inherit the land we had blessed to the East and the West'.

A dramatic and moving detail of the episode is given in Sura 10 (Yunus) 90. 'We parted the sea for the Israelites, then Pharaoh and his army followed them, filled with greed and enmity. Yet when drowning overwhelmed them, Pharaoh said: 'I believe that there is no God but the God in whom the Israelites believe; I am among those who submit myself to Him'.

This account of the conversion of Pharaoh has provided an issue for theologians and mystics who have debated for centuries whether Pharaoh's profession of faith was accepted or not.

The crossing of the sea leads inexorably to Mt. Sinai, where Moses is summoned away from his people, to be addressed by God on the mountain, and for the Divine Law to be entrusted to him.

This awesome event occurs after the Israelites have begun to grumble at Moses. They pass by a people who worship idols, and say to him, in Sura 7 (al-Aᶜraf) verse 13 'Make for us gods such as the gods of these people'. Moses addresses them:

138. You are an ignorant people.
139. What these people have is vain, and what they do is empty.
140. Do you really seek any god other than The God, He who has given you more favours than other people on earth, and saved you from the people of Pharaoh!

The Qur'an (v. 141) continues: We commanded Moses to fast for thirty nights, to which we added another ten. Then, after these forty nights the time his Lord had appointed came, and Moses said to his brother Aaron: Take charge of the people in my place. Act well, and do not follow the way of those who do evil upon the earth.

The next and central episode, with Moses on the mountain, follows swiftly:

143. Thus when Moses came to the point we had decreed, and His Lord spoke to him, he said: 'My Lord, let me look upon you'. He replied: 'You shall not see me, but look at the mountain. If it stands firm in its place, then you shall see me'. But when his Lord revealed himself to the mountain, he shattered it to dust.

Moses collapsed as one struck by lightning. When he recovered he said: 'Praise be to you. I turn to you. I am the first of those who believe in you'.

144. God said to him: 'Moses, I have chosen you out of all mankind for my message and for my words. So take what I have given you, and be thankful'.

....

These scenes are communicated in the Qur'an with tremendous power through the extraordinary rhetorical instrument that is Arabic. There are many further facets of meaning and internal relationships that could be explored: the style of the speakers — the initial gentleness of Moses in first addressing Pharaoh, and the bragging arrogance of Pharaoh, something akin to that attributed to Herod in the miracle plays. There is Moses' courage in speaking to God, setting as it were his terms if he is to accept his vocation, and at the same time his fear to go before Pharaoh in case Pharaoh mocks at his message, or recognizes him as the murderer who had fled years before, and finally his rashness in asking to see God. Then there is the loving kindness, the compassion of God to Pharaoh's mother, who sets him adrift in the Nile, but with the consolation that he will be returned to her — and the human touch of her almost revealing the assurance she has been given, a revelation that would imperil the divine plan. There is both the modesty and yet initiative of the daughters of Shu[c] aib whom Moses helps. There is Moses' sense of humility and total dependence on God.

Rich and varied as they are, these comments only touch the surface of the Qur'anic narrative, within which are still many levels of spiritual meaning.

For those of us brought up in the Hellenic tradition, there is a tendency to look in a text, even a sacred text — to use Frithjof Schuon's words — for 'a meaning that is fully expressed and immediately intelligible. In the Islamic tradition, on the other hand, there is often a very highly developed love of verbal symbolism, and a capacity to read in depth. The revealed phrase is ... an array of symbols from which more and more flashes of light shoot forth the further the reader penetrates into the spiritual geometry of the words: the words are reference points for a doctrine that is inexhaustible'.[6]

Schuon also speaks of the role of commentaries springing from the oral tradition which accompany revelation from its beginning — intercalating missing, though implicit parts of the text, specifying in what relationship or in what sense a given thing should be understood, and explaining its diverse symbolisms, often simultaneous or superimposed one on another. In short they form part of the tradition ... they are the sap of its continuity, even if their committal to writing, or in certain cases their re-manifestation occurred only at a relatively late date in order to meet the requirements of a particular historical period.[7] The commentaries in fact provide the link between the revealed word and the understanding of the word in the community, which indeed is a crucial part of its meaning.

There is a great tradition of Qur'anic exegesis which has followed diverse lines of development, and explored different aspects of the Qur'an. In every case this tradition has grown out of the sayings and explanations attributed to the prophet himself and to his companions which elucidate the significance of words and phrases, sets out the context in which they are to be understood, and serves as a guide to its legal provisions and to the probing and exploration of the spiritual values implicit in it, in the events it narrates, and the personalities who have a role in it.

The Qur'anic episodes relating to the prophets have in some cases been brought together in compilations of stories about the prophets, in others they are scattered throughout the work of the great commentators as they explore and try to come to terms with these great heroes of the spiritual life. The living sap of the oral tradition binds them together, and discovers new dimensions of meaning.

The reputable compilers of stories make use of the scholarly apparatus of careful lines of transmission that is the basis of traditional Islamic scholarship. But story-telling too is a technique of religious instruction, an art form in its own right. al-Tha[c]labi,[8] (d. 1035) for example, himself author of a major work of exegesis has, in his compilation *Qisas al-anbiya'* (stories of the prophets)[9] brought together so much carefully chosen information on Moses, that his presentation of him has been called a masterpiece in its own right, and an outstanding "novel of holiness". Yet he can allow his imagination to rove to give an earthy realism to the story. Pharaoh for example, was so terrified at the form of Moses' staff changed into serpent, that he had forty violent bouts of diarrhoea in a day![10]

The great 12th century commentator Fakhr al-Din al-Razi[11] summarizes much useful information as to how the Muslim community saw Moses.

He explains, for example, why this story was revealed to Muhammad: to strengthen his heart in the face of difficulties by telling him of the experience of the prophets before him, in particular Moses, because the tests and trials he endured were very great, in order to comfort Muhammad, and to support him in the hardships he too had to bear.[12]

At once we see a major function of the reference to earlier prophets in the Qur'an, and with it an aspect of Muhammad overlooked in the more triumphalist accounts of his life: that he was a man who suffered, and who needed the strength and consolation that the Qur'an provided.

al-Razi then takes the phrase from Sura 20 (Ta Ha), 'When he (Moses) saw a fire', and sets out the background to the story, details that make it easier for others to understand. He tells how Moses asked permission from his father-in-law (and employer) Shu[c]aib (Jethro in Exodus) to return to Egypt to see his mother. Shu[c]aib gave permission, and Moses set out. On the way, his wife gave birth on a cold winter night. It was the eve of Friday, and they had lost their way. Moses tried to kindle a fire with a drill stick, but it would light, and while he was busy with it, he suddenly noticed a fire in the distance. Al-Suddi, one authority al-Razi cites, says that Moses thought it a fire lit by shepherds, others say that he saw the fire in a tree, although the Qur'an furnishes no evidence of this ... he made his way towards it.[13]

al-Razi included a report from ibn [c]Abbas (the prophet's cousin) who says: 'He saw a tree, green from its base to its summit as though it were a white fire. He stood in wonder at the brilliant light of the fire, and the brilliant green of the tree. The fire has no effect on the green, and the abundant sap of the tree has no effect on the brightness of the fire, then he heard the praises of angels, and saw a mighty light.[14]

Another authority he quotes says that Moses thought it a fire that someone had lit, and he gathered twigs, to light a torch from its flames. Moses looked up at its branches, and lo, there was a brilliant green in the sky, and then a light between heaven and earth, with rays that dazzled his sight, and when Moses looked at it, he put his hands over his eyes, and a voice called him 'Moses' ... he responded 'At your service'. 'I hear your voice, I do not see you, where are you?' He replied: 'I am with you, in front of you, behind you, and totally encompass you. I am closer to you than your very self'.

Then Satan put a doubt into his mind, and said, 'how do you know that it is the voice of God you hear'. He replied: 'because I hear it from above, below and behind, from my right and my left, just as I hear it from in front of me, thus I know it was not the voice of any created thing'.[15]

al-Razi then gives some of the reasons offered for God's command: Take off both your sandals, you are in the Holy Valley of Tuwa'.

One explanation, attributed to Muhammad's cousin and son-in-law [c]Ali, is that as his sandals were of dead donkey skin, he was ordered take them off out of reverence for the Holy Valley. Another is that he should bestow upon his feet the blessing of the holy ground. A third is that to show his reverence for the valley, he should tread it only barefoot, out of awe for it and as an act of humility on hearing the voice of his Lord.

al-Razi then gives some examples of the more elaborate interpretations evolved by the 'referential' or 'allusive' tradition of exegesis:

One is that in sleep, one's two sandals are understood as referring to wife and child, thus the order 'take off your sandals' means: have no further regard for wife and child, and let not your heart be not burdened with care for them.

Another is that to remove one's sandals means to have no further heed for either this or the world to come. In other words, it is as though Moses is ordered to be totally absorbed in the knowledge of God, and not allow his mind to be attracted to anything other than He.

In this tradition, the 'Holy valley' is understood as the holiness of Almighty God, and the purity of his might. In this context the order means, once you have reached the ocean of gnosis, have no further concern with created things.

The last example al-Razi gives is more elaborate: Moses, having come to the holy valley has passed beyond the limitations imposed by reason on human knowledge of God. His sandals stand for the two premises on which rational argument for the existence of God is based — the necessity for a first cause and a principle of order — and he has no further need of them. Thus it is as if God is saying: you have reached the Holy Valley, and this stands for the ocean of the knowledge of God and the copiousness of His Divinity.[16]

It will be noted how the elements presented build up on common, everyday realities — a man lost on a winter's night, unsuccessfully trying to start a fire, the sight of a fire in the distance, and then suddenly the splendour of the fire in the tree which heralds the divine words: 'I, indeed I am your Lord'. There is a parallel development in the order of presentation of possible reasons for the order 'Take off both your sandals'. The first is the simple, ritual one that they were made of donkey skin, the last is that it is an order to abandon attachment to all created things, to pass beyond the limits of reason, and to plunge into the sea of gnosis. It is there that al-Razi stops. He explicitly resists the temptation to explore the heights and depths of mystical experience. He refers to it, identifies it, and leaves it.

This does not mean that he leaves out or understates anything of the awe or terror of the encounter, or of the solace that God brings. He comments on the words 'I have chosen you, so listen to what is to be revealed': The command 'listen to what is to be revealed' contains the ultimate in awe and majesty. It is as though God said to him: an awesome, terrifying task has been laid upon you, so prepare for it, and devote all your mind and all your thoughts to it. The words 'I have chosen you' on the other hand express the ultimate in gentleness and mercy. Thus the first expression brings to him the ultimate in hope and the latter the ultimate in fear. al-Razi then turns to explain God's question to Moses: 'What is that in your right hand'?

Why should God ask about the staff, al-Razi wonders, and answers his own question: because God can use a simple thing for extraordinary purposes. Thus, he goes on, Almighty God, when he intended to use the staff to show noble signs such as changing it into a snake, or using it to strike the sea and part it, or to strike the rock, so that water would spring from it, he first showed it to Moses as though to say to him: Moses, do you know what it is that you have in your hand? It is wood, that can neither harm nor help. Then He changed it into a huge snake, and by this means showed those with intelligence the perfection of his power and the extent of his might, which were such that he could display these great signs from the simplest thing that Moses had on him.[17]

al-Razi, however, has also a keen awareness of human emotions and reactions to circumstances, whether grief, joy or perplexity. Moses had undergone a great spiritual experience. God had shown him the light mounting from the tree up to heaven, had made him to hear the praise of the angels and then to hear his words. He then treated him with force and gentleness. He treated him with gentleness first, by his words 'I have chosen you' and then force by imposing on him awesome responsibilities. As a result of all this, Moses was totally perplexed and bewildered, and hardly knew his right hand from his left. And for this reason, God said to him: 'What is that in your right hand, Moses', so that he would realize that his right hand was that in which he held his staff. The point of the episode then is to show that God realized that Moses was overwhelmed by bewilderment in the divine presence, and to bring him back to earthly reality, asked him about something as down to earth and commonplace as the staff, something about which he could make no mistake.[18]

This is a perception of the kindness of God for his creatures in the text of the Qur'an, his understanding of their perplexities and need for encouragement. It is an insight worthy of an experienced spiritual director.

al-Razi was not the first to put into words this insight, or to possess such skill in understanding of the human heart and its needs. Such instances of psycho-spirituality which bring us a remarkable sense of closeness with human experience across the centuries are explicitly documented in Islam from very early times.

Muqatil b. Sulaiman (d. 767) for example, shows how early the Qur'anic passages concerning Moses aroused in many Muslims a desire to meditate on Moses' experience as a means of access to a direct relationship with God, in such a way that later he would be seen as a prototype of the perfect mystic, called to enter into the mystery of God. Of the burning bush, Muqatil says that the fire Moses saw was the light of his Lord, and that the voice ordered him to remove his shoes because the place became holy when God revealed his presence there.[19]

A slightly later contemporary of Muqatil, Ja'far Sadiq, gives a vivid account of how Moses was sure that his call came from God. Moses, Ja'far says, is shown the light of God in the form of fire, and he was sure it was God because the light 'overwhelmed me and submerged me so that it seemed that everyone of my hairs was summoned by a call that came from all directions, and offered itself in response.[20]

Abu 'l-Hasan al-Nuri (d. 907) in explaining the words — 'I have given you love from myself' — (Qur'an 20:39) — presents God as saying to Moses: Reserve your heart for my love. I have chosen it as a dwelling place for this. I have set out there a desmene of my knowledge and built a house of faith in myself. I have made to rise in your heart a sun, which is desire for me, a moon which is love for me and stars which are my visitations. I have likewise placed in your heart a cloud which is meditation on me, and made to rise a wind which is the aid I give you. Then, out of my beneficence I have sent down upon it rain. I have sown there the seed of my sincerity, and made to grow the trees which are obedience for my sake. Their leaves are fidelity, and the fruits which hang from them are the wisdom born of intimate dialogue with me.[21]

This phrase 'intimate dialogue' is certainly a reference to the Qur'an, Sura 19 (Maryam) verse 52: 'We brought him close to us and spoke to him as to a friend', one of the most beautiful references to the manner in which God spoke to Moses, the Arabic word *najiyan*, suggesting a marvellous degree of intimacy.

It is striking the degree to which our authors are concerned with Moses' reactions as a man to his extraordinary experience. al-Tha'labi tells how at the sight of the burning bush 'Moses was filled with awe, and a violent fear seized him when he saw this huge smokeless fire blazing within the hollow of a green tree'. Yet it was a terror to be followed by a deep interior peace.[22]

The encounter on Mt. Sinai is even more dramatic, for on that occasion, Moses made that most daring of requests to his Lord. 'Let me see you', (Qur'an 7:142). God's answer is like a parable in action. You (as you now are) shall not see me, unless the mountain stands firm in my presence. God reveals himself to the mountain, it shatters, and Moses collapses in a faint.

al-Razi does not touch on the mystical implications of this episode. His principal concern is to argue against those who use it to deny the possibility of ever seeing God, even on Judgement Day. He draws attention however to God's words to Moses after he had recovered from the faint: 'I have singled you out from all mankind for my message and my words (7:144) so accept what I have given you, and be thankful', and adds in explanation: When God refused Moses' request to see him, he prepared for him various great favours that were his to bestow on him, and commanded him to be thankful for them. Thus it was as if he had said: I have refused your request to see me, but I have given you immense favours of such and such a kind, so do not be grieved because you have not seen me. Rather, look on all the other favours that I have singled out for you alone, and be thankful. And this was to comfort Moses for not seeing him.[23] Again it will be noted how al-Razi draws attention to the kindness of God to his creatures.

The Qur'anic build up to this extraordinary scene is very brief. A striking feature is Moses preparation. He is ordered to fast first for 30 nights, and then for another 10 (Qur'an 7:142). The great mystic al-Hallaj (d. 922) has developed a marvellous picture of a spiritual journey out of this period of 'forty nights'. He gives a sublime picture of the role of Moses, and his encounter with the burning bush elaborated in his book of lyrical prose passages, al-Tawasin.[24] Moses, he sees as a type of spiritual pilgrim. To make his way towards Reality, he has to make himself an exile, following narrow ways, marked out by fire, — and the burning bush was such a fire — alongside undulating deserts. This image of Moses as a pilgrim has a counterpart and support very early in the Christian tradition, where it is to be found in Origen and Gregory of Nyssa.[25]

al-Hallaj commences his meditation on Moses when 'at the predestined time', Moses concludes his service with his father-in-law — Jethro in the Judaic, Shu^{C}ayb in the Muslim tradition — and sets out on the journey back to Egypt through narrow ways, amid rolling deserts and loses his way. Lost in the darkness of a winter's night, he sees a fire. A later commentator understands this, and the approach to the fire as Moses' entry into the mystical domain of intimacy with God. To approach the fire Moses has to leave behind his own, his wife and child, and approach the fire alone. In the rabbinic tradition too, it will be remembered, after his encounter with God in the fire, Moses led a celibate life.[26] Moses, al-Hallaj says, leaves his own, because the ultimate Reality wished to take him for Its own. Thus the approach to the burning bush teaches the secret of the path to the mystical union, and al-Hallaj explains: Cast far from you created nature in order that in Reality you become He, and He becomes you. This is because it was not the bush which spoke, nor the seed from which it sprung: it was the uncreated word of God.[27]

This spiritual tradition sees the burning bush various ways. One group, the *nuzayris*, according to that extraordinary visionary Massignon, see in it the figure of Muhammad.[28] Other Sufis see in it the figure of every believer attentive to the word of God in him.

For al-Hallaj, the uncreated voice speaking through the created bush is a guarantee that God himself may speak on the tongue of the mystic. My role, al-Hallaj says is to represent the bush. The burning bush, at one and the same time flame created and voice uncreated becomes the symbol of a mystical union in which human subject and divine subject make an exchange such that one gives testimony of the other according to the reality of the one and only witness, God.[29]

A later author al-Ghazali, (d. 1111) without the visionary intoxication of al-Hallaj, sees the mountain on which the burning bush is situated as a symbol of the stability and grandeur of the spiritual world. The valleys that run through it, pathways for the dispersal of water symbolize the various levels of perfection to be attained by those who quench their thirst in this spiritual world. The Qur'an refers to the right side of the valley, and it is from the right side of this high valley, that the beneficient waters flow to the lower valleys.

This holy valley of Tuwa (Sinai) is, al-Ghazali points out, (echoing al-Hallaj) the first stage of the entrance of the prophets into the world of holy transcendence, far from the troubles of the senses and the imagination, where they are ordered to turn the face of their souls towards the one reality, and to abandon all thought of both worlds, this, and the one to come, for this sole reality.[30]

There are various traditions which explain why Moses put his daring request: 'My Lord, let me see you'. Muqatil, the early commentator, says that when Moses had heard the word of his Lord, he found it very sweet, and it was this sweetness that aroused in him the desire to see God.[31] Ja^{C}far Sadiq says that Moses asks to see God because seeing the shadow of the word of God on his heart, he feels so at ease with his Lord, as to ask to see him. 'You shall not see me' replies God, because 'the perishable has no access to the imperishable'. Thus if Moses falls in a faint at the sight of the mountain become dust, what would happen to him if he saw his Lord directly.[32]

In the various sources we find elaborations of God's reply, 'You shall not see me'. al-Tha^{C}labi, for example, extends the dialogue, and God's words continue: Man is not able to look upon me in this world. Anyone who looks on me dies. Moses replies: 'My God, I have heard your voice, and I yearn for the sight of you. And that I look on you and then die, is better for me than that I live, and not see you'.[33]

How God spoke to him is not revealed. Abu Sa^{c}id al-Kharraz (d. 899) notes that Moses was the only man called to come close God, and remarks: God looks on his friends from behind a veil, otherwise they would be annihilated like the mountain — and thanks to the veil, the strong can receive spiritual fruits (fawa'id) which transform them from within, without destroying them.[34]

There are various references to God speaking to Moses from behind a veil. al-Tha^{c}labi quotes Wahb as saying: Between God and Moses were seventy veils, and God lifted all of them but one, and Moses was alone with the word of God, and filled with longing, yearned to see him, so he said, 'My Lord, let me see you'.[35]

Ibn Taymiyya too explains that God spoke to Moses from behind a veil. But through this veil he heard God speak to him directly, whereas the other prophets received revelation by *Iha*, God spoke to them in a dream, or by the mediation of an angel:[36]

Moses' fall in a faint is interpreted in various ways. All agree that it is the climax of an extraordinary vocation. Ibn ^{c}Abbas glosses the word sa^{c}iqan as meaning simply a faint. Other authorities such as Qatada say that Moses was struck dead, but was revived. Wahb, on the other hand, tells how all the celestial hierarchies from the first to the seventh heaven pass before Moses so that he will not collapse lifeless. Some tell him of his audacity in desiring to see God; others, by their terrifying aspect sow in him fear and terror, others make him hear the praises of the one who dies not recited by voices that ravish his heart. Lord, says Moses after this, I believe you are my master, and I am convinced no one can see you and live. If the sight of angels ravishes the heart, how much the more You.[37]

Of special interest is the ambivalence of some of the angels towards Moses, and their resentment at his arrogance. al-Tha^{c}labi quotes al-Waqidi's report: 'When Moses fainted, the angels said 'What right does the son of ^{c}Imran have to ask for a vision of God', and continues: 'in one of the books it is stated that the angels of the heavens and the earth came up to Moses after his faint, and began to kick him and to say: son of menstruating woman-kind, do you expect to look on the Lord of Might'.[38]

This animosity of the angels to this experience of Moses and his mediation of the Torah has a counterpart in the rabbinic tradition, which has them complaining, using words taken from the Psalms: 'What is man, that thou art mindful of him' and 'What is this off-spring of woman who has come up on high'?[39]

Two great scenes we have described are directly related to Moses' commission to preach the true religion to Pharaoh on the one hand, and to present the divinely revealed Law, the Torah, to the Israelites, on the other. These are essentially practical matters. But the dramatic character of their presentation in the Qur'an, and the way in which they were orchestrated in the living oral tradition deriving ultimately from Muhammad and the companions, shows in Moses a dimension which both transcends his role as law-giver and the allegorical and spiritual insights that the early Sufis attribute to him. This dimension derives from the Qur'an itself, which gives in Sura 18 (al-Kahf) 65-82 an account of Moses' encounter with a mysterious figure, a saint, identified as al-Khidr, the Green One, by many recognized also as a prophet. At a superficial level, this passage might be considered simply as a midrashic type of episode to show how God's knowledge is greater than that of men who know divine providence only in part. Yet it exercises an extraordinary power of attraction, and generations of exegetes have shown how deeply it is integrated into the texture of the Qur'an, and discovered in it layer upon layer of meaning.

The introduction to the story is brief. Moses vows to find his way to the meeting point of the two seas, to meet, so the commentators tell us, a wise man. He takes his servant with him. The place where they are to meet him is where they lose a salted fish that they have brought as provisions. They discover that the fish is missing when after a night's sleep, they prepare for breakfast. It is at this point that Moses' servant suddenly recalls a rock, some distance back, where the fish miraculously returned to life, leapt out of the basket, and swam away. They retrace their steps to this spot. The Qur'an continues the story:

65. The two of them met one of our servants to whom we had given our favours, to whom we had taught an understanding ours to give.
66. Moses said to him, "May I follow you so that you can teach me a right understanding of what you have been taught".
67. He replied, "you will not be able to bear me with patiently,
68. for how can you bear with patiently what you do not fully understand?"
69. He said, "If God so wills, you will find me patient, I will not disobey you in anything".
70. He replied, "Then if you follow me, do not ask me about anything before I explain its meaning to you".
71. So they set out. But when they were on board a ship, he made a hole in it. (Moses) said, "Did you make a hole in it to drown those on board? You have done a terrible thing!"
72. He replied, "Did I not say that you would be unable to bear with me patiently?"
73. Moses said, "Do not punish me for my forgetfullness, do not impose on me something too difficult for me to bear".
74. Then they continued on their way until, when they met a boy, he killed him. Moses said, "Have you killed an innocent without the excuse of retaliation? You have done an evil thing".
75. He replied, "Did I not say to you that you would not be able to bear with me patiently?"
76. Moses said, "If I question you about anything after this, be my companion no longer. From my side you have ample excuse for that".
77. Then the two of them continued on their way until, when they came to the people of a village, they asked them for food, but the villagers refused to welcome them as guests. Then they found there a wall on the point of collapse and he shored it up. Moses said, "If you had wished, you could have earned a wage for that".
78. He replied, "This is the parting of the ways between you and me. I will tell you the meaning of what you could not bear with patiently:
79. As for the ship, it belonged to some poor men who worked at sea, and I wished to damage it. Behind them was a king seizing every ship by force,
80. and as for the boy, his parents were devout believers, and we feared that he would burden them with arrogance and unbelief,
81. so we wished that their Lord would give them in place of him one better than he, more virtuous and faithful.
82. and, as for the wall, it belonged to two orphan boys in the village; beneath it was a treasure chest belonging to them both and their father was a righteous man, so your Lord desired that they should come of age and discover their treasure as a blessing from your Lord. I did not do it of my own initiative. That is the meaning of what you could not bear with patiently".

This mysterious person is identified by the commentators as al-Khidr, the Green One. Why did Moses wish to meet him? al-Razi explains that Moses asked God 'Who is there who knows more than I?' And God directed him to look for al-Khidr. al-Razi alludes to mystical dimensions in the story, but takes the matter no further, remarking that in his exegesis it is not possible to discuss them.[41]

Muqatil gives much the same information, thus indicating that this material is early. He argues, on the basis of the Qur'anic text 'one of our servants to whom we have given mercy' that al-Khidr is a prophet, glossing mercy (*rahma*) as a grace (*ni^{c}ma*) and says that this particular *ni^{c}ma* is prophecy, (*nubuwwa*). For Muqatil, then, al-Khidr is a prophet, and if his knowledge is superior to that of Moses, it is because God has made differences between the prophets, referring Sura 17 (al-Isra') ad v.55: 'We have preferred some prophets over others. To some, (Muqatil says), God has spoken, to some he has put in their charge the birds and the mountains; to one he has given a great kingdom, to another the power to raise the dead and cure the lepers and the paralyzed; yet another he has raised to heaven. To each he has given something not given to the others — this is the meaning of preferring one to another'.[42]

His title, al-Khidr, the Green, is explained in various ways. In a saying of Muhammad, he was called al-Khidr because on one occasion when he sat on a white pelt, it shook beneath him, and became green. Mujahid reports that he was called al-Khidr because wherever he prayed, all around him became green'.[43] It should be noted that 'He who wears green' has always been an epithet for those who live on the highest possible spiritual level — be they angels, the prophet, or al-Khidr himself — the guide of mystics in a very special sense'.[44] Appointed as guide and mentor to Moses, he had a role in inspiring mystics on their journey, answering their questions, and investing them with the Sufi cloak, an investmment regarded as valid in the tradition of Sufi initiation, and invested no less a person than Ibn 'Arabi himself'.[45]

How does al-Khidr perform his role, and what is Moses' relation to him? The sinking of the ship, the killing of the child, and rebuilding of the wall seem random acts, and Moses judges them at a commonsense rational level — why drown the crew of a ship that has given them passage? Why kill a boy without even the excuse of retaliation (a legists' point this). Why rebuild a wall free of charge when they are desparate for food in a village that refuses them hospitality?

In each case he has broken his word to al-Khidr and lost sight of the larger design. He had failed the test that al-Khidr designed for him, although al-Khidr had warned him 'How can you bear with patiently what you do not fully understand', and misunderstood his mentor's actions on no less than three occasions. It is the shock of realizing he has been wrong and the resulting perplexity that is to open his mind to new levels of understanding, new, infinite perspectives, extending beyond what God had already taught him. This psychological shock at the realization being wrong as a means of opening the mind to faith and spiritual insight occurs elsewhere in the Qur'an. In the encounter of Bilqis, the Queen of Sheba, with Solomon (Qur'an 27:41-44), in affairs of this world, she shows herself his equal. It is when she makes a mistake imagining that the polished glass she has to walk across to approach Solomon's throne is water, that her self-confidence is shaken, and out of the resulting perplexity she recognizes Solomon's prophetic role, and accepts his religion.

Yet this is not an end to the matter. al-Tha^{C}labi shows how all three tests were related to events in Moses' earlier life, thus demonstrating how profoundly this episode is integrated into the Qur'an. He has al-Khidr saying to Moses: "Moses, do you reproach me for wrecking the ship, fearing that those on board would drown, and forget yourself, that when you were a child, and helpless, your mother cast you into the Nile, and God preserved you! You reproach me for killing the boy, without cause, yet you killed an Egyptian without cause; and you reproached me for not taking a wage for repairing the wall, and you forget that you yourself, when you watered the herd of Shu^{C}ayb, did so without taking a wage, counting only on a reward from the Almighty King".[46]

The mystic Abu Sa^{C}id al-Kharraz draws an important lesson from this encounter, explaining that al-Khidr's role is to heighten the spiritual awareness of Moses in his public role as prophet and law-giver. This is because the prophet faces a special temptation to pride just because of this public role, and the need constantly to refer to himself as the recipient of the message, an urgent message that he has to communicate to mankind. His awareness of this vocation and personal role is a test analogous to that to which Iblis (Satan) failed when in Qur'an 7:12 he explains why he refused to bow to Adam, saying 'I am better than he'. The saint does not fail this test, and one aspect of the role of al-Khidr is to alert Moses to it, as well as to awaken in him a deeper spiritual understanding.[47]

The clarity with which these spiritual directors perceived the dangers implicit in a high vocation is striking. (One might wonder whether Prime Ministers and Archbishops, not to mention professors, might benefit from such counsel).

It is the great mystic Muhyi 'l-Din Ibn Arabi however, who brings the most striking psychological insights into his discussion of Moses' vocation. In examining his views, it should be mentioned that Ibn Arabi's theosophy is unacceptable in many parts of the Muslim world. His spiritual and psychological insights however can be separated out from his theosophy, usually more to their advantage rather than the reverse.

Indeed, some of his analyses of the life of Moses are of an extraordinary poetic as well a profound spiritual beauty. One of his goals in writing on Moses, as on the other prophets in his work *Fusus al-Hikam*[48] is to show that everything has a purpose and that evil has no absolute existence. His purpose is to reconcile outward appearance with inner reality, or from another standpoint to discover the inner meaning of outward phenomena. Moses was placed in a box and set adrift in the Nile. The outward act was one that could be expected to lead to death by drowning. In fact it resulted in the infant's escape from death in Pharaoh's pogrom.[49] In the same way, the outward aspect of al-Khidr knocking a hole in the boat, suggested that he intended to drown those abroad it; inwardly it was to save the men and their means of livelihood from the depredations of an evil king.[50] Outwardly, Moses' killing of the Egyptian was an evil act, and he fled out of fear to save himself from punishment. Inwardly it was for a higher purpose. Moses' flight was for the love of life. True, it meant escape from execution;[51] but it was also an act that would set in train a series of events that would lead to the rescue of the Israelites from Egypt, the drowning, and salvation of Pharaoh, and ultimately the Epiphany on Mt. Sinai.

Moses, Ibn Arabi says, was impelled into movement by the love of salvation, for the principle of movement is always love, no matter how the observer may be confused by outward appearances. ... The movement which is the existence of the world itself, is a movement of love, as is indicated by the word of God uttered by the prophet: I was a hidden treasure, I wished to be known, and I created the world that I might be known ... the movement of the world from non-existence to existence is in reality the movement of love revealing itself'.[52] It is as an illustration of this principle that ibn 'Arabi sees the inner meaning of Moses' flight.

But Moses was also a means of salvation for Pharaoh. When as an infant he was taken from the Nile, at first Pharaoh wished to kill him but his wife restrained him with the words 'a soothing of the eye to me and to you' (28:9). He 'soothed the eye of Pharaoh' because it was thanks to him that when on the point of drowning God gave him faith, and he exclaimed: 'I believe that there is no God other than the God in whom Moses and the Israelites believe, and I submit myself to him' (Qur'an 10:90). Thus God took him, purified, without a stain of sin upon him, for he took him at the moment of his acceptance of faith, before he committed any sin. For Islam wipes out what precedes it. He was made a sign of God's solicitude for whomever he wishes, so that no-one should despair of the kindness of God Qur'an (12:87). Had Pharaoh been one of those who despaired, he would not all of a sudden have believed.[53]

It is the saving of Moses from the water of the Nile that ibn ᶜArabi sees as the inauguration of his career. God saved Moses from the pain of confinement in the box in which he was placed in the Nile, and rent apart the darkness of nature by what he gave him of divine knowledge, even though leaving him within nature.[54] Moses then was saved by divine knowledge, just as those who are dead in ignorance come to life by knowledge. This in the interpretation that Ibn'Arabi gives to the words of the Qur'an, (6:122) (and one who was dead, we restored him to life, and made for him a light by which he could walk among men, and this is *huda*, guidance).[55] He then goes on to explain how this guidance is given: Man is led to a state of perplexity, of confused helplessness and thus realizes that existence is perplexity ... and that this perplexity is instability, ... it is anxiety (tension) and movement, and movement is life. Thus there is no inertia and no death; there is existence, and no non-being. This is the way in which water brings life and movement to the earth, as the Qur'an says (22:5): 'You see the dry earth, and when we send down water upon it, it trembles, conceives and produces all kinds of species in beauty'.[56]

In other words, just as water to the dead earth, so is perplexity to man. It is creative. As I said earlier, it was perplexity — that brought Bilqis (The Queen of Sheba) to accept the religion of Solomon; perplexity that Moses experienced at the burning bush, and perplexity that brought him to an awareness of the dimensions of knowledge beyond his experience.

These later developments might at first sight seem far removed from the literal meaning of the Qur'an, but they have roots early in the history of Islam. There is the tradition ascribed to Muhammad transmitted from ibn^{C}Abbas through Abi b. Ka^{C}b, who said: Whenever he mentioned anyone in his prayer, he began with himself, and on that day he said: 'May God have mercy upon us, and on my brother Moses. Had he stayed with his companion (al-Khidr) longer, he would have seen wonder upon wonder. But he had said: If I ask you anything after this, do not accompany me any more.' This occurs in al-Tha^{C}labi, but the tradition is also used by Ibn ^{C}Arabi.[57]

Thus it is clear that the episode with al-Khidr has a wide range of meanings, moral, psychological and mystical. In the Ibn Arabi frame of reference, al-Khidr becomes as it were the inward aspect of spiritual understanding, to the outward aspect of divine truth expressed in the form of the Law represented by Moses.

Frithjof Schuon puts it somewhat differently: 'Moses represents the Law, the particular and exclusive form, and al-Khidr, universal truth, which cannot be grasped from the standpoint of the 'letter', like the wind of which thou 'canst not tell whence it cometh and whither it goeth'.[58]

This survey of Moses, while giving some idea of the importance of Moses in the Muslim tradition, has attempted to show the richness of the diverse ways in which he was understood, and in which he inspired the religious imagination in Islam. If this, in its fullness is added to the traditions he has inspired in Judaism, and in Latin and Greek Christianity, whether in story, prayer, hymn of praise or iconography, the corpus of material he has generated is staggering. What a commentary on the history of these three traditions, that in sharing such veneration for this chosen shepherd, they have found so much to quarrel about with such disastrous results! No wonder that an Sumatran poet writing in the 30's, a devout Muslim, could liken Isaac and Ismael to two shafts of light from a singe jewel, Abraham. God, the master jeweller, he complains remaining indifferent throughout the centuries to the competing claims of their respective progeny. Rather than vex himself with the problem, to be on Sinai, close to God, like Moses, would be sufficient'.[59]

There is much for every religious tradition to share in the story of Moses. There is no need to limit its meaning or significance to the Judaeo-Christian-Islamic matrix. In almost every religious tradition, from the time of the Buddha, and before a period, exile or self-exile is required of the future teacher. Siddharta, the future Buddha, perplexed at the sight of poverty, sickness, old age and death, left home and family to seek enlightenment. Moses was lost in the mountains. He needed warmth and light. His flint and drill stick could not help him, and he looked for fire. In the fire, he found God. For, as Ibn ^{C}Arabi puts it: God speaking to Moses, appeared to him in this form because Moses had been searching for fire. God appeared to him in the form of what he sought, so there would be no danger of his wandering astray from him. For when God brings some one close to him, he attracts that person to him in a form that (at first) he does not recognize, just as Moses, in need of fire, through this need was drawn to God without realizing it.[60] And God spoke to him.

FOOTNOTES

1. Exodus, 15:21-22 (Translation: the Jerusalem Bible).
2. Youakim, Moubarac, *Moise dans le Coran* in *Moise l'homme de l'alliance*, Cahiers Sioniens, Paris, 1954, p. 375.
3. David Daitches, *Moses, The man and his Vision*, New York, 1975, pp. 9-10.
4. Charles Cutler Torrey, *The Jewish Foundation of Islam*, Ktav Publishing House, Inc., New York, 1967, p. 93 and p. 105 respectively.

5. See Bell & Watt, *Introduction to the Qur'ān*, Edinburgh Paperbacks, Edinburgh, 1977, pp. 109-113.
6. Frithjof Schuon, *Understanding Islam*, Unwin Paperbacks, 1979, (second impression), p. 59.
7. Schuon, *Islam*, p. 46.
8. al-Nisapurī, Abū Ishaq Ahmad b. Muhammad b. Ibrahim al-Tha'labī, d. 1035.
9. *Qisas al-Anbiyā' al-musammā bi 'l-'arā'is*, al-Halabi, Cairo, 1347 (A.H.)
10. al-Tha'labī, *Qişaş*, p. 128.
11. Fakhr al-Dīn Abū 'Abd Allāh Muhammad b. 'Umar b. al-Husain, al-Rāzī, 1149-1209.
12. al-Rāzī, *al-Tafsīr*, 22, p. 14.
13. al-Rāzī, *al-Tafsīr*, 22, p. 15.
14. al-Rāzī, *al-Tafsīr*, 22, p. 15-16.
15. al-Rāzī, *al-Tafsīr*, 22, p. 17.
16. al-Rāzī, *al-Tafsīr*, 22, p. 17.
17. al-Rāzī, *al-Tafsīr*, 22, p. 25.
18. al-Rāzī, *al-Tafsīr*, 22, p. 25.
19. Paul Nwyia, *Exégèse Coranique et Langage Mystique*, Recherches 49, Beirut, 1970, p. 83.
20. Nwyia, *Exégès Coranique*, p. 179.
21. Nwyia, *Exégès Coranique*, p. 328. (A passage quoted by Haydar Amoli in *Jāmi' al-asrār* in the form of a hadīth transmitted by Wahb ibn Munabbih, V, p. 513).
22. al-Tha'labī, *Qişaş*, p. 124.
23. al-Rāzī, *al-Tafsīr*, 14, p. 235.
24. Louis Gardet: 'L'experience interieure du prophet Mūsā (Moise) selon les sufīs' in G.C. Anawati et Louis Gardet, *Mystique Musulmane Aspects et Tendances — Experiences et Techniques*, Paris, 1961, p. 263.
25. Gardet, *Mūsā*, p. 263.
26. Wayne A. Meeks, *The Prophet King Moses Traditions and the Johannine Christology*, Brills, Leiden, 1967, p. 207.
27. Gardet, *Mūsā*, pp. 265-266.
28. Gardet, *Mūsā*, pp. 266.
29. Gardet, *Mūsā*, pp. 266.
30. Gardet, *Mūsā*, pp. 265.
31. Nwyia, *Exégèse Coranique*, p. 86.
32. Nwyia, *Exégèse Coranique*, p. 183.
33. al-Tha'labī, *Qişaş*, p. 140.
34. Nwyia, *Exégèse Coranique*, p. 254.
35. al-Tha'labī, *Qişaş*, p. 140.
36. Nwyia, *Exégèse Coranique*, p. 88, f.n. quoting Ibn Taymiyya 'Risāla ba'alabakiya' in *Majmū'āt al Rasā'il*, Cairo, 1328, pp. 402-403.
37. Nwyia, *Exégèse Coranique*, pp. 86-87.
38. al-Tha'labī, *Qişaş*, p. 140.
39. Meeks, *Prophet-King*, pp. 205-206.
40. al-Rāzī, *al-Tafsīr*, 21, p. 144.
41. al-Rāzī, *al-Tafsīr*, 21, p. 150.
42. Nwyia, *Exégèse Coranique*, p. 90.
43. al-Tha'labī, *Qişaş*, p. 153.
44. Annemarie Schimmel, *Mystical Dimensions of Islam*, University of North Carolina Press, 1975, p. 102.
45. Schimmel, *Mystical Dimensions*, p. 106.
46. al-Tha'labī, *Qişaş*, p. 159.
47. Nwyia, *Exégèse Coranique*, p. 47.
48. *Bezels of Wisdom*, or, in view of the content, *The Wisdom of the prophets*. Ed. A.A. Affifi al-Halabi, Cairo, 1946. A French translation of extracts fromthe work has been made by Titus Burckhardt, *La Sagesse des Prophetes*, Editions Albin Michel, Paris, 1955. Reference to page numbers in this translation are placed in brackets following page references in the Arabic text.
49. Ibn Arabi, *Fuşūş*, p. 199 (154).
50. Ibn Arabi, *Fuşūş*, p. 203 (162).
51. Ibn Arabi, *Fuşūş*, p. 204 (164).
52. Ibn Arabi, *Fuşūş*, p. 203 (162).
53. Ibn Arabi, *Fuşūş*, p. 201 (156).
54. Ibn Arabi, *Fuşūş*, p. 202 (159).
55. Ibn Arabi, *Fuşūş*, p. 199 (154-155).
56. Ibn Arabi, *Fuşūş*, p. 199-200 (155).
57. Ibn Arabi, *Fuşūş*, p. 205 (166).
   al-Tha'labī, *Qişaş*, p. 157.
58. Schuon, *Islam*, p. 81.
59. Amir Hamzah, *Njanji Sunji*, Jakarta, 1954, p. 7.
   'Alas, my Beloved
   For me this is all without use.
   For me there is only one desire
   To feel you close beside me
   As did Moses on the peak of Sinai'.
60. Ibn Arabi, *Fuşūş*, pp. 212-213 (178).

ZWI WERBLOWSKY

JERUSALEM: HOLY CITY OF THREE RELIGIONS

The relationship of Comparative Religion and Theology has long been the subject of much earnest, searching, and at times also partisan debate that was not always devoid of *odium theologicum*. For some (including, if I may say so, myself), theology is the handmaid of Comparative Religion; in other words: theology, as the intellectual elaboration of the beliefs of a religious group, is one of the bricks out of which—together with other bricks such as ritual, mythology, personal experience, social institutions—the total fabric of religion is made up. For the theologian, Comparative Religion is the handmaid—whether in terms of a *theologia naturalis*, or of a *theologia religionum*, or of apologetics, or of simple and straightforward polemics. A representative of what the late Dr. Strong called the "New Theology", and which we today would call a totally "open" theology, would no doubt consider Comparative Religion a very welcome and, indeed, indispensable handmaid, because the "science of religion" (as he called it) could show us the "laws according to which religion has developed and continues to develop. . . . It compares the religions and shows us what is the distinguishing genius of each, and how one form of religion has influenced another".[1] It will be my task tonight to show, by taking up one particular theme, how different—albeit closely related—forms of religion have influenced one another in one particular matter, and what was the distinguishing genius of each. I shall leave it to the theologians to draw the lessons, if any, suggested by these comparisons. In a sense, of course, we all are theologians, as Dr. Strong always insisted, i.e. human beings drawing lessons from our knowledge, and making judgments in terms of our experiences of reality and of our ultimate values. Living in a secularized and still secularizing age which partly has lost the sense of holiness, partly turned away from the traditional articulations of holiness because of their unholy irrelevance and abuse, and which partly is struggling to regain a holiness that would permeate the very secularity of our lives rather than ensconce itself in geographically or ritually delimited areas—nobody can help being a "theologian" of sorts, making his judgments, acknowledging his values, and committing himself to his choices.

One way in which people have experienced and, as it were, crystallized their sense of holiness, was in their relation to space.[2] There are holy lands —that is lands that are considered holy by virtue of the bond that binds human groups to the earth on which they live. It is a bond of gratitude and love that frequently, and at times imperceptibly, turn into veneration. Some of you may have visited the temple in Benares in which the object of worship is—a map of Mother India. There are holy places as distinct from holy lands, places where the divine became manifest, in one way or another, to the eyes of believing men and women, and which were cherished or revered as concrete, tangible, spatially defined testimonies to the reality of the divine as it had become visible in experiences or traditions of theophanies, revelations, miracles, or the lives of saintly men. There are holy cities as distinct from holy places: cities that acquired their holiness as a result of historical circumstances and events, or cities that are holy because either in theory or in actual fact they were constructed so as to reflect cosmic reality—a kind of microscopic spatial reflection of the cosmos and its underlying divine reality as conceived and spelled out in mythological tradition.[3] There are cities which are holy because they harbour and possess a holy object or shrine. We think of Mecca, Benares, Lhasa, Angkor, Rome and many others. As a modern example we may instance Tenri (near Nara, in Japan), which is a holy city not only because it is built around the "navel of the earth", the sacred *kanrodai,* but also because it is constructed according to a divine plan.

Tonight we shall turn our attention to one city only, but one to which three major, and related, religions are bound by bonds of veneration and love. We shall try to understand what Jerusalem has meant to Jews, Christians and Muslims, and what it means to them today. We shall attempt to see the differences in the nature of the bond, in the origins of the sacred character, and in the quality and functions of the holiness involved.

Let me turn to Islam first because here the problem is, in some respects, the most intriguing. The sanctity of Jerusalem in Islam is a fact. Jerusalem is *al-Kuds* ("the Holy One"), or *al-Kuds al-sharifa* ("the noble holy one") as it was referred to by medieval Arab travellers and writers. The problem that interests us here is how the city came to acquire that place in Muslim consciousness, and in a religion the founder of which exercised his ministry in south-western Arabia. (To obviate any possible misunderstandings, permit me to add here a parenthesis to the effect that I shall address myself to this problem as an "unbeliever". What are facts to the believing Muslim, are not necessarily so to the critical historian and student of Comparative Religion). The general outline of the answer is simple and obvious enough, though the details prove to be more complex. There is little doubt—in the eyes of the aforementioned unbelieving historian—that the Prophet Muhammed never was in Jerusalem. It is equally beyond doubt that the Prophet and his message were profoundly indebted to Christian and Jewish influences. Scholarly opinion differs regarding the extent and the relative contributions of the Jewish and Christian influences respectively, as well as regarding the forms of Judaism and Christianity which the Prophet encountered during his formative years when his message, as it were, incubated and matured. Was it, for instance, the "normative" Judaism which we know from the classical sources of the period, or some form of local or sectarian Judaism? This, incidentally, might also explain the "garbled" versions in which some Jewish and Christian, including Biblical, traditions re-appear in the Kur'an. But be that as it may, there is little doubt that for many of his central ideas (e.g. monotheism, the day of judgment, man's moral responsibility for his actions) the Prophet was indebted to a Christian and Jewish legacy.

The holiness of Jerusalem was part of that legacy, and indeed the original direction of prayer (*qibla*) was not towards Mecca but to Jerusalem —'*ula al-qiblatheyn* ("the first of the two qiblas"). This is not the occasion to discuss the origin of this first *qibla* and the reasons for the subsequent change to the direction of Mecca and the *Ka'aba* (cf. Kur'an, Sura 2:136f.). There is an abundant literature on the subject, both historical and theological, which I need not summarize here.

Nevertheless we must turn our attention, however briefly, to the famous passage in the Kur'an, Sura 17:1 "Praise be to Allah who brought his servant at night from the Holy Mosque to the Remote Mosque, the precincts of which we have blessed". Again we need not discuss here the original meaning of this verse, though I for one am convinced that the reference is to an exstatic viz. visionary ascent to a heavenly sanctuary.[4] The idea of a heavenly sanctuary too is well-known in Jewish and Christian tradition where, however, this notion was sometimes associated with that of a heavenly Jerusalem. Hence some scholars have persuasively argued that even the original meaning of the kur'anic text implied some kind of reference to Jerusalem, albeit the celestial one.

It is, however, not the debated original meaning of this kur'anic passage which must claim our attention here, but the interpretation which it was given already in early Islam. According to this interpretation, the Prophet Muhammad was miraculously transported from Mecca to Jerusalem, and it was from there that he made his ascent to heaven, the *mi'radj*. (The references to revelations granted to the Prophet and described Kur'an, Sura 81:19 ff. and 53:1 ff., were consequently merged with the journey referred to in Sura 17:1). The events of this nocturnal journey (the *isra'*) were subsequently embellished by a luxuriant growth of legend, which included the Prophet's miraculous winged mount, al-Buraq, and many more picturesque details. But the gist of the story—as relevant to our purpose— is simple, and if I may put it, somewhat irreverently, into the language of modern air travel, it is this: there are no direct flights from Mecca to Heaven; you have to make a stopover in Jerusalem. By this interpretation, and by this fusion of the *isra'* and the *mi'radj*, Islam linked itself to the traditional holiness of Jerusalem in Christianity and Judaism, and integrated it into its own religious system.

For the historian there arises the problem how to account for the growth of these beliefs and traditions. Why, where, and when exactly did they develop? It matters little for our purpose that not all Muslim traditions are unanimous on the subject, that some of these traditions are patently late fabrications, and that even in later times some audacious and near-heretical spirits actually denied the literal occurrence of these events, either by flat rationalist rejection or by mystical allegorisation. We are interested here in the central, orthodox, mainline tradition of Islam for which *al-mi'radj haqq,* the tale of Muhammad's ascent to heaven, including the preceding nocturnal journey to Jerusalem, is literally true. This belief has nourished Muslim dogmatics, piety and devotion for centuries, although in this respect too tensions and struggles are evident.

For there had occurred an important event that decisively affected and changed the status of Jerusalem, and influenced its consolidation as a centre of Muslim devotion. That was the conquest of the city by the Khalif Omar in or about the year 638. Unlike the early days of the Medinese period, when Jerusalem was outside the orbit of Muslim society, and the original *qibla* was due to purely ideological factors, Jerusalem was now part of the *dar al-Islam,* the Muslim *oikoumene.* The many Christian churches and places of pilgrimage in the city (including the traditional site of Christ's ascension), and its role as a centre of Christian devotion and piety, could not but act as a challenge to the Muslims. Jewish influences too may have played a part, as evidenced by traditions such as e.g. that concerning the dialogue between the conqueror of Jerusalem, the Khalif Omar ibn al-Khattab, and Ka'ab al-Akhbar, a Jewish convert to Islam, as recounted by the 10th century historian al-Tabari. Indeed, attempts to make the city compete with Mecca or Medina, were more than once branded by opponents as "Jewish".[5] The Khalif Omar seems to have erected a house of prayer near the holy *sakhra* (the "rock") on the site of the former Jewish temple, and about fifty years later, in the year 691, the Umayyad khalif Abd al-Malik ibn Marwan built the mosque (falsely called the Mosque of Omar in popular parlance) which to this day is one of the glories not only of Islam but of religious architecture in general. The Jewish word for the Temple became one of the Arabic descriptions of Jerusalem: *Beyt al-Makdis* (or *Beyt al-Mukaddis*), *sharrafahu Allah*—"the House of the Sanctuary, may Allah glorify it".

The history of the mosque, its repairs and renovations, need not detain us here. What matters is the fact that when Abd al-Malik (or his son al-Walid) built the large mosque at the southern end of the *Haram*—probably on the foundations of a Byzantine church—and this mosque came to be called *al-Aksa* ("the Remote Mosque"), the identification of the site with the "farthest (or remote) Mosque" in the kur'anic account of the *isra'* was definitive and complete. For a long time scholars have held the growing emphasis on the sanctity of Jerusalem to have been due mainly to pragmatic considerations of Umayyad politics, and even the eminent Goldziher[6] lent the weight of his great authority to this view. Abd al-Malik, it was asserted, was interested in boosting the sanctity of Jerusalem in order to counter the influence of the rebellious counter-khalif in Mecca, ibn Zubayr. Modern scholarship—and I am in private duty bound to emphasize the contribution of scholars from the Hebrew University of Jerusalem in this matter—has abandoned this interpretation, and tends to accept the testimony of the ancient Muslim writers to the effect that the underlying motives were essentially religious.[7] Jerusalem had begun to play an increasingly important role in Muslim piety, and if there was an element of competition, it was not so much with ibn Zubayr and Mecca as with the Christian churches in Jerusalem and especially the noble dome of the Anastasis (unfortunately known in western Christendom under the name of the "Holy Sepulchre"), the splendour of which the Muslims wanted to outdo with an even more glorious sanctuary. This is explicitly stated by a great lover of Jerusalem and an illustrous fellow-Jerusalemite (though he lived a thousand years ago), the 10th century Arab geographer and historian al-Mukaddasi, and I see no reason to disbelieve his testimony.

The sanctity of this holy site acted like a magnet, and an increasing number of cosmological, eschatological[8], and legendary-historical beliefs as well as devout practices came to be associated with it. After the conquest of Jerusalem by the Crusaders, a new kind of—one is tempted to call it "Zionist"—literature began to flourish in the Islamic world: the *fadha'il al-Kuds*, tracts singing the praises and virtues of Jerusalem. It will not do to describe this *genre littéraire* simply as propaganda designed to rouse enthusiasm for a Muslim reconquista. No doubt this factor helps to explain the quantity and dissemination of this kind of literature, but its existence as such and the underlying ideas belong to the sphere of Muslim piety and devotion. As a matter of fact, the *fadha'il* literature, though it flourished in the Crusader period,[9] actually had its beginnings before the Crusades. When a modern Muslim scholar asserts that "the earliest work of this class is by a contemporary of Saladin",[10] then I am pleased to point to the work of scholars at the Hebrew University of Jerusalem, which has definitely established the earlier date of some *fadha'il al-Kuds* compositions.[11]

Islam, therefore, provides us with perhaps the most impressive example of how a holy city can acquire a specific holiness on the basis of what—to the unbelieving outsider at least—is mere legend, superimposed, no doubt, on an earlier, traditional, sanctity of the place. Whereas in the case of Christianity historical facts (i.e., the life and death of Jesus) created religious facts (e.g., the resurrection and ascension), and both combined to create "holy places", the Islamic case is the exact opposite. Beliefs and piety created religious facts and these, in their turn, produced historic facts which, for the contemporary student of religion, culture and even politics, must be deemed, to all practical intents and purposes, as real as any other kind of "hard" fact. Certainly in Islam, which does not make the distinction between the religious and the secular (including the political) spheres in the way Christianity has made it, religious facts have implications which legitimately spill over into the political sphere. This remains true even where the religious dimension is subject to abuse and manipulation by purely political interests.

I have just mentioned the *fadha'il al-Kuds* literature and its remarkable flowering during the Crusader period, i.e. at a time when Christian longing for the Holy Land and the terrestial Jerusalem—as well as some other, less laudable and less Christian, impulses—had reached fever pitch. Christian enthusiasm for the Holy City celebrated its most un-Christian triumph in the Crusader conquest of Jerusalem in the year 1099. Muslim enthusiasm in turn triumphed with Saladin's conquest of the city and the removal of the golden cross from the top of the dome where the Crusaders had planted it. But the Christian attitude to the Holy Land and to the Holy City is far more complex, and was not always and unequivocally of the crusading type. To illustrate this ambiguity, let me begin with an incident from the times of the Second Crusade.

In the year 1129 or thereabouts, an English clerk by name of Philip from the diocese of Lincoln set out on a pilgrimage to the Holy Land. On his way to Jerusalem he stopped at Clairvaux. Shortly afterwards the Bishop of Lincoln received a Letter from the Abbot of Clairvaux, announcing the good tidings that Philip had arrived safely and very quickly at his destination, and that he intended to remain there permanently. "He has entered the holy city and has chosen his heritage. . . . He is no longer an inquisitive onlooker but a devout inhabitant and an enrolled citizen of Jerusalem". But this Jerusalem, "if you want to know, is Clairvaux. She is the Jerusalem united to the one in heaven by whole-hearted devotion, by conformity of life, and by a certain spiritual affinity."[12]

The true home of the Christian—according to the medieval conception—is the heavenly Jerusalem. Not that he must despise the terrestial Jerusalem, but the true terrestial Jerusalem which is "united to the one in heaven" is wherever the perfect Christian life is lived. We recognise in this letter the voice of the same Abbot of Clairvaux who refused the offer, in 1131, by the Crusader King of Jerusalem, Baldwin II, of the site of St. Samuel (also known as Mountjoy or Mons Gaudii northwest of Jerusalem, encouraging the Premonstratensians to establish themselves there instead of the Cistercians. Yet the same Bernard also preached the Second Crusade and helped to establish the new order of the Knights Templars. Here we have, in a nutshell, the late medieval version of what is a fundamental Christian ambiguity or, if you prefer, dialectics.

Indeed, for many centuries Christianity had been caught between the horns of the dilemma of the heavenly *versus* the earthly Jerusalem.[13] The New Testament itself exhibits a marked tendency towards what might be called a "de-territorialization" of the concept of holiness, and a consequent dissolution of spatially localized notions. It is not the Temple and its Holy of Holies that is the centre, but Christ; it is not the Holy City or Land that constitute the "area" of holiness, but the new community, the body of Christ.[14] Yet for later generations of Christians, the land in general and Jerusalem in particular were the scene on which the most uniquely momentous events of history had been enacted. The mystery of the incarnation and redemption had taken place here. The divine act of salvation, for all its universal—and according to some early fathers, cosmic—significance here had its local habitation and incarnate manifestation. The nativity and the events preceding it, Christ's childhood and manhood, his ministry and preaching, the consummation of this ministry in his passion, resurrection and ascension, the birth of the Church on Pentecost and the beginnings of the first Christian community—all these took place on definite spots in this particular city and land, no matter whether the sites associated with these events by later tradition were historically "authentic" or not.

Small wonder, then, that Christians have always cherished Palestine as a "holy land", and Jerusalem as a "holy city", and that pilgrims have at all times come to visit the sites associated with the mystery of salvation and to permeate their souls with the blessings of this mystery at the very place of its earthly and historical manifestation. Yet at the same time the aforementioned "de-territorializing" tendency also asserted itself, and many of the great spiritual figures in the history of Christianity expressed doubts about what seemed to them an at least potentially crude, unspiritual, and hence unsound approach to the mystery. Commenting on the words of Jesus "if any man thirst, let him come unto me and drink" (John 7:37), St. Augustine wrote:[15]

When we thirst, then we should come—not with our feet but rather with our feelings; we should come not by wandering but by loving. In an inward way to love is to wander. It is one thing to wander with the body, and a different thing to wander with the heart. He who wanders with the body, changes his place by the motion of the body; he who wanders with the heart, changes his feelings by the motion of the heart.

There were other voices warning against pilgrimages, and casting doubt on their value. St. Gregory of Nyssa wrote in one of his letters[16] "advise therefore the brethren to ascend from the body to God, rather than from Cappadocia to Palestine", but he himself did make a pilgrimage to Jerusalem. St. Jerome, although he chose to spend the better part of his life in Bethlehem, declared[17] 'the heavenly sanctuary is open from Britain no less than from Jerusalem, for the kingdom of God is within you", and many later mystical writers suggested that pilgrimages were not always or necessarily conducive to sanctification. Protestantism has taken up this strand in the Christian tradition, emphasizing and elaborating it, and I need not remind you of the Puritan poet's jeer in his description of the paradise of fools,[18]

Here Pilgrims roam, that stray'd so far to seek
In Golgotha him dead, who lives in Heav'n.

Others dreamed of a terrestial but omnipresent Jerusalem, a Jerusalem that could be built "in England's green and pleasant land". But again, as if to illustrate the aforementioned built-in Christian ambivalence in this matter, it was Protestant scholarship which gave the main impetus to the modern study of biblical archeology and antiquities.[19]

By and large, however, Christian piety has acted on the assumption that the movement of the body and that of the heart were not incompatible and that, on the contrary, the former could stimulate and promote the latter. But this is only part—and perhaps the lesser part—of the story. We already encountered one main Christian *Leitmotiv* in St. Bernard's letter to the Bishop of Lincoln: the idea of the heavenly Jerusalem, which is the real and essential one, and of which any possible earthly Jerusalem is but a pale terrestial reflection. The origins of this notion of a heavenly Jerusalem go back to the Judaism of the Second Temple period, and I shall soon have to say a word on this, as well as on the development of this idea in post-Temple, Tannaitic and Amoraic (i.e. rabbinic) Judaism.[20] Mount Zion and the city of the living God are explicitly identified with the heavenly Jerusalem in Hebrews 12:22, and there is no need for me to quote at length from the apocalyptic vision of the glorious celestial Jerusalem, shining with gold and studded with sapphires, as described in ch.21 of the Revelation of St. John. This chapter has had a lasting influence on Christian symbolism, but one may, perhaps, venture to generalize by saying that this influence exerted itself mainly in line with the aforementioned spiritualizing and de-territoralizing tendency. Jerusalem is essentially the heavenly Jerusalem, and the heavenly Jerusalem is the archetype of the Church. Like every city which is a *metropolis*, i.e. in both the literal and the archetypal sense a mother to her children, so the heavenly Jerusalem too, "the Jerusalem which is above", is, in the words of the Apostle Paul (Gal. 4:26), "the mother of us all". In fact, the city as the mother, i.e., the celestial Jerusalem which is the mother of us all, is identical with the *mater ecclesia*. The liquidation, to all practical intents and purposes, of concrete historical eschatology in the centuries between *Revelation* and St. Augustine, produced a Christian image of the heavenly Jerusalem which is purely spiritual. This heavenly, spiritual entity, of which the Church in this world is an earthly reflection, is the abode of God who dwells in the midst of his faithful and sanctified people. This spiritual view of humanity united to God, expressed largely in allegorical and homiletical imagery, was only partly counterbalanced by the traditions of popular piety, pilgrimages, and such outbursts of enthusiasm as witnessed by the Crusader period.

It would be a worthy subject of a special lecture to examine the songs of Zion in Christian poetry. Who has not listened with emotion and a pounding heart to the yearning for salvation voiced in many a negro spiritual that sings of Jerusalem; or has not felt an elation of spirit at listening to the strains of the German chorale *Jerusalem, Du hochgebaute Stadt*. And as for *Jerusalem the Golden,* associated in the minds of most Israelis with Naomi Shemer's wonderful song which, since 1967, has become an even more genuine expression of Israeli feeling than the national anthem, few of them, I suspect, are aware that a poem of that name is an old favourite in the hymn book of the Anglican Church, going back, in its turn, to a more ancient medieval hymn. Whenever a new church is consecrated— for a church is meant to reflect that heavenly church in which all the children of God are assembled—the following beautiful hymn is sung in the Latin rite:

Urbs Jerusalem beata
Dicta pacis visio
Quae construitur in coelis
Vivis ex lapidibus
....
Plateae et muri ejus
Ex auro purissimo.

But perhaps the most beautiful and moving of all Christian poetry on the subject is a song Abelard wrote, not in honour of Heloise, but in honour of that perfect day which is eternal Sabbath and eternal joy. This ultimate Sabbath day, Abelard identified, in the wake of traditional symbolism, with the heavenly Jerusalem, the one serving as a cosmic-temporal, the other as a cosmic-spatial symbol of ultimate bliss and perfection :

O quanta qualia
  Sunt illa sabbata
Quae semper celebrat
  Superna curia
Quae fessis requies
  Quae merces fortibus
Cum erit omnia
  Deus in omnibus
Vera Jerusalem
  Est illa civitas
Cuius pax iugis est
  Summa iucunditas.

I do not know what Abelard would have said had he known that this combination of the symbolism of Jerusalem and the Sabbath, coming to him from the treasury of Christian imagery, would later produce some very odd sectarian phenomena. The great revival that swept many Bantu tribes in South Africa (and about which Bishop Bengt Sundkler has given us such a fine book),[21] produced hundreds of churches and sects which in part have the word Zion in their name, and in part even use the six-pointed "Star of David" as a symbol, some of them carrying such curious names as "The Apostolic Jerusalem Church in Sabbath in Zion". Fortunately for me, and for you, this aspect of the matter does not come within the scope of the present lecture.

Christian hymnology is almost exclusively heavenly. In the words of the medieval poet, Jerusalem is the

Urbs Sion unica, mansio mystica, condita coelo.

To the extent that Jerusalem also has a terrestial, geographical dimension as a holy city, it is mainly in its quality of a memento of holy events that occurred at certain places—"holy places"—therein.

The Jewish tradition is very different. I need not go here into the question of the pre-history of Jerusalem, the "foundation of [the deity]

Shalem", and its role as a holy city viz. cultic centre in pre-Israelite, Jebusite and even pre-Jebusite times. For our present purpose it suffices to remind ourselves of the fact that Jerusalem does not form part of the earliest Israelite traditions as reflected in the corresponding strata of the biblical record. Jerusalem was not the major cultic centre of either the patriarchal or the early Israelite period after the conquest. There were Shilo, Beth El, Shechem and others. The episode of the meeting of Abraham with Melchisedek, the priest-king of Shalem (Gen. 14), probably reflects later, post-Davidic ideology, bent on cementing the association of the Holy City with the ancestor of the nation. Jerusalem entered Israelite history and historico-religious consciousness under David. The story of the conquest of the city, as well as the reasons that prompted David to turn her into a symbolic centre—ritually as well as politically—are too well known to require rehearsing here. Suffice it to say that David made Jerusalem the cornerstone of the religious and cultic, as well as the national unification of Israel. In the words of Prof. Shemaryahu Talmon,[22] "Jerusalem thus became the symbol and the most significant expression of the transition from 'peoplehood' to 'nationhood' and 'statehood'. But it was never exclusively subjugated to, or identified with, the new social phenomenon. Therefore, when the state ceased to exist, Jerusalem did not lose its importance and symbolic meaning for the Jewish people. The city which in antiquity had experienced one decisive transformation of her significance, could easily adapt and readjust to ensuing different historical situations. She has, in fact, done so for many hundred years without losing her prestige and symbolic value that had been conferred on her by David". Indeed, the amazing and historically crucial aspect of the story is the depth and tenacity with which the "Jerusalem consciousness" (as I would call it) struck roots in Israelite feeling, belief and theology. Jerusalem was the city which God had chosen, and the chosenness of this city was as much part of God's covenant with his people as his covenant with David and his seed, and it was as permanent as his covenant with nature (cf. Jeremiah 31:34-39; 33:14-26).

The meaning of Jerusalem as it subsequently determined Jewish self-understanding and historic consciousness is spelled out in the Prophets and in the Book of Psalms. Jerusalem and Zion are synonymous, and they came to mean not only the city but the land as a whole and the Jewish people (viz. its remnant) as a whole. When the author of *Lamentations* bewails the destruction of the "daughter of Jerusalem" and the exile of the "children of Zion" he obviously means the people; and when the prophet known as the Second Isaiah rhapsodically exults in the rejoicing of Zion as her sons return unto her from the dispersion, he clearly means the people and the land as historic entities. City, land and people become one in a grand symbolic fusion. Zion, viz. Jerusalem, is the "Mother" also in Jewish symbolic language, and the same figures of speech which Christian idiom uses in connection with the *mater ecclesia,* are used by the ancient rabbis of *keneseth Yisra'el*, identified with Zion and Jerusalem as the mother. These symbolic equations are a permanent feature of Jewish experience since the days of the Psalmist. The identification of Zion and Jerusalem with the widowed, sorrowful and mourning mother, who one day will exult and rejoice again as her children are gathered back unto her, is one of the main motives of traditional Jewish imagery since that pattern was set by the Second Isaiah. The talmudic sages merely spelled out more explicitly in their many dicta on the subject that which was already implicit in the prophets and in many Psalms. The prophet's word (Is. 49:14) "And Zion said 'the Lord has forsaken me'" is paraphrased in the Talmud[23]—as a matter of course—"the congregation of Israel said ...". The perfect liturgical expression of this symbolism occurs in the Jewish wedding service, where one of the liturgical benedictious reads "May she who was barren [*scil.* Zion] be exceedingly glad and exult when her children are gathered within her in joy. Blessed art thou, o Lord, who makest Zion joyful through her children". Another version of the same benediction has the closing words "who makest Zion joyful and rebuildest Jerusalem". Similarly one of the benedictions recited every Sabbath after the reading of the prophetic lesson says: "Have pity on Zion which is the home of our life.... Blessed art thou, o Lord, who makest Zion rejoice in her children".

Time does not permit even a cursory review of the role of Zion, or Jerusalem, in the daily liturgy, in the grace after every meal, and in the poetry and homiletical writings of medieval Judaism. The point which I wish to emphasize here is the semantic role of a geographical term for naming an historical entity, but in such a way that history remains anchored in a concrete, geographical centre, in terms both of origin (the covenant of the promised land and the chosen city) and subsequent catastrophe and suffering (exile, dispersion), and of eschatology (restitution and future return). Rabbinic tradition took up and developed in its own peculiar way the notion of a heavenly Jerusalem that had begun to evolve in the intertestamentary period. But the rabbinic priorities are reversed when compared to the Christian scheme, where the symbolism of the heavenly Jerusalem tends to dominate. Liturgical devotion, popular piety, religious symbolism, messianic hope—also in its 19th and 20th century secularized forms—are directed first and foremost to the earthly Jerusalem as a symbol of the ingathering, on this earth, of the people to their promised land. A most striking rabbinic saying almost goes out of its way to invert the usual apocalyptic cosmology, according to which the earthly Jerusalem is but a reflection of the heavenly one. According to this midrash[24] "you also find that there is a Jerusalem above, corresponding to the Jerusalem below. For sheer love of the earthly Jerusalem, God made himself one above". In other words, the earthly Jerusalem does not reflect a heavenly archetype, nor does it derive its significance from the fact that it mirrors a celestial reality. It is a value in itself, and as such serves as the archetype of

God's heavenly Jerusalem. According to this tradition, spiritual fullness can never be attained by playing down the historical sphere with its material, social and political realities. The ideal, restored Jerusalem of Jeremiah's vision is a city, nay a political centre, bustling with life and with people: "For if ye do these things indeed, then shall there enter by the gates of this house [i.e. city] kings sitting upon the throne of David, riding in chariots and on horses,he, and his servants, and his people" (Jer. 22:4). We may note in passing the plural "kings sitting upon the throne" in Jeremiah's utopia. The eschatological notion of the *one* messianic Son of David had not yet evolved. To quote Prof. Shemaryahu Talmon once more: the idea of the celestial Jerusalem as it was conceived by Jewish thinkers, and even by mystic fancy, never lost its touch with down-to-earth reality. A definite strand of this-worldliness ... seems to permeate normative Jewish religion in all its ramifications".[25] The earliest reference to a heavenly Jerusalem in talmudic literature[26] puts the following, somewhat surprising, words into the mouth of God himself, who is made to say: "I will not enter the heavenly Jerusalem, until I have entered the earthly Jerusalem first".

If it is true, as I have suggested, that the synonymous terms Jerusalem and Zion have symbolized the historical reality of a people and of its bond to a land, then we may, perhaps, also come closer to an understanding (though not necessarily to an affirmation) of the modern, secularized stages of this history. The modern Jewish national movement took its name not from that of a country or a people, but from that of a city: Zionism. The hymn of the Zionist movement, which in 1948 became the national anthem of Israel, speaks of the "eye that looks toward Zion" and of the millenial hope of a return to "the land of Zion and Jerusalem". The anthem, known as *ha-Tiqvah* ("Hope"), is very poor poetry indeed, but in all its awkwardness and sentimentality it somehow catches the essential awareness of the Jewish people that at its centre there is an indissoluble bond with the land, and that at the centre of this centre is Zion, the City of David. Jerusalem and Zion are geographical terms beyond mere geography, but not without geography: they are "the local habitation and the name" for an historic existence and its continuity—an existence which for the religious Jews has religious dimensions and which for the secular Jew is capable of a secularized re-formulation.

Permit me, in conclusion, to reflect on the practical, even political implications of what has been said so far. Jerusalem, which popular etymology has interpreted, surely with laudable intentions but with little philogical or, for that matter, historical justification, as the "city of peace", has seen more bloodshed, warfare, hatred, conquests and internecine strife than perhaps any other city. Today too, in this allegedly secularized age, religious arguments and symbols are marshalled and pressed into the service of political aspirations and the clash of conflicting nationalisms. Surely the student of Comparative Religion should beware of playing into the hands of partisan politics and propaganda. No religious or historic experience, however authentic and genuine, and however normative for the group that affirms it, can claim normative value and validity for the bearers of other experiences possessing their own and distinct symbolic articulations. But Comparative Religion can help us to understand: to understand the varieties and depths of emotions; the distinct types of symbolic and mythical realities involved; and the options, possibilities and limits which each religious group experiences within its own symbolic framework.

In one important respect there seems to be a crucial difference between the Jewish relationship to Jerusalem on the one hand, and that of Christianity and Islam on the other. The difference has, I think, been most lucidly expressed by Prof. Krister Stendahl, when he wrote:[27]

> For Christians and Muslims that term [scil. holy sites] is an adequate expression of what matters. Here are sacred places, hallowed by the most holy events, here are the places for pilgrimage, the very focus of highest devotion. . . .
> . . . But Judaism is different. . . . The sites sacred to Judaism have no shrines. Its religion is not tied to "sites" but to the land, not to what happened in Jerusalem but to Jerusalem itself.

The Christian tradition has, indeed, preserved much of the amplitude and many of the biblical resonances of the word Jerusalem, though these have been muted by the specifically Christian "de-territorialization" of the concept, a shift from a geographical to a personal centre, and—more generally —an orientation towards the universal categories of persons and community. Moreover, the spiritual emphasis came to be focused on the Heavenly Jerusalem, with the earthly Jerusalem being not much more than a memento of the holy events enacted there. Hence no political issue can possibly arise—unless the churches relapse into a Crusader mentality, into an antiquated triumphalism masquerading as "spiritual interests", or into sheer hypocrisy that tries to make political profit from a symbolism and message that are alleged to be purely religious and universal.

The case of Islam is different again. The fact that a non-Muslim critical historian will consider the Muslim bond to *al-Kuds* as based on pure legend is, as I have argued before, utterly irrelevant. *Al-Kuds,* together with the traditions of the *isra'* and the *mi'radj*, is firmly rooted in the very heart of Muslim belief and piety. It is part of the supreme event in religious history: the ministry of Muhammad as Allah's messenger and the seal of prophecy. But this fact also has political implications; for Islam, taken on its own terms, never claimed to make the same kind of distinctions between the religious and secular sphere that are so characteristic of the Christian tradition. Hence Muslim political interests in Jerusalem never have the unpleasant overtones of hypocrisy which Christian claims on the Holy City so frequently have. It is true that for Islam Jerusalem is not a holy city in the Jewish sense of that expression. Strictly speaking it is a question of a holy site in Jerusalem. But the very fact that the noble *haram*, "the surroundings of which we have blessed", is there, creates an almost natural presumption that it should be part of the *dar al-Islam.* The nature of this presumptive right may, perhaps, require re-examination in the light of the self-confessed secular quality of modern Arab nationalism that is shared by Muslim, anti-Muslim revolutionary, and Christian Arabs alike. But although the argument may have lost much of its genuinely religious dimension, the appeal to the sanctity of Jerusalem is still powerful enough to arouse enthusiasms and to inflame passions.

For the Jewish people, as we have seen, Jerusalem is not a city containing holy places or commemorating holy events. The city as such is holy and has, for at least two and a half millenia, served as the symbol of the historic existence of a people hunted, humiliated, massacred, but never despairing of the promise of its ultimate restoration. Jerusalem and Zion have, as I said before, become "the local habitation and the name" for the hope and meaning of Jewish existence, and of its continuity from the days when, according to the authors of the biblical books, God spoke of a certain place that he would choose, to the days of the return which—however improbable it might seem—was never in doubt for the Jew. Understanding the symbolic function of Jerusalem in Jewish tradition, we come to see that even the avowed secularist's use of this symbol has a measure of legitimacy about it, unparalleled in other traditions. When Jewish secularists say "Jerusalem", it is, *mutatis mutandis,* like the opening word of General de Gaulle's famous speech after the liberation of Paris: *Paris*—where *Paris* meant France and the French people, their history, their agony, and their liberation. There is, of course, the not insignificant difference that "Jerusalem" has far deeper roots in the Jewish soul, and as a symbol has a certain transcendental reference, unlike anything comparable in other societies.

Nevertheless I have chosen this last example advisedly, because there is something profoundly disturbing about it. Can we, should we, in the second half of this 20th century, make use of religious and/or secularized symbols that easily become catchwords drawing a dubious vitality from their mythological roots? Can we engage in constructive and morally responsible politics by making ourselves prisoners of symbolisms, however venerable and hallowed? Can we bring holiness into our personal lives and into our collective living by a mythology of holiness which all too easily degenerates into partisan sloganeering? These are questions not easy to answer, for symbols cannot always be dismissed with a cavalier wave of the hand as "mere" slogans or mythological anachronisms. Sometimes they are the repositories of both the conscious and the unconscious life-giving truths of a community. Today, whilst life in Jerusalem is normal and even shows signs of growing amity, on the personal level, between the different sections of the population, on the international and political level Jerusalem is not so much a symbol of holiness and of peace, as of strife and conflicting aspirations. Those who love Jerusalem and seek its peace, and in the first place all those that like to call themselves children of Abraham and for whom the word "Jerusalem" is still pregnant with meaning, will surely not forget that part of this meaning was expressed more than two and a half millenia ago by the Prophet Isaiah (1:27): "Zion will be redeemed by justice, and its inhabitants by righteousness".

NOTES

1 Quoted from C. R. Badger, *The Reverend Charles Strong and the Australian Church* (Melbourne, 1971), pp. 290-291.
2 Cf. e.g., Mircea Eliade, *The Sacred and the Profane* (1959), ch. 1 "Sacred Space and Making the World Sacred".
3 Cf. Werner Müller, *Die heilige Stadt* (1961). Müller's study is interesting and stimulating in many ways, but many of his statements and theories on the subject of *Der Berg Zion und der Schöpfungsfelsen* (p. 179 ff.) are wrong and utterly untenable.
4 This thesis was put forward by I. Horovitz in several papers as well as in his art. *Mi'radj* in the first ed. of the *Encyclopaedia of Islam*. The literature on the role of Jerusalem in Islam is immense. More or less full bibliographies can be found in the relevant encyclopaedias (and especially in the *Encyclopaedia of Islam*) s.vv. *al-Kuds, Isra'* and *Mi'radj*, as well as in the articles referred to below, nn. 7, 8 and 10. Lest anyone think that the Hebrew public in Israel needs enlightenment on the subject, I would refer here—among the more recent publications—to the two excellent (Hebrew) articles by H. Z. Hirschberg, "The Temple Mount in the Arab period (638-1099) in Jewish and Muslim Traditions and in Historical Reality", in *Jerusalem through the Ages* (Proceedings of the 25th Archaelogical Convention of the Israel Exploration Society), 1968, pp. 109-119, and by H. Lazarus-Yaffeh, "The Sanctity of Jerusalem in Muslim Tradition" in *Molad* N.S.iv, no. 21 (August-September 1971), pp. 219-227.
5 To call something "Jewish" was, in mediaeval usage, one of the most convenient methods of discrediting it; cf. the habit of orthodox Christian writers of denouncing millenarian tendencies as reprehensible "judaizing".
6 I. Goldziher, *Muhammedanische Studien* ii (1890), p. 35 f.
7 S. D. Goitein, "The Sanctity of Jerusalem and Palestine in Early Islam", in *Studies in Islamic History and Institutions* (Leiden, 1966), pp. 135-148, summarizing his many earlier researches and publications (mainly in Hebrew) on the subject.
8 This aspect of the matter deserves, perhaps, greater emphasis than it is usually given. The role of Jerusalem in Muslim belief and feeling is not exhaustively explained by exclusive reference to certain miraculous events in the Prophet's life. Jerusalem is also the place of the final *dénouement* of the history of this world; it is the centre and locus on which all eschatological beliefs and ideas are focussed. The eschatological associations are perhaps no less important—for the ordinary Muslim believer—than the "historical" associations with the Prophet's ministry.
9 Cf. E. Sivan, "Le caractère sacré de Jérusalem dans l'Islam aux XIIe-XIIIe siècles", in *Studia Islamica* xxvii (1967), pp. 149-182, especially p. 152 f.
10 A. L. Tibawi, "Jerusalem: its place in Islam and Arab History" in *The Islamic Quarterly* xii (1968), pp. 185-218. The quotation is from p. 196.
11 Prof. M. Kister has discovered a MS. of what may well be the earliest work of this genre in a mosque in Acre. The tract (the existence of which had been known before, since it is mentioned by the 14th century author al-Maqdisi) was composed in Jerusalem not later than 410 H/1019-1020. Al-Wasiti's text is currently being prepared for publication (as an M.A. thesis for The Hebrew University of Jerusalem) by Mr. Y. Hason. See also E. Sivan, "The Beginnings of the *Fada'il Al-Quds* Literature" in *Israel Oriental Studies* i (1971), pp. 263-271.
12 Letter 64 in the Benedictine ed. (P.L. vol. 182, coll. 169-70); English translation in Bruno Scott James, *The Letters of St. Bernard of Clairvaux*, 1953, pp. 90-92.
13 Cf. J. Prawer's (Hebrew) article "Christianity between the Heavenly and the Earthly Jerusalem" in the volume *Jerusalem Through the Ages* (see above, n. 4), pp. 179-192.
14 On this subject see W. D. Davies, "Jerusalem and the Land: the Christian Tradition" in M. M. Tanenbaum and R. J. Z. Werblowsky (edd.) *The Jerusalem Colloquium on Religion, Peoplehood, Nation and Land* (Jerusalem, 1972), pp. 115-154; cf. also the contribution of Canon M. Warren in the same volume, pp. 187 ff.

[17] Epistle 58 (P.L. vol. 22, col. 581).
[18] John Milton, *Paradise Lost* iii, 476-7.
[19] J. Prawer, in the article cited above, n.13.
[20] See my article "Jerusalem—Metropolis of all the Lands" in the volume *Jerusalem through the Ages* (see above, n.4), pp. 172-178, and E. E. Urbach, "The Heavenly and the Earthly Jerusalem in Rabbinic Thought", *ibid.,* pp. 156-171. The latter article also has a full bibliography.
[21] B. Sundkler, *Bantu Prophets in South Africa,* 1948 (2nd augmented ed. Oxford, 1961).
[22] S. Talmon, "Die Bedeutung Jerusalems in der Bibel" in W. P. Eckert, N. P. Levinson and M. Stöhr (edd.), *Jüdisches Volk—Gelobtes Land* (1970), pp. 125-132. The article has also appeared in an English version in *The Journal of Ecumenical Studies* viii (1971), pp. 300-316. The quotations in the present paper have been translated directly from the German original. The passage quoted is from p. 142 in the German text.
[23] B. *Berakhoth* 32b.
[24] *Midrash Tanhumah.*
[25] *Loc. cit.,* p. 144.
[26] B. *Ta'anith* 5b.
[27] Krister Stendahl, in *Harvard Divinity Bulletin,* autumn 1967.
[15] *In Ioannis Evangelium,* Tract xxxii (P.L. vol. 35, col. 1642).
[16] P.G. vol. 46, col. 1013.

METHODOLOGY

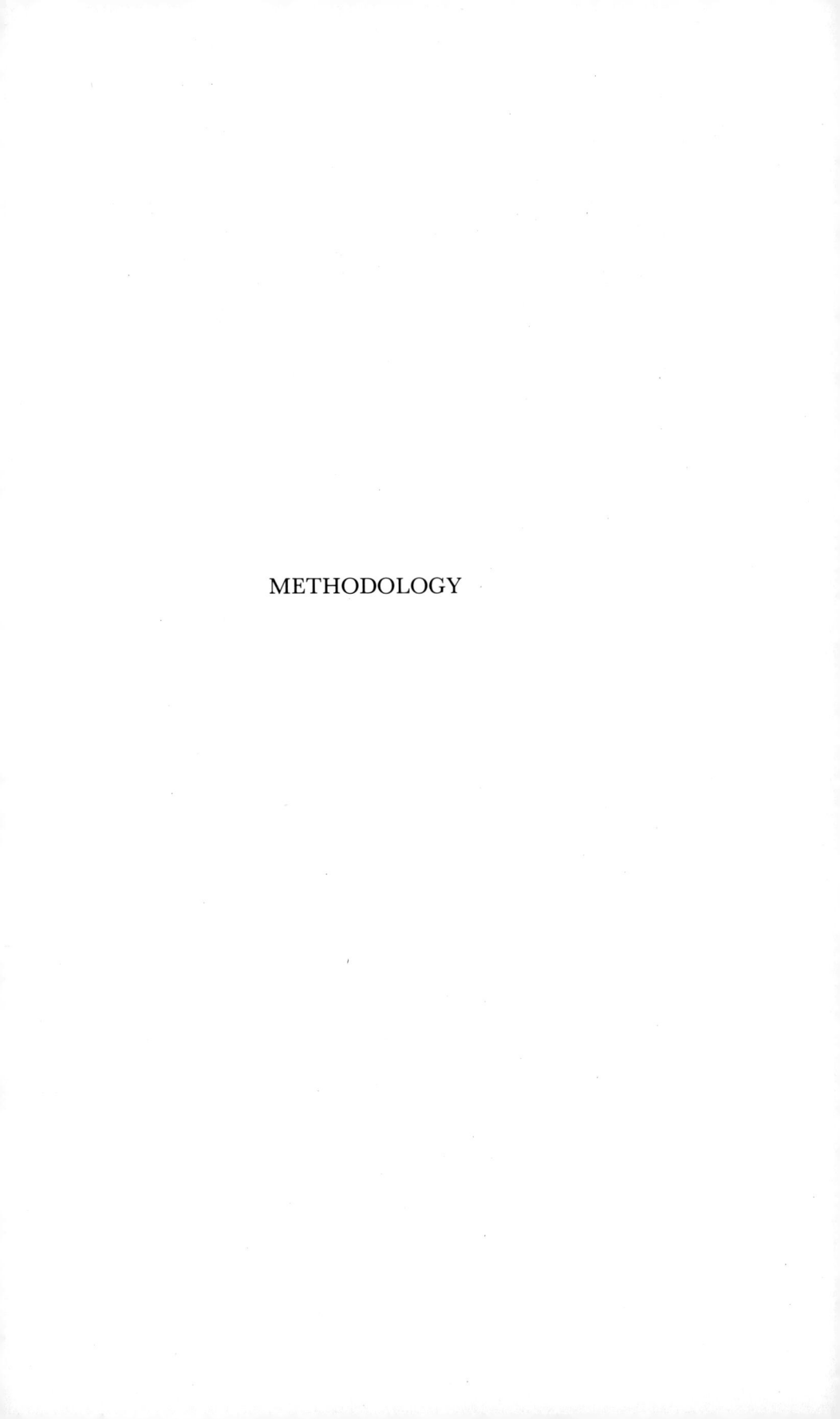

ERIC J. SHARPE

UNIVERSAL RELIGION FOR UNIVERSAL MAN

When in 1956 it was decided that there should be formed the Charles Strong (Australian Church) Memorial Trust, both as a memorial to the life and work of Dr. Charles Strong and as a continuation in some form of the work of the Australian Church itself, the first of the issues to which the new Trust addressed itself was defined as being the "promotion of liberal Christian religion and of friendship with other faiths".[1] For it was one of Charles Strong's own convictions that "the religion called Christianity, however noble and beautiful may be its teaching, is one among many religions". Christianity he asserted, "cannot cut itself off from other religions, but must take its place with them in God's 'education of the human race'."[2]

It is now almost a century since Strong made this particular affirmation, and I am honoured as a historian of religions, and as one much of whose time has been spent in the investigation of the encounter between Christianity and the religious traditions of India, to have been asked to deliver the Charles Strong Memorial Lecture on this occasion, and in front of this distinguished audience.

Christianity, so Strong believed, could if given the opportunity develop into "the Universal Religion". Therefore what I intend to do is to begin with this notion, that of "universal religion", and to examine some of its presuppositions from the standpoint of a historian and phenomenologist of religion. Specifically I shall try to show that "universal religion", as the Western liberals of the late nineteen and early twentieth centuries understood and spoke of it, though an attractive and widely sought-after ideal, may not turn out to be quite what its advocates expected, and that in so far as there *are* universals in the world of religion, they may not be the universals for which the liberals are looking. I shall illustrate my argument with material drawn from the Christian and the Hindu traditions, separately and in interplay. But first let me refer once more to a statement made by Charles Strong.

In his book *Christianity Re-Interpreted*, published in 1894, there is this passage, which speaks of a re-interpreted, "liberal" Christianity; to liberal Christians, he claims, ". . . it seems that the letter of Christianity must die if Christianity is to live, and become the power of God to bear the world onward to a new and fuller day. Never, it is felt, will Christianity escape from its present difficulties, its provincialisms and traditionalisms, and become the Universal Religion . . . until — shaking itself free from the letter of bibles and creeds and rubrics — it boldly declares itself to be a new 'Spirit of Life' . . ."[3]

At the end of the last century, statements of this kind were being made by very many liberals of all religious persuasions. They rest on certain well known assumptions. Human experience is one, though diverse in its outward manifestations; human evolution has come from one source and is moving in one general direction; human institutions — among them religion — fall into universal categories. Surely, therefore, it was argued, there must be a universal religion waiting, like a law of nature, not to be invented but to be discovered. Or perhaps uncovered, for religion appeared always to have existed as a notable fact of human experience, even though it had in the course of time attracted to itself all manner of accretions — myths, rituals, laws, conventions, doctrines and dogmas, hassocks and hymnbooks. To Charles Strong, and to many others of his day, Christianity could *become* that universal religion, provided that it was able to shake itself free from its provincialism, and from the letter of "bibles and creeds and rubrics". To another Charles of a different cast of mind, Charles Gore, ". . . if the true meaning of the (Christian) faith is to be made sufficiently conspicuous it needs disencumbering, reinterpreting, explaining."[4] In either case, the underlying assumption is that if the "disencumbering" could be done properly, the truth of universal religion would shine out to universal man. It is already there at the heart of Christianity, though it cannot necessarily be seen as such.

In 1893, the World's Parliament of Religions in Chicago had provided a startled world with a vast public manifestation of the power of liberal thinking in the world of religion. Its initial intention had been to present to the world "the religious harmonies and unities of humanity", and to help to bring about "the unity of the race in the worship of God and the service of man" — the vision which Alfred Lord Tennyson had contemplated in his *Akbar's Dream*.[5] Again and again in the two huge volumes of the Parliament's official proceedings we find this world vision apostrophised, though in the end its values and ideals are usually those of liberal Christianity. Christianity, stated John Henry Barrows in his opening address, "has in it such elements and divine forces that it is fitted to the needs of all men"[6] — and it is because of this conviction that the Parliament has been organised as "a Congress of Universal Religion".[7]

It would not have been possible, however, to have mounted this "menagerie of religions" (as one of its many detractors called it) had it been believed that the religions of the world other than Christianity had nothing to contribute to its final result. On the contrary: it was assumed that all the religions of the world had their place in God's great emerging scheme. One may be permitted to doubt whether the majority of the Oriental and other exotic visitors who came to Chicago in 1893 knew precisely why they were supposed to be there; but the organising committee knew. In the new industrial age, ably symbolised by the "windy city" on the shores of Lake Michigan, there was emerging a new world culture; what, then, could be more appropriate than that an attempt should be made to evaluate the role of the religions in the moral and spiritual development of the world; and what more inevitable than that liberal Christianity should exhibit its own credentials for the world to see? Equally, in a culture founded on the principle of open competition, there was bound to be (however energetically the organisers might try to deny it) some feeling of the market-place throughout the parliament. World brotherhood founded on mutual acceptance was affirmed, to be sure; but the organisers "expressly disclaimed" the notion that all the religious exhibits were to be treated as being of equal merit.[8] And in the end, Chicago came to resemble a multi-cultural showcase, an American religious version of the Great Exhibition of 1851, at which all were invited to draw their own conclusions about the range and pragmatic effectiveness of the exhibits.

That this particular attempt to arrive at universal categories in religion saw the light of day at this particular time was, no doubt, fortuitous. Perhaps an idea had found its *kairos*, its due time, as well as its due place. London in 1851 would hardly have been the place. There had certainly been a religious element in the Great Exhibition of that year, and Queen Victoria had been pleased with a "nice sermon" which she had heard three days after the opening of the Exhibition, preached on the text: "And He hath made of one blood all nations of men to dwell on the face of the earth."[9] But this was hardly the equivalent of the Chicago event, and Queen Victoria was recognisably not a Mid-westerner.

Beneath the surface there may have been a link, however. That human history is one history, and human religion one religion, was far from unknown to the West in 1851. For some considerable time rationalists had been urging that at the heart of every religion there were universals, deposits of the light of the divine reason in the human heart and mind. By the light of nature, one eighteenth-century Deist had written, " . . . every man perceives that there is a God, that is, a being of infinite goodness, wisdom, justice, mercy, power, who is eternal, immutable and perfect"; and to worship that Deity is "natural religion", a rational and moral conviction built into the fabric of the Universe: "the dictates of natural religion are universal, and plain to all men".[10]

I am sure that I do not need to argue on this occasion that convictions of this kind were part of the common intellectual property of the European and American intelligentsia throughout the eighteenth and nineteenth centuries, or that, as Basil Willey has said, ". . . it was possible for the religious to relegate the traditional mythology to a limbo of the mind, according to it a kind of poetic belief, while dwelling with the daylight part of their minds upon the rational interpretations."[11] Nor do I need to describe again the well known stages by which during these same centuries the world was gradually opened up to critical scrutiny, with its religious and social systems emerging, one after another, to take their places on the modern human stage. The initial tendency was, of course, for each to be treated by the West with caution, horror, amazement or fascination, depending on the presuppositions of the observer. As time went on, however, more and more attempts were made to bring these infinitely variable manifestations into some kind of order. That order might be developmental, as in the systems of a Hegel or a Comte, or evolutionary, as in the syntheses of Spencer and the Darwinians. But in every case, what was being sought was a law by which to classify and order masses of apparently disparate material; evolution appeared to provide that law. The cause of religion need not suffer thereby, for if the work of the eighteenth and nineteenth centuries added up to anything at all, it seemed (at least to Christian liberals) to lead to ". . . a wider and truer view of God, whose presence in all human history we can realize as our fathers could not possibly do."[12]

The West's notion of universal religion, therefore, was from the first linked with belief in emergent human reason. Whatever in human religious history was not reasonable might be observed, but there was no call for its retention; there might on the contrary be every reason for it to be rejected as a mark of the emancipation of the human mind. Natural religion *was* universal religion. The actual concrete observables of any particular religious tradition were at best symbols of values and principles, at worst mindless corruptions. Given religion, Max Müller believed, man had responded by inventing ever more grotesque myths; given a universal, he had created a menagerie of incompatible particulars. Religion might be evolving, moving toward deeper insights; equally religions may be, and probably are, in decline, becoming progressively more deeply enmeshed in their own errors and sophistries.

The total effect of this habit of mind we can now see to have been to drive a wedge between the ideal of religion — natural, moral, universal — and the actualities of the religions — local, variable, contingent. By the turn of the present century, the Western liberal rationalist (and bearing in mind the example of Ram Mohun Roy, some great minds who were not of the West) assumed a position rather like this, almost as a matter of course. In 1900 we find Adolf von Harnack asserting, in what became the great manifesto of Liberal Protestantism, that "It is to *man* that religion pertains — to man, as one who is in the midst of all changes and progress himself never changes."[13] As far as Christianity was concerned, his task he saw as being to penetrate to the essence of the tradition (the lectures in German were of course called *Das Wesen des Christentums*), by separating out "kernel and husk".[14] And of course the criteria by which this operation was to be carried out were rational criteria: the kernel is that which is in accordance with the mind of man and of God; the husk is that which is born of fear, fantasy and faith when it slides towards gullibility. And what could be done for Christianity could be done equally well for other religious traditions. They too could be subjected to critical analysis and be made to yield up their universal secrets.

This habit of mind has proved itself to be extremely tenacious. To take only one example, W.E. Hocking's book *Living Religions and a World Faith* (1940) similarly divides religion into two broad categories: the universal, which is characterised by freedom, rationality and essential insights; and the particular, which is known by its limitations, its irrationality, and its nervous insistence the local. The rational side of religion, claims Hocking, is constantly moving towards unity, attempting to reform itself in accordance with its own ideals; for the non-rational he seems to hold out very little hope. The rational has no need of organisations in which to express itself; the non-rational breeds organisations, which rapidly grow corrupt and are in constant need of reformation. Yet the two are not unrelated, for "Within the piety of the common people of every land ... there is this germ, the inalienable religious intuition of the human soul. The God of this intuition is the true God: to this extent universal religion has not to be established, it exists."[15]

It is not easy to say what Hocking meant by "the inalienable religious intuition of the human soul", but I suspect that he may have meant some vague deistic sense of God allied to an equally vague sense of moral obligation. Both, however, are rational senses. Man is close to God in so far as he is a thinking being, and his deep intuitions are the germs of rational thought. The trouble is, that on these true foundations man has erected a great many diverse ramshackle superstructures, expressive of nothing save human weakness and human inability to think. Between Skelton in the 1740's and Hocking in the 1940's, therefore, there is a long and for the most part unbroken chain of rationalist tradition, affirming that the outward manifestations of religion are least of all to be trusted to provide a true measure of the essence of religion. It may appear at first sight that John Hick is saying substantially the same thing when in his widely-read book *God and the Universe of Faiths* (1973: pb 1977) he asserts that the faiths of the world represent "diverse encounters with the same divine reality". Different cultures give rise to different theological and philosophical systems. "These resulting large-scale religio-cultural phenomena (he goes on) are what we call the religions of the world. But must there not lie behind them the same infinite divine reality, and may not our divisions into Christian, Hindu, Muslim, Jew, and so on, and all that goes with them, accordingly represent secondary, human, historical developments?"[16] Actually, however, there has taken place — between Hocking and Hick — a shift of emphasis. Hick is not, or at least not overtly, a neo-Deist. But nor is he an absolute innovator.

Just before the first world war, the Swedish scholar Nathan Soderblom, shortly to become Archbishop of Uppsala and one of the fathers of the modern ecumenical movement, held two chairs of the history of religion simultaneously, one in Uppsala and the other in Leipzig. These were the most productive years of Soderblom's scholarly career. As well as his book *Gudstrons uppkomst* (1914), which used to be fairly widely known in its German version as *Das Werden des Gottesglaubens* (1916), but was regrettably never translated into English, there appeared in 1913 an important essay, *Naturliche Theologie und allgemeine Religionsgeschichte*, which was published in an expanded Swedish version in 1914, but which again failed to find a translator into English. It is this shorter essay to which I would now like to call your attention.

The burden of this essay is that "natural theology", or the "universal religion" of our subject was never anything other than a beautiful illusion, an intellectual mirage.[17] It began among the radical wing of the rationalists, who contrasted a simple but exalted religion of the natural, rational experience of God with the distortions which had been imposed on that experience by later doctrinal systems, chiefly Christian.[18] All very well as an intellectual theory, this theory simply did not stand up to close examination. David Hume had been among the first to suggest that while exalted conceptions of God are perhaps possible to the human mind, these possibilities are seldom or never realized — an observation once made, incidentally, by the author of the *Book of Wisdom*. Actually to examine the world of the religions does not confirm the Deist's theories. Rather it does the opposite:

> What a noble privilege is it of human reason to attain the knowledge of the supreme Being; and, from the visible works of nature, be enabled to infer so sublime a principle as its supreme Creator? But turn the reverse of the medal. Examine the religious principles, which have, in fact, prevailed in the world. You will scarcely be persuaded that they are anything but sick men's dreams: Or perhaps will regard them more as the playsome whimsies of monkies in human shape, than the serious, positive, dogmatical asseverations of a being, who dignifies himself with the name of rational.[19]

But more important for Soderblom was the witness of Friedrich Schleiermacher, whose celebrated *Reden* first appeared in 1799. Speaking to religion's "cultured despisers", Schleiermacher had urged, with much eloquence and not a little repetitiveness, that the heart and the universality of religion was to be sought, not in any particular doctrinal construction or intellectual synthesis but in an emotional apprehension of the oneness of all true being, beyond names, forms and systems. Religion, he had maintained, had nothing whatever to do with the Deistic notion of a Universal Lawgiver, whose presence might be inferred from the contemplation of laws; religion is rather " . . . to have life and to know life in immediate feeling . . . a life in the infinite nature of the whole, in the One and in the All".[20] Again and again Schleiermacher had returned to individual feeling as the sole arbiter of universal religious truth. "The sum total of religion is to feel that, in its highest unity, all that moves us in feeling is one; to feel that aught singular and particular is only possible by means of this unity; to feel . . . that our being and living is a being and living in and through God."[21]

In Soderblom's view — and he might equally well have taken his illustrations from any one of a company of assorted nineteenth century Romantics, among them Carlyle, Emerson and Thoreau — the bubble of Deism had been pricked, once and for all, by Hume and Schleiermacher. Natural religion had been abolished, shown up as the abstraction it always was.[22] There could therefore be no more talk of a rational universal religion at the heart of the religious traditions of the world.

But Soderblom was not merely conducting a work of demolition. One might imagine that as a scholar, he was saying that we ought to abandon all thought of universals in religion, and concentrate instead on purely local manifestations of religion in those areas which we know we can master. But this was not at all what he was trying to say. For he went on to make the rather startling suggestion that the space left vacant by the dismissal from the scene of "natural religion" or "natural theology" *can* be filled — by comparative religion, or more properly, by *Allgemeine Religionsgeschichte*. Scholars are in purpose of discovering, he claimed, "a new inner unity for all genuine religion"[23] — a unity which does not however consist in a set of shared notions about the nature of Deity. "For what is universal in the history of religion (he writes) reveals itself not in a minimum of rational truths, which the religions of the world have forgotten or corrupted, and on which revelation is able to continue to build; on the contrary, *what is universal lies in what for the most part constitutes the irrational in religion* (my italics), and which can never be separated from the concrete forms it takes in sacral institutions or in historical expressions of devotion."[24]

It is irritating to have one's head cut off by a sword of sharpness which one cannot see, and not a few liberal rationalists continued (and continue) to ignore the signs, and to act as though nothing had happened; yet their heads were off for all that! The notion of *rational* universal religion had been flatly contradicted, first by Hume and Schleiermacher, then by the Romantics, and subsequently by Soderblom, Rudolf Otto and their followers. All said, in effect, that there *is* a universal in religion, but that it is not rational in its nature, and cannot be deduced from the laws of nature. Rather it is man's instinctive emotional reaction to the riddle of the world, a direct non-rational experience of something (or someone) not himself, and not reducible to natural, rational categories. Soon, indeed, all the talk was of the numinous, the *mysterium tremendum*, *mana* and mysticism.

****

The shift in opinion, away from a rationally conceived universal religion grounded on moral principles, and toward a non-rational universal religion founded solely on the experience of the believing individual, parallels closely the shift away from historicism and towards phenomenology in the comparative study of religion. It was not so much that historical studies were abandoned altogether; such was very far from being the case. But less reliance was now placed on history and its cause-and-effect categories as an "open sesame" which would reveal the ultimate nature of things.

I do not wish on this occasion to go over again the history of the rise of the phenomenology of religion as an independent approach within the comparative study of religion. I would remind you merely that in its beginnings, the phenomenology of religion was little more than a "systematic" counterpart to the history of individual religious traditions, which assumed that the historical work had already been done, and that fresh light could be thrown on the nature of "religion-as-such" by dealing with the material not in historical sequence, but by phenomena or by groups of phenomena. Husserlian phenomenology at first played practically no part in its approach, and indeed became important (or at least an irritant) only when a later generation of scholars began to doubt their capacity to know and understand anything, and especially the innermost faith of other human beings. As such, we have no particular reason to discuss it in this context.

For a variety of reasons, phenomenologists of religion have always been a little difficult to pin down, and even to identify satisfactorily. Like mystics, saints and bushrangers, they are more often taken dead than alive. In 1940, however, Eva Hirschmann, under the guidance of Gerardus van der Leeuw, compiled a survey of the work of ten phenomenologists of religion: and her thesis may at least serve as a check-list of those scholars who in the first half of the century might be placed in this category, even though some of them made no use whatsoever of the language of phenomenology.[25] Without going through the work of all ten (which would be tedious and time-wasting), it is very striking how many of them are, explicitly or implicitly, disciples of Schleiermacher. None is content merely to assemble, classify and arrange material. All are aiming, in their various ways, to prove a point, and that point is usually the primacy of the unique, self-authenticating religious experience. Again and again they return to the concept of "the holy", *das Heilige, det heliga*, and to the "adjectival" use of the same term in connection with people, places, times and seasons. If I may quote from one of the less well known of their company, the Dane Edvard Lehmann, after expounding the concepts of "power" and "value", he goes on to say that "In practical terms we describe the union of power and value as *the holy* (or 'the sacred') and we have thereby come to the fundamental word of religion (*det religiosa grundordet*), that which we encounter at every stage of religion in one or another form as an expression of what is essential."[26] We may also recall Soderblom's categorical statement that "Holiness is the great word in religion; it is even more essential than the notion of God ... From the first, holiness constitutes the most essential feature of the divine in a religious sense ... Not the mere existence of the divinity, but its *mana*, its power, its holiness, is what religion involves.[27]

One might without much difficulty assemble a catalogue of similar statements from descriptive phenomenologists. They suggest that at least in its earlier phase, phenomenology was almost as much a psychological as a historical or other discipline. It would be well to bear in mind, however, that in its early phase, although it attempted to pass beyond history, phenomenology was nevertheless an evolutionary science. Van der Leeuw, for instance, was much influenced by Levy-Bruhl, spoke often of "primitive mentality" and "pre-logical vestiges" in "our logical society" and maintained that the scholar, if he paid attention to these "survivals" in his own mentality, would have a means whereby to begin to understand them in the mentality of others.[28] Of course, it is a common characteristic of all evolutionists to regard themselves as the highest point reached by the process thus far, and to range phenomena on an ascending scale, beginning with the essential, the core, the nerve, the germ, and culminating in whatever the observer sees as being its greatest refinement hitherto. This is natural enough, though some later commentators, perhaps most notably Geo Widengren, have criticized the proto-phenomenologists for the unacknowledged (so he asserted) evolutionary assumptions, on the ground that this meant that their work was in no way value-free, whatever they might claim.[29] In the last analysis, they were theistically committed, but approached theism psychologically, as a process of progressive apprehension of God.

It is easy to overlook the fact that the "classical" phenomenologists were Christian theologians, and to miss the vital point of their commitment to a theistic (not however a Deistic) concept of universal religion. In the hands of a Soderblom, an Otto, a Heiler, a van der Leeuw, the universal dimension of religion which the phenomenological study discloses is that of man's encounter with the "wholly other", which is conceived as "the holy". Again to take an example, Friedrich Heiler writes in 1949 that "The manifold religious manifestations, ideas and experiences (*Erscheinungsformen, Vorstellungen und Erlebnisse*) point beyond themselves; they tend towards a final objectivity which is transcendent, which lies behind and above all concrete and spiritual phenomena. This objectivity is the Holy . . . "[30] And we may add that even in the case of those phenomenologists who do not follow Schleiermacher, but rather line themselves up with the *Hochgottglaube* tradition of Andrew Lang and Wilhelm Schmidt, the study of the manifestations of religion point back to an original apprehension of, or at least belief in, an undifferentiated High God who is the creator, the guardian of law and the ultimate source of all life. Geo Widengren, for instance, though he breaks with Darwinian evolutionism, does not break with the idea of a historical process in religion. To be sure, he does not use the language of universal religion; but it is difficult to avoid the impression that his version of *Hochgottglaube* might well serve the interests of theistic religion — as it did in the work of Father Schmidt.

It is my impression that, despite all that is said these days among scholars on the subject of the phenomenology of religion, few of the classical phenomenologists are in fact read at all closely. Their presuppositions are all too easily forgotten as a result.

The great shift in scholarly opinion which has taken place in the years since the war is hard to characterize in a few words. But it may consist in a movement away from the acceptance of firm goals and the belief that those goals may be achieved if only the abundantly available material can be arranged and classified in a new way, and toward a deep uncertainty about the possibility of the observer's knowing anything at all about human religiosity, particularly if he or she happens to be a member of a Western society. This is of course more than just a scholarly problem in isolation from other problems; it has political, economic and racial dimensions — in fact it is a cultural problem in the widest sense of that word. Whereas the classical phenomenologists of religion were historians first and theorists second, concerning themselves for the most part with the broad vistas of religion in its older forms, present-day scholarship has become more and more *nutidstillvand* (oriented towards the present, Carl-Martin Edsman's term).[31] It has become inextricably involved in the complex and difficult issues surrounding "inter-religious dialogue", and painfully aware that religion, whether universal or particular, is open to a wide variety of culturally and theologically (or Buddhologically) determined judgements. The difficulties facing the present-day scholar might perhaps be summed up as consisting in the awkward fact that he no longer has a monopoly on method or interpretation. There was in the past little likelihood of an ancient prophet, priest or king arising up to condemn errors of fact or ungenerosities of treatment; today the Western scholar must constantly be prepared to defer to the judgement of those who live within the tradition he is studying.

The consequences are there for all to see. The Christian or Western idealist scholar can no longer assume that his notion of universality in religion is the only competitor in the field. Nor can it readily be assumed that universal notions are always convergent. To be sure, there are those for whom the only possible universal is a *philosophia perennis*, independent of cultural forms and interpretations. But the pre-suppositions of this are less Western than Hindu, and it may therefore be appropriate to consider briefly how the Hindu regards the question of universal religion.

****

In point of fact, of course, Hindu views on this subject are highly variable. There is on the one hand a sharply focussed universalism which claims universal validity for a particular received tradition, assuming contrary views to be simply defective: the International Society for Krishna Consciousness provides us with an example. All that is necessary, on this view, is for the whole of mankind to accept Krishna as one embodiment of Godhead, to practice *japa*, to accept *prasad*, to sing and dance. The *Srimad Bhagavatam* and the Gita contain the sum total of all that man needs to know for his salvation.[32] The demand is for submission; the reward is certainty — just as in Fundamentalist Christianity.

But it is elsewhere in the Hindu tradition that the universals are most persuasively stated. Ram Mohun Roy was perhaps a Vedantin only in a qualified sense; his sources of inspiration were Muslim and Unitarian Christian, as well as Hindu. His major attack was directed against image worship, which he regarded as an affront to "the all-perfect Author of Nature" and "utterly subversive of every moral principle".[33] Theism, however, is a natural and in some sense an easy option to the Hindu, as well as to the Muslim or Christian: " . . . to read the existence of the Almighty Being in his works of nature, is not, I will dare to say, so difficult to the mind of a man possessed of sense, and unfettered by prejudice, as to conceive of artifical images to be possessed, at once, of the opposite natures of human and divine beings . . . "[34] This, however, is not Vedanta — at least not Advaita Vedanta. Nor, for that matter, is the universal "religion of man" expounded by Ram Mohun's spiritual descendant Rabindranath Tagore.

Tagore, like Ram Mohun Roy, passed far beyond popular tradition in his search for universals, speaking of " . . . timid orthodoxy, its irrational repressions and its accumulation of dead centuries"[35], and of the static, artifical averages of belief fostered by religious institutions.[36] The human element in religion, he believed, had introduced " . . . a mentality that often has its danger in aberrations that are intellectually blind, morally reprehensible and aesthetically repellent".[37]

Perhaps not surprisingly, then, Tagore shows a great mistrust of the capacity of the human reason to arrive unaided at valid knowledge of the Divine. The individual rational mind has its uses, but leads rather in the direction of science than of religion: science "represents the rational mind of the universal man".[38] But beyond this rational mind, which is capable of the most horrific distortions and misapprehensions, there is "the universal human mind" which comprehends "all time and all possibilities of realization".[39] It is this universal human mind (which in some senses sounds a little like Jung's collective unconscious) which is able to intuit "the Eternal Spirit of human unity beyond our direct knowledge".[40]

But how is this knowledge of the universal man to be communicated? In Tagore's own case, what he seems to be saying is that it came through an aesthetic experience of Nature (and indeed we find him quoting Wordsworth in its support), as a result of which "I felt that I had found my religion at last, the religion of Man, in which the infinite became defined in humanity, and come close to me so as to need my love and co-operation."[41] But this is not the only channel along which saving knowledge can be communicated; equally it may come through the testimony of great men, great minds, "the messengers of Man to men of all countries".[42] Foremost among these he places, perhaps a little surprisingly, Zarathustra, who was "the first who addressed his words to all humanity, regardless of distance of space and time", proclaiming to universal Man that "the Sun of Truth is for all".[43]

And yet Tagore would not have been Tagore had he not supported his argument finally from that Brahmo tradition in which he had been brought up. His spiritual mentor was less Ram Mohun Roy himself (though of his reverence for Ram Mohun there could be no question) than his father, Debendranath; and it is fully in line with Debendranath Tagore's thinking that the ultimate source of universal religion should be the Upanishads. The message of *The Religion of Man* is almost summed up in a passage which reads: "The *Isha* of our Upanishad, the Super Soul, which permeates all moving things, is the God of this human universe whose mind we share in all our true knowledge, love and service, and whom to reveal in ourselves through renunciation is the highest end of life."[44] And more generally, it is *Advaitam* (the Supreme Unity) which to Tagore is *Anantam* (Infinitude) — the universals in face of which all that is partial and finite recedes into illusion and error.

And who has found this unity, this universality? To Tagore, the answer would presumably have been: very few. But in the devotional simplicity of the Bauls he claimed to have found a constant source of inspiration. He quotes their songs repeatedly, not as rational treatises but as statements of devotion to the One Universal. There is more here than a febrile seeking for proofs, though we might do well to remember that Tagore was only too willing to admit that his religion was "a poet's religion",[45] and that, more explicitly, "I am a singer myself, and I am ever attracted by the strains that come forth from the House of Songs".[46]

In Tagore — if we must seek for Western comparisons — we find ourselves closer to a Schleiermacher or an Otto than to a Deist, of whatever subtlety. His universal was based on a self-authenticating experience, rather than on a set of rational propositions. He saw little need to make pronouncements about the goal of all religions being the one Universal Being, or to clothe his theories in the language of Vedanta. His universal was an aesthetic universal, rather than a metaphysical, real not as an idea or a proposition, but as an experience. And as he so rightly observed on the last page of *The Religion of Man*, in respect to the process of Yoga as leading to a pure state of consciousness of undivided unity with *Parabrahman*: "There is none who has the right to contradict this belief; for it is a matter of direct experience and not of logic."[47] He might well have said the same of the *bhakti* tradition to which he himself belonged — that the experience cannot be contradicted.

It goes without saying, I think, that at the present time, the most characteristic universal interpretation of Hinduism is that which passes along the chain of tradition from Ramakrishna through Vivekananda and Aurobindo to Radhakrishnan and thence into the popular Hindu consciousness. I do not propose to expound it in detail on this occasion, however, except to say that like Tagore's aesthetic universalism, it rests on the foundation of immediate experience, and that it looks upon individual religious traditions as signposts, all pointing in the same direction. The point of convergence is of course the experience of *samadhi*, that intuitive awareness of the believer's oneness with the Ultimate Reality which is so like death itself, but which is still realizable in this life. It may be theistic, or it may not. Usually — and this despite the lip-service which is paid Shankaracharya — it is indeed theistic, affirming a oneness of oneself and a personally conceived ground of all being. Usually, too, it looks upon religious traditions as pointers to the one goal, as parallel though separate paths through the mists of *namarupa*, name and form, which will always be transcended in time by the true seeker.

The trouble, perhaps, is that in these terms there are so few who are true seekers, or as Aurobindo might have said, "Gnostics". Sarvepalli Radhakrishnan, for example, had a great deal to say about the universal dimension of Hindu belief, but only in respect of the *sanatan dharma*, and not of the actual forms which Hindu belief takes. Hinduism (and he unhesitatingly identifies the *sanatana dharma* with "essential" Hinduism) "seeks the unity of religion not in a common creed but in a common quest. "Let us believe (he urges) in a unity of spirit and not of organization".[47A] Of course he is reaching back here into the Vedantic tradition of the ultimacy of the Real *beyond* names and forms; but he sees all religions through this same mystical prism. The goal of all religion, to Radhakrishnan, is the mystic, non-rational, non-conceptual experience of the One. In this light, creeds and dogmas, words and symbols, historical events and persons, can have no more than an instrumental value. The unchanging substance of religion — all religion — is the evolution of man towards spiritual reality. This evolution, the quest, is " ... the eternal religion behind all religions, the *sanatana dharma*, the timeless tradition; ... it is our duty to get back to this central core of religion ... Our historical religions will have to transform themselves into the universal faith or they will fade away."[48]

The trouble, perhaps, is that believers who make up the historical religions show so few signs of wanting, or indeed being able, to do this. Hindus will be Hindus, Buddhists will be Buddhists, Christians (worst of all from Radhakrishnan's point of view) will be Christians. To be sure, there are Strongs and Hockings, just as there are Tagores, Aurobindos and Radhakrishnans. But they are few and unrepresentative. This inevitable recognition may, and often does, lead to a degree of impatience with those ordinary believers, who persist in "gazing into the heavens", looking there for signs, not of universal spiritual religion but for the Saviour, the Lord and the Law.[49]

It may lead to a still more marked impatience with those believers — usually Christians — who conceive of their tradition as being in some sense unique in the world of religion, or who persist in conducting a mission to humanity (as though the Radhakrishnans of this world were not in their own way missionaries!).

It is striking nevertheless, that when it comes to the primacy of experience in establishing religious universals, thinkers of East and West have repeatedly found one another. The traffic has been by no means one way, and it seems that the acknowledgement of the validity of one's own religious experience as an ultimate criterion has inevitably pointed in the direction of the acknowledgement of the equal validity of the religious experience of others, and of their equal right to evaluate that experience in the terms laid down by their own theological and cultural traditions. Perhaps the commentator may affirm his or her right to interpret the data in terms of a particular tradition (and this we must always acknowledge to be a legitimate right, just as one may be forced to interpret language, not in linguistic abstractions, but in the categories of a particular living language). But when this happens, there may be reasons why a member of another tradition objects to the statements which are made.

We must conclude, I think, that for a specific religious tradition — any tradition — to make claims about universality is emphatically not for that tradition automatically to pass beyond its own frontiers. It may believe that it is doing so. It may claim energetically to be doing so. But it is still speaking to the world in terms of its own self-understanding, its own concepts, myths, images and symbols. The Christian universalist is still a Christian; the Hindu universalist is still a Hindu. The arguments and the assumptions of the one do not appeal to the other. Hindus, for instance, are greatly offended when they hear Christians speak of Hindu quests being "fulfilled" in Christ, and if anything still more offended when it is suggested that without knowing it, they may be "anonymous Christians" — a form of words much used by Roman Catholic theologians of encounter since Vatican II. I am not suggesting, incidentally, that Christian theologians have no right as theologians to approach the encounter of religions in this way; merely that they may accidentally give much offence in so doing. At least it may be suspected that the right hand of fellowship extended toward the other tradition may be an iron fist hidden in a velvet glove. Let me give you a recent example.

Reviewing Richard Drummond's recent book *Gautama the Buddha*, which attempted to pass beyond the history of religions into theology, and to universalise Christianity without falling into syncritism, Bhibuti S. Yadav accuses the author of suffocating Buddhism to death: "This he does by first alienating the facts from their context, and then keeps on putting them in the wrong categories until they have a nervous breakdown".[50] The reviewer's point here is that Buddhist facts cannot be interpreted other than on the basis of the Buddhist totality. Buddhist questions must not be supplied with Christian answers, which in the terms in which they are given, appear to be totally meaningless. Yadav's highly detailed argument, which I cannot of course fully recapitulate, ends (somewhat emotionally) with the statement that "the concept of 'anonymous Christ', from the perspectives of Mahayana Buddhism and theistic Hinduism, is not theological; it is religious imperialism in the name of a very good God."[51] But the sword of criticism has two edges, and we may well recall, for instance, Hendrik Kraemer's criticism of Radhakrishnan's interpretation of Christianity as "a complete misunderstanding, sometimes even going to the length of disgust", and as the work of "an outsider, who lacks every trace of congeniality".[52]

This of course is the trouble. The student, whether or not he chooses to call himself a phenomenologist, a historian, an anthropologist, or whatever, is always an outsider, once he crosses the frontiers, and passes beyond the religious tradition and the culture to which he rightfully belongs. And the ultimate test may be the extent to which he is prepared not to judge, but simply to accept and try to understand what he finds on the other side, including the desire of the folk "over there" to address the world.

It is perhaps time now to attempt a brief summing up of the very disparate material we have passed in review, and to state some tentative conclusions.

First, concerning the Deistic type of universal religion, it is very doubtful whether from the phenomeno-logical point of view the "natural religion" in which the Deists so passionately believed, ever existed, other than as a Western intellectual construction. The degree of abstraction and intellectualization which it presupposed has never been an option, other than to a very few, and in its abrupt rejection of the forms and symbols of the believer's world it was setting itself up, not as an interpreter, but as a harsh critic of human religiosity. As Söderblom saw, Deist religion simply does not conform to the facts of human experience; at best, it is a device employed by secular man to try to preserve an abstract moral essence, while at the same time rejecting every means by which that essence finds expression, save the moral sense. This is from the phenomenological point of view a reduction, partly eliminating the existential, and wholly dismissing the social modes of religion in the interests of the intellectual and the ethical.

The experiential universal is also a reduction, though on this occasion what is devalued is the intellectual, the social and the ethical. There is still a certain attraction in this approach, it is true but it makes a fundamental mistake in assuming that religious experience is simply experience, and that it can be divorced from the question "experience of what?" The phenomenologist can on this matter at least affirm that religious experience, like religious faith, can be understood only within the tradition of which the person experiencing is a part. It is the tradition which again provides the individual with the terms, the symbols, the words, the images, in which experience is described and by means of which it is accounted for. And this holds good whether the tradition is "great" or "little"; it obtains among Mormons, Spiritualists or the Hare Krishna movement, just as it obtains among Roman Catholics, Sunni Muslims, Buddhists or Vedantins. Certainly you may say, if you like, that all religious experience is experience of a transcendent, just as you may say, as Ebeling says, that "Christian faith (or Hindu faith, or whatever) is not a special faith, but simply faith",[53] but these are the words of the intellectual analyst, and not of the believer — or of the phenomenologist, for that matter. Faith and experience alike, to the phenomenologist, are inextricably bound up with the object of faith, the means by which faith is transmitted, and the images in which it expresses itself. Similarly, the universal claims made from within a tradition are part of the total self-understanding of that tradition; they do not exist above or alongside, but within it.

The phenomenologist, it seems to me, can find a *raison d'être* precisely in his resistance to attempts to impose external intellectual criteria, and far-reaching judgements of value, on the world's religious traditions. Not that he will be free from presuppositions; but if he knows his trade he will at least be able to prevent preconceived notions from distorting the faith or the beliefs or the total integrity of other believers. What universals there are (and far be it for me to deny that there are religious universals, and perhaps even universal religions) reach his understanding not *in spite of*, but *through* the manifestations which he is studying. Perhaps we may never fully understand the faith of another human being, and perhaps we must maintain a certain agnosticism about how far our attempts are going to take us. That we are none of us models of impartiality or omniscience goes without saying. But it is none the less an exciting enterprise on which we are engaged — the ultimate meaning of which may well be as was once described by Gerardus van der Leeuw:

> "The religious significance of things ... is that on which no wider nor deeper meaning whatever can follow. It is the meaning of the whole; it is the last word. But this meaning is never understood, this last word is never spoken; always they remain superior, the ultimate meaning being a secret which reveals itself repeatedly, only nevertheless to remain eternally concealed. It implies an advance to the farthest boundary, where only one sole fact is understood: — that all comprehension is 'beyond'; and thus the ultimate meaning is at the same moment the limit of meaning."[54]

FOOTNOTES

1 C.R. Badger, *The Reverend Charles Strong and the Australian Church* (1971), p. 155
2 *ibid.*, p. 253
3 *ibid.*, p. 255
4 C. Gore (ed.), *Lux Mundi* (15th ed. 1904), p. vii
5 J.H. Barrows (ed.), *The World's Parliament of Religions I* (1893), p. 10
6 *ibid.*, p. 73
7 *ibid.*, p. 57
8 *ibid.*, p. 71f.
9 A. Briggs, *Victorian People* (1963), p. 42
10 Skelton, *Ophiomaches* I (1749), p. 43f
11 B. Willey, *The Seventeenth Century Background* (1962 ed.), p. 133
12 Moulton, *Religions and Religion* (1911), p. 16f
13 A. Harnack, *What is Christianity?* (3rd ed. 1904), p. 8
14 *ibid.*, p. 12
15 W.E. Hocking (ed.), *Re-Thinking Missions* (1932), p. 37
16 J. Hick, *God and the Universe of Faiths* (2nd ed. 1977), p. 143
17 N. Soderblom, *Naturlig Teologi* (1914), p. 45
18 *ibid.*, p. 42f.
19 D. Hume, *The Natural History of Religion* (ed. Root, 1956), p. 75
20 F. Schleiermacher, *On Religion* (1958 ed.), p. 35f.
21 *ibid.*, p. 49f
22 N. Soderblom, *op. cit.*, p. 51
23 *ibid.*, p. 65
24 *ibid.*, p. 66

25 E. Hirschmann, *Die Phanomenologie der Religion* (1940), *passim*
26 E. Lehmann, *Religionens varld* (1926), p. 58
27 *ERE* VI (1913), p. 731a
28 Hallencreutz, *Kraemer towards Tambaram* (1966), p. 112
29 G. Widengren, "Evolutionism and the Problem of the Origin of Religion", in *Ethnos* 10 (1945), pp. 57ff.
30 F. Heiler, *Erscheinungsformen und Wesen der Religion* (1949), p. 559
31 C.M. Edsman, " 'Nutidstillvand ', religionshistoria" in *Religion och Bibel* 28 (1969), pp. 39ff.
32 cf. *Back to Godhead* (the magazine of the Hare Krishna Movement), and Judah, *Hare Krishna and the Counter Culture* (1974), esp. pp. 79ff. Houriet, *Getting Back Together* (1971), pp. 331ff.
33 R.M. Roy, *Translation of the Veda* (1827), p. 149
34 *ibid.*, p. 142
35 R. Tagore, *The Religion of Man* (1961 ed.) p. 76
36 *ibid.*, p. 68
37 *ibid.*, p. 38
38 *ibid.*, p. 15
39 *ibid., loc. cit.*
40 *ibid.*, p. 11
41 *ibid.*, p. 60
42 *ibid.*, p. 44
43 *ibid.*, p. 51
44 *ibid.*, p. 15
45 *ibid.*, p. 67
46 *ibid .*, p. 55
47 *ibid.*, p. 128
47A Radhakrishnan, *The Hindu View of Life* (1965 ed.), p. 42
48 *idem, Eastern Religions and Western Thought* (1939), p. 180
49 *idem, The Hindu View of Life*, p. 25
50 Review in *Religion and Society* (December 1977), p. 72
51 *ibid.*, p. 79
52 H. Kraemer, *Religion and the Christian Faith* (1958), p. 129
53 G. Ebeling, *The Meaning of Faith* (1966), p. 28
54 G. van der Leeuw, *Religion in Essence and Manifestation* (1938), p. 680

ROWAN IRELAND

INTERPRETING BABEL

Towards a Sociology of Afro-Brazilian Cults

Charles Strong's deeply incarnational theology and his interest in comparative religion were linked in a way that might still lend inspiration to a modern sociologist. In his wide reading and discussions in the Religious Science Club of the Australian Church he was attempting to appreciate the working out, in precise historical circumstances, of what he called that "embryo spiritual nature akin to God"[1] of which he believed all men and women possessed. His own primary motivation may have been theological and his view of spiritual development too simply evolutionary for modern sociologists. But from his project in comparative religion it is possible to draw up a sort of preamble to a constitution for the sociological interpretation of religion. The provisions of such a preamble would be

(1) Assume that religion is to be found not in compendia of dogma but in the living of religious ideas in particular historical circumstances.
(2) Assume too that there is a contingency of lived religion on the varying conditions of life.
(3) Do not assume that contingency implies determination. Be as ready to find men and women shaping their lives and their relationships with one another according to their gods as to find them shaping, interpreting their gods according to their conditions of life.

Moving out from this preamble, our sociologists' constitution, I would say, would have to specify three essential moments in the sociological interpretation of any religion. Firstly, the moment of *reading* — from oral testimony and ritual and organization to a construction of the effective religious predispositions orientating members of the religious group in social action. Second the moment of *tracing out* — through biographical study, from the predispositions that have been read into the world, into daily lives. Third, the moment of *dialectical analysis* with its twin projects: on the one hand, the analysis of the effects of group patterns of religiously informed actions on systems of social, political and economic relations at local and national levels; on the other hand, analysis of the accretions of experienced social, political and economic processes on religion, shaping religion in terms of what options are available and congenial to or even forced upon social groups.

In addition to positive injunctions our constitution for the sociological interpretation of religion would require at least two caveats. Firstly the caveat against under-interpretation which would mean, in the case of the Afro-Brazilian religions I shall try to interpret today, that I would forget about analysis of their shaping and being shaped by modern Brazil, remaining content with reading them for their predispositional content and tracing out predispositions into everyday, local life. The second caveat would be directed against over-interpretation, which in my case, would be to forget about my fieldwork data about the Afro-Brazilian cults as lived at the local levels, to forget about the first two moments of interpretation, and to proceed to grand generalization about, say, the determinative effects of the cults on Brazilian class formation or the essential nature of the cults as cases of alienated religiosity.

Anyone attempting to abide by this constitution in the interpretation of Afro-Brazilian cults will have moments of despair. It would be easy if *the* Afro-Brazilian cult would come forward for the sociologists to examine. Instead, such is the exuberance of Brazilian *homo religiosus*, there is a Babel of cults and federations of cults, with different pantheons of spirits and profound variation in the way in which religion articulates with everyday life. It would be easier to interpret if Brazil would stand still and present us with a uniform set of 'conditions of life'. Instead, of course, Brazil is a Babel of jostling political economic tendencies, of drastic regional variation, of the manifold happenings of classes in conflict and formation.

Perhaps we could cope with Brazilian exuberance if the sociologists could come to order; if there were neat, agreed upon concepts which we could impose on the political economy and a spare checklist of theories to apply to religious phenomena. But, as you know, the sociology of religion is itself a Babel of rival conceptual foundations and theoretical towers. The Afro-Brazilian religions, themselves diverse, are met by Bryan Wilson's interpretation of them as thaumaturgical responses to the insecurities of modernization;[2] by Marxists' analysis of them as reflections of an illusory traumatized consciousness utilized by ruling classes to ensure dominance;[3] by evolutionists who classify the cults from primitive to modern and recognize in them the means for various groups to participate in modernizing Brazil.[4]

There was indeed a once-upon-a-time when the connection between broad historical processes in the society at large and what was going on down there in the cult seemed plain and simple enough. The macro-history of Brazil was the gathering triumph of modernity, and it was clear how the cults fitted in, or failed to fit in to that. Modernity was to have an economy like the British or the Yankees, a culture that was as scientific as Germany's is, and a people educated in European civilization, along French lines. The Afro cults were the antithesis of all of this: the legacy of slavery, the survivals of pre-scientific African society, the evidence of an African pre-scientific mysticism quite opposed to scientific rationality. The historical relationship between modernity and the cults was quite simple. As modernity advanced, ineluctably, so the cults would wither, by degrees, through quaintness to oblivion. Modernity was a Midas, and, as a later generation of social scientists might put it, indisputably the independent variable in the relationship with the cults.

But that sort of interpretation, though still heard in middle class clubs, and, curiously, in some of the cults themselves, won't do among sociologists. In the face of the flourishing of the cults, involving now not hundreds of thousands but many millions of participants, the disappearance hypothesis has been shelved. Or else the timetable has had to be modified, especially in view of the fact that the most rapid growth of the cults has occurred in areas of greatest modernity as described. In any case, as we have learned more about Brazil and more about the cults, we have learned to distrust the concept of global modernity and to distinguish the cults from one another. And so, Babel. Perhaps, though, we can pick our way through the ruins and enrich our understanding by attempting to apply our rules of interpretation.

It is no easy task, if only because the rules demand constant shuttling between the "micro" everyday world of the fieldworker and the "macro" historical political economy of the grand theorist. And it is exactly in the marriage of micro and macro sociology that my discipline most fails me. But I have promised only a movement *towards* in the title of my paper. And that I can deliver with a sort of compromise. As I move from reading and tracing out religious symbols in local lives and situations, I will refer to macro phenomena not as they may be grasped from the models of political economy but as they are in fact apprehended in individual lives and in a precise locality.

The "Real" Brazil?

Each of the characters to whom I shall introduce you is urged, cajoled and sometimes forced to fit in with the modern national security model of Brazil that the generals, through their control of the State, would make the *real* Brazil. The generals and their technicians outline that model in their own way, and, incidentally, some of them have traced out in chilling detail implications of their model for the disciplining of the Brazilian poor. But ordinary Brazilians are instructed in their part in the national security model through constant and pervasive messages which, I believe, amount to what may be called a national security code.[5] The code is enjoined upon ordinary Brazilians in a variety of ways — most directly in explicit propaganda and the rhetoric of public occasions; most effectively in the hidden curricula of educational and other institutions.

Key provisions of the national security code as it is received at the grassroots of Brazilian society may be defined on the basis of careful analysis of explicit messages received and message-laden occasions experienced. That analysis warrants at least another paper; but the provisions drawn out in such an analysis would include:

(i) the image of the good citizen as one who accepts and obeys rational bureaucratic authority and understands the necessity of a system of status and rewards grossly favouring those with formal qualifications over those with few qualifications in the modern urban sectors of the economy;

(ii) the equation of the State, the Nation and Society as being but different names for the same organic entity proceeding from one pure stream of history towards the one destiny of the successful national security State;

(iii) the belief that loyal citizens and legitmate groups will identify above all with the nation state and only secondarily or not at all with class or region or ethnicity;

(iv) the belief in formal, instrumental education as the source of all worthwhile wisdom and the means for progress away from individual and collective ignorance and poverty;

(v) the belief that civilization and Brazil's destiny among the A-grade league of nations can be achieved in the triumph of whiteness, Europeaness and hygiene over darkness, Indian-ness, African-ness and dirtiness; in the triumph of science and modern technology over emotionality and ignorance; in the taming and tapping of nature over against the wild unused jungles;

(vi) the conception of Brazilian history as essentially in accord with the history textbooks in which the remembered heroes are the great military commanders, the conquerors of the hitherland, the modernizers and defenders of order.

It must be stressed that these provisions and the national security code as a whole do not adequately describe the world-view of the Brazilian people. They rather define images, sentiments and beliefs which significant members of Brazil's ruling elites would like to see internalized by ordinary Brazilians. The national security code, once it is taken for granted as the common-sense view of the social order and the march of history, should help turn *one* vision of modern Brazil, the generals', into *the* Brazil. Ordinary Brazilians are bombarded with the national security code as part of the attempt by a ruling elite to define and engineer what modern Brazil should be. That much time and effort is invested in the bombardment suggests, however, that the battle is not over and won. The national security code must compete with other visions of what Brazil is and what it might become and other definitions of the role of the good citizen.

Those who are committed to the national security code feel it necessary to exert strong pressures on those naive, or uncivilized or potentially subversive or subverted enough not to accept it.[6]

Now, one line of interpretation of the Afro-Brazilian religions, faithful to our constitution, is indicated in two questions. Firstly, does each of the Afro-Brazilian cults as read in interview and ritual and traced-out in individual lives, constrain reaction to these pressures for Brazil of the national security code or mediate internalization of it? Secondly, to what extent is Brazil of the national security code shaping each of the cults?

I am going to introduce you to some Brazilians who introduced me to Brazil as they see it and to the Afro-Brazilian cults which shape their seeing. I met and lived with these Brazilians during the twelve months of 1977 when my family and I were engaged in fieldwork in the town we call Campo Alegre in the Northeast of Brazil. The town's twelve thousand inhabitants are mostly very poor, many of the rural labourers and fishermen earning less than the minimum wage of about $50 a month.

I was attempting to gather data which would allow me to interpret the religious factor in socio-economic change in the area. So I was interested not only in the fourteen Afro-Brazilian cults of the town but in folk and official Catholicism, the Assembly of God (the largest single organized religion in town), the Baptists and Jehovah's Witnesses. I attended the rituals of all these groups, interviewed religious leaders and followers for details of biography and belief and attempted to observe religion as it went out from religious centres into everyday life. I have found that the different religions do make a difference in the way in which the inhabitants of Campo Alegre cope with the challenges of poverty and rapid socio-economic change. But I have also found that it is difficult to generalize to religious groups. There is variety within the Assembly of God and, as we shall see, even more variety within the Afro-Brazilian cults. Hence the need to begin with individual believers and particular groups.

Pai Fuló

Pai Fuló, 79 years old, known as the *pai de santo*, literally the father of the saint, is the leader of a Xangô cult. Xangô is the name of an African spirit brought to Brazil, Cuba and other places in the Americas by West African slaves. Fuló's home is the centre for the cult and fixed to the rendered mud outer wall is a sign telling passers-by that this is a

    terreiro dos cultos
    africanos anago
    são joão
    batista

— the place of the African Nagô cults, St. John the Baptist. The naming encapsulates a great deal about Fuló and his cult. Fuló is insistent on the Africanness of his cult. He is himself clearly of African ancestry as are many though by no means all of his cult members. (Photo No. 1) The Nagô cults are Yoruba in origin and he stresses the point: the ritual chants of his house are in Nagô rather than Portuguese, because Nagô is the language to which the great African spirits respond. As a guardian and communicator of myth and ritual — the role that he considers central and most important — Fuló passes on to his followers, preferably while they are very young, enough Yoruba language and lore so that they will be able to bear their spirits into the world.

But note that this is the place of the African cults called St. John the Baptist. Fuló celebrates and recreates Africanness but uses the nomenclature of Christianity. In my first conversations with him he identifies himself as a member of the Holy Roman Catholic and

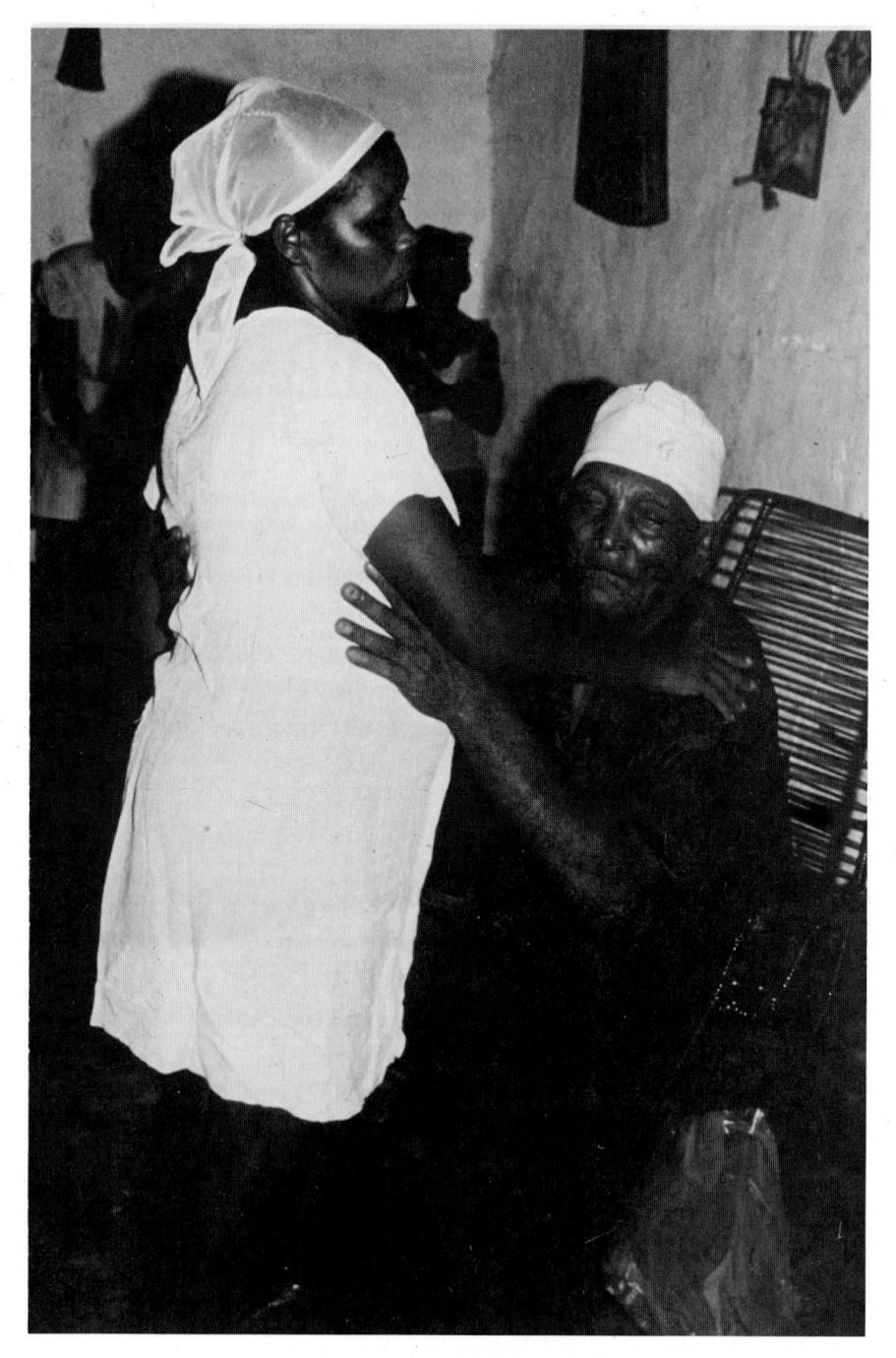

Photo No. 1 (see p. [4])

Apostolic Church — each adjective carefully enunciated so that the correct formula might banish doubt. He points out to me that each of the spirits whose image resides in the *pejí* room of his house has both an African and a Catholic saint's name — Yemanjá the spirit of the waters and mother of many of the other great spirits is Our Lady, Mary, the mother of Jesus. Xangô, whose name is popularly given to the whole cult, is represented by symbols of lightning and kingship but his character as dispenser of justice is emphasised in his identification as Saint Jerome.

In the naming of the house as in the naming and representation of the spirits, Fuló's Xangô adopts outward forms and labels from appropriated aspects of the dominant religious culture. But the character of the spirits and the concerns of the house in relationship to them remain, in the eyes of the group, essentially African. Fuló explains that he is not of the *cultura alta*, the high culture, even when, in my first conversations with him, he protests his good standing within it. He and his sons and daughters in the saint (*filhos e filhas de santo*) identify themselves with *Brasil selvagem*, savage Brazil, but they do not reject *Brasil selvagem* nor do they accept the valuation placed by the *cultura alta* on it.

They are continuing an old tradition, investigated by Roger Bastide,[7] in which the Catholic saints become masks for the *orixás* or African spirits and, in doing so, the *orixás* and the ways of life integrated around them may avoid suppression.[8] But it is the *orixás* who rule and the mode of life that they require that persuades in Fuló's group. Reinterpretation of the Christian saints and of the *cultura alta* in general has been accomplished in terms of the values, cognitions, modes of relationship between man and nature and man and man, distinctive of *Brasil selvagem*.

Indeed, if not in word, then in ritual action and symbol Fuló and his "family", seen in the photograph sharing a ritual meal (Photo No. 2), construct alternatives to much of the *cultura alta*. Their lives bear the stamp of poverty but though they do not politically attack "the system" head on, they reject its judgements of them and assert alternative identify for the poor. The Portuguese language itself is denied its superiority in the Nagô chants — and it is noteworthy that Nagô is used and taught by Fuló not as a priestly language for mystery and the arcane but for the acquirement of a counter culture: Fuló's Nagô does not mirror but exactly negates the function of the traditional priests' Latin. The group's blood sacrifices ignore modern urban Brazil's rules of hygiene and separation from raw nature — and for this alone members of other Afro-Brazilian cults label followers of Xangô ignorant and uneducated. But sacrifice, (Photo No. 3), Fuló explains, is one of the things that the spirits demand if they are to infuse their followers with their diverse strengths and protect them from harm.

Fuló and his group are even more profoundly counter-cultural in their social relations. In a society where, even at the local level, authority claims legitimation through formal qualifications and expertise, Fuló exercises traditional authority — authority based on wisdom passed on through the generations in deep personal relationships. Fuló does not intend, nor is he expected, to hoard his wisdom as an expert for specific functions; rather his standing relies on his transposing his wisdom from his life to as many other lives as he can. His proudest boast to me is that he has left communities of *filhos* and *filhas de santo* all over Brazil — that is to have fulfilled his roles as "ambassador of the spirits" and *Zelador* (watchman) of the wisdom of Africa and *Brasil selvagem*.

I do not want to suggest that Fuló's group is an antithesis of modern Brazilian society, or that its encodings of reality exactly negate the national security code. Fuló, as we have seen, and members of his family in even greater degree, are ambivalent towards a *cultura alta* that is itself multi-valent. Fuló, I would say, is teacher/father in a counter culture — but counter to what? If entirely counter to rational-bureaucratic authority then, for some members, only an alternative locus wherein to realise the continuing motif of patrimonialism in the *cultura alta*. Counter to the *exclusive* pretensions of those who buy white specific rationalist Brazil lock stock and barrel — and I intend the allusion to the gun — Fuló's Xangô does not yet arm for resistance, unless it is with a potent sense of independence and confident apartness grounded in ritually nurtured alternative history.

Photo No. 2 (see p. [6])

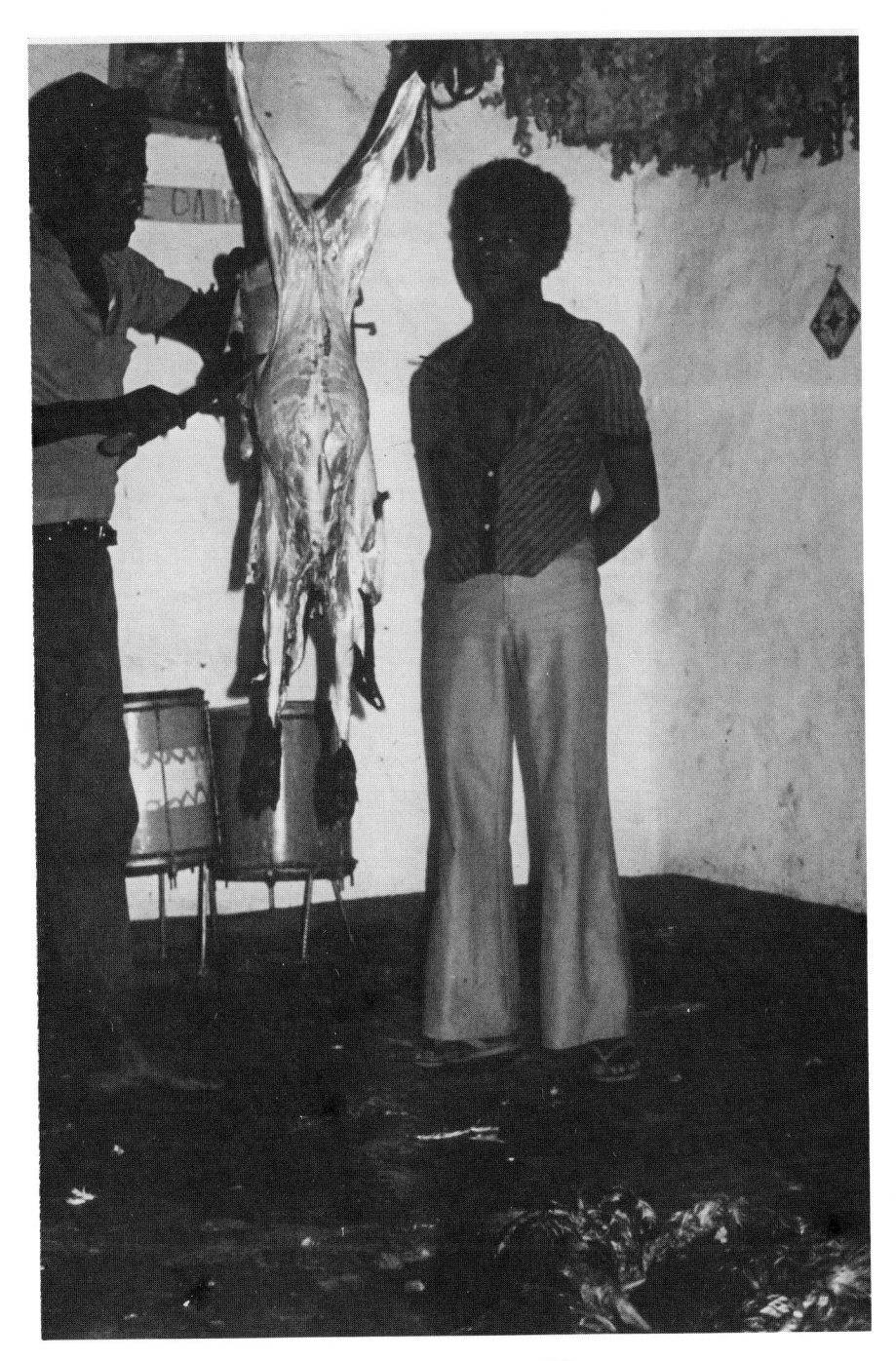

Photo No. 3 (see p. [6])

In merely introducing Fuló I have strayed unsystematically over the three moments of interpretation. Let me farewell him with a return to the first moment — the moment of reading — in which all the others must be grounded. I would invite you to read with me the *terreiro* of the cult, Fuló's house. In Figure 1 the first thing to note is that the ritual space, *the salão*, is located in a home: to receive the wisdom and strength of the spirits one has to become a member of a household. In the *salão* itself everything is moveable: it is a space for learning through community-in-motion rather than through the raised expert commanding, or pouring specific chunks of knowledge into empty vesels. The *pejí* is a place apart, but not for individual therapy: when a member of the group is performing his or her obligation to his spirit — which is also an obligation to the group involving provision of a high-protein meal for all participants — that member is secluded for a time in the special places of the spirits. But the obligation is fulfilled only when the member emerges from the pejí, bearing his spirit in trance out into the group to move and move with the others.

FIGURE I: FULÓ'S HOUSE

**TERRÈIRO DOS CULTOS
AFRICANOS ANAGÕ
SÃO JOÃO BATISTA**

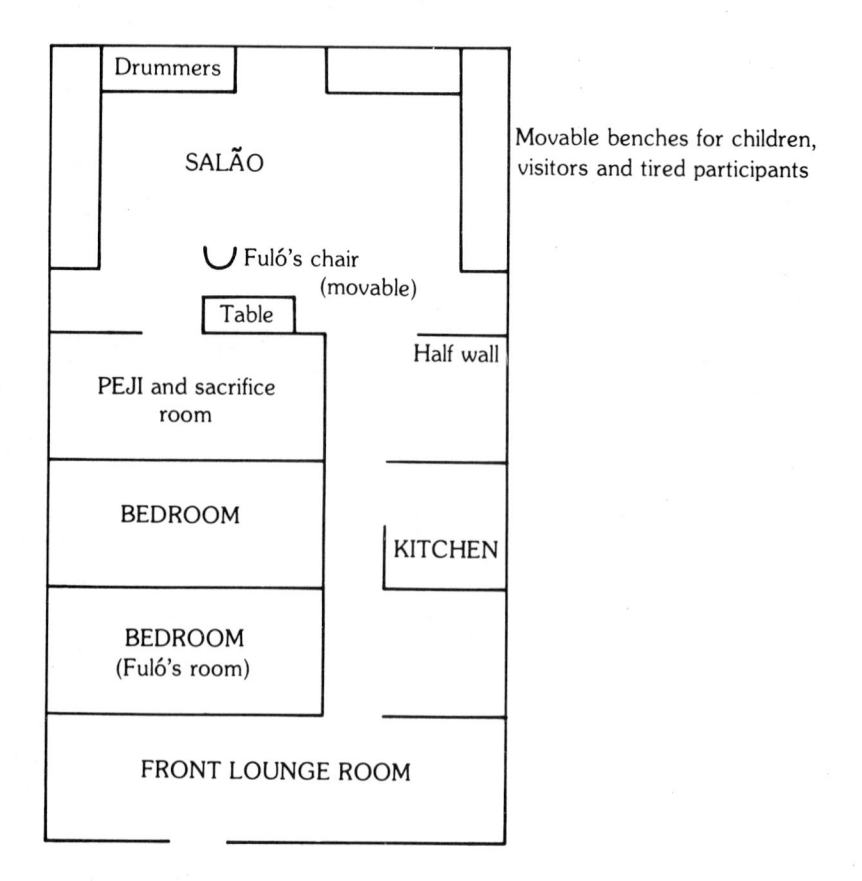

[Floor plan showing:
- Drummers area at top
- SALÃO (main room)
- Movable benches for children, visitors and tired participants
- Fuló's chair (movable)
- Table
- Half wall
- PEJI and sacrifice room
- BEDROOM
- KITCHEN
- BEDROOM (Fuló's room)
- FRONT LOUNGE ROOM]

A household for survival and community building

To "trace out", is to follow members of the group from the *terreiro* into the world. This requires presentation of biographies of members and accounts of how the group responds to the problems posed for its members by the Brazil of the national security code. These biographies do not admit of easy, uniform interpretation. But the lives of core members of the group do suggest a carrying out into the world of a critical stance towards the national security code. In dealings with neighbours, the bureaucrats, the rich and the powerful, they show a coolness borne of partly willful marginality and a resilience borne of confident identity.

Dona Rosária

In Figure 2 we can read a very different sort of group and a very different sort of leader in Dona Rosária. Dona Rosária comes to her spiritist Centre from Recife, the State capital, 40 kilometres away. She is bringing from her upper class suburb a message to the poor. In the Centre she dispenses enlightenment, therapy, and goods to the needy. Her centre was originally a large barn that was made available to her by the local prison authorities. She has transformed it to her purposes.

I would ask you to note several of its features. Two thirds of it is arranged as a classroom or lecture hall of the traditional kind. The top third is set apart for what Fuló would call the *cultura* alta, its personnel and its artifacts. Dona Rosária and visiting dignitaries speak from the table to an audience seated in rows: the very furniture is arranged for passive reception of messages from experts.

The remaining third of the building is reserved for other forms of dispensing from the *cultura alta*. In the cubicles, after hearing the message, Dona Rosária's audience may become clients. A client will enter into the cubicle and an expert in spiritual currents will dispense a therapeutic pass (as in Photo No. 4), and sometimes counselling based on the

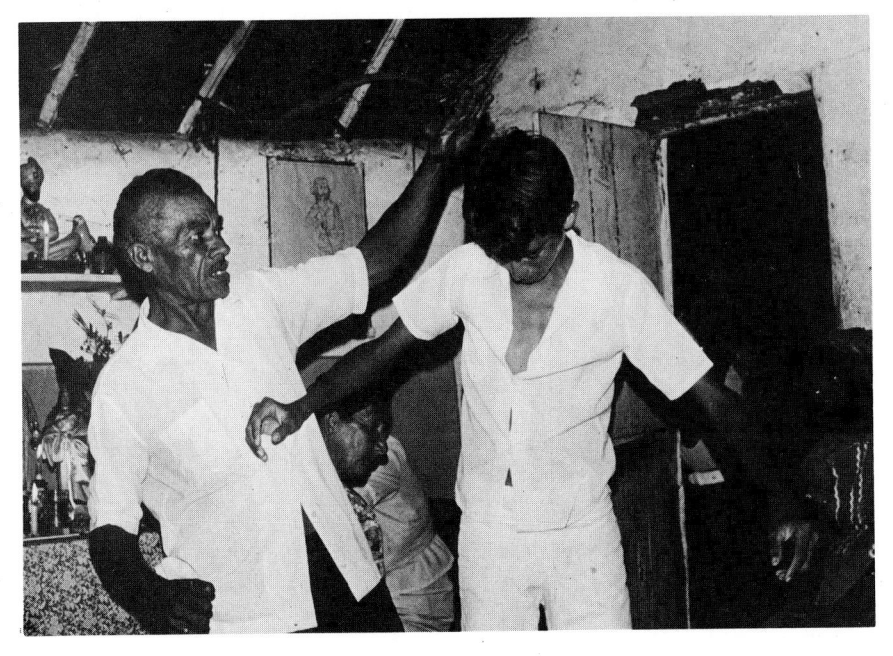

Photo No. 4 (see p. [10])

**FIGURE 2: CENTRO ESPIRITISTA
DONA ROSÁRIA OF THE
FEDERAÇÃO ESPIRITISTA,
ENCRUZILHADA**

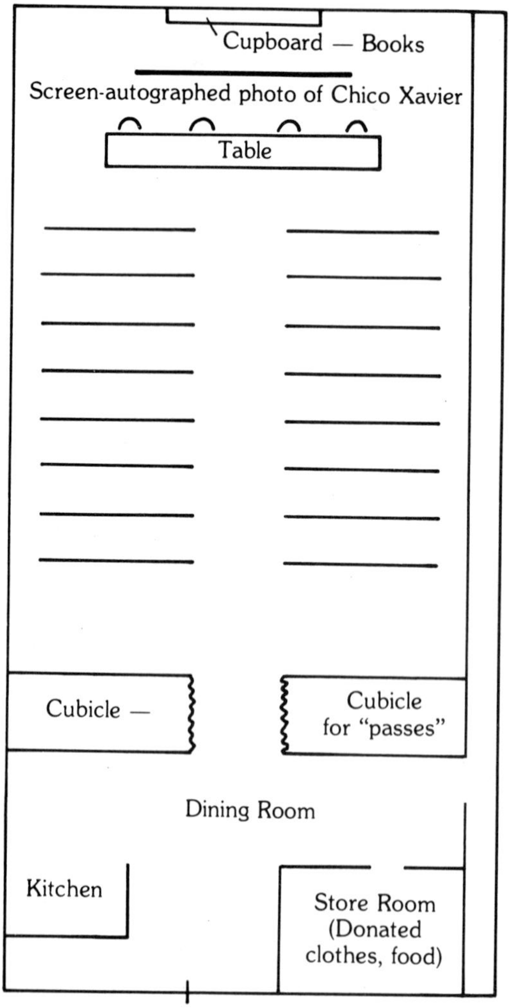

```
┌─────────────────────────────────────┐
│         Cupboard — Books            │
│  Screen-autographed photo of Chico Xavier │
│            Table                    │
│                                     │
│   ─────────        ─────────        │
│   ─────────        ─────────        │
│   ─────────        ─────────        │
│   ─────────        ─────────        │
│   ─────────        ─────────        │
│   ─────────        ─────────        │
│   ─────────        ─────────        │
│                                     │
│   Cubicle —        Cubicle          │
│                    for "passes"     │
│                                     │
│          Dining Room                │
│                                     │
│   Kitchen        Store Room         │
│                  (Donated           │
│                  clothes, food)     │
└─────────────────────────────────────┘
```

A school room for dispensing *Cultura Alta* to the Lower Orders wisdom passed on from the higher, purer spirits. Then, those in greatest need may be given food and even clothing brought by Dona Rosária from the Spiritist Federation headquarters in Recife.

Dona Rosária's spirit world is tidily arranged. It is elaborately structured from higher spirits, with Jesus Christ at the top, through the great departed thinkers of Western civilization down to the lower spirits — the old slaves, the cowboy spirits, the spirits of the street, and then the inarticulate caboclo and African spirits down finally to the evil spirits of darkness, including the African Exús. She professes the beliefs of the Afro-Brazilian cult known as Umbanda, though among Umbandistas hers is of the kind most heavily influenced by the nineteenth century European spiritualist Alain Kardec and the least continuous with more African cults like Fuló's Xangô or Bahian Candomblé. Her exemplar is the great white medium Chico Xavier, whose portrait hangs on the screen behind the table. Xavier has published books of prayers and revelations communicated by superior spirits. And the superior spirits are not African spirits of Xangô or the caboclo Indian spirits, the cowboys, ex-slaves and street spirits of the Umbanda groups — but spirits of departed white, professional representatives of the cultura alta.

Much of Dona Rosária's discourse departs from a framework of oppositions: spirit vs. flesh; whiteness, light, lucidity, science, Christ vs. blackness, darkness, ignorance, superstition, Satan. Like most Umbandistas she has borrowed the notion of Karma: success in this life is to prepare the spirit, in whatever walk of life, for a higher, purer existence in the extra-terrestrial plane and in the next incarnation.

There is more of Dona Rosária's spiritism and that of her followers to be read, but an outline of worldview and predispositions for social action has emerged, I hope. The predispositions may be traced out in the life of a neighbour who introduced me to the group — Maria José. Maria attends as often as she can for a complex of reasons. The existence of a spirit world that impinges on this is very real to her, but so is the experience that nothing must take you too far away from secure lines of patronage to Brazil of the cultura alta. Fuló's Xangô takes you too far away and offers nothing in return; Rosária's group offers needed strength from the spirits and a line for material patronage as well. The Centre itself is well lit, clean, comfortable and offers the schooling that seems necessary to get on but which is otherwise unavailable to the Maria José's of Northeast Brazil. From the Centre, her recent biography suggests to me, Maria José goes out hopeful that modernity will provide, distrustful of her judgement because convinced of her ignorance, accepting of many of the claims of the national security code — the beneficence of its representatives being demonstrated in Dona Rosária's dispensing of expensive powdered milk for her adopted boy.

Maria José may help us towards a dialectical analysis of both her own Kardecist Umbanda group and Fuló's Xangô. In particular she suggests an explanation for the correlative emergence of a military State engineering Brazil towards identity with the national security-code and the spectacular expansion of the Umbanda cult, partly at the expense of Fuló's Xangô and the cults like it. Insofar as Umbanda emerges out of a previous generation of African and Amerindian spirit-cults, it represents a triumphant reshaping of the spirit world in accordance with the national security code and the more diffuse cultura alta.

The Maria José's of Brazil find the re-shaping attractive because it promises a participation in the power, the comfortable ethos and even some of the material benefits of that world otherwise denied them. And so, the spirits usher in the generals' version of modernity having been first tamed and re-ordered by it. Dona Rosária, gentle soul, has become a medium for what Harvey Cox calls "the seduction of the spirit", in more ways than one.[9]

In Fuló's Xangô, on the other hand, the African spirits, or more particularly, the way of life integrated around them, encode reality such as to predispose at least skepticism towards claims based on the national security code. The spirits do not respond to the blandishments of scientism nor are they reached by experts and bureaucrats. They live in story and ritual, and rather less as signs to be manipulated. They are not themselves of the *cultura alta* — in fact Exú, one of the most powerful of them as controller of traffic between *the seen and unseen in Xangô*, has become in the more modern cults, and in the *cultura alta* itself, the lowest and darkest spirit of all, Exú-Satan.

The interpretation of the Afro-Brazilian in Campo Alegre cannot proceed only on the basis of a comparison of Dona Rosária's and Fuló's cults. That would be to tune out Babel prematurely and risk over-interpretation. The quest for pattern must proceed on the basis of at least a glance at some of the other twelve cults in the town.

Dona Dina

Dona Dina's cult is of the Umbanda type, though much less Kardecist than Dona Rosária's. Here, in photo 5, she is manifesting a caboelo spirit, as D. Rosária never would. Her *salão* is much more like Fuló's and one becomes a member through participation in ritual rather than through exhortation. Dona Dina is herself a poor, illiterate fishing lady and had no patronage to offer. She does, though, have what she and her clients believe to be special gifts of mediumship which can be drawn on by individuals to provide advice and prescription to deal with the troubles of poverty. Through her, clients, usually paying clients, may receive help — not from the higher spirits but from the spirits of wise, often rough-diamond Brazilian spirits like her preferred cowboy spirit.

In Dona Dina's cult there are certainly departures from the national security code: wisdom may reside in and come from the lower orders, for example. In the photo (No. 6) a member of her group is manifesting a bent old slave spirit who will listen to problems and occasionally give advice. On the other hand, Dona Dina is herself an expert in magic and often feared as such. She and her clients understand her central role as the providing of a service to individuals in trouble who need help to survive in the system. Hers is not the role of builder of an alternative community with an alternative culture. Her religious code does not predispose towards translation of private troubles into community issues. Her own discourse is full of the scientisms of the national security code and her spirit hierarchy conforms exactly to the social hierarchy of that code.

One of her clients, Biu, may help us "trace out" Dona Dina's cult into the world. Biu is an occasional client, seeking aid from Dona Dina when in trouble, but avoiding participation in the cult because of fear of falling into trances. When worried that her de facto husband might leave her and their young child, she goes along to Dona Dina for divination and advice, seeking, in the techniques of Afro-Brazilian religion, aid to deal with her private troubles. She does not go to cult leaders as frequently as some: the attempt at short range manipulation of everyday life through recourse to the spirits has not become for Biu a way of life. But consultation with Dona Dina and two other cult leaders is, for her, a normal part of crisis management. And in her interpretations of her own behaviour during crises in her life she has adopted the pathos[10] of Dona Dina's type of Afro-Brazilian spiritualism. She sees herself drawn by one or other of the spirits to attempt suicide or even to kill her child. It has become part of her everyday conception of herself that she is, at times, the passive victim of spirits who act on her. She does not interpret all her behaviour in this way, nor does she consistently attribute the behaviour of others to the workings of the spirits, as some of Dona Dina's other customers do. But she deals with the crises of poverty as though they were only private troubles generated by personal relationships with spirits who may be themselves manipulated from time to time through cult leaders. Dona Dina is Biu's science; the theology of the cult reinforces Biu's location of herself as one who is born to the travails of poverty, subject to the darker more malevolent lower spirits, needing expert help to hang on in modern, urban Brazil.

Maria Pretinha (Little Black Mary), another of the cult leaders whom Biu consults, sternly rejects the pathos with which Biu negotiates her world. Anybody may be acted upon by the spirits, usually for the better; but, as Maria argues, and proclaims in her well-

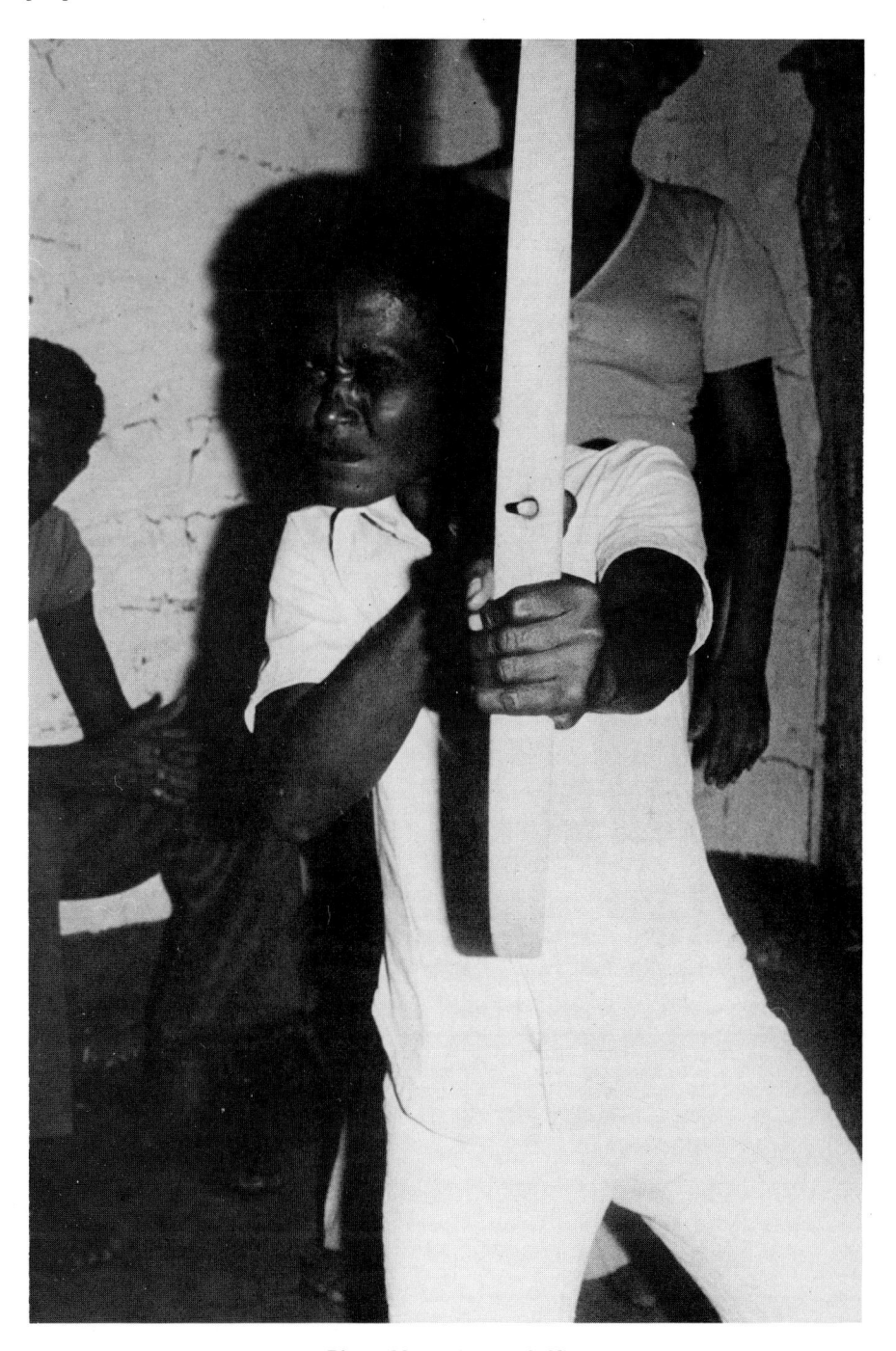

Photo No. 5 (see p. [13])

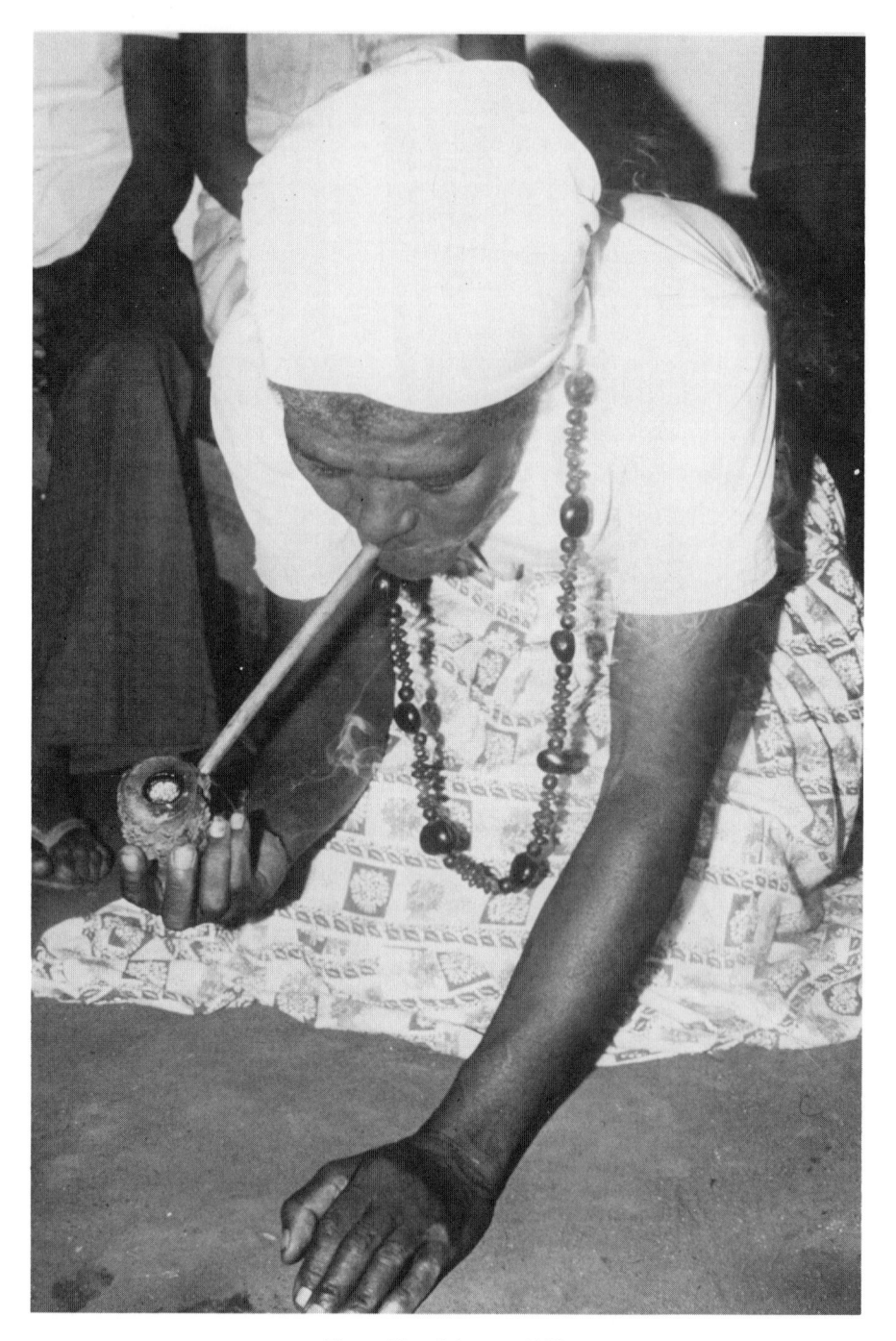

Photo No. 6 (see p. [13])

organized, if poverty-stricken life, people are ultimately responsible for their own actions, for their control over the spirits, for the purification of their own spirits. Maria Pretinha negotiates her world with irony, interpreting even her own sufferings as, in part at least, due to the still unconscious weaknesses or deficiencies in herself that she must discover and control. She goes out from her cult to assess and conduct life in a way that is strikingly similar to that of many members of the Assembly of God: insisting sternly on the necessity of traditional morality and self-discipline, allowing efficiency and order as the only legitimations of accepted hierarchy and political authority. Unlike most members of the Assembly, however, Maria Pretinha seems predisposed by her religion to distrust the claims of experts and professionals to a monopoly of wisdom. She is medium for a spirit who in his "terrestriel" life was a sort of city slicker, a wily operator from the lower urban classes who, despite his sins, picked up a lot of wisdom and who has developed as a spiritual and practical guide for the living through his relationships with other spirits since his death. Maria criticises her spirit for his remaining rough edges but also proclaims his merits as a sort of lower class hero who has battled upwards from vice and ignorance to a higher place of development. She insists that he knows and understands what many a learned doctor will never learn and points out that he dispenses counsel without pretensions and at a cheaper rate than the officials from the higher classes. He is wiser than they are too: he calls his clients not just to band-aid immediate problems but to turn to a new way of life; and most of his remedies, passed on through Maria Pretinha, involve clients in some sort of activity for their own spiritual development.[11]

Interpretation

There are many more cases to be considered along with Maria Pretinha, Biu, Dona Dina, Maria José, Dona Rosária and Fuló and his family. But the variations that constitute the Babel of the Afro-Brazilian cults in Campo Alegre has been sufficiently suggested by these cases to allow some interpretations of the Afro-Brazilian cults with a reduced risk of over-interpretation.

As I have read and traced out the array of cases I have been persuaded that there are two quite different divergent types of religiosity present in the cults and distinguishing different individual believers. In that neater world which will be the reward of all good sociological typologisers, each of the cults would fall tidily into one or the other type and we could predict that the religiosity of any one cult member would correspond to the religiosity characterising the cult. In fact I can suggest only tendencies along such lines.

One type of Afro-Brazilian religiosity evident in Campo Alegre is primarily communal. Those who experience this type of religiosity are called in teaching and ritual to become members of a distinctive historical community. The individual conceives of his or her development taking place in and through the community's collective access to the spirits who for all their power are dependant on and obliged to the living. Misfortune for the individual and the community as a whole, is explained in ironic terms — i.e. the sufferer will be held to have *some* responsibility for suffering and will have to take an active part in dealing with suffering. Leaders are conceived of as communicators of communal wisdom rather than experts in the esoteric or agents of higher culture.

The other type of religiosity is individual and instrumental in focus. Followers are involved in their cults as competitors to harness the power of the spirits to private ends.[12] The individual member seeks development by gaining competitive advantage and defensive cover through the expertise of the medium. His interpretation of misfortune and chosen remedies connote a disposition of pathos: the sufferer has been acted on by forces beyond normal personal control and restoration is sought in therapies in which the medium's client is passive. Leaders are primarily experts in the therapeutic techniques.

The spirits themselves are called on to serve for specified goals, rather than, as in communal religiosity, to draw participants into a way of life.

Fuló's religiosity is of the first, communal type; though I cannot claim that all who frequent his cult or consult him as a powerful medium share his orientations. Maria Pretinha too, despite her disinterest in the African spirits and her moralistic individualism, is much nearer the communal type than any of the other cult leaders. Dona Dina, though a medium for genuinely popular spirits, does not seek to construct community around them: she is primarily a religious expert for clients to whom she is plausibly powerful. Her followers, like Biu, approach her with a pathos she shares and hope to draw on the power which she in turn draws from the spirits. Dona Rosária, though as moralistic as Maria Pretinha, sets up herself and other visiting mediums as dispensers of therapy for the afflicted. She enjoins change of heart and modernity and uprightness but is not concerned to achieve these ends through the development of community. She and her spirits invite and entice Maria José upward, alone.

I am suggesting, of course, that the Babel of cults in Campo Alegre can be brought to some order, while remaining faithful to the requirements for sound reading and tracing out, by considering variety around these two types of religiosity. Attempting the final moment of interpretation, the types help me formulate propositions to be tested in analysis of biographies and collective action in Campo Allegre. Without hoping to clinch them in this paper, let me conclude by outlining some interpretative propositions for you.

The individualist-instrumental type of Afro-Brazilian religiosity is part and parcel of modern Brazil. In the cults in which it is dominant and in the lives of those who manifest it we may trace a Gramscian movement in which the powerful in Brazil, through their control over symbols and over the means for survival and success, are powerful even over the spirits. And, as the spirits are transformed — from exemplary historical heroes into colourful "inside-dopesters" — so they come to serve the powerful and help subordinate the less powerful. Afro-Brazilian religiosity of the individualist instrumental type at once predisposes towards a buying of the national security code (if not always *in toto*) and parades its successful hegemony (if sometimes incongruously).

The communal type of religiosity, by contrast, provides a vocabulary of motives, heroes, interpretations and meanings which predispose men and women to make their social worlds other than the powerful desire. Afro-Brazilian religiosity of the type approached with different pantheons of spirits and different emphases by Fuló and Maria Pretinha does not train revolutionaries to do battle with the generals. My claim is milder than that. It is that a minor theme in the Babel of Afro-Brazilian religion in Campo Alegre is incredulity before the claims of upper class modernity and the claims of the national security code. Perhaps that is subversive far beyond the intentions of Fuló or the suspicions of Dona Rosária.

FOOTNOTES

1. Quoted in C.R. Badger, *The Reverend Charles Strong and the Australian Church*, Abacada Press 1971, p. 310. See also Strong's address, "The new theology and its relation to sociology", *Ibid.*, pp. 283-286. Badger notes Strong's interests and views concerning comparative religion on p. 232.
2. Bryan Wilson *Magic and the Millenium*, Paladin Paperback 1975, Chapter 4, esp. p. 105.
3. E.g. Colin Henfrey, in *Dependency and Latin America: A Workshop*, Centre for Latin American Research and Documentation, Amsterdam 1973, pp. 262-301.
4. E.g. Carmargo, Candido Procopio Ferreira de, *Kardecismo e Umbanda*, Sao Paulo, Ed. Pioneira, 1961.

5. An excellent outline of the national security code as derived from the writings of some of the generals themselves may be found in José Comblin, *The Church and the National Security State*, Orbis Books, Maryknoll, New York 1979, Ch. 4.
6. Comblin *op. cit.* summarizes the views of key generals like Golbery e Couto, the head of the presidential household under several military presidents, regarding the necessity of education and pressures for the diffusion of the national security code.
7. Roger Bastide *The African Religions of Brazil*. Johns Hopkins University Press, Baltimore 1978.
8. I do not want to suggest that the symbolic masking is in any way either mechanical or cynical.
9. Harvey Cox, *The Seduction of the Spirit: the Use and Misuse of People's Religion*, Simon and Schuster, New York 1973.
10. I have found the distinctions between pathos, irony and tragedy made by Richard Niebuhr in his *The Irony of American History*, Charle Scribner's Sons, New York 1962, very helpful in formulating themes in Brazilian folk religions.
11. I have tried in this paragraph to keep close to translations of Maria's language. Phrases like "spiritual development", "learned doctors", "higher place of development" are hers.
12. In another context this competition theme in Umbanda cults hs been carefully analysed by Yvonne Maggie Vehlo in *Guerra de Orixa*, Zahar Editors, Rio de Janeiro, 1977.

ADDENDA

Page 3, line 41 (vi): hitherland *read* hinterland
Page 4, line 6 — section under Pai Fuló: anago *read* anagô
Page 6, line 26: identify *read* identity
Page 9, line 16: TERŘEIRO *read* TERREIRO
Page 9, line 17: ANAGŌ *read* ANAGÔ
Page 9 in diagram: PEJI *read* PEJÍ
Page 13, line 2 — section under Dona Dina: caboelo *read* caboclo
Page 16, line 11: terrestriel *read* terrestrial
Page 17, line 19: Campo Allegre *read* Campo Alegre

GRAHAM ROSSITER

STUDYING RELIGION IN AUSTRALIAN SCHOOLS

The Interface with Tertiary Religion Studies

Introduction

Since the formation of the Australian Association for the Study of Religions in 1976, there have always been some school teachers at the national conferences. It has been valuable for them to meet, and listen to, scholars in the academic field of Religion Studies. In addition, a small place has been available in the conferences for attention to the study of religion at school. It seems appropriate that this is a *small* place. It does not distract from the main business of the conference. Yet this presence is a useful point of contact between tertiary Religion Studies and Religious Education at school.

This contact has extended beyond the conferences. Members of the A.A.S.R. have made valuable contributions to the development of religion courses in schools. They have also been involved with the accreditation and inservice of such courses.

The invitation to deliver this lecture offers a special opportunity to bring to the attention of the A.A.S.R. Conference some of the current issues in the study of religion in Australian schools. I propose to look at the following questions. What *are* the key issues being negotiated in the development of religion as a subject in government schools? How do these developments depend on or relate to the field of tertiary Religion Studies? How do the developments and issues in religious education in church schools compare with those in the government schools? I hope to examine these questions in a way that may give tertiary religion scholars a feeling for the way religion teachers see and understand religious education in school, and in a way that may highlight points of contact between religious education and tertiary religion studies.

While there has been much debate about the most appropriate terms to use,[1] I will use the terms 'study of religion' and 'religious education' as simple synonyms for convenience. I recognise that there is need for much more discrimination in language if the different processes in the classroom are to be described accurately but that task need not be pursued here.

The lecture will be divided into three parts:
1. Issues in the study of religion in government schools
2. Issues in the study of religion in church-related schools
3. Interrelationships between religious education in government and church-related schools and the potential those relationships have for the long term development of religious education in Australian schools.

DEVELOPMENTS IN RELIGIOUS EDUCATION IN GOVERNMENT SCHOOLS IN AUSTRALIA

What then are some of the issues for the study of religion in government schools in Australia? These comments will be confined to the role of departmental religion teachers and to the place of religion in the general curriculum. The role of visiting denominational clergy or their representatives in government schools requires separate consideration.

The identity of Religious Education in Government Schools

When departmental teachers take religious education, they do so by virtue of their role as teachers and not as representatives of particular religions or churches. Hence one of their major tasks has been to differentiate their role at the level of intention. They must firstly differentiate between the intention of educating young people in religion and the intention of handing on a particular religious tradition and promoting the development of personal faith.

A new identity had to be developed for religious education. In a sense, a new 'paternity' had to be sought. Religious education, with its traditional roots in the religious purposes of the Christian churches and in Christian theology and Bible study, was uprooted. It had to develop new roots in fields that were not identified with Christian purposes. The most logical place to take root was in educational theory and practice. This would give religious education an *educational* identity rather than an *evangelising* one.

Finding a clear cut educational identity has not been easy. One of the problems has been "multiple identities" — or at least a "coat of many colours". The identities that religious education has assumed can be correlated with the different 'soils' in which it has taken root. For example: in the early 1970s, the philosophy of education of Paul Hirst provided a popular epistemological basis for religious education.[2] Hirst regarded religion as one of the distinctive forms of knowledge. Hence, initiating children into religion as a mode of thought and experience could be proposed as an educational basis for religious education. The formation of religious concepts became the practical aim for religion teachers.[3]

At about the same time, the field of the phenomenology of religion also provided a useful soil in which religious education could take hold. Phenomenology offered the claim of objectivity. Its study of world religions offered a seemingly less confessional basis than did Christian theology. Religious education thus sought an affinity with tertiary religion studies. Key people in this academic discipline in the United Kingdom made important contributions to religious education in school.[4] The scholars at the University of Lancaster would be good examples (Ninian Smart, Eric Sharpe).

The identities of religious education in government schools in Australia are encapsulated in the State Government reports and curriculum documents of the 1970s.[5] This type of religious education has had a short history by comparison with the 40 year history of its counterpart in the United Kingdom. It is not surprising then that a widespread public acceptance of the reports' proposals, and the establishment of religion in the curriculum of Australian public schools will take considerable time.

The major problems with implementing these proposals are political, and are not to do with the theory of R.E. However, as far as political acceptability goes (and you must remember here the acceptability at the levels of government, teachers in the State department and the public) the crucial question for R.E. is its identity.

To clarify the identity of religious education for government schools requires a clear statement of how it contributes to a child's education. I hope to show later that this clarification may also have much significance for church schools.

It is not always difficult to make a distinction at the level of intentions between educating in religion and handing on a religious faith. However, there are many difficulties in working out what this distinction means at the level of classroom practice. For example: It is possible that the *same* classroom processes used by a government school religion teacher will be used by a teacher in a Catholic school. I consider that the best contribution that classroom religion teaching will make to a church's purposes will occur when the activity is good education. Many of the problems in religious education in Catholic schools are really educational and not religious problems. Hence, any distinctions that might b e made between processes which educate a child in religion and those which presume personal faith can be of great importance to religion teachers in church-related schools, particularly Catholic schools.

The United Kingdom and the United States

In Great Britain in 1944, religious education became a compulsory subject in County schools. During the following 40 years, the evolution of an educational, as distinct from a confessional, basis for religious education has been slow. Most of the significant developments occurred during the past 15 years. In Australia, the corresponding developments are shown in the government reports on religious education in the 1970s. These reports evidently have strong roots in British religious education.[6] The work of Michael Grimmitt of the University of Birmingham has probably been the single most significant influence on Australian developments.[7] Another important factor in R.E. in the United Kingdom which is also having much influence in Australia is multiculturalism. However, recognition of the British influence is not to deny a distinctive Australianisation of theory with an overseas origin, as well as a distinctively Australian contribution in its own right.

One might ask: Have there been similar developments in religious education in public schools in the United States? Have these developments influenced Australian theory and practice?

In the United States there are courses in public schools in which religion is studied but these are not as comprehensive as they are in the United Kingdom or in Australia. It would appear that the political situation in the United States is such that the place of religion in public schools is interpreted too exclusively in terms of church and state. This inhibits an interpretation in terms of the function of religion in education. One theorist in that country suggested that the language of the debate was either too ecclesiastical or too anti-ecclesiastical.[8] This limitation prevented the development of a sound educational rationale for religious education in public schools. It situated key decisions about the nature of religious education in the law courts where the judiciary, rather than educational theorists, were to determine the language of religious education.

Curriculum Theory in Religious Education and the Interface with Tertiary Religion Studies.

One way of looking at religious education in government schools that may highlight points of contact with tertiary religion studies is to make use of the concept 'curriculum theory'.

Curriculum theory can be regarded as the 'clearing house' or 'middle ground' where expectations from various sources, including the academic disciplines, are evaluated to determine what implications they should have for the school curriculum. Curriculum theory is like an educational 'arbitration commission' where the claims of different interest groups are appraised so that balanced decisions can be made in the organisation of the total school curriculum.[9] The term may be unfamiliar to tertiary religion scholars. Within their departments, there is no special need to modify their academic discipline (which has an autonomy of its own) to fit in with an holistic view of the total curriculum of the university or college of advanced education.

And so the very idea of having a curriculum theory for schools poses a significant challenge for the tertiary religion scholar who is interested in religious education. The idea of curriculum theory is built on the principle that direct initiation of young people into an academic discipline (e.g. mathematics, biology, phenomenology of religion) is no longer a sufficient or satisfactory reason for including that discipline in the curriculum. To be initiated into the academic disciplines is no longer accepted as an adequate goal for education. Rather, learning experiences in the academic disciplines are required to show how they can be of instrumental value to the education and personal development of the child.

Those wishing to advance the place of religion in the curriculum need to show how studying religion can provide wholesome learning experiences in their own right; and to show how the study of religion contributes in both a general and a distinctive way to the aims that currently apply for a school curriculum.[10] Curriculum theory thus requires a clarification of the *educational* value of studying religion. In curriculum theory, the potential contribution of religious education is also assessed in relation to the findings of developmental psychology and learning theory. For example the question: How can the study of religion be made appropriate for particular stages of pupils' physical, intellectual, affective and moral development?

The 'arbitration function' of curriculum theory helps moderate the expectations that different interest groups have in the school curriculum. One of society's myths tends to regard the school as a powerful agent for changing social attitudes and renewing society. There is a tendency to introduce elements into schooling that will help young people solve in advance the problems they will face later in life. Consider, for example, the following letter to the Sydney *Sun* in July, 1984:

"What is needed is an education, even at high school level, on personal relationships.
"School curricula should include classes in 'living', with subjects such as 'making a marriage work', 'responsibility of parenthood', 'job-hunting', 'family break-up' and 'drug and alcohol abuse'.
"And why not also include counselling in responsible behaviour, self confidence and self esteem and coping with life generally?
"Some preparation for dealing with the problems of life is essential before our young people leave school and surely these subjects are relevant to everyday living and just as important as the subjects now taught in school."

The general public may expect driver education to reduce the road toll significantly; sex education to reduce the illegitimate birth rate; and personal development education to reduce the instability of marriage. It is not surprising then that some of the public might have unrealistic expectations of religious education. Some would expect religious education to improve church attendance, raise moral standards, eliminate injustice, prolong peace and perhaps increase the numbers of young people joining the ministry/priesthood and religious orders! Expectations such as these have a long history. Centuries ago, in England, when convicts were retained on the hulks, the only formal program for their rehabilitation was religious education. The Victorian Russell Report noted that the State parliamentarians, in a debate on religious education, considered that the teaching of religion in government schools might help decrease 'vandalism' and 'juvenile deliquency' while also inhibiting the spread of 'atheistic communism' throughout Australia.[11] These expectations may seem exaggerated. But, in practice, the future development of religious education in government schools depends very much on how realistic are the public expectations for the subject. The same applies even more so to religious education in church schools because much more is often expected in those schools.

Of the curriculum theorists in religious education, Michael Grimmitt has given special attention to the way in which the study of religion may contribute to personal development. It is significant that his most recent contribution in this direction resulted from work he prepared for the Seventh National Conference of the Australian Association for Religious Education.[12] Grimmitt ascribed great educational significance to the 'evaluative consciousness' of the pupils. They could evaluate religion in their own personal terms and in addition could evaluate themselves in terms of the religions being studied. In this way, Grimmitt considered that religious education helped pupils explore the spiritual dimension to their own consciousness.

An assessment of the potential contribution of religious education requires recognition that there is not one established, widely accepted curriculum theory to which it must answer. There are a number, each with its own distinctive emphases. The different emphases tend to underline the importance of different aspects of personal development. Some of the goals that are valued in contemporary curriculum theories are listed as follows To show justification for the place of religion in the curriculum there is need to show how the study of religion at school can help young people move towards these goals:

* skill development — the development of literacy; 'religious' literacy; the skill of non-judgemental description of the beliefs of a believer; skills for analysing and classifying religious phenomena;

* initiation into the academic disciplines — philosophy, theology, psychology of religion, history of religions, phenomenology of religion;

* critical rationality — to develop habits of critical, analytical and evaluative thought;

* moral autonomy — to develop responsible decision-making; to develop the young person's sense of self-determination, particularly in the areas of lifestyle, moral values and beliefs;

* self awareness — promoting self knowledge, self esteem, and self confidence;

* making meaning out of life — helping pupils to explore the dilemmas of the human condition and to consider the answers proposed by different religions;

* vocational orientation — specific preparation for later employment possibilities;

* consciousness-raising — deepening awareness of value-laden issues and of channels of negative and positive influence on people's lives; (note the similarity to critical rationality, but with a distinctive political emphasis);

* political awareness — increasing awareness of political issues and of the functioning of politics; motivation for political action;

* social justice — to become aware of injustices at local, national and international levels; shared action/reflection in the direction of protest against unjust structures;

* aesthetic development — exploration of the aesthetic and emotional dimensions of religious experience and religious traditions;

* assimilation, evaluation and transformation of cultural inheritance;

* multiculturalism — sensitive appreciation of cultural diversity.

The study of religion has much to gain and much to contribute when considered from the standpoint of these themes in curriculum theory. Religion is a sensitive, controversial, value-laden area of human culture. The study of religion can tap into pupils' personal thinking about life. It can engage pupils in challenging intellectual analysis, interpretation and evaluation. From an educational point of view, a powerful case can be prepared for the value of teaching religion in the curriculum.

Religion as an academic subject

In the past, the academic disciplines had control over the school curriculum, carving it up into subjects that corresponded with them. The 'academic subject' curriculum made secondary schools very dependent on the universities. A legacy of this dependence was still evident recently in the dominance of university personnel on subject syllabus committees. Given Australian political history, theology and religion studies have not influenced the curriculum in the same way as have academic disciplines like maths, english, sciences, etc. However, religion studies and theology have influenced the religion courses that are available in schools. Consider, for example, the influence of Ninian Smart. He considered that education should be 'seamless'. That is, education in schools should have the same principles as those which apply in the particular academic disciplines at the university.[13] This principle would make the study of religion in school continuous with the phenomenological study of religions at tertiary level.

Whereas Smart would seek to make the phenomenology of religion the 'parent' discipline for religious education, some educators would want to make religious education continuous with Christian theology. The Victorian Biblical Studies course has strong connections with contemporary biblical scholarship.[14] The recent Australian book, *When Religion Goes to School*, by Basil Moore and Norman Habel, would base religious education within the area of typological phenomenology.[15]

A further related issue is the pressure on Higher School Certificate religion studies courses to satisfy official accreditation and matriculation requirements. Where religion is a new subject seeking admission to the established group of subjects, there is a danger that its academic standard may be inflated to gain acceptance. If an H.S.C. religion studies course needs to look something like an Honours university course to be accredited, then, to that extent, its chances of appealing to even a small minority of Year 12 students may be diminished. The interests and needs of pupils need to be given a higher priority than the desire to advance the academic discipline of religion studies. This question of accreditation of religion studies courses needs further consideration in the light of structural changes to senior school curricula that are now in process or under consideration in most Australian States.

Evaluative Aspects of Religious Education

The 'evaluative' aspect of religious education refers to pupils' personal evaluation of the truth, worth or significance of the content being studied. This is distinct from the evaluation of pupil learning and from the evaluation of curriculum in religious education.

There has been some difficulty in balancing the need for both 'non-evaluative' and 'evaluative' approaches to religious education. Being 'non-evaluative' was regarded as an essental element of the phenomenological approach.[16] On the other hand, the importance of the evaluation of religion by pupils was also affirmed by religious education theorists.[17] One British writer expressed the claim this way:

"The basic beliefs of religions claim to be statements of truth and so they raise the issue of truth and falsehood ... Schools should raise this issue and enable pupils to make their own reasoned judgement about what they believe to be true. To suspend judgement would be to fail to come to terms with different and sometimes incompatible beliefs, to suggest that some form of syncretism was possible or simply to show insufficient concern for truth. No judgement need be seen as final and pupils should be encouraged to reassess their views."[18]

An obvious problem of imbalance arose where religion teachers adopted one of the evaluative or non-evaluative approaches while excluding the other.

Grimmitt was concerned that an uncritical use of the phenomenological approach would overload religious education with descriptive content from world religions while neglecting evaluative aspects which he considered were more relevant to the personal lives of pupils.[19] Grimmitt sought a balance between evaluative and non-evaluative aspects of religious education. He suggested two types of evaluation. Firstly, pupils should be encouraged to evaluate their understanding of religion in personal terms. Secondly, they should be encouraged to evaluate their understanding of self in terms of the religious content being studied.

Non-evaluative and evaluative activities in religious education should not be thought of as being contradictory; both are necesary and can be considered as performing useful functions during different phases of the study of religion. A temporary suspension of pupils' assumptions and judgements is required during the phenomenological phase of inquiry directed towards a sympathetic grasp of a believer's subjective understanding and feelings. In the next phase, when the focus shifts to pupils' understanding, evaluative questions about the internal consistency of the beliefs being studied can be more appropriately considered. Other evaluative aspects would include pupils' consideration of the value and the significance of the material for their own lives, or with respect to other frames of reference.

Pupils could be alerted to the need for rational evaluation and critique of religious beliefs. An approach which formalised the perspectives, principles and criteria involved in making evaluative judgements could help refine pupils' critical capacities in a way which contrasted with their own experience of prejudiced, irrational judgement making. Pupils could become more aware of their own prejudices, stereotypes and ignorance — factors which might have influenced their judgements in religious matters.

Helping pupils become more 'rational' about religion should not be interpreted as proposing reason in opposition to religious beliefs or that religious beliefs were irrational. This approach would, however, be open to criticising what some people might regard as irrational aspects of religious beliefs.

There is a need to spell out clearly the intended types of teaching transactions in an evaluative approach, the criteria invoked for judgement, the types of pupil response to be elicited, and the precautions to be observed. At present, the extent to which evaluative approaches are encouraged in the Australian government school programs in religion is obscure because of the use of vogue words like 'clarification' or 'review' of beliefs. If evaluative approaches are to be used responsibly, clearer specification of the intended classroom processes is needed.

The main role of an evaluative approach is to develop 'informed positions' for pupils on religious matters so that if they did wish to make judgements or commitments, these decisions should be more informed as a result of religious education. It is not the function of religious education to compel judgements, but rather to critically inform students who may or may not wish to pursue evaluative judgements.

This discussion of evaluative aspects of religious education touches many controversial issues because it is concerned with teaching for possible change in pupils' attitudes and values. There is a need for recognition that all education is concerned with personal change, and that it is not possible to engage in religious education without running the risk of changing beliefs and values. However, it is important to specify the types and limits of both the desired changes in pupils and the intended evaluative teaching procedures. The use of an evaluative approach needs to be balanced with awareness of the potential dangers in its misapplication and with an awareness of the need for other approaches and emphases which complement personal evaluation.

RELIGIOUS EDUCATION IN CHURCH-RELATED SCHOOLS

In terms of numbers of pupils in religion classes, numbers of classroom teachers involved and the time and resources given to the activity, the most serious attention given to religious education in Australia is in the church-related schools. Whether or not matriculation courses become firmly established in any State will ultimately depend on whether such courses gain acceptability and a following in these schools.

There is no need to detail here the many fine things that are being done in religious education in the church school sector.[20] Attention can be drawn to some of the critical issues that are being faced in trying to make it a more attractive and meaningful area of study.

Rather than attempt to show the fine differences in religous education in the 14 or so types of church-related schools in Australia,[21] the following will concentrate on the theory and practice in Catholic schools as a sizable example. This would need to be transposed into different keys with particular changes in emphasis to cover the situations in other school types. Nevertheless, the issues are still likely to be relevant in one way or another throughout the entire range of church-related schools.

Issues in Religious Education in Catholic Schools

The first impression one could readily take from a survey of religious education in Catholic schools is the extraordinary variety of approaches and activities that are employed.[22] While this variety in itself and the comprehensive expectations of what should be achieved are strengths of religious education in the Catholic system, these features are also sources of special problems.

One crucial issue is the extent to which the classroom teaching of religion is seen as a process in which religious faith is developed in pupils. Is it a religious experience which pressures personal faith on the part of pupils? Or is it an educational experience in exploring religion where any connections with personal faith are matters for the freedom of pupils? Answering these questions may not be difficult for this audience, but for many parents and teachers the practical implications of these questions remain very complex. The complexity comes from the desire that the Catholic school should not only provide a sound education in religious matters but also foster the development of a personal religious faith and practice.

These aims seem appropriate for the Catholic community to hold for its schools. The difficulty lies in seeing how the total range of experience in the school contributes to these goals. In particular, what contribution should the classroom study of religion make without compromising the freedom of pupils regarding their personal beliefs and commitments. A common problem is 'over-expectation'. Far too great a responsibility for the comprehensive religious development of young people may be ascribed to the classroom religion period. This problem is a special case of the more general problem of over-expectation for Australian schools that was mentioned in the first part of the paper.

Particular schools, and even teachers within any one school, will take a variety of positions on what to expect of classroom religious education. What follows will look at the question of expectations under a number of headings, namely: the language of religious education; freedom of the pupils; the place of teachers' commitments; and how faith, attitudes and values are taught.

The Language of Religious Education

In education generally, the words and concepts developed by authorities and theorists eventually filter down to the practitioners. To a large extent, the dominant language in a particular area influences the way practitioners think and talk about their work. Inevitably, this language has a formative influence on the expectations they develop for their teaching and it ultimately has a bearing on what and how they actually teach. It influences their presumptions about the types of responses they will seek from pupils. It provides the criteria for judging what has been achieved; it ultimately influences the way teachers feel about their work — 'Am I a success or a failure?'[23]

Not a small part of the difficulty teachers have with expectations for religious education in Catholic schools comes from the fact that this field is dominated almost exclusively by complex ecclesiastical lanuage. Language that is concerned with the Church's comprehensive ministry to Catholics of all ages, from all nations, in different situations, through a wide variety of agencies, may be applied uncritically to classroom religious education. There is a need to recognise that the classroom is but one part of one agency that deals with a small section of an individual's life.

One can readily find the following terms in use: catechesis, evangelisation, inculturation, religious socialisation, ministry, mission, conversion, witness, pastoral care, faith development.[24] Added to these are current themes like justice and peace, religious story empowerment. Some theorists make their distinctive contributions and have introduced further terms like 'shared praxis' and 'present dialectical hermeneutics'. While a competent teacher, given time, can master the terminology to help analyse religious education, it would appear that many religion teachers are mystified, confused and even oppressed by this language. Even where they are not familiar with many of the terms, they can still be influenced by the images and ideas that percolate down through the system. People may not be conscious of this domination by language or of the effects it may be having on their expectations, on their teaching practice, or on their perception and interpretation of problems.

There is a need for simpler educational language for describing processes of classroom religious education. This can provide a healthy balance to ecclesiastical language and expectations. It can help teachers and parents develop a clearer more realistic picture of what teaching religion in the classroom can do for pupils. In turn, this can help clarify expectations of what religious education can best contribute to the Church's overall purposes for Catholic schools.

Freedom of the Pupils

One valuable line of thought for religion teachers in Catholic schools is reflection on the nature of religious faith as suggested in Christian theology. An apprecation of the ultimate personal freedom required in any authentic Christian faith and appreciation of the Christian view that such a response is to an invitation by the mysterious Spirit of God, should caution teachers not to presume too much for the place of faith in the teaching process. This could help them avoid a naive view that in the classroom they are programming faith experiences, communicating religious faith or eliciting faith responses. Furthermore, this reflection can lead to a view of religious education as primarily concerned with informing pupils about religion, introducing them to religious issues, and contributing to their affective appreciation of religion. As a result of such religious education, young people should be in a more informed position to determine eventually what role faith and commitment might have in their own lives. This view sees any decisions about faith as generally beyond the focus and scope of the classroom, while, as in any subject area, pupils are free to discuss personal insights if they so wish.

Another useful line of thought for religion teachers is to consider the place of perceived freedom of inquiry in the classroom. Secondary students, especially the young adults in the senior school, are particularly sensitive about their personal freedom in matters of lifestyle, values and beliefs. The following example will be considered in some detail because it highlights in a distinctive way that respect for this freedom is probably the most crucial factor in secondary religious education in Catholic schools.

The example is from the experience of a colleague who taught a five period-per-week Religion Studies course as part of an alternative Year 12 program in a Catholic school in South Australia.[25] The teacher had the same class for the regular Catholic religious education periods provided for all Year 12 students. This arrangement provided her with a unique opportunity for comparing the students' perceptions of the two courses in the study of religion. It should be noted that the students doing the Religion Studies course were of average intellectual ability. They were not seeking entrance to university.

Initially, the students were cynical about the Religion Studies course. They were not pleased to be receiving a 'double dose of religion', more than twice the 'injection of religion' given to the other Year 12 students. However, as the course progressed they changed their minds on this question. They came to recognise that they were engaged in an open-ended inquiring study of religion which did not presume or require a particular faith commitment. Rather, they were involved in serious thought about world religions and they considered the connections that their study made with their own personal experience. Beginning with unfamiliar religions, they learned skills for studying religion impartially without the prejudice that is often associated with study of one's own religious tradition.

In this school-based, Board-approved subject, all of the documentation and student work were carefully scrutinised and moderated by officers of the State Education Department. The course had an educational rationale and was not justified on the grounds of handing on the Catholic faith tradition. The course aimed at knowledge and understanding of some world religions, including Christianity, and it encouraged students to make use of the study in clarifying their own religious beliefs.

These aims are not incompatible with what might be called Catholic aims for religious education, as far as the classroom is concerned. The overall Catholic aims for religious education also usually include a special place for prayer, religious practices and religious ethos of the school. The school also claims to 'sponsor' the development of a personal faith in pupils.

Consider now the young people's different perceptions of the two forms of religious education. They liked the Religion Studies course because it gave them the opportunity for a free, inquiring, critical encounter with religions as a significant part of human culture which previously had been a closed book to them. Furthermore, their experience and thinking about a number of contemporary human/religious issues were enriched.

What were their perceptions of the regular Catholic religion classes? This program, by comparison with similar programs in other schools, was a well-balanced one. Nevertheless, the students perceived the purposes and processes of this program as being different from those in the Religion Studies course. While not able to articulate the differences clearly, they sensed that the Catholic religion periods were designed for the 'getting' of religion while the Religion Studies course was more for the 'studying' of religion.

While the students were not antagonistic to the Catholic religion periods, the very existence of the alternative course seemed to highlight for them a difference in purposes. They seemed able to distinguish between 'a sympathetic, inquiring study of religions' and the 'attempted communication of religious faith'. The students even invented their own language to describe the difference. At times, they would ask their teacher — "Are you speaking to us as our Religion Studies teacher or as our 'Religion/Religion' teacher?"

It would appear that the difference had much to do with the perceived degree of freedom of inquiry in the two types of classes. In most Catholic schools where there is but one program of religious education, it is likely that students' freedom of inquiry remains a critical factor in religion classes. There are religion teachers who provide this freedom naturally in their conduct of classes. There are others who do not recognise that a subtle psychological pressure on students in terms of an expectation to agree with or stand by a particular viewpoint is very compromising to young people; it makes the religion classes counter-productive.

This interpretation also makes much sense of the experience of teachers who may deal with religious issues in other parts of the curriculum. It is not uncommon to hear a teacher say: "I teach more religion in my English literature class than I do in religion periods". It appears that the English class has an authentic freedom of inquiry for looking into religious issues where they arise. The English lesson is not regarded by the teacher or the students as an activity for communicating religious faith and values. The challenge for religion teachers in Catholic schools is to transpose the sense of authentic freedom experienced in the English literature class to religion classes. Until this happens, religious education is likely to be regarded negatively by students and, as a consequence, it could leave religion teachers anxious and dissatisfied about their work.

A further significant point can be drawn from the example. This has to do with the place of 'personalism' in the classroom — that is, the place for sharing of personal insights by pupils and teachers. In the Religion Studies course, the teacher made it clear that the students' task was to develop knowledge, understanding and a sympathetic appreciation of the religions being studied and to grapple with the religious issues that were involved. The class was educational and not devotional in orientation. Students were not required to state their own personal positions. The teacher was not directly concerned with responses which might indicate a deepening of religious faith. The irony in the situation was that these conditions which made it clear to pupils that 'faith responses' were not being sought, created the very freedom that they needed to be able to share insights comfortably at a personal level. The students were unanimous in noting that there was much more value in discussion in the Religion Studies classes than there was in the Catholic religion periods, even when the latter were given over to longer periods of group discussion. This suggests that a creative study of religions is not incompatible with healthy personal discussion — much in the same way as English and Humanities teachers would welcome pointed discussion during their lessons. Personal discussion can readily be generated in the classroom as the by-product of a study which has the spotlight on exploring content. A discussion is not always free when the spotlight is directly on the personal views of the students.

A free discussion is one which does not commit any contributor to a particular value position which he/she may comment on. This allows students to explore and even rehearse imaginatively what different value positions might mean without their comments being regarded as the 'taking' of that position. If religion classes are primarily for exploring religious issues, then the question of possible commitment decisions can be left to the students' own freedom, in their own time and on the stage of life which is much larger than the one represented in the classroom.

What do the above comments say about aims for religious education in Catholic schools? It can be suggested that more emphasis should be given to educational aims. There is a danger that a rationale which emphasises the development of personal faith (very prevalent in aims for religious education in Catholic schools) can create unrealistic expectations for religion teachers. They can neglect aims in the area of knowledge and skills while emphasising aims in the area of religious faith and values. Such an emphasis could leave teachers with an image of the religion class which is too devotional or too concerned with the religious views of the students. This could compromise students' freedom of inquiry and could initiate a syndrome of problems in religion classes which might elude the understanding of the teacher.

The Place of Teachers' Commitments in Religious Education

Should a teacher's own religious beliefs and commitments figure prominently in the study of religion at school? How should a teacher handle controversial religious issues in the classroom? What deference should be made to Church authority?

It is not uncommon to hear parents or teachers say "Only committed Catholics should teach religion in Catholic schools". The valuable place that committed Catholics can have in Catholic schools and the valued places for professionally committed teachers, whether religiously affiliated or not, need not be questioned here. What can be questioned is the adequacy of the comment when it is applied to the classroom teaching process.

There is danger that such a statement looks at religious education as a process for the direct communication of religious faith and commitment from teacher to pupil. It also tends to presume that being a 'committed Catholic' is an adequate qualification for a religion teacher. It can suggest that the teacher's religious beliefs could become the dominant source of content for religious education. There is also a danger that some self-righteous teachers, who feel they have a monopoly on the term 'commitment', can be encouraged by such a statement to present their own views in an authoritarian way.

It is quite unlikely that these issues would arise for the teacher of religion at tertiary level. However, at school, difficulties are associated with the responsibility that the school and its teachers have for the learning of young people. One suggested way of addressing the above-mentioned problems requires the development of a sound code of ethics for the religion teacher. Brian Hill of Murdoch University has provided guidelines on this question that have proved very helpful to religion teachers.[26]

The position Hill recommends is described as 'committed impartiality'. It allows the teacher to refer to his/her commitments as an appropriate contribution to the content when this is judged to be of educational value to the lesson and to the pupils. In this way, the teacher's commitments may be used as one element of data in the lesson along with other data. More than one point of view is presented. The teacher's position is not imposed or presented as 'weighted' evidence but is offered for consideration and evaluation by pupils on the same basis as other content. There is no pressure on the teacher to give his or her viewpoint on all the issues considered in class. Both teacher and pupils should be free to offer their reflections on commitments, and equally free not to make their personal views known to the class should they so wish. In this way, teachers' own beliefs and commitments can be valuable resources in religious education (as can the contributions of pupils) without becoming the major content. As regards the teachings of the Church, these can be presented clearly without imposing any moral pressure on pupils to accept them. An educational exploration of such teachings in the formal curriculum is quite different from a sharing of personal responses to such teachings in a voluntary commitment group.

What has been said above notes, in a brief way, some of the complicated ethical questions that a teacher faces when teaching a controversial subject like religion in a Church school. The code of ethics that was referred to has been spelled out in the writings on religious education in Government schools in Australia.[27] This is one practical example of the value that such materials can have for educators working in Church schools.

How can Faith, Attitudes and Values be taught?

Each of the three considerations above has pinpointed a different aspect of the one underlying problem — just how is the classroom teaching of religion expected to influence young people's faith?

It was suggested earlier that the best contribution that classroom teaching can make to religious faith is to inform young people about their own religious traditions, about religions and religious issues and not to focus on drawing a personal religious response from them. At the same time, this would allow personal freedom for discussion. Also, it would include scope for exploring the *affective* side of religion and for helping pupils in some way with their own affective or emotional lives.

The above reference to the affective lives of pupils sounds imprecise. Yet educators in all curriculum areas are trying to see how the classroom might make a valued contribution to the emotional development of pupils. Similarly, there is an interest in the development of attitudes and moral values. So, the difficulties that teachers in Catholic schools may have in seeing how classroom teaching influences the development of faith are part of a wider problem. Religion teachers are not the only ones interested in the potential of the classroom for promoting personal change in pupils.

Course accreditation procedures commonly require teachers to specify what 'attitudes' the course seeks to promote. However, the authorities have not clarified just what they understand by 'attitudes', just how they think attitudes are developed, just how classroom teaching/learning experiences might change attitudes and just which attitudes they consider desirable. Interest in personal and affective change through education shows up in thinking about areas such as moral development and moral education, personal development education; courses in living skills, self esteem, transition to work, and, most recently, education for human rights.

The interest in these personal, affective areas should be welcomed. It seeks a well-rounded education for young people by attending to more than just their intellectual development. However, so much emphasis has recently been placed on the affective and the personal, that any suggestion that education within the limits of classrooms is primarily *cognitive* may be readily challenged with the claim that this view is old fashioned. Nevertheless, a view of the schooling component of education as one part where the main emphasis should be on the cognitive development of children is well worth defending. This need not be construed as a return to a 'back to basics' in education.

It is much easier to propose affective and personal goals for education than it is to develop practices which will actually help pupils move towards those goals. Much remains to be done in many subject areas to clarify the pedagogy which would most appropriately and most effectively promote such development in children. Special care should be given to respect for their freedom and privacy. Care is also needed in the development of ethical guidelines for teachers so that their work in these areas will not be manipulative and that it will promote autonomy in pupils.

To summarise the comments made in this section, it can be noted that the particular problems in religious education in Catholic schools are not unrelated to more general problems in education for affective development and personal change. What has been learned from addressing the problems in the former context may be a useful guide for those who are trying to clarify the aims and practices of education for affective and personal development. Also, to reiterate the point made earlier, religious education in Catholic schools needs a healthy dose of educational thinking to compensate for the dominance of ecclesiastical language. Hence, one might hope that a wider debate and exchange of ideas in the areas of education concerned with personal and religious development would be profitable for many of the different interest groups and school types in Australian education.

INTERRELATIONSHIPS BETWEEN RELIGIOUS EDUCATION IN CHURCH AND GOVERNMENT SCHOOLS

When the new Religion Studies programs taught by State Departmental teachers were to be set up in Australia, they required a secular identity to differentiate them from confessional programs which aimed at handing on a particular religious faith. There was then a tendency to define the new identity over and against religious education in Church schools. This was most noticeable in South Australia where the State R.E. project was under considerable pressure from sections of the public to show that is was an educationally-based program and that it was not in any way a form of cover for evangelism.[28] This development tended to create a division between the Government schools and the Church schools as far as the teaching of religion was concerned. At times, presumptions were implied about the process of religious education in Church schools which were not always accurate.

For their part, religion teachers in Catholic schools hardly adverted to the new programs in Government schools. If they did, it was quite likely that they considered them to have too much content on world religions and too little on Catholicism. Some teachers would have found the programs unacceptable because they apparently did not give an overt place to the development of religious faith.

Consequently, there was little that might encourage religion teachers in these different sectors to look seriously into what they might have in common. They seemed separated by their apparently different rationales and purposes, different language, different content and perhaps even different teaching processes. This division remains generally true even though the national association of religion teachers, the A.A.R.E., has done much to promote some exchange between the sectors. The time needed to prepare their own teaching is often sufficient reason in itself to prevent educators from taking much interest in what is happening in another school, let alone in a different school sector.

Political pressures can have an influence on the apparent strength of the divisions between so-called 'confessional' and 'non-confessional' religious education. By contrast with the situation in South Australia, there is in Queensland a political pressure which tends to minimise the difference. The Queensland departmental religious education curriculum project was set up to improve the denominational teaching of religion in State schools.[29] Nevertheless, the project team developed a rationale for studying religion in State schools which is quite comparable with that of the South Australian R.E. project. The Queensland team claimed that religious education in the classroom, whether it served confessional purposes or not, remained essentially the same teaching/learning process, even if the content was varied. In a sense, this gave the Queensland scheme a foot in both the confessional and non-confessional camps. It was not surprising that their South Australian counterparts could be somewhat uneasy about this claim. A detailed analysis of the theory and curriculum documents for the projects in each State suggests that they are not only compatible but closely related genetically through their similarities with the theory of Michael Grimmitt.[30]

On one particular point, the New South Wales report on religious education differs from those in the other States.[31] It recommended that both confessional and non-confessional forms of religious education be developed in Government schools. The former was to be the responsibility of the churches and the latter of the State Department. Clearly, this report favoured the maintenance of a difference in nature between the two forms of religious education.

Sociologists could have a 'field day' in examining the theory for religious education in Australian schools. The question "Whose interests are best served by maintaining a division between so-called confessional and non-confessional religious education?" is a very pertinent one to ask.

As far as Catholic schools are concerned, there is a body of recent writing which suggests that the classroom teaching of religion, certainly not the complete role for religion in Catholic schools, should be a thoroughly educational activity and not over-burdened with unrealistic expectations about the communication of personal faith.[32] If this view is accepted, then there are good grounds in theory for seeing an extensive common enterprise for religion teachers in both Government and Catholic schools. Because religious education in schools related to the Anglican, Presbyterian and Uniting Churches is usually not as 'faith-oriented' in its purposes as it is in Catholic schools, there is less difficulty in including religion teachers from these schools in that same common enterprise.

Perhaps it is in the development of accredited religion courses in the senior school where the common nature of the task of religion teachers will be first accepted and made fruitful. One of the dangers to progress, however, could be in the exercise of power in determining the content. If content is dominated by material on world religions, this will not make the courses attractive to many Church schools. Those who favour such a loading towards world religions may be particularly interested in that field of study and they may also be somewhat prejudiced against the academic respectability of studying Christian theology and the Hebrew and Christian scriptures. (The academic calibre of the Victorian Year 12 Biblical Studies course should be enough evidence to show that these studies of theology and scripture can be treated as sound academic studies.) On the other hand, the courses should not exclude a detailed study of some world religions. Perhaps flexibility in the choice of content units that can be taught will be valuable for promoting the courses.

Conclusion

A recent paper on religious education in Australian school has noted:
"Religious education has always been a controversial area of curriculum in

schools. At times it has been criticised for being repressive, indoctrinatory and proselytising. It has also been praised for being informative, liberating, creative and fulfilling. Some pupils have found it painfully boring while others have found it fascinating and engaging. Both politically and educationally religious education is very complicated. Not the least of its difficulties are the different expectations of the activity arising from the varying perspectives and purposes of different interest groups such as politicians, clergy, educators, parents and young people."[33]

No doubt the teachers of religion at tertiary level will be relieved to find that their work area is not so fraught with such public controversy and high expectations as that of their colleagues who teach in schools. Perhaps this leaves the former more free to grapple with the complications of their own academic discipline. This paper has touched on some of the key issues in religious education in schools. In bringing these to the attention of tertiary religion scholars and teachers it may help further the public clarification of the purposes and practices of religious education in schools. Such a clarification is a long-term process. Yet it may eventually improve the quality of religion teaching in schools and it may extend the opportunity of young Australians to find that the study of religion can have a valued place in their education.

Notes and References

1. G.M. Rossiter, 1981. *Religious Education in Australian Schools*, Canberra: Curriculum Development Centre, Chs. 1-3.
   B.S. Moore, 1981. The nature of religious education, Ch.8, in *Religious Education in Australian Schools*.
   R.H. Elliott and G.M. Rossiter, 1982. *Towards Critical Dialogue in Religious Education.* Sydney: Australian Association for Religious Education.
   G.M. Rossiter, 1983. *An Interpretation of Normative Theory for Religious Education in Australian Schools.* Unpublished Ph.D. Thesis, Macquarie University, Sydney. Ch.3.
2. P.H. Hirst, 1965. Liberal education and the nature of knowledge, in *Philosophical Analysis and Education* Ed. R.D. Archambault). London: Routledge and Kegan Paul.
3. M.H. Grimmitt, 1978. *What Can I Do in R.E.?* Great Wakering: Mayhew-McCrimmon. Ch.3.
4. ibid.
5. *Australian Capital Territory*
   Interim A.C.T. Schools Authority, 1973.*Secondary Education for Canberra.* (Campbell Report). Canberra: Australian Government Publishing Service. (This Report referred only in part to religious education.)
   Interim A.C.T. Schools Authority, 1975. *Religious Education Workshop Report.* Canberra: Interim A.C.T. Schools Authority. This publication provided a rationale and guidelines for subsequent school-based developments in R.E.
   New South Wales
   New South Wales Government, 1980. *Religion in Education in New South Wales Government Schools: Report of the Committee appointed by the Minister for Education to consider Religious Education in N.S.W. Government Schools.* (Burns-Rawlinson Report). Sydney: N.S.W. Department of Education.
   Queensland
   Queensland Department of Education, 1972. Report of the Committee of Inquiry into Religious Education in State Schools. (Gutekunst Report). Presented to the Minister for Education but not released to the public.
   Mavor, I.G., Kelly, G.M., Munro, J.A., Nolan, E.H. and Read, G.T., (1977). *Religious Education, its Nature and Aims.* Queensland Religious Education Curriculum Project, Brisbane: Queensland Department of Education.

South Australia
South Australian Education Department, 1973. *Religious Education in State Schools.* (Steinle Report). Adelaide: Education Department of South Australia.
South Australian Education Department, 1976.*Soundings: Some views on religious education in South Australia.* Adelaide: Education Department of South Australia.
South Australian Education Department, 1977. *Evaluation of Religious Education 1976.* Adelaide: Education Department of South Australia.
South Australian Education Department, 1978. *Religious Education Syllabus R-12.* Adelaide: Education Department of South Australia.
Tasmania
Tasmanian Education Department, 1971. *Religious Education in State Schools.* (Overton Report). Hobart: Education Department of Tasmania.
Tasmanian Education Department, 1978. *T.E.N.D. Committee Report* (Tasmanian Education: Next Decade) (Tend Report). Hobart: Education Department of Tasmania. (Refers in part to religious education and values education).
Tasmanian Education Department, 1980. *Religious Studies Syllabus.* Hobart: Education Department of Tasmania.
Victoria
Victorian Government, 1974. *Religious Education in State Schools.* (Russell Report). Melbourne: Government Printer.
Victorian Government, 1977. *A Consideration of the Recommendations of the Russell Report: Report of the Committee on Religious Education.* (Healey Report). Melbourne: Government Printer.
Western Australia
Western Australian Education Department, 1977. *Religious Education in the Government Schools of Western Australia.* (Nott Report). Perth: Education Department of Western Australia.

6. For Example, Schools Council, 1971. *Religious Education in Secondary Schools. Working Paper 36.* London: Evans, Methuen Educational.
7. M.H. Grimmitt, 1978. *What Can I Do in R.E.?*
   M.H. Grimmitt, 1983. *Religious Education and Humanisation.* Sydney: Australian Association for Religious Education.
8. G. Moran, 1977. Two languages of religious education. *The Living Light 14*, 1, 7-15.
   G. Moran, 1978. Where now, what next?, in *Foundations of Religious Education* (Ed. P. O'Hare). New York: Paulist Press, p.99.
9. G.M. Castles and G.M. Rossiter, (Eds.) 1983. *Curriculum Theory and Religious Education. Sydney: Australian Association for Religious Education.*
10. M.H. Grimmitt, 1983. What does religious education contribute to the curriculum? in *Curriculum Theory and Religious Education.*
11. The Russell Report, p.8.
12. M.H. Grimmitt, 1983. *Religious Education and Humanisation.*
13. N. Smart, 1975. The exploration of religion and education. *Oxford Review of Education 1*, 2, 99-105.
14. Victorian Institute of Secondary Educatin, 1982. *Biblical Studies. Higher School Certificate Course Description.* Melbourne: Victorian Institute of Secondary Education.
15. B.S. Moore and N.C. Habel, 1982. *When Religion goes to School: Typology of Religion for the Classroom.* Adelaide: South Australian College of Advanced Education.
16. E.J. Sharpe, 1975. The phenomenology of religion. *Learning for Living 15*, , 4-9.
17. Schools Council Religious Education Committee, 1977. *A Groundplan for the Study of Religion.* London: Schools Council.
18. I.C. Hartland, 1979. Review of A Groundplan for the Study of Religion. *British Journal of Religious Education 2*, 2, 72-73.

19. M.H. Grimmitt, 1982. World religions and personal development, in *Curriculum Theory and Religious Education*.
    M.H. Grimmitt, 1983. *Religious Education and Humanisation*.
20. See *Religious Education in Australian Schools*, Chs. 3 and 6.
21. ibid.
22. G.M. Rossiter, 1982. Diversity of curriculum in religious education in Catholic schools. *Curriculum Perspectives 2*, 2, 5-14. (Also published in *British Journal of Religious Education 4*, 2, 88-98).
23. D. Huebner, 1979. The language of religious education, in *Tradition and Transformation in Religious Education* (Ed. P. O'Hare). Birmingham, Alabama: Religious Education Press.
    G. Moran, 1977. Two languages of religious education. *The Living Light 14*, 1, 7-15.
24. G.M. Rossiter, 1981. Stifling union or creative divorce? The future relationship between catechesis and religious education in Catholic schools. *Word in Life 29*, 4, 162-173.
    G.M. Rossiter, 1983. *An Interpretation of Normative Theory for Religious Education in Australian Schools*. Chs. 7 and 8.
25. M.L. Crawford, 1982. A Year 12 course on world religions in a Catholic high school: Contrasts with the regular education in faith program, in *Towards Critical Dialogue in Religious Education* (Eds. R.H. Elliott and G.M. Rossiter). Sydney: Australian Association for Religious Education.
26. B.V. Hill, 1981. Teacher commitment and the ethics of teaching for commitment, Chapter 10 in *Religious Education in Australian Schools*.
    B.V. Hill, 1982. *Faith at the Blackboard*. Grand Rapids: Eerdmans.
    B.V. Hill, 1982. The religious education teacher's commitment, in *Curriculum Development in Religious Education 2*. Perth: Australian Association for Religious Education.
27. See references in Footnote 5.
28. A.H. Ninnes, 1978. Two steps forward, one step back: Religious education in South Australia. *Learning for Living 17*, 4, 145-148.
    P.C. Almond and P.G. Woolcock, 1978. *Dissent in Paradise: Religious Education Controversies in South Australia* (3rd edition). Adelaide: Hartley College of Advanced Education.
29. I.G. Mavor, G.M. Kelly, J.A. Munro, E.H. Nolan and G.T. Read, 1977. *Religious Education, its Nature and Aims*. Queensland Religious Education Curriculum Project, Brisbane: Queensland Department of Education.
30. G.M. Rossiter, 1983. *An Interpretation of Normative Theory for Religious Education in Australian Schools*. Ch. 5(a) and (b).
    M.H. Grimmitt, 1983. *Religious Education and Humanisation*, Appendix 2.
31. New South Wales Government, 1980. *Religion in Education in New South Wales Government Schools: Report of the Committee appointed by the Minister for Education to consider Religious Education in N.S.W. Government Schools*. (Burns-Rawlinson Report). Sydney: N.S.W. Department of Education.
    See G.M. Rossiter, 1983. *An Interpretation of Normative Theory for Religious Education in Australian Schools*. Ch. 5(e).
32. R.M. Rummery, 1975. *Catechesis and Religious Education in a Pluralist Society*. Sydney: E.J. Dwyer.
    G.M. Rossiter, 1981. Stifling union or creative divorce? The future relationship between catechesis and religious education in Catholic schools. *Word in Life 29*, 4, 162-173.
33. G. Moran, 1981. *Interplay: A Theory of Religion and Education*. Winona: St. Mary's Press.
    K. Scott, 1981. Collapsing the tensions. *The Living Light 18*, 2, 167-169.
    G.M. Rossiter, 1982. Diversity of curriculum in religious education in Catholic schools. *Curriculum Perspectives 2*, 2, 5-14.

ISBN 90 04 07863 0